MW00998264

What Readers Are Saying About
Cocoa Programming: A Quick-Start Guide for Developers

Cocoa Programming is powerful because Daniel Steinberg teaches us the brilliant way Cocoa and Objective C are constructed and commonly used—just what you'd expect from a seasoned, native, local resident.

▶ **Eric Freeman**
   Author, Head First Design Patterns

Over the years, as a programmer experienced in many different languages and paradigms, I've come to dread the process of learning new programming languages and technologies. It's really hard to find a teacher who can speak to experienced programmers without boring us to tears with oversimplification or taking too much prior knowledge for granted. In this book, Daniel Steinberg has proven to be such a teacher. *Cocoa Programming* exposes the beauty of the Cocoa environment with just enough detail and explanation to help you "get it" the first time.

▶ **Chad Fowler**
   CTO, InfoEther, Inc.

If you are writing applications for the Mac, the iPhone, or the exciting new iPad, this book will get you started. The programming model for all three platforms is essentially the same, and this book will teach it to you. Get this book so you have a solid foundation to write the next big hit.

▶ **Bill Dudney**
   Gala Factory Software

This book is perfect for seasoned developers looking to get started with Cocoa development. Daniel gives you a solid foundation that will allow you to build the next great Mac or iPhone application.

▶ **James Frye**
   Developer, Tasty Cocoa Software LLC

If you're new to Mac programming or switching from iPhone development, start reading this book now! *Cocoa Programming* covers topics other books don't and puts it all together through great examples where you actually learn it and don't just read it.

► **Jake Behrens**
Software Engineer, Snafl

As a recently initiated iPhone developer with several applications under my belt (and seasoned web applications developer), this book was a perfect fit for my desire to use my knowledge to create robust, functional, and lightweight Cocoa applications. Daniel Steinberg captured my attention early on with his brilliance and kept me intrigued from one chapter to the next. I had no choice but to write my first Cocoa application while reading and felt I walked away with more than just a solid foundation upon which to build. This book will be a mainstay in my library for sure.

► **Kevin J. Garriott**
Developer II—Mobile Applications, Rockfish Interactive

One of the best flowing programming books I've ever read. The chapters just naturally follow one after another. The book is a whole, in much the same way the Cocoa framework is a whole. Both reflect a single, clear, concise voice.

► **Craig Castelaz**
Principle Software Engineer

Cocoa Programming

A Quick-Start Guide for Developers

Cocoa Programming
A Quick-Start Guide for Developers

Daniel H Steinberg

The Pragmatic Bookshelf

Raleigh, North Carolina   Dallas, Texas

Many of the designations used by manufacturers and sellers to distinguish their products are claimed as trademarks. Where those designations appear in this book, and The Pragmatic Programmers, LLC was aware of a trademark claim, the designations have been printed in initial capital letters or in all capitals. The Pragmatic Starter Kit, The Pragmatic Programmer, Pragmatic Programming, Pragmatic Bookshelf and the linking *g* device are trademarks of The Pragmatic Programmers, LLC.

Every precaution was taken in the preparation of this book. However, the publisher assumes no responsibility for errors or omissions, or for damages that may result from the use of information (including program listings) contained herein.

Our Pragmatic courses, workshops, and other products can help you and your team create better software and have more fun. For more information, as well as the latest Pragmatic titles, please visit us at

http://www.pragprog.com

ISBN-10: 1-9343563-0-1

ISBN-13: 978-1-9343563-0-2

Printed on acid-free paper.

P1.0 printing, April 2010

Version: 2010-4-7

Contents

Chapter 1

Introduction

As I finished up the final walk-through of our new house, a woman called to me from across the street. "Tonight's our annual progressive dinner," she shouted. "Come meet the neighborhood."

I followed along and met our new neighbors all at once. It went fast and was a bit overwhelming, and there was a ton of information, some of which I was able to sort out later. Mostly, it made me feel a lot better about my new neighborhood. I knew the questions to ask, and I had met the people who could answer them for me.

That's the goal in this book. It's not a guide for tourists that lists the things you'd want to see if you were only going to live with Cocoa for a day. It's not a comprehensive almanac that lists every API class by class and method by method. This is designed to get you through those first weeks and months of moving to Cocoa.

This is the coding equivalent of finding out where to go for coffee, which streets are safe to walk on at night, and which teacher to request for your kids. Once you get a feel for the neighborhood, you'll have more questions, but you'll know where and how to get them answered.

1.1 Moving In

Moving to Cocoa is like moving to a new neighborhood. You need to figure out where everything is and get used to the local customs. You'll find that some aspects of developing Cocoa apps for Mac OS X are very similar to what you've been doing, while other aspects feel very strange.

In this book you'll get a feel for working with the following:

- *Objective-C*: The language of Cocoa development

- *Xcode, Interface Builder, and Instruments*: The tools for Cocoa development
- *Cocoa*: The frameworks full of existing classes created by Apple that will give your applications the features and polish of your favorite Mac OS X applications

What, you ask, is a framework? A *framework* is a directory that contains some related set of resources. You can think of a framework as a library or a package, but it can also contain image files, documentation, localization strings, and other constructs that you'll learn about later in this book. You'll see in Chapter 2, *Using What's There*, on page 11 that we bring in all the resources for programming web applications by adding the WebKit framework to our project.

Frameworks are kind of like what you know already and kind of different. For now you can think of them as libraries, and you'll be fine. You'll learn about many ideas in Mac OS X development that are close to what you already know. You'll be tempted to hold on the way you used to do things. Don't. You don't want to be the only one driving on the wrong side of the road. It's not good for you, and it's not good for others sharing the same road.

No one likes a new neighbor who goes on about how good it was where they came from. It's the same here in OS X. It isn't that the old-timers are being mean. It's just that they have a way of doing things. You will have an incredible amount of power at your fingertips to quickly develop native Mac OS X applications if you embrace Objective-C, use the development tools, and take advantage of the Cocoa frameworks. You will tend to get much further much more quickly if you use what is provided for you and follow local customs rather than fight with the culture.

Use Objective-C. Sure, you can write Cocoa applications in other languages. But for now, learn the native language. There is a lot of support for new developers on the various Apple lists[1] and in the support documentation, tutorials, and sample code accessible from Xcode. You will have an easier time of getting your question answered if you use the lingua franca of Cocoa development.

---

1. For a comprehensive list, visit http://lists.apple.com/. You will probably want to subscribe to the http://lists.apple.com/mailman/listinfo/cocoa-dev list. Also look for lists that serve specific areas that you target in your application. If you have a specific need that is only temporary, you can also search the archives.

What About the iPhone and iPad?

In this book we mainly target Mac OS X development. For the most part, these are the same techniques, tools, and APIs you will use to target the iPhone and iPad. There are differences that I've highlighted in a couple of the iPhone chapters, but for the most part this book focuses on desktop Cocoa and assumes that you'll find it fairly easy to move from Cocoa development for Mac OS X to developing for the mobile platforms.

Use the tools that Apple provides for Cocoa development. In your old environment, you may have popped open a terminal window and used vi or emacs along with gcc and gdb, or you may have used an IDE like Eclipse. For Cocoa app development, use Xcode to write, compile, debug, and run your code. Use Xcode to create, build, and manage your projects. You'll even use Xcode to create and edit your data models. You'll use Interface Builder (IB) to create your GUI and to wire up the various components. You'll use Instruments to improve the performance of your application. You can find most of your favorite command-line developer tools in /usr/bin/, but you still want to use Apple's dev tools when you are creating a Cocoa app.

Finally, use the built-in frameworks as much as you possibly can. Before you think about writing any code, take a look at what Apple has provided for you. Your first impulse should always be to use what is there.

To emphasize this last point, your first project will be to build a simple web browser with Apple's WebKit framework.[2] The browser will include a text field where the user can enter a URL and a web view that renders the web page. You will also add Forward and Back buttons for navigating through sites you have already visited. Because you are taking advantage of the WebKit framework, you can accomplish all of this without writing any code.

Working with the new language, tools, and APIs is going to feel a bit odd at first. They are unfamiliar, so your first instincts won't always be right. but in no time you'll be typing in what you assume the method

---

2. I got the idea for starting with this example while editing Chris Adamson's "ten-minute browser" example in *iPhone SDK Development* [DA09].

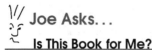

Joe Asks. . .

Is This Book for Me?

This book is for the experienced programmer who is new to the Mac or iPhone platform.

You understand basic programming concepts but just don't know how they apply in this setting. You know a language that has a structure somewhat like C, but you don't know Objective-C. You understand object-oriented programming, just not in this setting. You want to learn all the techniques for working with the Cocoa frameworks, but you are comfortable reading the documentation to explore the specific APIs that you need in your app. Finally, you have a Mac and are currently running Snow Leopard.

By the way, if you are a new programmer, start with our book by Tim Isted, *Beginning Mac Programming*, which is available at http://pragprog.com/titles/tibmac/.

name is and find that it is, in fact, correct. Once you tune yourself to the Cocoa frameworks, you'll find that they tend to obey the *principle of least surprise*: you'll usually find what you expect to find.

This is not a comprehensive book in any way. This book doesn't cover every nook and cranny of Objective-C. I don't take you click by click through all that you can do in Xcode nor do we walk through the entire set of APIs. This book gets you up and running and gives you enough context to find the answers you need as new questions arise.

1.2 Learning the Language

When you first learned to speak a new language in school, you probably translated everything back and forth from and to your native language. After a lot of work, you began to master the vocabulary and the grammar and you became comfortable with the native usage patterns and idioms. Without noticing it, one day you found yourself thinking in your new language while you were speaking or reading it.

The same is true about Objective-C, the language of Cocoa. The syntax is different, but much of it is similar to languages you use now. You need to be as careful of being fooled by the similarities as you are of being challenged by the differences.[3] You can get used to the square brackets and the way that code is structured pretty quickly. You also have to get comfortable with the common patterns that Cocoa programmers use.

In Chapter 3, *Methods and Parameters*, on page 35, we'll get you comfortable reading some Objective-C. We'll start with messages because sending messages is the core of Cocoa programming. Even experienced object-oriented programmers lose sight of this. We tend to think that OO is all about the objects.

Objective-C sits on top of C, but it owes many of its ideas to Smalltalk. It helps to reread Alan Kay's 1998 reminder on the Squeak mailing list every now and then in which he expresses his regret at coining the term *objects* because it encourages people to focus on the wrong thing.[4] Kay explains that "The key in making great and growable systems is much more to design how its modules communicate rather than what their internal properties and behaviors should be."

1.3 Installing the Tools

Check that you have installed the free developer tools. By default the installer puts the developer applications, documentation, examples, and other files in the Developer directory at the root level. Even though the developer tools are free and included on the install discs that come with Mac OS X, they are not installed by default. Check the Developer directory to make sure they are installed. Also select Xcode and choose File > Get Info or press ⌘I to bring up the info window for Xcode. Check the version number. The examples in this book assume you are running at least Xcode 3.2.

Get the most recent developer tools (including beta releases) by joining the Apple Developer Connection (ADC) at http://developer.apple.com/. You *should* join the ADC. There is currently a free membership level that gives you access to much of the prerelease software. There are also paid membership levels that come with different benefits.

---

3. One of the great selling points for Java was also its weakness. Its syntax was familiar. C programmers could easily write Java code. But they often wrote Java code that looked a little too much like C code. The same is true for many other programming languages including Objective-C. Objective-C sits on top of C, so you could write pure C code. Don't.
4. http://lists.squeakfoundation.org/pipermail/squeak-dev/1998-October/017019.html

Starting Fresh

You might have problems if you are moving to Snow Leopard from an earlier version of Mac OS X or if you are moving to the developer tools installation that features Xcode 3.2 from an earlier version of the developer tools. These problems manifest themselves in different ways but are often surface when dealing with nib files.

The fix is simple. First uninstall your old developer tools, and then do a clean install of the new developer tools. Problem solved.

We'll spend most of our time in this book in Xcode and Interface Builder. You'll write your code in Xcode and design the data models that we'll use later in the book. You'll use Interface Builder to create the look of your application and to connect your visual components to the code containing your business logic.

Even though those two applications get most of the attention, you get a lot of other tools for free. For example, before you release an application into production, you're going to want to take some time to exercise it with profiling tools such as Instruments and Shark. You'll also find audio tools, graphic tools, other performance tools, and a slew of utilities. When you install the developer tools, you've also installed a ton of command-line tools as well.

1.4 Exploring the Frameworks

We're going to play quite a bit with the Cocoa frameworks. When you can, you should use the objects and classes that Apple provides before you struggle to write the code yourself. In the beginning, you will find yourself writing a lot of code to do something you've seen other applications do on Mac OS X. An experienced Cocoa developer will look at your code, make a face, and suggest, "Why don't you just...?" As much as you may hate to hear it, their two lines of code will do everything that your 400 lines did. That's just the way it's going to be.

And then one day it will all make sense to you.

That doesn't mean you will know the two lines of code you need to write. But fifty lines in, you'll be aware that you're working too hard. You will know that those two lines probably exist. When you don't know what to do yourself, you'll know where to go to find help.

You'll find your favorite paths into the documentation. I tend to hold down the Option and Command keys (⌥ ⌘) and double-click a class name or a method name to view the docs for the class or method. You can also right-click or Control-click part of your code and get a pop-up context-sensitive help menu that can include refactorings, links to definitions, and other available actions. You don't need to memorize these key bindings; you can always navigate to the docs using the Xcode menus.

You will find great third-party web sites, and you can join the *cocoa-dev* mailing list that you can find at http://lists.apple.com. Lurk first to get a feel for the list. And when you have really tried to figure out something for yourself, go ahead and ask a question that explains what you've done and what you don't understand or are hoping to learn.

1.5 In This Book

There are four sections in this book. The first section is an introduction to Cocoa, Objective-C, and the tools. The second section takes you to a level where you are comfortable with the fundamental techniques of creating a Cocoa application. The third and fourth sections consist of material that can wait. It's essential that you understand the concepts presented there, but you need to wait until you have some experience.

In the first section, you'll start to use Xcode and Interface Builder. You'll get used to the rhythm of bouncing back and forth between them. We'll start in Chapter 2, *Using What's There*, on page 11 with a web browser that you create without writing any code at all. Between there and Chapter 9, *Customizing with Delegates*, on page 147, you'll master the basics of Cocoa and Objective-C.

In this first section, you'll learn to create and call methods and over-come any fear you might have of the funny-looking syntax with its square brackets and colons. You'll design classes in Xcode and cre-ate objects in Xcode and in Interface Builder. You'll embrace proper-ties and the dot syntax and use automatic garbage collection wherever you can. You'll learn the rules of reference counting for situations—like iPhone apps—when you need to manage memory manually. You'll be introduced to the two fundamental patterns in Cocoa development:

delegation and MVC. At the end, we'll take a deep breath and then reimplement our web browser for the iPhone.

You'll start the second section of the book in Chapter 11, *Posting and Listening for Notifications*, on page 181 with a new application that listens for when other applications on your computer start and quit. You'll react to notifications sent by the workspace your application runs in and how to send notifications of your own. You'll create protocols that describe what methods a class might implement, and you'll create delegates to add behavior to objects without subclassing. You'll read and write information in key-value pairs to a dictionary—this is a technique that we'll build on in big ways in the third section of the book.

One of the keys to the second section is modularity. We break methods, classes, and even nibs into small pieces. By the end of this section, we will have five nib files in this application to organize your main menu, window, preference panel, and two views. One of the views will be a custom view you learn to create partially in Xcode and partially in Interface Builder. A key to this modularity is the separation of the model, view, and controller. You'll see this highlighted in our chapter on custom views, in our work with tables, and in Chapter 18, *Changing Views*, on page 277 where we let the user switch between two different views in the same window.

The third section focuses on more sophisticated ways in which to send and receive messages. You'll begin with Chapter 19, *Key Value Coding*, on page 291. Key Value Coding (KVC) allows you to decide which method you are calling at runtime based on user input. KVC works perfectly with properties and allows you to treat your objects as if they were dictionaries and your properties as if they were entries in the dictionary. You'll see what I mean when we get there.

You can go even further and use Key Value Observing (KVO) to register to listen for changes in a property's value. This low-ceremony notification sets the stage for Bindings and Core Data. In the early parts of the book, you will have learned to use Interface Builder instead of code to create your views. This section lets you remove much of your controller code and even some of the model code.

This book begins with you creating an application with almost no code. You then spend the bulk of the book mastering different coding techniques. By the end of Chapter 23, *Categories*, on page 361, you will again be writing less code. This time, however, you will understand sophisticated techniques that allow you to create powerful and flexible applications by writing only the code that is required.

The fourth section is a brief one that introduces blocks and two methods for working with concurrency. In Chapter 24, *Blocks*, on page 377, you will learn a new construct that was added to Snow Leopard. Although I am assuming you are developing in Snow Leopard, all of the techniques you learn up to this point apply to code you are deploying to Leopard as well.[5] If you use blocks in your code, you cannot target Leopard or the iPhone. You are restricted to Snow Leopard and above.

I wrestled with whether to cover concurrency in this book. It's such a difficult thing to get right in your code, and I could have written an entire book on this topic. My advice is simple: don't use threads directly. First, reach for operation queues, and if they don't meet your needs and if you are on Snow Leopard or above, go ahead and work with dispatch queues.

As you can see, the book focuses on techniques and not APIs. By the end of this book, you should be well positioned to take on any Cocoa task. Even though you might not have learned about the specific problem you need to tackle, you'll have enough experience to find the right place in the Apple documentation and figure out how to do what you need to do.

Welcome to the neighborhood. I'm so glad you're here. I can't wait to see the cool applications you develop after you read this book.

---

5. The APIs may differ, but the techniques are the same.

Chapter 2

Using What's There

We're going to start by creating a web browser that looks like this:

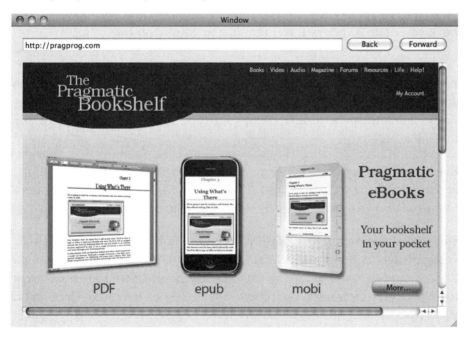

We'll create our browser without writing a line of code. It won't be fancy, but it will mostly work. You'll be able to type in URLs to load your favorite websites. You'll be able to navigate around the sites by following links the way you would in an ordinary browser, and you'll be able to use a couple of buttons to move forward and backward through your browsing history.

In this chapter, we'll use Interface Builder and off-the-shelf components to build our browser. We'll pick a couple of buttons, a text field, and a special component for displaying web pages from a library. We'll drag these components onto our window, arrange them the way we want them to look, and make sure they visually behave right when we shrink or stretch the window. We'll then use Interface Builder to enable the behavior we want. Once we get everything working the best we can for now, we'll take a quick look behind the scenes at some of the backstage magic.

2.1 Creating Your Project in Xcode

As we bounce back and forth between IB[1] and Xcode in these first few chapters, you'll get a feel for what each is for. Mostly, you'll use Xcode as an IDE to work on your code, your data model, and your project. The work you do in Xcode will feel familiar to you if you use other IDEs.

As you might expect, you'll create your GUI using Interface Builder. You'll also use Interface Builder to connect the elements of the GUI to data sources, to other GUI elements, and to methods described in code. You're going to spend almost all of your time in this first example using Interface Builder.

Even though you won't write any code for this SimpleBrowser example, you'll need to create the project from Xcode. Start Xcode, and create a new project using either ⌘ ⇧ N or File > New Project.[2]

You'll be presented with a variety of options for project templates that you can use to develop applications for the iPhone or for Mac OS X. Choose Mac OS X > Application > Cocoa Application. Leave the checkboxes unselected for creating a document-based app or for using Core Data. Click the Choose button or just press ↵.

I have saved the project as SimpleBrowser in ~/Dev/UsingWhatsThere/. You can choose another name or location if you prefer.

---

1. This is short for Interface Builder and is pronounced "I.B." but written IB.
2. You'll find Xcode in the /Developer/Applications directory. You will use it enough that you should drag it to the Dock to create a shortcut. Also, remember you can always use Spotlight by clicking the magnifying glass in the far right of the menu bar.

Your new project should look something like this:

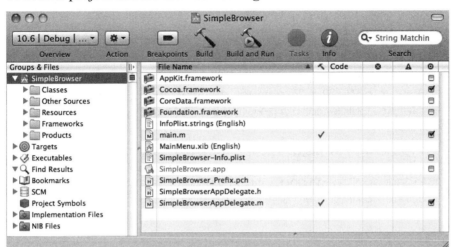

There's quite a bit of infrastructure automatically created for you. We're going to ignore almost all of these files for now. In this chapter, you'll do all of your work in the MainMenu.xib file.

Your SimpleBrowser application doesn't do anything yet, but you can take it for a test-drive. Click Build & Run, and after a moment of compiling and linking, you'll see an empty SimpleBrowser window and a menu bar populated with the standard set of menus and menu items. You may also notice that SimpleBrowser.app is no longer highlighted in red in Xcode because the file now exists. Quit SimpleBrowser,[3] and let's get started on creating the interface.

2.2 Creating the Appearance with Interface Builder

Double-click MainMenu.xib (English) in the Xcode window. This is your main nib file. A nib file contains all of the work you do in Interface Builder. You create, configure, and connect objects using graphical tools in Interface Builder. Each nib file is essentially a freeze-dried object graph that is reconstituted at runtime. This first application will have a single nib file. Later in the book you'll build more complicated applications with more than one.

Nib files used to be stored in a binary format and had the extension nib. They are now stored as XML during development so that they work bet-

---

3. Closing the window doesn't quit the application. You need to stop the task from within Xcode, or while SimpleBrowser is active, you can press ⌘Q or use the menu to quit.

Joe Asks...

Shouldn't We Be Writing Code?

Anything that can be done in Interface Builder can also be done in code. But, in general, anything that can be done in Interface Builder should be done in Interface Builder and not in code.

If you follow this rule as strictly as possible, then most of the time when you are coding, you will be writing code that is specific to your application and not general-purpose code. There probably is nothing special about the way in which you need to instantiate and place buttons in your application—so use Interface Builder to do so.

In this chapter, we are only using common visual components such as windows, buttons, text fields, and web views. We don't need to create our own classes because Apple has created them for us and included (most of) them in the Cocoa frameworks. We are going to create instances of these visual elements and arrange them so they look right in Interface Builder.

By the end of this chapter, you'll see that we can also use Interface Builder to connect a button to the action it performs. The web view that Apple provides us with already knows how to go to a provided URL and to navigate back and forward in the browser history. We'll use this built-in behavior for now and delay writing code until we want to customize the behavior of the browser.

ter with version control. You still should only interact with these files using Interface Builder so the persistence format is transparent to you. The only difference you'll see is that the XML versions use the xib extension. Despite this change, they are mostly still referred to as nib files (pronounced "nib" and not "N.I.B."), although some people pronounce xib files as "zibs."[4]

SimpleBrowser consists of a single window with off-the-shelf components. You'll fill the MainMenu nib with a web view for rendering the

---

4. The name *nib* comes from the acronym for NeXT Interface Builder. Interface Builder and the framework that has become Cocoa were developed at NeXT Computer. Also, when you create a release, the xib files are compiled into nibs.

websites, a text field for entering their addresses, and two buttons for navigation.

You started Interface Builder when you double-clicked MainMenu.xib. You should see several windows. One has the information for your menu bar, and another is titled MainMenu.xib and contains the File's Owner and First Responder. The one you care about is empty except for the words *SimpleBrowser* in the title bar. This is the window we'll use to hold all of our visual elements.

Open the Library using either ⌘ ⇧ L or Tools > Library. The Library is where you'll find all the objects that Apple provides for you as well as objects that you will create in Xcode. You can navigate to the elements you want, or you can use the search box at the bottom of the window to filter the results. To see the components that Apple provides, check that the Objects tab is selected at the top and that Library is selected in the drop-down list just below the tab. Here I've typed *text* to find the text field box I want to use for URL entry.

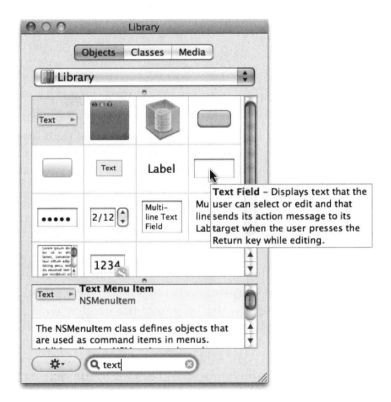

You can right-click the middle panel of the Library window to configure it. I've chosen to show the icons, but we can instead show the icons and labels or show the icons and descriptions for the GUI elements. Whichever view you choose, you can always get additional details like those shown in the box in the preceding figure by hovering your mouse over one of the components.

Click the text field in the library, and drag it to your empty window. As you drag the text field around the window, you will see blue guidelines that help you place elements according to Apple's Human Interface Guidelines.

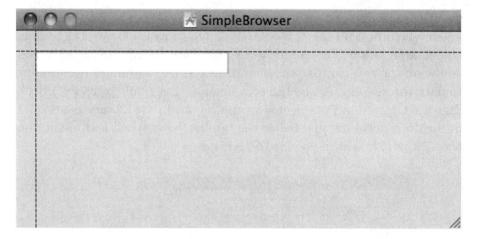

Place the text field in the top-left corner of the window using the left and top guidelines. You may need to increase the size of the window by dragging the bottom-right corner of the window to the right and down. You need enough room for two buttons to the right of the text field. Take a look back at the browser on the first page of this chapter to be reminded of what you are building.

Go back to the Library, and clear the word *text* from the search box on the bottom. Make sure the Objects tab is selected at the top, and use the control just below the tab to navigate to Library > Cocoa > Views & Cells > Buttons. You will see a dozen different buttons. They are all instances of the class NSButton, but they are each used in different situations. As you click each one, the text at the bottom of the window changes to let you know which type of button you have selected. You want the Push button.

Click the Push button in the Library, and drag it to the right of the text field you just placed in your window. You should see horizontal blue guidelines that make sure you are on the same line as the text field, and as you move the button closer to the text field, a vertical blue line will appear at the left side of the button to indicate that you have the right separation between the elements.

Go back and grab another Push button from the library, and drag it to the right of the other button. The top row of your window should now contain a text field and two buttons. We'll be making some more adjustments to these three elements, so you'll have a chance to refine their size and placement later.

You have one more element to place. Go back to the Library, and find Library > Web Kit. This is not under Cocoa. It is part of a separate framework that you will have to link into your project later using Xcode. This framework contains a single visual element called WebView. This is the element in which the web page will be rendered. Click the icon that looks like Safari's, and drag it into your window. Position the web view to occupy the rest of the window. You should now see something like this:

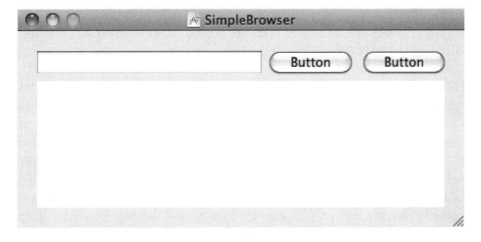

Take a moment to resize and rearrange the buttons, text field, and web view so that everything looks the way you want it to look.

It's easy to lose sight of the big picture while following all of these "click here" and "drag there" directions. In this section, you've selected the objects you need for your application's interface from a palette and positioned them in the main window as the user will see them at launch time.

Save your work using either ⌘ S or File > Save. Close the Library window. You won't need it for the rest of this chapter.

2.3 Testing the Interface with the Cocoa Simulator

You should pause now and then to play with your interface to make sure it is behaving the way you want it to behave. You first need to have Interface Builder selected as your application (click any IB window). Start the Cocoa Simulator using either ⌘ R or File > Simulate Interface.

Nothing is wired together, so you can't check behavior yet. For now, all you can test is that the application looks right. Resize the window. Make it really big. Make it really small.

The items probably don't behave the way you want them to behave. When you make the window really big, you expect the web view to grow accordingly. When you stretch the window out wide, you expect the buttons and text field to stay close to each other and to have the text field grow to make up the difference.

The problem is, you haven't told the application how you want the components to behave as the window is stretched and shrunk. Quit the simulator with ⌘ Q or Cocoa Simulator > Quit Cocoa Simulator.

Let's fix how the size of the components change when the window is resized. You'll need to open the Size inspector in IB. You can do this with ⌘ 3. (You use ⌘ 3 because the Size inspector is the third tab in the inspector window.) You can also use your mouse to choose the Size inspector with Tools > Size Inspector. If the inspector is already open, you can select the third tab from the left.[5] That's the one with the icon that looks like a ruler. You can also open the inspector using ⌘ ⇧ I or Tools > Inspector. In any case, if you select a button and the Size inspector, you should see something that looks like the screenshot on the next page.

To change the size settings for a component, you select the component and then make adjustments in the Size inspector. For now we're making adjustments to the "autosizing" settings. You should experiment with setting the four struts, the I-beam shapes, on the outside of the inner square.

---

5. There are lots of ways to get to each of the inspectors. I present more than one because some people like menus and others like keyboard shortcuts. Choose the one you like the best.

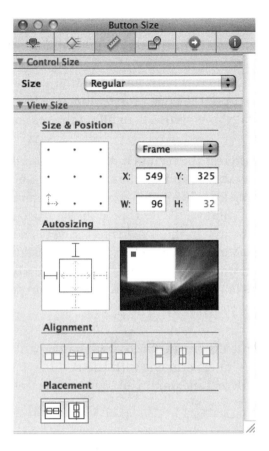

As you turn them on and off by clicking them, the animation on the right will show you the results of making the changes. This is how you control which sides of the component are anchored when the window grows and shrinks. You should also experiment with turning the horizontal and vertical springs on and off inside the inner square. This is how you control the direction in which the component will stretch and shrink when the window size changes.

Here are the settings for both buttons, for the web view, and for the text field:

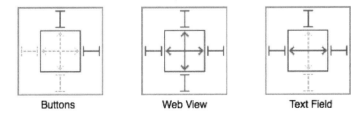

Buttons   Web View   Text Field

As the window grows and shrinks, the top of each of the elements will stay the same distance from the top of the window. The right side of both buttons will stay the same distance from the right side of the window. The text field will grow horizontally so that its two sides can stay the same distance from the edge of the window. Finally, the web view will grow horizontally and vertically to fill up the rest of the window.

Save your work, and test the results in the Cocoa Simulator. Shrink the window all the way down, and then expand it back out. Chances are, that will make your interface behave badly. You should set the minimum size for your window. To do this, quit the Cocoa Simulator, and select the Window object. In the Size inspector, you'll see a Window Size section. Select the Minimum Size checkbox, and click the Use Current button. Save your work. Now the user will not be able to shrink the window beyond its current size. If you'd like, you can set the maximum size for the window in the same way.

Again, test your results in the Cocoa Simulator. While you are here, take a few minutes to experiment with the settings for the struts and springs, and try different maximum and minimum sizes for the window.

2.4 Finishing the Interface

You still have two buttons labeled Button. One way to change a button's label is to double-click the button and type the new name. Another way is to use the inspector and select the Attributes tab. This is the inspector's leftmost tab—the one with the slider icon. You can also access this tab using ⌘ 1 or Tools > Attributes Inspector.

Set the title for the leftmost button to Back by selecting the rectangle to the right of Title and typing *Back* in the data-entry field. When you select another area of the inspector, you will see the title of the button changes. While you're at it, set the keyboard equivalent for this button to ⌘ ← by clicking the gray rectangle next to the label Key Equivalent and then typing the left arrow (←) while holding down the Command key (⌘).

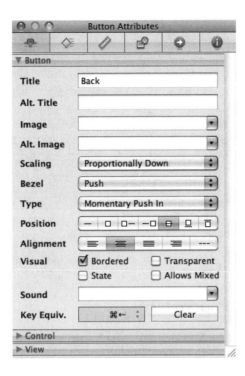

Set the title for the other button to Forward and its keyboard equivalent to ⌘ →. Next, select the Window, and set its title to SimpleBrowser.

Finally, let's provide the user with a default value and a hint of how to use our browser. Set the title of the text field to http://pragprog.com either by double-clicking it or by selecting it and setting the value of the title field using the Attributes inspector. Also use the drop-down list in the text field's Attributes inspector to set the value of Action to Sent on Enter Only. This configures the text field to send its value when the user presses Enter.

Where is the text field's value sent when the user hits Enter? We haven't set that yet.

You're now done creating all of the visual elements of the interface for SimpleBrowser. Use the Cocoa Simulator to take another look at the browse and adjust the sizes of the window or any of the components. Your browser still doesn't do anything—but we will fix that in the next section.

Reading the Nib

All of the work you have done so far is stored as XML in the MainMenu.xib file. There is no reason for you to directly read or change the XML you've generated. This is a format meant to be created and interpreted by Interface Builder. For kicks, you may want to open the file in your favorite text editor and take a look around. You can find the text field, the two buttons, and the web view. It's not pretty, and you wouldn't want to have to interact with your GUI setup this way, but it may be reassuring that the format is one that you can poke around in if you want. Quietly close the file without saving any changes. We'll take another look at MainMenu.xib before the end of the chapter.

2.5 Wiring Up the Components

You've used Interface Builder to select and configure the visual elements you will use in this application. You've placed them in your window, changed their appearance, set default values, adjusted their sizes, and set up how they would adjust as the window size changes. Now you are ready to wire them together.

For example, you want to connect the Back button to the web view. When you click the button, you want the web view to display the contents of the previous URL. Your average button isn't going to know a thing about web views. A web view, however, should know how to move back in its history and should be able to be triggered by some outside source. So, you just need to wire up the web view's ability to go back to this button's clicks.

Similarly, a text field shouldn't know about URLs and web views. If a text field had to know about everything it could supply text for, the API would be huge and brittle. But a web view should know how to get a URL from a string from some other element. So, we just need to wire the web view's "get the URL from a string" ability to the component providing the string.

Connecting the Web View

It doesn't always work, but it helps to think of who knows what. In this case, most of the knowledge is in the web view. Much of what an object can do is revealed to you in Interface Builder by the Connections inspector.

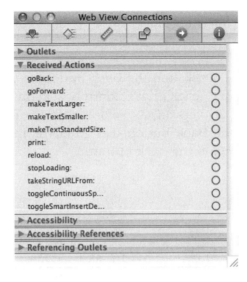

To see some of what a web view can do, select the web view in the layout window, and open the Connections inspector. With the web view selected, if the inspector is already visible, you can click the blue right arrow to open the Connections inspector tab. You can also press ⌘5 or navigate to Tools > Connections Inspector. The previous figure shows the actions that the web view can receive. Those are the only ones we'll need for now.

This next step feels like magic to me.

Click inside the circle to the right of goBack: in the Connections inspector, and hold the mouse button down. Drag the mouse pointer over to the Back button you created. You should see a blue line appear as you begin to drag. As your mouse hovers over the Back button, a gray box will appear with the words *Push Button (Back)*. Release the mouse, and you will have made a connection.

Here's a slow-motion replay. A WebView knows how to go back in the browser history. The button knows how to initiate an action when it is pressed. We've used the Connections inspector to connect them. Now that we've made the connection, whenever a user clicks the Back button, the WebView's goBack: method is called, and as a result, if there is a previous page in the browser history, it will be loaded.

Look back at the Connection inspector. The circle you clicked next to goBack: is now filled in. Also, goBack: is now visually connected to Push Button (Back). See the *x* to the left side of Push Button (Back)? Click it. You've just broken the connection.

You can reconnect goBack: and the Back button as you did before, or you can right-click or ^-click (that's Control-click) the web view to bring up a heads-up display version. As before, click the circle next to goBack:, and drag to the Back button. Let go of the mouse, and you've reconnected goBack: and the Back button.

We have two more connections to make. Select WebView again, and use the Connections inspector or the heads-up display.

1. Connect the goForward: received action to the Forward button. This will enable the user to click the Forward button to move forward in the browser history.

2. Connect the takeStringURLFrom: received action to the text field. This lets the user type a URL into the text field and click Enter to load the web page.

When you are done, the Connections inspector should look like this:

As if you don't have enough options, you can also make these connections in the opposite direction. For example, choose the Back button and look at its Connections inspector. In the Sent Actions section, you should see the single entry, selector:.[6] Select this, drag the connection back to the WebView, and let go. A gray box with all the web view's actions should pop up.

Choose goBack:. You have now successfully made the connection in the opposite direction. You will soon develop a rhythm around your favorite method and direction. Stick with whatever you are most comfortable doing.

Testing the Browser in the Simulator

Save your work, and open it in the Cocoa Simulator. Click in the text field, and hit ↵. The Pragmatic Programmer home page should appear. Enter another URL, and hit ↵. Although this mostly works, I have a couple of quick notes:

- Don't forget to include http://, because this is just a very basic web browser.

---

6. A selector is the name of the method being called, and the colon indicates that the method takes a single argument. You'll learn a lot more about selectors in Chapter 3, *Methods and Parameters*, on page 35.

- Don't choose overly complicated pages or pages that need authentication. This is a *very* basic web browser.[7]

- Once a second page appears, you can hit the Back and Forward buttons to navigate back and forth between the two pages.

This is great! At least here in the simulator, you have a working web browser.

Our browser doesn't have some of the features you might expect to see in even the sparest of browsers. For example, you don't get any feedback when a page is loading. When you first run SimpleBrowser, you might think that nothing is happening until, after a pause, the page appears. Also, the URL doesn't change when you hit Back and Forward. If you load http://pragprog.com and then http://apple.com and then hit the Back button, you will see the Pragmatic Programmer's home page even though the URL will still read http://apple.com. We'll take care of these problems in the next few chapters.

2.6 Fixing the Build

It feels like you're done. You can play with your application in the Cocoa Simulator. All of your work in Interface Builder is correct and complete, and you have no code to write for this SimpleBrowser project. You don't, however, have an application that you can give to someone else to run on their machine. You need to go back to Xcode and create a release.

In Xcode, click Build & Run. The build succeeds, and it looks as if SimpleBrowser starts to load. The icon bounces in the Dock for a while, but nothing is happening. Depending on how you're set up, you might find yourself in the debugger with a stack trace and a warning.

Arrggghhhh. Click the Stop button, or choose Run > Stop.[8] We need to add WebKit.framework.

I mentioned earlier we'd have to link it in. We could have done it when we dragged the WebView from the Library into our window. Chances are that you'll be more likely to remember it now that you see the problems

---

7. The point of this example is not to build a robust web browser but to use a web browser as an example application that allows us to introduce you to Cocoa programming. Currently, for example, you won't be able to load pages that include Flash.
8. If your installation of Xcode doesn't look like mine, you can always customize the toolbar by choosing View > Customize Toolbar.... Also, you can make many adjustments from Xcode > Preferences.

 **Joe Asks...**

How Would I Have Known to Add the WebKit Framework?

Start by opening the debugger with either Run > Debugger or ⇧ ⌘ Y. Depending on how you've configured Xcode, you may also see an icon that looks like bug spray that you can click. In the top-left corner of your Xcode window, you will see the warning that the application is

```
TERMINATING_DUE_TO_UNCAUGHT_EXCEPTION
```

The stack trace isn't very helpful, but if you look at the Console, you will see the problem pretty quickly. Open the Console using ⌘ ⇧ R or Run > Console. You'll see a gdb prompt. Scroll back past a listing of the stack. Just above this you will see a series of lines that each begin with a time stamp, the word *SimpleBrowser*, and brackets around an identifier that includes the process number. Once you pare away all of this information, you should be left with something like this:

```
An uncaught exception was raised
-[NSKeyedUnarchiver decodeObjectForKey:]:
               cannot decode object of class (WebView)
Terminating app due to uncaught exception
               'NSInvalidUnarchiveOperationException'
```

A-ha! The problem is with unarchiving a WebView object. Your nib is essentially an archive of objects and their connections. You need to load the WebKit framework so that the WebView can be successfully reconstituted.

that can come up. See the *Joe Asks...* on this page for an explanation of how you might have diagnosed the problem yourself.

When we dragged the WebView instance from our library, we saw that it is part of the WebKit framework but not part of the Cocoa framework. I would have assumed that Xcode would automatically have added the WebKit framework to the corresponding project to link against, but it doesn't. You need to do that yourself.

From the project view, select the Frameworks folder in the SimpleBrowser group. You should see four frameworks have already been added to the project, but if you look at the rightmost column, you'll see that only Cocoa.framework is active for our target.

Right-click or ^-click the Frameworks folder, and choose Add > Existing Frameworks....

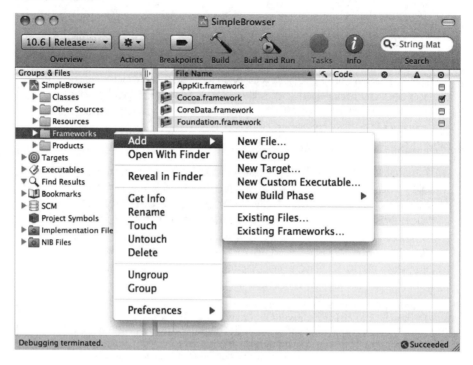

Choose WebKit.framework, and make sure that once it is added that the target checkbox is selected.[9]

Congratulations! You can now build and run your application from within Xcode.

2.7 Sharing Your Browser

Now that you've gone to all that work to create a working browser, you'd like to share your application with your friends—at least the ones who are running Mac OS X. Make sure that your Active Build Target setting is set to Release and not Debug. You can do this from Project > Set Active Build Configuration > Release or using the Active Build Configuration dropdown in Xcode if you have set Xcode's preferences so that this is visible.

---

9. You can also add a framework by selecting a target either with Add > Existing Frameworks ... or on the General tab you get after selecting Get Info.

Once the build target is set, click Build & Run again. This time, your SimpleBrowser application should build, link, and launch fine. Look inside your project's build/Release directory.

You should see your SimpleBrowser application. Because we chose Release as our target instead of Debug, this file can be distributed and run on other machines. The easiest way is to right-click the Simple-Browser file inside the build/Release directory and choose the Compress "SimpleBrowser" option. That creates SimpleBrowser.zip, which you can send to a friend.

2.8 Exercise: Rinse and Repeat

In this chapter you created a working web browser without writing any code. You took advantage of Apple's WebKit framework to do most of your work for you. You spent much of the time getting the application to look right and just a few click-and-drags at the end to get the behavior you need.

You learned how to make this all work in discrete steps, but that's not the way you will tend to work. If you were doing this again from scratch, you would combine steps. When you drag in your first button, you would probably immediately name it Back and connect it to the web view.

Although you will be tempted to skip this exercise, you will benefit greatly from starting from scratch and re-creating this web browser. With no one telling you step-by-step what you need to do next, the pieces will start to fit together. Take five minutes to make your own web browser, and you will reinforce what you have learned.

2.9 The Nib File

All the work you did in this chapter is captured in a nib file. A *nib* is an archive of objects. In Cocoa, nib files contain all the information you need to bring your UI elements to life at runtime. A typical Cocoa application will have many nib files that are loaded only as they are needed to create instances of the objects that make up your user interface and, as you'll see in Chapter 8, *Creating a Controller*, on page 129, nonvisual objects as well.

The nib file represents the graph of objects you built using Interface Builder so that your interface and other objects captured in the nib can be reconstructed each time your application begins. You will work in Xcode to define your classes, and you will instantiate classes into objects in either Xcode or Interface Builder. A nib file that you create in Interface Builder is a frozen graph of objects that will be brought back to life at runtime.

We'll return to Interface Builder and nib files throughout this book. You'll also find a great deal of information on them in Apple's *Interface Builder User Guide* [App08e]. Scott Stevenson also has a nice quick-start tutorial of creating a different application with no code.[10] It currently uses Xcode 3.1, so what you'll see in Snow Leopard will be slightly different from what he shows you.

The Document Window

Let's take a look at the objects in the MainMenu nib. Double-click Main-Menu.xib to reopen it in Interface Builder. This time, open the Document window using the menu item Window > Document or using the keyboard shortcut ⌘0.

I prefer the List view mode, which you select using the middle of the three tabs in the upper-left corner. I've also opened up the disclosure

---

10. http://cocoadevcentral.com/d/learn_cocoa/

triangles for the Window object and the objects it contains. This hierarchy includes all of the GUI components we placed in the layout window.

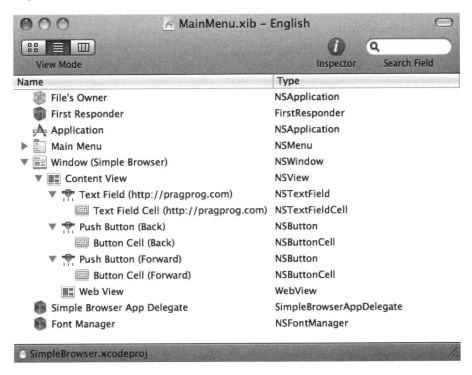

Look at the Window hierarchy, and you will see that the window contains a content view that contains the four components we dragged on the window. The nib also contains the main menu and a bunch of nonvisual elements. I'm not going to talk about what each of them does right now, but I wanted to show you this view of the objects in the nib because we're going to use it later to connect visual and nonvisual elements. This window will help us connect what we build in Interface Builder to the code we write in Xcode. It is also a handy way to select components that are nested in the layout window. Also, if you lose the layout window, you can double-click the Window (SimpleBrowser) item in the Document window, and the layout window will come to the front.

The XML Representation of the Nib

The Document window gives us one view of the nib file. For another, let us look at the actual XML that is used to persist the nib during development. Let's start with a quick look back at creating and using the nib we built in this chapter.

Our particular nib contains two buttons that are each instances of the class NSButton. If you search the Interface Builder Library for *NSButton*, you won't just find one button. You should see a dozen or more buttons like the ones shown here:

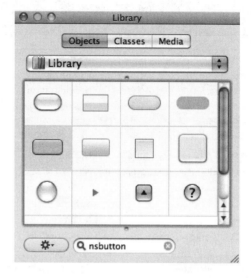

When you drag an NSButton from the Library and place it in the view, you are creating an instance of the NSButton class. You could start with any one of the NSButtons you see previously in the figure and turn them into the instance of NSButton that you want. But Apple presents you with a palette of buttons that look very different. That means that you aren't really focused on finding an NSButton as you browse through the library. You are looking for a button that has a particular look or is used in a particular way. This means that you look for components from your end user's point of view.

You select, place, and configure your button. You can figure out at least part of the information that is stored by reading the XML.

We're going to open MainMenu.xib with a text editor just to take a look around. You will never need to do this again to view what's in a nib file. More importantly, promise me you will never change anything in a nib file while it's open in a text editor. Interface Builder is the only tool you should use to create, view, or modify nibs.

If you haven't already, open MainMenu.xib with a text editor. Search for the text *NSButton* and look for this part of the file that describes the look of your Back button:

UsingWhatsThere/SampleNib/MainMenu.xib

```
<object class="NSButton" id="164086064">
        <reference key="NSNextResponder" ref="439893737"/>
        <int key="NSvFlags">265</int>
        <string key="NSFrame">{{277, 258}, {93, 32}}</string>
        <reference key="NSSuperview" ref="439893737"/>
        <bool key="NSEnabled">YES</bool>
        <object class="NSButtonCell" key="NSCell" id="941085700">
                <int key="NSCellFlags">67239424</int>
                <int key="NSCellFlags2">134217728</int>
                <string key="NSContents">Back</string>
                <reference key="NSSupport" ref="640083843"/>
                <reference key="NSControlView" ref="164086064"/>
                <int key="NSButtonFlags">-2038284033</int>
                <int key="NSButtonFlags2">268435585</int>
                <string key="NSAlternateContents"/>
                <string type="base64-UTF8" key="NSKeyEquivalent">75yCA</string>
                <int key="NSPeriodicDelay">200</int>
                <int key="NSPeriodicInterval">25</int>
        </object>
</object>
```

This describes an object of type NSButton. The x and y coordinates as
well as the height and the width are in the line with the NSFrame as the
key. The NSButton object also contains an object of type NSButtonCell. We
haven't talked about NSButtonCells, but you can see that that's where
the button name and the keyboard shortcut are set.

The nib file also contains objects that represent the connections you
made. For example, search for the string takeStringURLFrom:. You should
see this part of MainMenu.xib:

UsingWhatsThere/SampleNib/MainMenu.xib

```
<object class="IBConnectionRecord">
        <object class="IBActionConnection" key="connection">
                <string key="label">takeStringURLFrom:</string>
                <reference key="source" ref="1029174864"/>
                <reference key="destination" ref="109215417"/>
        </object>
        <int key="connectionID">459</int>
</object>
```

You can search on the reference numbers for the destination and the
source and see that this snippet describes a connection from the Web-
View object with the label takeStringURLFrom: to the destination NSTextField
object. In the next chapter, we'll learn to say this a little differently.
As you'll see in the next chapter, this just means that the target (the

WebView object) is being sent the message takeStringURLFrom: with the NSTextField object passed in as the sender.

In our particular case, the nib object life cycle is straightforward. When the application starts up, the object graph is loaded into memory and unarchived. The components are initialized. Then all of the connections between the objects are made, and the main menu is displayed.

Of course, any useful application has its share of code as well—that's the next stop on our tour.

Chapter 3

Methods and Parameters

So, you've built a working web browser. On one hand, you're feeling pretty good about yourself. You just dragged and dropped and connected some dots together and had yourself a web browser. That's power.

On the other hand, it doesn't feel like real programming. A *real* programmer wouldn't use a bunch of GUI tools. Real programmers would build the objects with their bare hands. They would say "Arrrr" and make other pirate sounds while they wrestle with memory management. You aren't going soft on me, are you? Come to think of it, you haven't even built yourself a "Hello, World!" program yet.

Your "Hello, World!" program will have to wait until the next chapter. Before you start creating your own objects in code and writing your own methods, you need to get comfortable reading the Objective-C that sends a target an action and navigating the API documentation to find out which messages you can send to objects in the Cocoa APIs. This chapter is your introduction to messages in Objective-C and Cocoa.

3.1 Sending Messages Without Arguments

Back in Section 2.5, *Wiring Up the Components*, on page 22, you used Interface Builder to create a connection from your Back button to the goBack: received action in your web view. As a result, every time the Back button is clicked, the web view's goBack method is called.[1]

---

1. You might notice that I've introduced a slight simplification by dropping the : at the end of goBack. I'll fix that in a little bit, but it's going to make it easier for us in the beginning.

Let's assume you have instantiated the two objects involved in this action. You have an instance of NSButton named backButton and an instance of WebView named myWebView. When the user clicks the Back button, essentially this message is sent:

```
[myWebView goBack]
```

The square brackets and everything in between make up the *message expression*. In this simplest of cases, there are only two parts: the receiver and the message. The myWebView object is the receiver. It is the target—the object to which you are sending the message. In this example, the message is goBack.

We are sending a message with no arguments. In this form, the call will look like this:

```
[receiver message]
```

Depending on the programming language you use now, this might look like a function call or method call. In other words, in your own language the following Objective-C message:

```
[myWebView goBack]
```

looks something like this:

```
myWebView.goBack()
```

As you would expect, you can chain messages together in much the same way as you would chain methods. In Java or C#, you might write something like this:

```
myWebView.oneMethod().anotherMethod()
```

This invokes oneMethod() on myWebView, and then anotherMethod() is called on the result.

In Objective-C you would write this same fictional code as follows:

```
[[myWebView oneMethod] anotherMethod]
```

You read these nested calls from the inside out. First the message oneMethod is sent to myWebView. Then the result of this call is the target of the message anotherMethod.

What messages can you really send to myWebView? You'll spend a lot of time looking through the documentation of Apple's APIs. Let's take a look at the docs for WebView and find a description of this goBack method.

3.2 Reading the Docs

Apple includes a comprehensive set of documentation to help you figure out what to use and how to use it when you develop your Cocoa Apps. You can access the docs from Xcode using Help > Developer Documentation. Of course, you can make your way through the documentation without my help—I just want to point out some of what you'll find as a way of encouraging you to look.

Type *webview* into the search box in the upper-right corner of the Doc viewer and experiment with the different results you get depending on whether you choose to search through the doc sets for iPhone, Mac OS X, Xcode, or some combination.[2] You can also choose whether you are interested only in results that start with, contain, or match the search string exactly.

You can narrow your search in many ways. For now, choose to limit the doc sets to the Mac OS X 10.6 Core Library, enable all languages, and choose Exact. The returned results will be grouped under the headings API, Title, and Full Text like this:

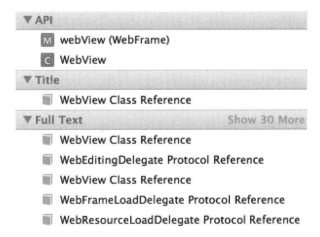

Our first two results under API are the webView method from the Web-Frame class and the WebView class. The only entry under the Title heading and the first entry under the Full Text heading also take us to the docs for the WebView class.

---

2. The docs as well as the way in which you search them and filter the results changed in Snow Leopard. The instructions here are for Xcode 3.2 (and above), which was released with Snow Leopard. If you are using Leopard or earlier, the differences should be clear.

We get more results under Full Text because *webview* occurs in the title of only one document, but it appears in the body of more than thirty documents.

If you change your Doc Sets setting to include iPhone docs and you select Contains instead of Exact, you will also see the iPhone equivalent of the Cocoa WebView, the UIWebView class, in each of these categories.

Select the line containing the WebView class to see the class reference for WebView. Here's the top of the listing:

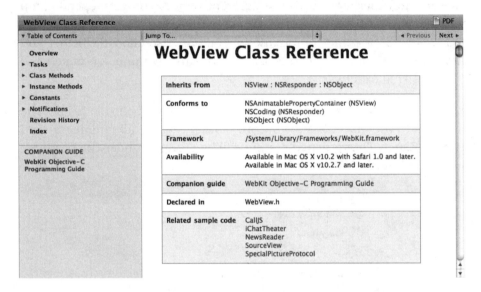

On the right side you can trace the inheritance from WebView back to the Cocoa root class NSObject. WebView extends NSView, which extends NSResponder, which in turn extends the root class NSObject.

You also see what framework you'll need to include to use the class. Objective-C uses header files[3]—in this case, WebView is declared in WebView.h, which is part of the WebKit framework. The Availability section of the method description will let you know whether a method is available if you want to target older versions of Mac OS X.

---

3. If you aren't familiar with header files, don't worry. Section 8.4, *Declaring an Outlet and an Action*, on page 134 and the material leading up to it should give you a good feel for how and why they are used.

You can search the document for specific method names, but there are three links in that gray box on the left side that will help you figure out how to use a Cocoa class.

- *Overview*: This is a quick summary of what the class is for and how you should use it. It contains links to specific methods that need to be called out and classes that often collaborate with the one being described.

- *Tasks*: You can get alphabetical listings of the class and instance methods later in the documentation, but this is a grouping of the methods by what they do, in other words, by the tasks you might want to perform. For example, the screenshot that follows shows the methods used for moving back and forward. I've hovered my mouse pointer over the canGoBack method to bring up the tooltip describing the method.

Moving Back and Forward

```
- setMaintainsBackForwardList: ⓘ
- backForwardList ⓘ
- canGoBack ⓘ
- goBack ⓘ    Returns whether the previous location can be loaded.
- goBack: ⓘ
- canGoForward ⓘ
- goForward ⓘ
- goForward: ⓘ
- goToBackForwardItem: ⓘ
```

- *Companion Guide*: Apple often has one or more comprehensive documents that gives examples of using instances of this class to accomplish some programming task. In this case, you are given a link to the *Web Kit Objective-C Programming Guide*.

In addition to the Tasks listing of all the methods, you can also see a list of the class methods and a list of the instance methods. There are also lists of constants and available notifications.

Let's take a quick look at a listing for a method.

If you click the goBack method (and not the goBack: method below it), you'll see something like this:

goBack

Loads the previous location in the back-forward list.

- (BOOL)goBack

Return Value
YES if able to move backward; otherwise, NO.

Availability
Available in Mac OS X v10.2 with Safari 1.0 and later.
Available in Mac OS X v10.2.7 and later.

See Also
- backForwardList
- goForward
- goToBackForwardItem:

Declared In
WebView.h

This is a quick description of what the method is designed to do followed by the method signature:

- (BOOL) goBack

The minus (-) indicates that goBack is an instance method. A plus (+) is used to label a class method. We haven't talked about objects and classes much yet, but when we do, you'll see that you send a class method to the WebView class and an instance method to an object of type WebView.

The return type of goBack is BOOL. You can see by the Discussion section that in Objective-C the two boolean values are YES and NO and not true and false. In addition to being the way experienced Objective-C programmers write code, you'll want to use YES and NO to make your code read more conversationally.

3.3 Methods with Arguments

If you look back at the list of tasks for moving back and forward, you should see two methods for going back that look almost identical. There's the goBack method we just looked at, and there's the goBack: method.

These two methods are completely different. The trailing colon on the goBack: method indicates that it takes a single argument.

Look up the goBack: method in the WebView class reference. Its signature is very different from the no-argument goBack method:

goBack:

An action method that loads the previous location in the back-forward list.

- (void)goBack:(id)*sender*

Parameters
sender
  The object that sent this message.

Discussion
This method does nothing if it is unable to move backward.

Availability
Available in Mac OS X v10.2 with Safari 1.0 and later.
Available in Mac OS X v10.2.7 and later.

See Also
– goForward:

Declared In
WebView.h

When you connected your Back button to the web view, you chose this goBack: method as the action. You'll see this type of signature a lot with methods designed to be called by GUI components. The sender argument is a handle back to the calling object. The type of sender is upcast to id. This is the generic type for Cocoa. Any pointer to an object is at least of type id. Having a handle to the sender allows us to communicate with the object that called goBack: no matter what its type. We'll look at a typical example of how you might take advantage of this in Section 3.6, *Links Back to Yourself*, on page 45.[4]

Here's how you call a method that takes a single argument:

```
[myWebView goBack:self]
```

If you are still translating back and forth between Objective-C and another language, you might be used to something like this:

```
myWebView.goBack(this)
```

---

4. The return type of goBack: is IBAction. We're going to wait until Chapter 8, *Creating a Controller*, on page 129 to talk about what that means. For now, you can treat it as a void.

Let's use a method with more arguments to help you better understand the differences. WebView contains a method with the rather lengthy name searchFor:direction:caseSensitive:wrap:. That is the entire method name. In other languages, this might be called searchFor, but in Objective-C the description of all the arguments is included as part of the method name. Separate the method into pieces that end with a colon. When you call the method, you need to supply one argument for each colon. The method signature makes this clearer because it specifies the return type of the method and the type of each of the arguments.

```
- (BOOL)searchFor:(NSString *)string
        direction:(BOOL)forward
    caseSensitive:(BOOL)caseFlag
             wrap:(BOOL)wrapFlag
```

Here's how you might use it:

```
[myWebView searchFor:myString direction:YES caseSensitive:NO wrap:YES]
```

The equivalent in Java or C# might be something like this:

```
myWebView.searchFor(myString, true, false, true)
```

Newcomers to Objective-C tend to be more put off by the colons and by having arguments mixed in than they are by the square brackets. I completely understand. I think part of the difficulty comes when a method is short enough to list on one line. Instead, you might find it easier to read if we use this more vertical orientation:

```
[myWebView searchFor:myString
           direction:YES
       caseSensitive:NO
                wrap:YES]
```

Here we are following the Objective-C code formatting standard and aligning the colons. It makes it easy to see the method name as the combination of the elements to the left of the colon and that the arguments sit to the right side of each colon.

The Objective-C version might look like named parameters, but they are not. The order of the arguments cannot be changed. You can't leave any of them out. The method name is searchFor:direction:caseSensitive:wrap:, which is also called the *selector* because it is used at runtime to select the method that will be called.

You will come to really appreciate the fact that you don't have to recall what the parameters true, false, and true refer to as you do in the Java or C# versions. In the Objective-C version, you know that you are conducting a search for a given string that is not case sensitive in the forward direction with wrapping enabled.

Your Cocoa code should be readable. A month after you've written a method, you should be able to quickly reconstruct your intent and understand what the method does. In WebView, you can see the method moveToBeginningOfSentenceAndModifySelection:. The name of a method might be longer than its implementation—but what the method does is immediately clear to anyone who invokes it in code or connects to it using Interface Builder.

You'll find more information about methods in the "Objects, Classes, and Messaging" chapter of Apple's *The Objective-C Programming Language* [App09f]. There's also a nice entry on Stack Overflow about passing multiple parameters in Objective-C.[5] You should also check out Apple's *Coding Guidelines for Cocoa* [App06] for guidelines on naming methods. Matt Gallagher has a nice post on Cocoa with Love about method names.[6]

3.4 Dynamic Binding

Let's take a look behind the scenes at what happens when an Objective-C message is sent. The simplest of cases, as shown here:

```
[myWebView goBack]
```

is converted at runtime to the following function call:

```
objc_msgSend(myWebView, goBack)
```

The receiver is passed in as the first argument and the selector as the second. The more complicated message, as shown here:

```
[myWebView searchFor:myString direction:YES caseSensitive:NO wrap:YES]
```

is converted at runtime to this function call:

```
objc_msgSend(myWebView, searchFor:direction:caseSensitive:wrap:,
                                    myString, YES, NO, YES)
```

Again, the receiver is passed in as the first argument, and the selector is passed in as the second. The parameters are passed in as the remaining function arguments.

---

5. http://stackoverflow.com/questions/722651/how-do-i-pass-multiple-parameters-in-objective-c
6. http://cocoawithlove.com/2009/06/method-names-in-objective-c.html

Here's more than you need to know: at runtime, the selector is matched to an entry in the dispatch table for the object's class, which points to the memory location of the procedure that implements the requested method. If no selector exists in that class, then the search continues in the class' superclass and on up the tree to the root class. For more information on this, read Apple's *The Objective-C 2.0 Programming Language*, which you can access from Xcode's Documentation window.

3.5 Problems Sending Messages

There are two basic things that could go wrong with a simple message in Objective-C: either the receiver may not exist, in which case it has the value nil, or the object may be valid but may not understand the message being sent to it. You may get a compiler warning when you try to build the application, but neither type of error will break the build or prevent someone from trying to run the application.

In the first case, you are sending a message of the following form:

```
[nil someMessage];
```

You won't get an error at compile time or exception at runtime. Also, if someMessage returns an object, pointer type, or most valid numeric types, then this message returns 0.

In the second case, you are sending a message like this:

```
[validObject someMessageItDoesNotUnderstand];
```

This time the application will terminate when the receiver is sent a message it doesn't understand.[7] This problem snuck by you at compile time but has led to a runtime exception. If validObject is an instance of the fictional class CustomClass, you'll see a message like this in the console:

```
*** -[CustomClass someMessageItDoesNotUnderstand]:
                 unrecognized selector sent to instance 0x109280
*** Terminating app due to uncaught exception 'NSInvalidArgumentException'
```

---

7. An object will "understand" a message if it or one of its superclasses declare and implement the corresponding method.

This tells you that the message someMessageItDoesNotUnderstand was sent to an instance of CustomClass and that CustomClass does not implement that method.

So, why wasn't this caught at compile time? It probably was. You will most likely get a warning that CustomClass may not respond to the message someMessageItDoesNotUnderstand.[8]

There are times that we will take advantage of the dynamic typing and dynamic binding and other times that we will find it helps to take advantage of the help the compiler can give us if it knows the types we are targeting. One way to avoid runtime errors is to become familiar with Apple's docs so that you are sending objects messages they understand.

3.6 Links Back to Yourself

We used the WebView method takeStringURLFrom: to use the URL the user types into the text field for the web view. The takeStringURLFrom: signature looks a lot like the goBack: method's.

```
- (IBAction)takeStringURLFrom:(id)sender
```

Assume that we have an instance of WebView named myWebView and the text field is an instance of NSTextField named addressField. Then when the user enters a string in the text field and hits ↵, something like this message is sent:

```
[myWebView takeStringURLFrom: self]
```

You might want to visualize this as a message from the text field with the target as the WebView instance.

takeStringURLFrom: self

---

8. There are times that you can carefully ignore this warning. You may know that at runtime validObject will not be an instance of CustomClass but will be an instance of a class that can handle someMessageItDoesNotUnderstand.

The web view receives this message and prepares to load a new web page. First it needs to get the string containing the URL from somewhere. As a result of the message it just received, it knows from where. The WebView object sends a message back to the object sending the takeStringURLFrom: message asking for its string value.

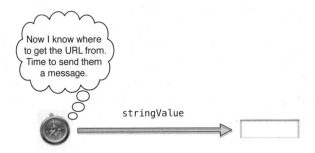

The WebView object sends this message:

```
[sender stringValue]
```

The web view sends a message back to the object sending the takeString-URLFrom: message asking for its string value. The sender is a valid object, and we assume its type is such that it will respond to the stringValue message, but the compiler can't check this for us. We can't know the type of the sender at compile time, and yet everything works fine at runtime.

The web view then tries to load the URL provided as a string in response to this message.

3.7 Exercise: Multiple Connections

You can see this in action by modifying the SimpleBrowser project. We're going to throw out this version when we are done, so make a copy of the existing SimpleBrowser project so you can do all of your work in this copy.

Let's work through this one together. When we're done, you'll have connected the web view to more than one text field and have given it the ability to take its string URL from any of them.

Open the nib file in this copy of your project, and add two text fields with different default addresses so the application looks like this when it's running:

In Interface Builder, select the web view, and use the inspector to look at its connections. There should be a connection between the received action takeStringURLFrom: and your first text field, and the circle should be filled in as before.

But we know how takeStringURLFrom: works. The first thing it does is send a message back to the component that called the method. So, there's no reason we can't connect this received action to multiple elements. Drag from the filled-in circle to one of the two text fields you added at the bottom of the window. Drag one more time from the filled-in circle to the other text field you added. Your web view is now ready to take its URL from any of the text fields. You can see the multiple selections here:

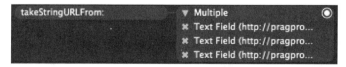

Save your work, and test your modified application. You can enter URLs from any of the text fields. In fact, you could have mixed and matched the type of visual components that you used to pass in the URL. The component just needs to be able to respond to the message stringValue with a string containing a valid URL.

Before moving on, you may want to save a copy of this project and revert to the version we had before adding the two text fields. Go ahead and close this project; we're not going to need the browser example for the next three chapters.

Now that you know how to read methods in Objective-C, you can write a few of your own to customize the behavior of the SimpleBrowser. Before we get back to our browser, we're going to take a little time to explore classes, objects, instance variables, and properties.

Chapter 4

Classes and Objects

We're going to set our browser example aside for a few chapters. Now that you can read methods, it's time to write a few of our own. This is the chapter where you begin to write Objective-C code. You'll start with a fairly basic "Hello, World!" application and learn to create classes, objects, variables, and methods.

Remember that our purpose is not to create a great "Hello, World!" application. The output of our program won't change very much during the course of the chapter. The point is our progression through using different techniques. You'll use one of Apple's classes and then create one of your own. You'll communicate with these classes using class methods. You'll then create an instance of a class and use instance methods to communicate with these objects. After we've regained our self-respect as *real* developers, we'll return to our web browser example in Chapter 8, *Creating a Controller*, on page 129 and customize the behavior by writing our own code.

4.1 Creating "Hello, World!"

Let's create our "Hello, World!" project in Xcode. Remember in Xcode you create a new project with File > New Project or ⇧ ⌘ N. Choose the Application > Cocoa Application template, leaving all the check boxes unselected, and name the project HelloWorld. Click Build & Run, and after a pause, an empty window will appear. The application works; it just doesn't do anything. Quit HelloWorld, or stop the tasks from within Xcode by clicking the stop sign, by choosing Run > Stop, or by pressing ⇧ ⌘ ↵.

We aren't going to talk much about memory until Chapter 6, *Memory*, on page 89. Even so, I want you to get into the habit of turning on automatic garbage collection for every new Cocoa project. In Xcode, choose Project > Edit Project Settings. This will open the Project Settings window. Choose the Build tab, and start to type the word *garbage* into the filter. You won't need to type very much of it to see the Objective-C Garbage Collection setting.

Use the drop-down tab, and select Required. Close your settings, and now your project supports automatic garbage collection.

4.2 Logging Output to the Console

For now we're going to ignore the GUI and write directly to the Console using NSLog(). You will pass in an NSString to NSLog() to be printed to the Console window.[1]

Instead of just enclosing the string to be printed in quotes, you need to indicate an NSString like this:

```
NSLog(@"Hello, world!");
```

In other words, you need to put the @ before the open quote to signal the start of a Cocoa NSString. If you forget to include the @, you will get a compiler warning that you are passing an argument from an incompatible pointer type. Unfortunately, the syntax coloring for the quoted material without the @ is exactly the same as it is with the @, so this omission can be tough to spot.

---

1. Many of the core classes such as NSString begin with NS, which stands for Apple. Actually, NS stands for "NeXTSTEP," and these classes were not renamed when Apple purchased NeXT. Objective-C does not have namespaces, so we often begin a class name with a two- or three-letter identifier. The same convention is also followed for many C functions such as NSLog().

Functions

NSLog() looks nothing like the square brackets, colons, targets, and actions we saw in the previous chapter.

It shouldn't. NSLog() is not an Objective-C method—it is a C function. Objective-C sits on top of C. Although you should prefer to use the Objective-C style of sending messages to classes and objects, you can also use good old-fashioned C for getting things done.

You'll see a lot of C-style functions when you work with system-level calls and with APIs that work with graphic objects. You can recognize C functions because they use ordinary parentheses to capture their arguments, and you just call the function without a target. In this chapter, I'll point out the differences now and again, and soon you'll get used to the mixture of C and Objective-C constructs.

In a traditional C "Hello, World!" application (or even in older versions of Cocoa "Hello, World!" applications) that you might have seen, you would put this line in main(). Your program has a main() in the file main.m, which you can find in Groups & Files in the Other Sources directory.

`Classes/HelloWorld1/main.m`

```
#import <Cocoa/Cocoa.h>

int main(int argc, char *argv[])
{
    return NSApplicationMain(argc, (const char **) argv);
}
```

We're going to leave main.m alone. We aren't going to ever add to it or modify it. All of the action for main() is contained in the call to the function NSApplicationMain(). In our case, this function creates an instance of the NSApplication class and loads the MainMenu nib. In other words, it launches the application.

If you're a C programmer, you'll be tempted to put more of your programming logic here in the main() function. Don't. There is a new place for this customization, the application delegate. You're going to see a lot of this delegate pattern throughout this book.

This first time through, I'm going to gloss over the details, but the big idea is that the NSApplication class knows a lot about how an application should behave in general. It can't possibly know how any particular application should behave. One solution would be for us to subclass NSApplication and override the appropriate methods with our custom behavior. We tend to take a different approach in Cocoa applications. We assign a delegate object to the NSApplication and implement only those methods we need to implement. And what's a delegate? You can think of it as an assistant class that the main class passes work to. When the main class, in this case Application, needs something done, it calls a method in its delegate class.

Fortunately, the Cocoa Application template created an application delegate for us named HelloWorldAppDelegate. You'll find the source files in the Classes folder under Groups & Files.[2]

The Cocoa Application template has created the files HelloWorldAppDelegate.h and HelloWorldAppDelegate.m, which together define the class HelloWorldAppDelegate.

Inside HelloWorldAppDelegate.m, there is a method named applicationDidFinishLaunching: that contains the following comment:

```
// Insert code here to initialize your application
```

Add the log line in place of the comment like this:

Classes/HelloWorld1/HelloWorldAppDelegate.m

```
#import "HelloWorldAppDelegate.h"
@implementation HelloWorldAppDelegate
@synthesize window;

- (void)applicationDidFinishLaunching:(NSNotification *)aNotification {
    NSLog(@"Hello, World!");
}
@end
```

---

2. If you don't find these files, you are probably using Xcode version 3.1 or earlier and need to move to Xcode 3.2 or later.

How is this method ever called? We don't call it explicitly from main(). In fact, we don't explicitly call it from anywhere.

The simple explanation is that at runtime after the application finishes launching, the application object sends its delegate the message applicationDidFinishLaunching:. The slightly longer version is what you saw in the previous chapter; if the delegate didn't implement this method, then there would be a runtime error when it is called. So, what really happens is the application object checks to make sure the delegate implements the method, and if it does, then it sends the message.

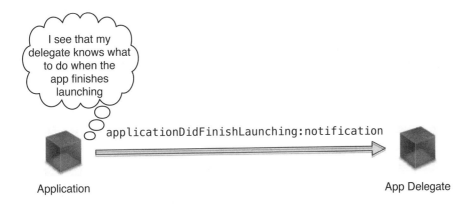

To run the application, first show the Console with Run > Console or ⇧ ⌘ R. Next, clear the Console by selecting Run > Clear Console, by pressing ^ ⌥ ⌘ R, or by clicking the Clear Console button if it is visible. Finally, click Build & Run (or use the keyboard shortcut for this, ⌘ ↵).

HelloWorld should start up, the empty window will appear, and the Console should contain a line indicating the time at which the session started followed by a line with a time stamp, the process ID, and the string we created. Mine looks like this:

```
HelloWorld[19673:10b] Hello, world!
```

Once you've admired your achievements for a bit, you can quit HelloWorld and get back to work.

4.3 Using an Existing Class

We've got a "Hello, World" app printing out nicely to the Console. As our next step, we'll create a text field in code, add it to our window, configure it a little, and then display "Hello, World!" in this text field. Remember, our goal is not to print out "Hello, World!" in a text field. If that were our only goal, we could just drag the widget out of the library in Interface Builder and type in the phrase *Hello, World!*[3] The rule of thumb for Interface Builder is simple: any time you *can* use Interface Builder, you *should* use Interface Builder. There is nothing you can do in Interface Builder that can't be done in code. There is no reason to avoid Interface Builder for any but very esoteric cases.

This is one of those cases. Our goal in this section is to gain experience in using code to instantiate, configure, and use a class that we didn't write. Then we'll be ready to create and use our own class.

To make things a bit easier, double-click MainMenu.xib to start Interface Builder, select your window, and use the Size inspector to set the width of the window to 580 and the height to 90. It's unfortunately easy to select the view by mistake if you click the inside of the window. If you click the title bar for the window, then the title bar for the Size inspector should say *Window Size*.

I've set the maximum and minimum size of the window to be these dimensions as well so that the user can't resize the window. There's nothing magic about these dimensions, but it will help us if we know the size of the window when we create and place a label.

So, think back to what happened when we placed the text field at the top of the window in our SimpleBrowser example. You grabbed a text field from the library and dragged it to the window and dropped it. It was automatically added to the view hierarchy. Your Document window looked something like this:

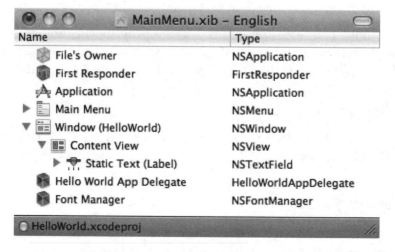

---

3. A side benefit of creating a text field in code in this example is that it should help convince you to use Interface Builder whenever you can.

Although you probably didn't pay attention at the time, the window contains a ContentView. When you dropped the text field onto the window, you were creating an instance of NSTextField, and you were adding it as a subview of the ContentView.

You then repositioned the text field and changed the text to display what you wanted. Here's how we might do this in code:[4]

Classes/HelloWorld2/HelloWorldAppDelegate.m

```
#import "HelloWorldAppDelegate.h"
@implementation HelloWorldAppDelegate
@synthesize window;

-(void)applicationDidFinishLaunching:(NSNotification *)aNotification {
    NSRect labelLocation = NSMakeRect(20, 20, 540, 50);
    NSTextField *label = [[NSTextField alloc] initWithFrame:labelLocation];
    [label setStringValue:@"Hello, World!"];
    [[self.window contentView] addSubview:label];
}
@end
```

First, we create an NSRect that holds the information for the size and location of the label. This matches the work we did using Interface Builder in Chapter 2, *Using What's There*, on page 11, where we resized the text field or set its dimensions in the Size inspector. Notice that NSMakeRect() is a C function and not a method. This is fairly typical when we work with graphic elements. Although this is certainly too much information for now, an NSRect or an NSPoint is a C struct and not an Objective-C object. There will always be a corresponding C function such as NSMakeRect() or NSMakePoint() to create and configure these elements.

Next we create an instance of NSTextField named label and set its location and dimensions to those described by the labelLocation variable. We set the label's string value to be Hello, World! and add the label as a subview of the window's content view.

---

4. I'll assume for now you understand that self.window refers to the current object's window instance. I'll explain the dot syntax in Chapter 5, *Instance Variables and Properties*, on page 73.

Click Build & Run, and you should see something like this:

I'm not very happy with the current state of this project. Sure, the output looks ugly, and we'll fix that, but mainly I'm concerned with the state of the code. Let's refactor it a bit.

4.4 Refactoring Code

Now and then it helps to step back from your code and look to see what could use some cleaning up. Now that I look at it, I don't like the name labelLocation. Of course, we could get rid of the variable completely and just inline the creation of the NSRect without using an explanatory temporary variable. That would be one solution.

If instead we choose to rename the variable, then we need to take into account that it's not just the location of the label but also its size. As you might have guessed from the method name initWithFrame, these two pieces of information are collected in an NSRect and called a *frame*.

Let's use Xcode to change the variable name from labelLocation to label-Frame. In this case, it would be easy enough to make the change by hand, but I'd like to introduce you to how you might use Xcode to perform a couple of refactorings.

I don't know if you've noticed it yet, but when you click labelLocation (go ahead, click it), all instances of labelLocation are underlined.[5] If you hover your mouse around the labelLocation you've selected, slightly to the right, you will get a drop-down arrow. This is the same interface you see when you hover over a phone number or an address that is part of an email you read in Mail.app. Click the arrow, and you should see the options shown here:

```
-(void)applicationDidFinishLaunching:(NSNotification *)aNotification {
    NSRect  labelLocation                          50);
    NSTextField *label = [                    ithFrame:labelLocation];
    [label setStringValue:    Edit All in Scope
    [[self.window contentVi   Find in Project
}                             Jump to Definition
```

---

5. Here labelLocation appears only once, but you get the idea.

Choose Edit All in Scope. Both instances of labelLocation are high-lighted. Change Location to Frame in one of them, and you'll see that they both are changed to labelFrame.

Next, although it doesn't look to be a problem right now, the applicationDidFinishLaunching: method could easily get out of hand. I like to have small, cohesive, easy-to-understand methods. Let's perform a quick refactoring and pull out these four lines into a separate method:

```
NSRect labelFrame = NSMakeRect(20, 20, 540, 50);
NSTextField *label = [[NSTextField alloc] initWithFrame:labelFrame];
[label setStringValue:@"Hello, World!"];
[[self.window contentView] addSubview:label];
```

Again, we could easily do this refactoring by hand, but let's use Xcode's refactoring tools. Select exactly those four lines, and choose Edit > Refactor ..., press ⇧ ⌘ J, or Control-click and select Refactor... in the menu that appears. The refactoring dialog box will appear and, after analyzing the code you selected, will present you with a drop-down list of available refactorings.

Choose Extract. The default signature of the new method is -(void) extracted_method. Change it to -(void) createLabel. Click the Preview button. You will get a list of all the files where there are changes. In this case, the only changes that will result from this refactoring are in HelloWorldAppDelegate.m. There are four changes noted. Click HelloWorldAppDelegate.m in the refactoring window, and you should see this preview:

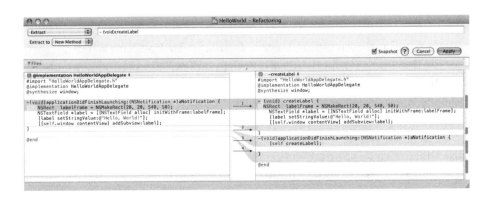

Click the Apply button to complete the refactoring.

Here is the HelloWorldAppDelegate.m file that results:

```
Classes/HelloWorld3/HelloWorldAppDelegate.m
#import "HelloWorldAppDelegate.h"
@implementation HelloWorldAppDelegate
@synthesize window;

-(void)createLabel {
    NSRect  labelFrame = NSMakeRect(20, 20, 540, 50);
    NSTextField *label = [[NSTextField alloc] initWithFrame:labelFrame];
    [label setStringValue:@"Hello, World!"];
    [[self.window contentView] addSubview:label];
}
-(void)applicationDidFinishLaunching:(NSNotification *)aNotification {
    [self createLabel];
}
@end
```

Now applicationDidFinishLaunching: is nice and clean. It consists only of a call to createLabel. Four quick notes:

- There is no reason that createLabel had to be a method. I could have chosen during the refactoring to make it an ordinary C function.

- Remember that we call methods by sending messages to objects. In this case, the target of the message createLabel is self, which points to our current instance of HelloWorldAppDelegate.

- If createLabel had instead been defined to be a C-style function, we would have replaced [self createLabel]; with createLabel();.

- The refactoring tool will place the new method in the source code above the line where the method is called. Think of the compiler as reading your source code from top to bottom. When it gets to the line in which the method is called, the compiler needs to have already encountered the implementation of the method. If a method occurs in the source code below where it is called, you will get a compiler warning.

Now that we've separated the code that creates the label, I don't mind adding a bit more code to configure it the way I want. I'll add code some of the customization I would have done in Interface Builder using the Attributes inspector.

Classes/HelloWorld4/HelloWorldAppDelegate.m

```
- (void) createLabel {
    NSRect  labelFrame = NSMakeRect(20, 20, 540, 50);
    NSTextField *label = [[NSTextField alloc] initWithFrame:labelFrame];
▶   [label setEditable:NO];
▶   [label setSelectable:NO];
▶   [label setAlignment:NSCenterTextAlignment];
▶   [label setFont:[NSFont boldSystemFontOfSize:36]];
    [label setStringValue:@"Hello, World!"];
    [[self.window contentView] addSubview:label];
}
```

I've set the label so that the user can't select or edit it. I've centered the text and made it both bold and 36 point. The outcome looks a little bit better, but we're not going to win an Apple Design Award any time soon:

You don't want to write a lot of code like this. Anything you can do in Interface Builder can also be done in code. In general, though, if you *can* do something in Interface Builder, then you *should*. Always choose using Interface Builder over writing code.

4.5 Creating a New Class

Let's create a class of our own. We'll create a class named Greeter and send it messages. Then we'll use the class to instantiate an object and send this object messages.

All classes are created in Xcode. You can create instances of the classes in Xcode or Interface Builder, but the classes are created in Xcode.

From Xcode, select the Classes folder under Groups & Files so that the files you create will appear inside this folder. Choose File > New File..., or press ⌘N. Choose to create a Cocoa > Objective-C class that is a subclass of NSObject. The description should say that you are creating "An Objective-C class file, with an optional header which includes the <Cocoa/Cocoa.h> header." Click Next.

Organizing Files

At the left side of your Editor window you should see a section labeled Groups & Files. You may need to use the disclosure triangle next to your application's name to reveal folders labeled Classes, Other Sources, Resources, Frameworks, and Products.

When you create a new class in Xcode, the implementation and header files will appear in whatever directory is selected. If none is selected, they will appear in the top level under the application name. There is no correspondence between where the files actually live on the disk and where they appear in this organizer. The organizer works more like playlists in iTunes than like mailboxes in Mail.

Create other folders if you like, but for small projects you want to keep your source code in the Classes folder. Either select Classes before you create a new class or drag the files into the folder afterward.

Name your file Greeter.m.[6] Also, make sure that the checkboxes to create Greeter.h and to target HelloWorld are selected. Generally, if you accept the defaults, you should be OK. Click Finish. You've now generated the header file Greeter.h and the implementation file Greeter.m.

The header file contains the public interface for the Greeter class. You use it to tell other people how they can interact with your class. At the top of the file you'll often import the header files of other classes your class might want to use. In this case, Xcode has already included the directive to import Cocoa.h, which includes the header files for all of the Cocoa classes you might need to use.

---

6. Begin class names with an uppercase letter, and use camel case. Begin variable names and methods with a lowercase letter. Remember to check out *Coding Guidelines for Cocoa* [App06], which includes Apples documentation on naming classes, variables, methods, and functions.

Here's the header file with two comments I've inserted to help our discussion:

`Classes/HelloWorld5/Greeter.h`

```
#import <Cocoa/Cocoa.h>

@interface Greeter : NSObject {
    // you'll declare instance variables here
}
    // you'll declare methods here

@end
```

Everything between @interface and @end is the description of the public interface for the Greeter class. Greeter : NSObject indicates that the Greeter class directly extends the root class NSObject. WebView, in contrast, is a subclass of NSView, which in turn is a subclass of NSResponder, which is a subclass of NSObject. Unless you specifically override it, you benefit from inheriting the behavior of any of your superclasses. The behavior that is common to all objects is specified in the root class NSObject. You will sometimes have to look in the documentation of a superclass to find methods that are available to objects created from your class.

In the header file, the comments I've added to the template code show that you add the declaration for your instance variables inside the curly braces, and you declare your methods between the closing brace and the @end.

Here's Greeter.m, the implementation file you just generated:[7]

`Classes/HelloWorld5/Greeter.m`

```
#import "Greeter.h"

@implementation Greeter

@end
```

The file begins by importing the header file for Greeter. Other than that, you won't see anything other than the beginning and end markers for the class implementation. Notice that in this file you don't specify that the Greeter inherits from NSObject.

---

7. Note the suffixes of the two files Greeter.h and Greeter.m. The h is for header, and the m is for implementation. You'll find this and other fun facts in the Objective-C FAQ at http://www.faqs.org/faqs/computer-lang/Objective-C/faq/.

You will use this combination of the Greeter.h and Greeter.m files to define the Greeter class. A class's header file contains the information you are happy to share publicly. Other classes will import this header file so they know which messages they can send this class. The implementation file contains the part of the class that is no one else's business. The header file tells others what they can ask this class or objects of this type to do. The implementation hides away the details of how this work is accomplished.

4.6 Creating and Using a Class Method

In this iteration of "Hello, World!" we're going to define a new class but not create any objects from it. In practice, we will usually create one or more objects from a class and work with these instances. I want you to see this progression so that you'll know how to create and use both class methods and instance methods.

The Greeter class will have the class method greeting. We can call this method without instantiating Greeter. In other words, the target of the greeting method is the class Greeter and not an object of type Greeter. You'd call it like this:

```
[Greeter greeting];
```

Declare your class method in Greeter.h. You'll use + (NSString *) in front of the method declaration to indicate that greeting is a class method that returns an NSString. You will declare your class methods between the closing brace and @end.

Classes/HelloWorld6/Greeter.h

```
#import <Cocoa/Cocoa.h>

@interface Greeter : NSObject {
}
▶ +(NSString *) greeting;
@end
```

The method returns an NSString containing our greeting. Here's the implementation file:

Classes/HelloWorld6/Greeter.m

```
#import "Greeter.h"

@implementation Greeter
▶ +(NSString *) greeting {
▶     return @"Hello, World!";
▶ }
@end
```

You need to make two changes to HelloWorldAppDelegate.m. You have to import the header file for Greeter so that the compiler doesn't complain when you try to call greeting. You also have to set the label's string value to be whatever you get back by sending the message greeting to the class Greeter.

Classes/HelloWorld6/HelloWorldAppDelegate.m

```
#import "HelloWorldAppDelegate.h"
▶  #import "Greeter.h"
@implementation HelloWorldAppDelegate
@synthesize window;

- (void) createLabel {
    NSRect  labelFrame = NSMakeRect(20, 20, 540, 50);
    NSTextField *label = [[NSTextField alloc] initWithFrame:labelFrame];
    [label setEditable:NO];
    [label setSelectable:NO];
    [label setAlignment:NSCenterTextAlignment];
    [label setFont:[NSFont boldSystemFontOfSize:36]];
▶   [label setStringValue:[Greeter greeting]];
    [[self.window contentView] addSubview:label];
}

-(void)applicationDidFinishLaunching:(NSNotification *)aNotification {
    [self createLabel];
}
@end
```

Click Build & Run, and the results should be exactly the same as before. When you're ready, quit the application, and let's change this application to create objects and to use instance methods.

4.7 Creating a New Object

Next, we're going to create a new object and call an instance method. Because we configured the project to use garbage collection, there are a whole bunch of memory management details you don't have to worry about right now. I'll wait to show you those until Chapter 6, *Memory*, on page 89 because the details are a bit dry yet still important if you ever want to work in a non-garbage-collected Cocoa application or want to develop applications for the iPhone where garbage collection isn't supported.[8] Because garbage collection is enabled, we just make a few small changes in our code to create an object of type Greeter.

---

8. Actually, memory management won't be the first detail I'll gloss over. You may have noticed an asterisk (*) or two float by without a comment. We also haven't talked about what happens when an application first starts up. How is it that our browser appeared

First, change the header file Greeter.h to change the + to a - to declare the greeting method as an instance method instead of a class method:

Classes/HelloWorld7/Greeter.h

```
#import <Cocoa/Cocoa.h>

@interface Greeter : NSObject {
}
► -(NSString *) greeting;
@end
```

Make the corresponding change of + to - in the implementation file Greeter.m, or your compiler will complain that you declared an instance method that you didn't implement (it will not complain that you implemented a class method that you didn't declare).

Classes/HelloWorld7/Greeter.m

```
#import "Greeter.h"

@implementation Greeter
► -(NSString *) greeting {
    return @"Hello, World!";
}
@end
```

Now it's time to actually create your first object and call an instance method. Change the createLabel method in HelloAppDelegate.m to look like this:

Classes/HelloWorld7/HelloWorldAppDelegate.m

```
Line 1  - (void) createLabel {
    -       NSRect  labelFrame = NSMakeRect(20, 20, 540, 50);
    -       NSTextField *label = [[NSTextField alloc] initWithFrame:labelFrame];
    -       [label setEditable:NO];
    5       [label setSelectable:NO];
    -       [label setAlignment:NSCenterTextAlignment];
    -       [label setFont:[NSFont boldSystemFontOfSize:36]];
    ►       Greeter *greeter = [[Greeter alloc] init];
    ►       [label setStringValue:[greeter greeting]];
    10      [[self.window contentView] addSubview:label];
    -   }
```

The right side of code in line 8 is the template code you will use to create new objects. Here the variable greeter points to the object of type

---

all ready to work and the system knows that HelloWorldAppDelegate is where we should be creating our initial objects in code?

Greeter that you are creating. You create the object in two steps, as you can see by the nested call:

```
[[Greeter alloc] init]
```

The class method alloc is responsible for allocating the memory and returning an object whose initial values are set by the instance method init. In the following line, you send the message greeting to greeter and use the returned value as the string displayed in your label.

4.8 Further Refactoring

We won't do this throughout the book, but I wanted to give you a feel for the rhythm of writing Cocoa code. You seldom get things right the first time, so you code a little and then clean things up when you notice code getting out of hand.

It feels a little odd to me that the createLabel method is responsible for creating the Greeter object. One way to try to tease these two apart is to think of how I might describe the action at a high level from within the applicationDidFinishLaunching: method. Let's try this:

```
Classes/HelloWorld8/HelloWorldAppDelegate.m
```

```
-(void)applicationDidFinishLaunching:(NSNotification *)aNotification {
    Greeter *greeter = [self greeter];
    NSTextField * label = [self labelWithText:[greeter greeting]];
    [[self.window contentView] addSubview:label];
}
```

In this code, you can see that we start by obtaining a Greeter object from another method named greeter, which won't do much for now. Then we create and configure a label that has as its text the results of sending the Greeter object the message greeting. Finally, we take that label and add it to the window's content view as a subview.

Once I've mapped out what my class looks like, I can now fill in the details. I can see I need to make the following by the way I've called the code that creates the label:

- I've changed the name of the method to labelWithText:.

- The method now takes the text it is going to display in the label as a parameter.

- I'm expecting the method to return the label to me so that I can add it as a subview in applicationDidFinishLaunching: and not within the method that creates the label.

We can easily make those changes to the newly named labelWithText: method:

`Classes/HelloWorld8/HelloWorldAppDelegate.m`

```
▶ - (NSTextField *) labelWithText: (NSString *) labelText {
      NSRect  labelFrame = NSMakeRect(20, 20, 540, 50);
      NSTextField *label = [[NSTextField alloc] initWithFrame:labelFrame];
      [label setEditable:NO];
      [label setSelectable:NO];
      [label setAlignment:NSCenterTextAlignment];
      [label setFont:[NSFont boldSystemFontOfSize:36]];
▶     [label setStringValue:labelText];
▶     return label;
   }
```

We also need to add a greeter method that creates and returns a Greeter object:[9]

`Classes/HelloWorld8/HelloWorldAppDelegate.m`

```
- (Greeter *) greeter {
    return [[Greeter alloc] init];
}
```

We'd kind of like our applicationDidFinishLaunching: method to come at the top of our code so people can glance at it and get an idea of what the class does. Remember, the compiler reads your code from top to bottom. If the applicationDidFinishLaunching: were at the top, the compiler would complain that it doesn't know about the greeter method or the labelWithText: method. The program would still run fine, but you would have these warnings.

We could declare the greeter and labelWithText: methods in the header file, but they really aren't part of the public interface. We'll learn other tricks, but for now we'll leave the applicationDidFinishLaunching: method at the bottom.

4.9 Initializing Your Objects

When we create a new Greeter object, we allocate memory, and then we call the init method. But you've seen the Greeter. It doesn't have an init method of its own. When you call init on an instance of Greeter, you are really calling init on Greeter's superclass NSObject.

---

9. We could leave the creation of the Greeter object inlined as part of the applicationDidFinishLaunching: method. I've split it out to emphasize small methods and to provide more experience with creating methods and sending messages.

All this inheritance worked fine because Greeter didn't have any of its own variables to initialize. There was nothing that was in a Greeter that wasn't already in an NSObject that needed initialization.

Let's change that. Let's add an instance variable named name to Greeter. Remember, we need to add a declaration between the curly braces in the header file Greeter.h.

`Classes/HelloWorld9/Greeter.h`

```
#import <Cocoa/Cocoa.h>

@interface Greeter : NSObject {
    NSString * name;
}
-(NSString *) greeting;
@end
```

What are we going to do with our new variable? First, we're going to need to set its value when the object is initialized. We're going to have to write our own init method in which we set the value of name to World. Then we're going to have to change the implementation of greeting so that it inserts the value of name between *Hello,* and *!*.

We'll go through the following code slowly starting with init:

`Classes/HelloWorld9/Greeter.m`

```
Line 1  #import "Greeter.h"

        @implementation Greeter

5       -(NSString *) greeting {
            return [[NSString alloc] initWithFormat:@"Hello, %@!", name];
        }

        -(id) init {
10          if (self = [super init]){
                name = @"World";
            }
            return self;
        }
15      @end
```

Let's start with line 10. It sure looks wrong. You might think that there should be a double equals between self and [super init], but this really is an assignment and not a test for equality. So, what's going on in the assignment?

```
self = [super init];
```

Reading from the right, when you initialize an object, the first thing you do is make a call to the superclass's init method. You assign this initialized object to self, and then you test that self is not nil. If it isn't, then go ahead and customize it as we've done in line 11. This lets you start with all the initializations you had before you started writing this method and then fill in the additional initializations on top of them. Finally, you return your object in line 13.

You'll often see this slightly more verbose way of accomplishing the same thing:

```
- (id) init
{
    self = [super init];
    if (self != nil) {
        name = @"World";
    }
    return self;
}
```

If you use this second version, I prefer you replace if (self != nil) with if(self).[10]

Now let's look at line 6 in the greeting method. We are returning a formatted string. This is similar to what you've seen in many other languages. You create a string with placeholders like %d in it. You follow the string with a comma-separated list of the values that replace the placeholders in the string.

In our case, we are using a new Cocoa type %@, which displays a string representation of a Cocoa object (as specified in its description method). In our case we have this:[11]

```
[[NSString alloc] initWithFormat:@"Hello, %@!", name]
```

This means we replace the %@ with the value of name, which is currently World.[12] Our result is Hello, World!.

---

10. For a full discussion of self and [super init], see Matt Gallagher's article at http://cocoawithlove.com/2009/04/what-does-it-mean-when-you-assign-super.html. It's also informative and entertaining to read Wil Shipley's article on using self= [super init], which you can find at http://www.wilshipley.com/blog/2005/07/self-stupid-init.html. Be sure to read to the end where he concludes it's a good thing to use.
11. If you already know about memory management in Objective-C, you'll see that I am introducing a memory leak here. It's deliberate and is taken care of by the garbage collector, and later we'll talk about what to do when we don't have a garbage collector.
12. For more details on formatted strings, you can look up the method stringWithFormat: in the docs. This points to an article called "Formatting String Objects" with some examples

Click Build & Run, and the program should again work exactly as before.

4.10 Logging Objects

Sometimes you want a quick view of the state of an object at particular points in a program. A quick-and-dirty solution is to use NSLog() together with %@ to log the string description of the object. Unfortunately, Apple can't know what you want to log for your custom objects. For example, add this highlighted line to log the value of the newly created Greeter object:

Classes/HelloWorld10/HelloWorldAppDelegate.m

```
-(void)applicationDidFinishLaunching:(NSNotification *)aNotification {
    Greeter *greeter = [self greeter];
►   NSLog(@"Greeter: %@", greeter);
►   NSLog(@"This occurred in %@ at line %d in file %s.",
►               NSStringFromSelector(_cmd), __LINE__, __FILE__);
    NSTextField * label = [self labelWithText:[greeter greeting]];
    [[self.window contentView] addSubview:label];
}
```

Click Build & Run. Unfortunately, the Greeter object doesn't know how to describe itself, so you inherit the default behavior from NSObject. You'll see something like this:

```
Greeter <Greeter: 0x10044d520>
```

This is just the class name for the object along with its memory location. This probably isn't very useful, but you can always specify how you want an object to display itself by overriding the description method. To help with debugging, I've also added information to display the name of the method and the file and current line number.[13]

Classes/HelloWorld10/Greeter.m

```
-(NSString *)description {
    return [[NSString alloc] initWithFormat:@"name: %@ \n created: %@",
            name, [NSDate date]];
}
```

---

of how you might use the method. There is also a linked comprehensive list of string format specifiers.

13. For more options, see Apple's technical Q&A titled "Improved logging in Objective C" at http://developer.apple.com/mac/library/qa/qa2009/qa1669.html.

Now the Greeter knows how to describe itself, so when you rerun the application, you now see something like this:

```
Greeter: name: World
 created: 2010-02-10 15:57:35 -0500
This occurred in applicationDidFinishLaunching: at line 27 in file
/Volumes/Data/Prags/Bookshelf/Writing/DSCPQSL/Book/code/Classes
/HelloWorld10/HelloWorldAppDelegate.m.
```

There's no set style for implementing the description method. Include whatever data you anticipate might be useful to you or others who will want a string description of your class. You can see in this log message how Apple has implemented the description method for the NSDate class. The display consists of the year, month, day, time, and time zone.

4.11 Exercise: Other Initializations

As always happens with this example, after a while you'd like to greet something other than the whole world. Fortunately, we're in great shape to do so. To greet anyone we want, we need to be able to reset the name variable.

One way to add a bit of flexibility would be to create a second init method. This one would take the name as a parameter. The convention is to provide a more descriptive method name that begins with *init*. We could call it initWithName:.

Take a minute to do just that. Declare an initWithName: method that takes an NSString * as its only parameter and returns an id in the Greeter header file. In Greeter.m, implement the initWithName: method to set the value of name to the string that is passed in.[14]

Each class should have a designated init that all other inits call. Refactor our current init method to call initWithName:, and pass World as the value of the parameter.

Click Build & Run, and our application should run just as it has.

In HelloWorldAppDelegate.m, rename the greeter method greeterFor that takes an NSString * as its only argument and creates a Greeter using Greeter's initWithName: method.

---

14. I haven't said anything about id yet. Think of it as a type that can stand in for any possible object type, and I'll explain a bit more about it in Chapter 5, *Instance Variables and Properties*, on page 73.

Click Build & Run, and you should see a more personal greeting.

4.12 Solution: Other Initializations

Add this declaration to the Greeter header file as we are adding a new initialization method to the public interface:

Classes/HelloWorld11/Greeter.h

```
#import <Cocoa/Cocoa.h>

@interface Greeter : NSObject {
    NSString * name;
}
-(NSString *) greeting;
-(id) initWithName:(NSString *)newName;
@end
```

For Greeter.m, add this method:

Classes/HelloWorld11/Greeter.m

```
-(id) initWithName:(NSString *) newName {
    if (self = [super init]){
        name = newName;
    }
    return self;
}
```

Once you learn about properties in the next chapter, you'll use something a bit more robust than the following:

```
name = newName;
```

You'll use a property to set the value of the name and take care of the memory management while you're at it.

You can now refactor the init method to call initWithName: to eliminate the duplicated code:

Classes/HelloWorld11/Greeter.m

```
-(id) init {
    return [self initWithName:@"World"];
}
```

This method replaces greeter in HelloWorldAppDelegate.m:

Classes/HelloWorld11/HelloWorldAppDelegate.m

```
- (Greeter *) greeterFor:(NSString *) personName {
    return [[Greeter alloc] initWithName:personName];
}
```

Adjust applicationDidFinishLaunching: to call this new method:

Classes/HelloWorld11/HelloWorldAppDelegate.m

```
-(void)applicationDidFinishLaunching:(NSNotification *)aNotification {
    Greeter *greeter = [self greeterFor:@"Maggie"];
    NSLog(@"Greeter: %@", greeter);
    NSTextField * label = [self labelWithText:[greeter greeting]];
    [[self.window contentView] addSubview:label];
}
```

Click Build & Run, and you should see something like this:

In this chapter, you've created and used your own classes and objects. You've created custom initializers, class methods, instance methods, and instance variables. Now let's take a step back and look at some of the issues we've swept under the carpet.

Chapter 5

Instance Variables and Properties

Messages are a big deal in this book. So far, we've sent messages that ask an object to perform a task like saying hello or initializing itself with a particular name. In this chapter, we're going to look at messages that get or set the state of an object's variables.

Many of your objects will have instance variables to store state. Often that state is internal to your object—you don't want it exposed to other objects. But sometimes you do want other objects to be able to examine and possibly set the value of one or more instance variables. Think back to some of the variables we set in Interface Builder using the Attributes inspector. We set the text for the buttons as well as the key equivalent. In the previous chapter, we set certain attributes such as the font size and justification for our text field in code. These publicly visible instance variables are *properties* of the object. Objective-C 2.0 has a mechanism for generating the getters and setters that let other objects access them.

We'll start with instance variables and expose them with a getter and a setter that we declare and write ourselves. We'll then generate the declaration automatically using the @property directive and implement them automatically using the @synthesize directive. You'll then learn to call the accessors differently using the new dot syntax.

5.1 Pointers

Take a look back at the header file for Greeter:

Properties/HelloWorld12/Greeter.h

```
#import <Cocoa/Cocoa.h>

@interface Greeter : NSObject {
    NSString *name;
}
-(NSString *) greeting;
-(id) initWithName:(NSString *)name;
@end
```

Every time you see the type NSString, it is followed by a space and an asterisk (*). In particular, consider the declaration of the instance variable:

```
NSString *name;
```

In Objective-C, variables that refer to objects are really pointers. The * is how we indicate that name is a pointer. We could declare our variable in either of these two ways:

```
NSString* name;     // OK, but
NSString *name;     // this form is preferred
```

In Objective-C we tend to put the * right before the variable name.

We are careful to always use the * to mark an object's variable as being a pointer, but we're more casual when we talk about them. We'll tend to say that name is an NSString, but really name is a pointer to an NSString.[1]

We use pointers in method declarations as well. For example, here's how you'd declare an instance method named greeting that returns a pointer to an NSString:

```
-(NSString *) greeting;
```

Again, in casual conversation, we would more likely say that greeting returns a string, but the code makes it clear that we're actually returning a pointer to an NSString.

Finally, look at the declaration of our custom init method:

```
-(id) initWithName:(NSString *)newName;
```

---

1. If you're coming from Java, the same thing is true there, but we pretend there are no pointers in Java. Then you have some explaining to do when you throw your first NullPointerException.

This declares an instance method named initWithName:. The method takes a pointer to an NSString named newName as its only argument.

The return type ofinitWithName: is id. We use id to mean a pointer to any type when we don't want to specify exactly what that type is. In other words, id is what we use in Objcctive-C to point to an instance of a class. We used id in Section 3.3, *Methods with Arguments*, on page 40 as a parameter type.

```
- (IBAction) goBack:(id) sender
```

This was the message sent to the WebView when the Back button was clicked.[2] The way we wired it up, the sender of the message was an NSButton *. We could have introduced a completely different element and used it to initiate the goBack: message, so the type of the sender would have been different. We capture this need for flexibility by setting the type of the sender to be id.

You don't write id * because id is a pointer. This can be confusing because id stands in for pointers like NSButton * and NSString *. But id appears without the asterisk.

In our example, we use id as the return type for any init name (including our own initWithName: and others), as described in Apple's *The Objective-C Programming Language* [App09f].

5.2 Working with Nonobject Types

Objective-C sits on top of C, so you can use the primitive C types such as int and long and float, and so on. But you also come across other types that aren't primitives but also are not first-class objects.

For example, if you look at the first line of the labelWithText: method in HelloWorldAppDelegate.m, you'll see this:

```
NSRect  labelFrame = NSMakeRect(20, 20, 540, 50);
```

You probably didn't think much about this when we first typed it in, but now it looks as if it might be missing its *. It's not. If you check the docs, you'll see that an NSRect is a struct consisting of an NSPoint and an NSSize. These are each in turn defined to be structs consisting of two CGFloats. Follow the docs one more step, and you see that CGFloat is

---

2. We'll look at theIBAction return type in Chapter 7, *Outlets and Actions*, on page 111. An IBAction is the same as a void except that Interface Builder is able to expose some information to us. Check in the docs, and you'll see that IBAction is #defined to void.

typedef'd to be a float for code running under 32-bit and a double for code running under 64-bit. In any case, a variable of type NSRect is not a pointer, so there's no *.³

This can get confusing. An NSNumber is an object, while an NSInteger isn't. You need to consult the docs to see which is which. Here's how you might declare two variables where one is an NSNumber while the other is an NSInteger:

```
NSNumber *income;
NSInteger age;
```

Objective-C also has a BOOL type for handling booleans. We tend not to do tricky and unreadable arithmetic for logical calculations. Instead, we think of a BOOL as having one of the values YES or NO. We're particularly careful not to use words like *true* or *false* when talking about booleans. We don't want people thinking we're from out of town.

5.3 Getters and Setters

We can easily get and set the value of name inside the Greeter class. In the first highlighted line in the following example, we are getting and printing out the value of name, and in the second highlighted line we are setting its value:

Properties/HelloWorld12/Greeter.m

```
#import "Greeter.h"

@implementation Greeter
-(NSString *) greeting {
    return [[NSString alloc] initWithFormat:@"Hello, %@!", name];
}
-(id) initWithName:(NSString *) newName {
    if (self = [super init]){
        name = newName;
    }
    return self;
}
-(id) init {
    return [self initWithName:@"World"];
}
```

---

3. There is a great explanation of objects and simple C structures in the answer to this Stack Overflow question http://stackoverflow.com/questions/2189212/why-object-dosomething-and-not-object-dosomething. The answer is written by Apple engineer Bill Bumgarner who posts under his standard username: bbum. It's always worth seeking out his posts on Stack Overflow and his contributions to various other lists such as the *cocoa-dev* list at http://lists.apple.com. From time to time he summarizes his thoughts on his blog at http://www.friday.com/bbum/.

```
-(NSString *)description {
    return [[NSString alloc] initWithFormat:@"name: %@ \n created: %@",
            name, [NSDate date]];
}
@end
```

If we wanted to allow other objects to get and set the value of name, we would declare a getter and setter in the Greeter header file and implement them in the implementation file.

The getter is an instance method that returns the current value of the name instance variable, so the return type must be NSString *. The getter doesn't take any parameters. The only thing left to worry about is what to call it. In Objective-C the getter for the property xyz is also named xyz. You don't insert *get* into the name at all.

The setter is also an instance method. It doesn't return anything, but it needs to take the new value of name as an NSString * that we'll call name. As for the method name, in Objective-C the setter for the property xyz is named setXyz. In other words, you start the name with *set* and follow it with the variable name with the first letter converted to uppercase.

Add these declarations for the accessors to your header file:

Properties/HelloWorld13/Greeter.h

```
#import <Cocoa/Cocoa.h>

@interface Greeter : NSObject {
    NSString *name;
}
-(NSString *) greeting;
-(id) initWithName:(NSString *)name;
▶ -(NSString *) name;
▶ -(void) setName:(NSString *) name;

@end
```

There's not much to the getter. You've probably written code like this in your sleep:

Properties/HelloWorld13/Greeter.m

```
-(NSString *) name {
    return name;
}
```

If we ignore memory management for the moment, there's not much more to the getter than that:

Properties/HelloWorld13/Greeter.m

```
-(void) setName:(NSString *) newName {
    name = newName;
}
```

We can now change the direct calls to the instance variable into calls to the getter and setter. For example, in the construction of the formatted string, we call the getter like this:

Properties/HelloWorld13/Greeter.m

```
-(NSString *) greeting {
    return [[NSString alloc] initWithFormat:@"Hello, %@!", [self name]];
}
```

And in the initWithName: method, we call the setter like this:

Properties/HelloWorld13/Greeter.m

```
-(id) initWithName:(NSString *) newName {
    if (self = [super init]){
        [self setName: newName];
    }
    return self;
}
```

Even more important, you can now access the name property from other objects. Here's a silly example that I've added to HelloWorldAppDelegate.m:

Properties/HelloWorld13/HelloWorldAppDelegate.m

```
-(void) setUpperCaseName:(Greeter *) greeter {
    NSLog(@"The name was originally %@.", [greeter name]);
    [greeter setName:[[greeter name] uppercaseString]];
    NSLog(@"The name is now %@.", [greeter name]);
}
```

I've used the getter [greeter name] in every line of this method. The setter setName: is used in the middle line of the method to take the value of the name and transform the name to uppercase.

To see this work, you'll have to add a call to this method from applica-tionDidFinishLaunching: like in the highlighted line here:

Properties/HelloWorld13/HelloWorldAppDelegate.m

```
-(void)applicationDidFinishLaunching:(NSNotification *)aNotification {
    Greeter *greeter = [self greeterFor:@"Maggie"];
        NSLog(@"Greeter: %@", greeter);
    NSTextField * label = [self labelWithText:[greeter greeting]];
►   [self setUpperCaseName:greeter];
    [[self.window contentView] addSubview:label];
}
```

Click Build & Run, and you'll see output like this:

```
The name was originally Maggie.
The name is now MAGGIE.
```

Now let's introduce properties and start reducing and simplifying our code.

5.4 Converting the Accessors to Properties

Let's take stock of where we are. We've exposed an attribute of the Greeter class named name that we can get and set. We've done this in three steps:

1. Declared an instance variable name in the header file.
2. Declared a getter and a setter named name and setName: in the header file.
3. Provided mostly boilerplate code to implement the methods in the implementation file.

Now we'll use Objective-C 2.0 properties to make changes to these last two steps and in some cases eliminate the first step.

Replace the declarations of the getter and the setter with this:

Properties/HelloWorld14/Greeter.h

```
#import <Cocoa/Cocoa.h>

@interface Greeter : NSObject {
    NSString *name;
}
-(NSString *) greeting;
-(id) initWithName:(NSString *)name;
► @property(copy) NSString *name;

@end
```

Ignore the copy in parentheses following the compiler directive @property for now. You should read the rest of that highlighted line as declaring a property of type NSString named name. As it stands, that line declares a getter named name and a setter named setName:.

If you click Build & Run right now, your code will work exactly as before. You will be able to call the getter and setter from HelloWorldAppDelegate without any warnings or errors. In other words, this @property directive is declaring your getter and setter—in fact, it is doing more than that, as you'll see in Section 5.6, *Property Attributes*, on page 83.

There wasn't anything special about the way in which we implemented the getter and setter methods. In fact, the compiler can create the implementations for us if we ask it to do so. Replace your implementation of the getter and setter with this highlighted line:

Properties/HelloWorld14/Greeter.m

```
#import "Greeter.h"

@implementation Greeter
```
▶
```
@synthesize name;
```

The @synthesize directive tells the compiler to implement the methods that were declared in the corresponding @property directive.

So, let's look back on our three steps of creating properties. We declare an instance variable in the header file between the curly braces. We declare the getter and setter in the header file outside of the curly braces by using the @property directive. So far, we are just declaring a variable and a property (in other words, the accessor methods), so that's why we do so in the header file. Now it's time to implement the methods we declared for the variable we declared. Implementations go in the .m file, so that is where we put the @synthesize directive.

Click Build & Run, and the program should work exactly as before. In other words, the getter and setter are being correctly generated.

5.5 Dot Notation

Now that you've declared and synthesized your properties, you should call them differently. When you want a getter, I want you to use dot notation instead of the method-calling syntax you've been using.

In other words, replace this:

```
[self name]
```

with this:

```
self.name
```

To see this in the wild, it means that you are changing to this high-lighted line in the greeting method:

Properties/HelloWorld14/Greeter.m

```
-(NSString *) greeting {
►    return [[NSString alloc] initWithFormat:@"Hello, %@!", self.name];
}
```

Similarly, you will replace this version of the setter:

```
[self setName:newName];
```

with this:

```
self.name = newName;
```

That changes the initWithName: method to this:

Properties/HelloWorld14/Greeter.m

```
-(id) initWithName:(NSString *) newName {
    if (self = [super init]){
►        self.name = newName;
    }
    return self;
}
```

In each case, the method invocation form and the dot syntax form behave identically. In fact, the dot syntax is just syntactic sugar that compiles down to the method invocation form. You'll find, however, that if you consistently use the dot syntax for getting and setting properties, your code will become easier to read.

This kind of feels as if we've come full circle. Looking at the setter for example, we began by setting the variable directly like this:

```
name = newName;
```

Then we introduced a setter. You now were told to use the setter method to set the value of underlying instance variable like this:

```
[self setName:newName];
```

 **Joe Asks. . .**

Why Should I Bother Using the Dot Syntax?

There has been a fair amount of controversy over this issue. Some people object to the fact that when you write code like this:

```
self.name = newName;
```

you are making a method call even though it doesn't look as if you are. That's true, but the advantage of using the dot syntax is that getting or setting a property is a different activity from sending a message to an object even if underneath the mechanism is the same. The dot syntax clarifies your intent.

When you send a message like this:

```
[greeter greeting];
```

it is clearly completely different from setting or getting the value of a property. You'll find that Apple embraces the dot syntax in its modern APIs. As you look at the tasks for a given class, you'll see that many of them are actually properties. After you've used the dot notation for get and set for a while, you'll find that your code is easier to read and to more quickly understand.

At http://eschatologist.net/blog/?p=160, Chris Hanson explains passionately and in greater detail why you want to use dot syntax for properties.

And now we've declared and synthesized a property, so you now set the value of the variable like this:

```
self.name = newName;
```

We haven't come full circle. When you use self.name = newName, you are using the setter method and not directly setting the underlying variable.

You want to use the property and not the variable to take advantage of the various settings we will soon add to the property. This is one of the most common mistakes with properties. You go to all the trouble of declaring and synthesizing a property, and then you forget to use self and end up using the instance variable directly and not the property.

Even more important, we can access this property from HelloWorldAppDelegate. First, I want you to take a fresh look at HelloWorldAppDelegate:

Properties/HelloWorld14/HelloWorldAppDelegate.h

```
#import <Cocoa/Cocoa.h>

@interface HelloWorldAppDelegate : NSObject <NSApplicationDelegate> {
    NSWindow *window;
}
@property (assign) IBOutlet NSWindow *window;
@end
```

Now that you know about properties, you can recognize that the variable window of type NSWindow is declared as a property. If you look at the top of HelloWorldAppDelegate.m, you'll see that it's synthesized, and you might remember that at the bottom of applicationDidFinishLaunching: we accessed it as a property when we added the label to its content view.

```
[[self.window contentView] addSubview:label];
```

Once you refactor the code in the setUpperCaseName: method to take advantage of the dot syntax, it should look like this:

Properties/HelloWorld14/HelloWorldAppDelegate.m

```
-(void) setUpperCaseName:(Greeter *) greeter {
    NSLog(@"The name was originally %@.", greeter.name);
    greeter.name = [greeter.name uppercaseString];
    NSLog(@"The name is now %@.", greeter.name);
}
```

5.6 Property Attributes

The general form of the property declaration looks like this:

```
@property(attribute1, attribute2,...) PropertyType propertyName;
```

The attributes are how you indicate what sort of accessors you want created when you synthesize them.

One set of attributes lets you determine whether you want to generate a getter and a setter or just a getter. By default, you will generate both, so you don't need to use the attribute readwrite, but if you want to just generate a getter, you will use readonly.

Another set of attributes is useful for setting the accessor names. This is often used in the case of a boolean. You may have a variable named highlighted. The default getter name for this would also be highlighted, but a more natural name for a BOOL would be isHighlighted. You change the name of the generated accessors with the getter and setter attributes like this:

```
@property(getter=isHighlighted) BOOL highlighted;
```

If you have a boolean property, you need to make this change in order to follow the naming conventions that are used by the system to enable some of the dynamism you'll learn about later in the book.

We haven't yet talked about memory management, so it's going to be a bit tricky to cover your options for the memory attribute. The following should tide you over until we get to Chapter 6, *Memory*, on page 89. The choices are assign, which is the default; retain; and copy.

Essentially, here are the differences. You want to use assign for all nonobject types. Suppose you have a property of type NSInteger named age. If you choose assign, your setter will look something like this:

```
-(void) setAge:newAge {
    age = newAge;
} //assign
```

For object types, you are really dealing with pointers. The first thing we determine is that the old and new pointers don't point to the same object. If they don't then, as you'll see in the next chapter, we need to let the runtime know that we're no longer interested in the object the variable used to point to. We do that by sending the release message to our variable.

Now we have two options. If the variable supports copying, we can make a local copy of the object and work with it without changing the value of the object that was passed in. More formally, we can use copy only if the property type conforms to theNSCopying protocol. NSString does,[4] so when we use the copy attribute, our setter looks something like this:

```
-(void) setName:newName {
    if (name != newName) {
        [name release];
        name = [newName copy];
    }
} //copy
```

---

4. Check the docs up at the top, and you'll see it listed under Conforms To.

The other option is to set our property's underlying variable to point to the object the argument is pointing to. This is the pointer version of assign, and if it weren't for the memory management, the implementation would be exactly the same. Suppose we have a property named buddy of type Greeter. The setter looks something like this:

```
-(void) setBuddy:newBuddy {
    if (buddy != newBuddy) {
        [buddy release];
        buddy = [newBuddy retain];
    }
}   //retain
```

These rules apply for both iPhone and Mac OS X development. If you are taking advantage of the garbage collector, then you don't need to worry about retaining and releasing variables, so you can use assign anywhere you would have used either assign or retain.[5]

You have one more attribute to set if you want to declare a property to be nonatomic. By default, accessors are atomic. When your property is atomic, access to that property is thread safe. In a desktop app where you are using the garbage collector, this comes at very little cost. When you aren't using the garbage collector, then in a getter you will have to set an object-level lock, retrieve the value you want, release the lock, and then return the retrieved value. The details for implementing an atomic setter in this situation are similar.

When you are writing code for the iPhone, you won't have a garbage collector available. If you access properties a lot, you will feel a dip in performance. So when we declare our properties for the iPhone, we will tend to set the attribute nonatomic, and when we are developing for the desktop, we will use the default setting. For more information, read the "Declared Properties" chapter of Apple's *The Objective-C Programming Language* [App09f].

5.7 Exercise: Adding Properties

Add these three properties to Greeter: an NSInteger named age, a Greeter named buddy, and a BOOL named upperCase.

---

5. I'm assuming that your Mac OS X applications will target Leopard and above, so you will be using the garbage collector. For desktop applications, your two memory attribute choices are assign and copy.

For the purposes of this exercise, assume that you aren't using garbage collection and so need to make a distinction between assign and retain.

Use the correct attributes so that there is a getter but no setter for age and so that the getter for upperCase is called isUpperCase.

5.8 Solution: Adding Properties

All of the hard work is in the header file. You need to declare the three instance variables and then declare your properties like this:

Properties/HelloWorld15/Greeter.h

```
#import <Cocoa/Cocoa.h>

@interface Greeter : NSObject {
    NSString *name;
    NSInteger age;
    Greeter *buddy;
    BOOL upperCase;
}
-(NSString *) greeting;
-(id) initWithName:(NSString *)name;
@property(copy) NSString *name;
@property(assign, readonly) NSInteger age;
@property(retain) Greeter *buddy;
@property(assign, getter=isUpperCase) BOOL upperCase;

@end
```

The name variable is an NSString, which conforms to NSCopying, so we use the copy attribute.

Both age and upperCase are primitives, so we use assign. Because we are only generating a getter for age, we also use readonly. To follow the correct naming convention for booleans, we specify that the getter for uppercase should be isUpperCase by adding getter=isUpperCase.

The buddy property is a Greeter. It is a pointer to an object that doesn't conform to NSCopying and so we use retain as the memory attribute.

In the implementation file, add the names of your three new properties to the @synthesize line, and separate them with commas. Note that we've also initialized the upperCase variable in initWithName::

Properties/HelloWorld15/Greeter.m

```
#import "Greeter.h"

@implementation Greeter
```

```
@synthesize name, age, buddy, upperCase;
-(NSString *) greeting {
    return [[NSString alloc] initWithFormat:@"Hello, %@!", self.name];
}
-(id) initWithName:(NSString *) newName {
    if (self = [super init]){
        self.name = newName;
        self.upperCase = YES;
    }
    return self;
}
-(id) init {
    return [self initWithName:@"World"];
}
-(NSString *)description {
    return [[NSString alloc] initWithFormat:@"name: %@ \n created: %@",
            name, [NSDate date]];
}
@end
```

You can also use separate @synthesize directives for each property if you prefer:

```
@synthesize name;
@synthesize age;
@synthesize buddy;
@synthesize upperCase;
```

We have one last simplification to make to our code.

5.9 Removing Instance Variables

If you're running on a machine set to 64-bit and you are targeting 64-bit machines only, then you can eliminate your instance variables and let the runtime synthesize them for you. Unfortunately, this has not been backported to the 32-bit runtime.

Since the 64-bit runtime can infer the underlying instance variables from the @property and @synthesize directives, you would not be adding information by declaring the instance variables yourself. Worse, you could be introducing a possible source of error. Also, if you have no instance variable backing your property, then the compiler can let you know if you mistakenly try to access the variable directly rather than use the property accessors. In other words, if you try to get the background color using backgroundColor and not self.backgroundColor, the compiler can now flag your error.

So, let's remove the instance variables backing our properties. First, let's check your project settings. Open them from the menu bar with Project > Edit Project Settings. Choose the Build tab, set the Architectures setting to 64-bit Intel, and select the checkbox to build the active architecture only.

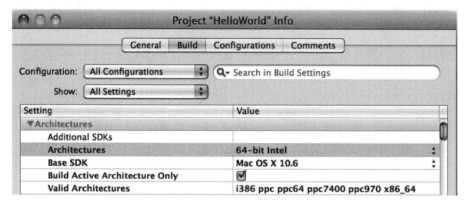

Now you can remove the instance variables from the header file:

`Properties/HelloWorld16/Greeter.h`

```
#import <Cocoa/Cocoa.h>

@interface Greeter : NSObject {
}
-(NSString *) greeting;
-(id) initWithName:(NSString *)name;
@property(copy) NSString *name;
@property(assign, readonly) NSInteger age;
@property(retain) Greeter *buddy;
@property(assign, getter=isUpperCase) BOOL upperCase;

@end
```

Click Build & Run, and the application should run exactly as before. If you get warnings after removing the instance variables, then check that you are running under 64-bit and that your project settings are correct.

You can remove the instance variables that back properties if you are developing for the iPhone,[6] but not if you are developing on or for the 32-bit Mac OS X runtime.

---

6. At the time of this writing, you can remove the variables when targeting the iPhone, and your code will work on the device. The removal of variables is not yet supported on the simulator.

Chapter 6

Memory

You've learned how to create objects in Interface Builder and in code. You've seen how to send messages to objects, and you've used properties to change the state of some of your objects. In this chapter, you'll learn the rules for managing memory in your Cocoa applications.

Whenever you create an object, you're using a small chunk of memory. If, at some point later, you're no longer using that object, you want to make sure that that memory chunk is no longer spoken for. Over the lifetime of a program, you may end up creating thousands or millions of transient objects. If you don't arrange for these to be tidied up, all that memory will just be wasted (and, what's worse, unavailable to other applications). So, as responsible developers, we make sure that all these waste objects are returned to the pool of available memory.

If you fail to reclaim objects you're no longer using, your application leaks memory. Over time, it will grow and grow, sometimes to the point where it can no longer run (or it prevents other programs from running).

On the other hand, if you reclaim an object that is still being used, there's a chance that this object will be overwritten by other code that grabs the reclaimed memory—this will lead to data corruption.

And that's what this chapter is about—how to organize things so that memory is reclaimed when it is no longer needed but not before.[1]

---

1. As you follow along in this chapter, every once in a while your program may fail when it shouldn't or not fail when it should. Select Build > Clean All Targets..., and try to run again.

6.1 Reference Counting

Reference counting is the technique we use to manage the memory of objects ourselves. The rules for memory management are simpler to express than to apply:

- If you own an object, you are responsible for releasing it when you are finished with it. Claiming ownership of an object increases its reference count. Releasing that object decreases the count. An object is unused when its reference count is zero.

- If you don't own an object, you should never release it.

If you violate the first rule, you cause a memory leak. If you violate the second rule, then you could be causing an object to disappear while others still need to send it messages.

So, when do you own an object?

Any time you create a new object using alloc, you own the object and need to release it when you are no longer using it. There is also a class method named new, which is a combination of alloc and init. In other words, the following does exactly the same thing:

```
Greeter *host = [[Greeter alloc] init];
```

as the following:

```
Greeter *host = [Greeter new];
```

We tend not to use new in Objective-C even though it's available. The point here is that when you use it, you own the object. The reference count is increased by one, and you are responsible for releasing it when you are finished with it.

You may also want to take ownership of an object that has been created elsewhere. When you are given an object you need to hold on to, you are responsible for sending a retain or copy message to the object. This increases its reference count by one. Whether you create an object using alloc or new or if you hold onto one using retain or copy, you now own that object and are responsible for releasing it when you no longer need it.[2]

---

2. You'll soon see that if instead you create an object using a class method, you have not retained that object. It is autoreleased. If you want to hold onto the newly created object, you must explicitly retain it.

When you are done with an object, you are responsible for sending a release message to the object. This decreases its reference count by one. When an object's reference count is zero, its dealloc will be called to clean up the object resources and release the memory.

You never call the dealloc method directly. You can't know if someone else is holding a reference to the object that you would be destroying. You just call release to signal that you are no longer interested in this object. If everyone plays by the rules, then when no one is interested in the object, its reference count will be zero, and dealloc will be called.

That's all there is to it. Those are the rules for when the reference count is increased or decreased. Although the rules for manual memory management are straightforward, you can find more information in Apple's *Memory Management Programming Guide for Cocoa* [App09e] and *Garbage Collection Programming Guide* [App08d].

6.2 Finding Leaks with the Clang Static Analyzer

To make things easier up to this point, you might remember that I had you turn automatic garbage collection on. To cause a leak, we need to turn garbage collection off. Choose the menu item Project > Edit Project Settings, and on the Build tab, filter for the garbage collection setting. Set the value of Objective-C Garbage Collection to Unsupported.

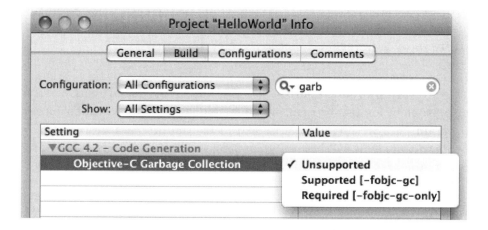

Now let's cause a deliberate memory leak.

To start with, I'm going to remove the GUI code from HelloWorldAppDel-egate. Clean up HelloWorldAppDelegate.h like this:

Memory/HelloWorld17/HelloWorldAppDelegate.h

```
#import <Cocoa/Cocoa.h>

@interface HelloWorldAppDelegate : NSObject <NSApplicationDelegate> {
}
@end
```

Reduce the implementation file so that all it does is create a Greeter object and log it:

Memory/HelloWorld17/HelloWorldAppDelegate.m

```
#import "HelloWorldAppDelegate.h"
#import "Greeter.h"

@implementation HelloWorldAppDelegate

-(void)applicationDidFinishLaunching:(NSNotification *)aNotification {
    Greeter *host = [[Greeter alloc] initWithName:@"Maggie"];
    NSLog(@"Greeter %@", host);
}
@end
```

We caused the problem, so we can certainly see what's wrong. We created an instance of the Greeter class using alloc and point to this object with the variable host. The reference count is one. We never send the release message to host, so its reference count never reaches zero, and the memory is never reclaimed.

This is a very short and short-lived program, so this doesn't cause much of a problem for us. You can imagine that it is part of a much bigger program, and we might have to search for the problem first. In Snow Leopard, this leak will be pretty easy for you to detect using the Clang Static Analyzer.

Run the Clang Static Analyzer by choosing the menu item Build > Build & Analyze or using the keyboard shortcut ⇧ ⌘ A.

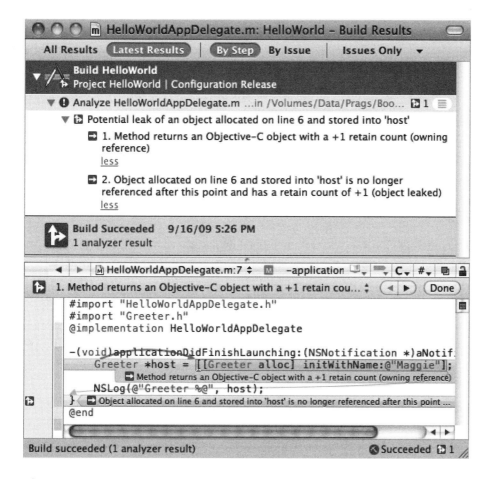

The report tells us that an object has been allocated and stored into host with a retain count of 1. You may see three problems reported instead of the one pictured previously—if you click each, you'll see that they are reporting the same issue, and when we fix it, they will all disappear. After host is used in the log statement, it is never referenced again. That's our memory leak. The Greeter object is instantiated and used and then hangs around for as long as the GUI window remains open without ever being used again.

6.3 Fixing the Memory Leak on Mac OS X

To fix the memory leak on Mac OS X, go back to your project settings, and change the setting for Objective-C Garbage Collection from Unsupported to Required.

Click Build & Analyze, and the memory leak has disappeared.

Whoa—you just learned a whole new way to manage memory. No need for reference counting and balancing your new, alloc, retain, or copy with a release. In this book, I'm assuming that you are deploying to Leopard or later, so the advice is that simple:

Turn garbage collection on.

People who have mastered reference counting feel that trusting the garbage collector is an affront to them as programmers. It's not. If you are programming for Mac OS X, turn on the garbage collector, and leave reference counting behind.

The first garbage-collected system I worked with was Java. Back in the really old days of Java, everything would come to a halt when the garbage was collected. In fact, there was an animation that would appear on the screen. It was a bulldozer collecting stuff.

For a while people would study the byte code generated by the compiler and look for little optimizations. One of them involved turning for loops around so that instead of incrementing from 0 to some limit, it was more efficient to decrement from that limit to 0.

But while we were learning these clever little hacks, the garbage collector was getting better at optimizing for situations that naturally arose. It turned out that our clever little hacks were now making it harder for the garbage collector to do its job.

That's kind of where we are now with Cocoa on the desktop.

That said, you still need to understand reference counting. We'll soon explore an iPhone example where you have no other choice but to manage your memory manually. First I want to show you what the garbage collector can and can't help with when it comes to the memory attribute for properties.

6.4 Properties and Garbage Collection

Now that we have garbage collection turned on, let's reconsider the property declarations in the Greeter header file:

Memory/HelloWorld17/Greeter.h

```
#import <Cocoa/Cocoa.h>

@interface Greeter : NSObject {
}
```

```
-(NSString *) greeting;
-(id) initWithName:(NSString *)name;

@property(copy) NSString *name;
@property(assign, readonly) NSInteger age;
@property(retain) Greeter *buddy;
@property(assign, getter=isUpperCase) BOOL upperCase;

@end
```

If the memory management is being taken care of for us, can't we just eliminate the memory attribute from the property declarations like this?

Memory/HelloWorld18/Greeter.h

```
@property NSString *name; //this line is not correct
@property(readonly) NSInteger age;
@property Greeter *buddy;
@property(getter=isUpperCase) BOOL upperCase;
```

If you build, you'll see that the answer is "mostly."

Remember, the default memory attribute is assign, so we could have already eliminated the attributes for age and upperCase. When garbage collection is turned on, there is no effective difference between retain and assign, so we no longer need to specify the memory attribute for buddy.

When you build, you get this warning:

```
Default 'assign' attribute on property 'name' which implements
'NSCopying' not appropriate with -fobjc-gc-only.
```

The problem is that even though name is declared to be an NSString, it could also be of type NSMutableString, which extends NSString. An NSString is immutable, so you can use copy but not retain, whereas you would use retain but could use either for an NSMutableString. Because of the possible ambiguity, you need to explicitly declare the memory attributed for name.

Memory/HelloWorld19/Greeter.h

```
▶ @property(copy) NSString *name;
  @property(readonly) NSInteger age;
  @property Greeter *buddy;
  @property(getter=isUpperCase) BOOL upperCase;
```

The compiler will warn you when these problems arise. Mostly you will find yourself having to explicitly declare copy when working with NSString as well as the collection classes NSArray, NSDictionary, and NSSet. Each of these has a subclass that is a mutable version.

Don't worry if this isn't clicking for you yet. I mainly want you to be prepared when the compiler complains about this problem later in the book. The main place you will have to think about managing your memory is when creating apps for the iPhone, iPod touch, and iPad. For the remainder of the chapter we'll look at an example of an iPhone app.

6.5 Creating a Flashlight

Currently, if you are targeting the iPhone or iPad, you have to use reference counting and manage the memory yourself. Let's build the iPhone version of our HelloWorld project so that we can experiment with some of the rules you've learned.

You need to register to become an iPhone developer at http://developer. apple.com/iphone. It's free but requires that you agree to Apple's terms. When you are ready to deploy to your phone or distribute on the App Store, you'll need to join one of the programs that cost money.

If you are not registered as an iPhone developer, you can just continue to work with our current example; just set garbage collection back to being Unsupported.

Create a new project in Xcode (File > New Project...). This time choose the iPhone > Application > Window-based Application template. Make sure the checkbox for using Core Data is unselected, and click Choose. Name the project Flashlight, and choose Save.

Click Build & Run, and the iPhone Simulator will launch and run your application. You should see a plain white screen with the status bar at the top. Congratulations, you've built a flashlight. People have sold these on the App Store.

We need to copy the header and implementation files for the Greeter class. Select the Classes folder in Groups & Files. Choose the menu item Project > Add to Project.... Navigate to where you've stored your HelloWorld project, select Greeter.h and Greeter.m, and click the Add button. Select the check box to copy the items to the Flashlight applications folder if needed, and click the Add button. You've added the Greeter class to this project.

Your FlashlightAppDelegate.m file should look much like your HelloWorldAppDelegate.m file did.

You should have this:

```
Memory/Flashlight1/Classes/FlashlightAppDelegate.m
```

```objc
#import "FlashlightAppDelegate.h"
#import "Greeter.h"

@implementation FlashlightAppDelegate
@synthesize window;

- (void)applicationDidFinishLaunching:(UIApplication *)application {
    Greeter *host = [[Greeter alloc] initWithName:@"Maggie"];
    NSLog(@"Greeter %@", host);
}
@end
```

Click Build & Run, and you'll see there are problems to fix.

First we get an error in Greeter.h that there is no file or directory named Cocoa/Cocoa.h. For the iPhone, the framework that includes the GUI and the underlying frameworks is UIKit/UIKit.h. Here we don't need any of the graphical bits, so we're just going to import the Foundations framework. Replace

```objc
#import <Cocoa/Cocoa.h>
```

with

```objc
#import <Foundation/Foundation.h>
```

in Greeter.h. The other problem is an artifact of us running on the simulator. We need to explicitly declare our instance variables. Here is the corrected Greeter.h file:

```
Memory/Flashlight1/Classes/Greeter.h
```

```objc
#import <Foundation/Foundation.h>
@interface Greeter : NSObject {
►    NSString *name;
►    NSInteger age;
►    NSDate *today;
►    BOOL upperCase;
}
-(NSString *) greeting;
-(id) initWithName:(NSString *)name;

@property(copy) NSString *name;
@property(assign, readonly) NSInteger age;
►  @property(copy) NSDate *today;
@property(assign, getter=isUpperCase) BOOL upperCase;

@end
```

I've also replaced the buddy object of type Greeter with an NSDate named today.[3] I'll use it to create an actual time stamp when the Greeter object is created.

Memory/Flashlight1/Classes/Greeter.m

```
#import "Greeter.h"

@implementation Greeter

@synthesize name, age, today, upperCase;
-(NSString *) greeting {
    return [[NSString alloc] initWithFormat:@"Hello, %@!", self.name];
}
-(id) initWithName:(NSString *) newName {
    if (self = [super init]){
        self.name = newName;
        self.upperCase = YES;
        self.today = [NSDate date];
    }
    return self;
}
-(id) init {
    return [self initWithName:@"World"];
}
-(NSString *)description {
    return [[NSString alloc] initWithFormat:@"name: %@ \n created: %@",
            self.name,self.today];
}
@end
```

Click Build & Run, and you should see your flashlight again along with the same output to the Console that you saw in the desktop version. Click Build & Analyze in the simulator, and you should see the same memory leaks reported as before.[4] We'll focus on the one that appears in FlashlightAppDelegate.m.

6.6 Finding Leaks in Instruments

Whole books could and should be written about Apple's performance and debugging tools. I just want to take a minute to show you how the Instruments application could also have identified the memory leak in FlashlightAppDelegate.m.

---

3. I've used the convenience constructor date instead of alloc and init. By the end of the chapter you'll understand why.
4. I'll assume that you are running all of your performance tools against the simulator. You can do that for free. You need to pay to deploy apps to your device.

You have already done a Build & Run, so there is a product available for us to run in Instruments. In Xcode choose the menu item Run > Run with Performance Tool > Leaks. The Instruments application will launch, and your Flashlight application will launch from within Instruments. Almost immediately you should see a vertical blue line in the top row of the Instruments window as objects are being allocated. About ten seconds later, you should see a red line with a series of blue lines in the second row of the Instruments window. The red line represents the number of leaks discovered, and the blue lines represent the bytes that have been leaked.

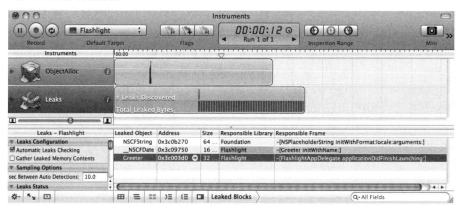

The leak happened much earlier, but the default setting is to sample for leaks every ten seconds. By default the Object alloc data is reported in the lower-right portion of the Instruments window. Select the Leaks instrument at the top left, and you should see the leak information. You can see in this sample output that the leak is reported to originate in FlashlightAppDelegate's applicationDidFinishLaunching: method. That is enough information for us to find the leak, although if you double-click the line reporting the leaked Greeter object, you will be taken to the offending lines in the source code. Now that we know where the leak is, let's fix it.

6.7 Fixing the Memory Leak on the iPhone

Memory management is a balance of many constraints. The most elementary is that you don't want to release the memory for an object while something else might still be pointing to it. On the other hand, you don't want to create a memory leak by hanging on to objects long after no one needs them anymore. The way to accomplish this in Objective-C is through reference counting.

You've seen briefly that when you create an object of type Greeter with code that looks like this, the reference count is set to one when alloc is called:

```
Greeter *host = [[Greeter alloc] initWithName:@"Maggie"];
```

That is exactly the error being reported by Build & Analyze. It knows that you increased the reference count to one and never used the variable again. It wants you to acknowledge that you have no further interest in the variable. You do that by calling this:

```
[host release];
```

This decrements the reference count by one. In our case, that's enough. The reference count for host will be zero, and its dealloc method will be called to clean up the object resources and release the memory. Send the release message to the host object when you know that you won't need it anymore. In our case, you would do it here:

Memory/Flashlight2/Classes/FlashlightAppDelegate.m

```
- (void)applicationDidFinishLaunching:(UIApplication *)application {
    Greeter *host = [[Greeter alloc] initWithName:@"Maggie"];
    NSLog(@"Greeter %@", host);
    [host release];
}
```

Click Build & Analyze, and this particular memory leak is now gone. Next let's take a minute to look at what happens when you make the other key memory mistake. What happens when you try to send a message to an object that has been freed?

6.8 Using Zombies

So far, we've created an object of type Greeter, we've printed its contents to the Console, and we've freed that object. Now let's deliberately send this freed object another message. We'll just print its contents to the Console again like this:

Memory/Flashlight3/Classes/FlashlightAppDelegate.m

```
- (void)applicationDidFinishLaunching:(UIApplication *)application {
    Greeter *host = [[Greeter alloc] initWithName:@"Maggie"];
    NSLog(@"Greeter %@", host);
    [host release];
    NSLog(@"Greeter %@", host);
}
```

Choose the menu item Build > Build & Debug. You should see a boilerplate message in your Console window followed by something like this:[5]

```
Greeter name: Maggie
 created: 2009-09-18 14:24:43 -0400
objc[11179]: FREED(id): message respondsToSelector:
                        sent to freed object=0x3b06760
Program received signal:  ''EXC_BAD_INSTRUCTION''.
```

This is so unhelpful. We only know which object has been freed because we freed it ourselves to demonstrate this, but in a large program where objects are coming and going, it would be harder to track down the offending object.

We're going to use zombies to help us out here. To enable them, select Executables > Flashlight in Groups & Files. Right-click the file, and choose Get Info; or, with Flashlight selected, press ⌘ I. Choose the Arguments tab, and at the bottom you should see the "Variables to be set in the environment:" text.

Add an environment variable by clicking the + button at the bottom-left corner. Enter *NSZombieEnabled* for the name of the variable and *YES* for the value.

Close the window. Click Build & Debug again. This time you should see this in the Console:

```
Greeter name: Maggie
 created: 2009-09-18 16:13:57 -0400
*** -[Greeter respondsToSelector:]:
            message sent to deallocated instance 0x380d950
```

This time the zombie helps us see that the type of the object is a Greeter. This technique helps a lot when debugging and trying to figure out which freed object you are messaging. Before going on, remove the variable that enables NSZombies. You don't want to be holding onto these objects when you deploy your application.

---

5. If you don't see this message, try to do a Build > Clean All Targets, and click Build & Run again.

6.9 Cleaning Up in dealloc

When the reference count for an object reaches zero, its dealloc is called. This is where you clean up the resources used by your object. For example, in Greeter there are two pointers to objects that we own: name and today. We need to send each a release when our Greeter object is about to be destroyed. We do this by overriding the dealloc method:

Memory/Flashlight5/Classes/Greeter.m

```
-(void) dealloc {
    [name release];
    [today release];
    [super dealloc];
}
```

Note that in the init method we let the superclass do its initialization before we did our custom initialization. Here we clean our custom objects up first and end with a call to [super dealloc].

You can add this line to your dealloc to output a quick message to the Console window when your Greeter object is being freed.

```
NSLog(@"In Greeter dealloc.");
```

If you are a belt and suspenders type of person and want to make sure that there's no chance that you end up sending a message to a freed object, then you may want to set the variables to nil after you release them like this:

Memory/Flashlight6/Classes/Greeter.m

```
-(void) dealloc {
    [name release];
    name = nil;
    [today release];
    today = nil;
    [super dealloc];
}
```

Here you are releasing the instance variable and setting it to nil. You can combine these steps using the corresponding property like this:

Memory/Flashlight7/Classes/Greeter.m

```
-(void) dealloc {
    self.name = nil;
    self.today = nil;
    [super dealloc];
}
```

As you'll see in the next section, self.name = nil will both release name and set it to nil.[6]

6.10 Retain and Release in a Setter

Here's an example of the retain-release pattern you'll use when changing the value of an object.[7] Suppose you already have created an object named greeter of type Greeter. An idiomatic setGreeter: method using the retain-release pattern would look something like this:

```
- (void) setGreeter: (Greeter *) newGreeter {
    if (newGreeter != greeter) {
        [newGreeter retain];
        [greeter release];
        greeter = newGreeter;
    }
}
```

You are being sent the object newGreeter. You want to own it to do something with it, so it is your job to retain it. On the other hand, you are about to set the variable greeter to point to the object referenced by newGreeter.

First, check to make sure the pointers aren't pointing at the same memory location. If they are, then there is nothing to do. If not, then go ahead and set greeter to now point to the object referenced by new-Greeter.

You are going to need to hold on to the object that newGreeter points to, so you send it a retain message. On the other hand, you don't need the object that greeter points to anymore, so you release it. Now you set greeter to point to what newGreeter points to. Even though you are never going to use the variable newGreeter again, you are going to use what it pointed to. This whole retain-release cycle was retaining and releasing what the variables point to and not the variables themselves.

This retain-release method of memory management does have parallels in everyday life. For example, the conference hotel where I wanted to stay was completely booked. They put me on the waiting list, and I

---

6. There are potential consequences that could come up if you are using Key Value Observing and someone else is still registered to listen to changes in the object being released and set to nil. I tend to just send the variable the release message in dealloc and leave it at that.

7. You saw this briefly when we were looking at property memory attributes in the previous chapter. This version is slightly different, and now you better understand the retain-release cycle.

booked a room at a nearby hotel. I entered all of this information in iCal. Fortunately, a room opened up at the conference hotel. Think for a minute about the order in which you make the changes, and you will see that it corresponds completely to how you handle memory in Objective-C.

First I retained a reservation for the new room in the conference hotel. Then I released my existing reservation at the nearby hotel. Finally, I reset the information in iCal to contain the information about the changed reservation. So if you think of the iCal event as our variable, I retained the object the variable would point to, I released the object the variable currently points to, and then I set the variable to point to the new object.[8]

If you use a property for greeter with the memory attribute set to retain, then the setter generated for you at compile time will follow the pattern. This is another reason that you should take advantage of properties rather than directly accessing the underlying instance variables: let the properties help you manage the memory correctly.

6.11 The Autorelease Pool

There's another situation we haven't taken care of yet. To see this problem, let's create the instance of the Greeter object in a separate method in FlashlightAppDelegate.m.

Memory/Flashlight8/Classes/FlashlightAppDelegate.m

```
#import "FlashlightAppDelegate.h"
#import "Greeter.h"

@implementation FlashlightAppDelegate
@synthesize window;

- (Greeter *) greeterFor:(NSString *) personName {
    return [[Greeter alloc] initWithName:personName];
}

- (void)applicationDidFinishLaunching:(UIApplication *)application {
    Greeter *host = [self greeterFor:@"Maggie"];
    NSLog(@"Greeter %@", host);
    [host release];
}
@end
```

---

8. To stretch the metaphor, having a travel agent is the analog of turning on automatic garbage collection in this hotel reservation example.

Click Build & Run, and the application behaves correctly. It creates the new object, displays it properly, and then releases it and calls dealloc.

```
Greeter name: Maggie
 created: 2009-09-17 14:12:09 -0400
In Greeter dealloc.
```

If instead you click Build & Analyze, you'll see that two problems are flagged in FlashlightAppDelegate.m. You'll usually see this problem when the method that returns an object (in our case greeterFor:()) is defined in a different class than the object that calls it. For this example, both halves of the transaction are included in the same object, and that's why we successfully created and released the object when we ran the example. The Clang Static Analyzer, however, is identifying a potential problem by looking at the two methods, greeterFor:() and application-DidFinishLaunching:(), separately.

▼   **Build Flashlight**
     Project Flashlight | Configuration Debug

  ▼ ❶ Analyze FlashlightAppDelegate.m ...in /Volumes/Data/Prags/Bo... 2 ≡

    ▼ Potential leak of an object allocated on line 8

       1. Method returns an Objective-C object with a +1 retain count (owning reference)
       less

       2. Object returned to caller as an owning reference (single retain count transferred to caller)
       less

       3. Object allocated on line 8 is returned from a method whose name ('greeterFor:') does not contain 'copy' or otherwise starts with 'new' or 'alloc'. This violates the naming convention rules given in the Memory Management Guide for Cocoa (object leaked)
       less

  ▼ Incorrect decrement of the reference count of an object is not owned at this point by the caller
     less

       1. Method returns an Objective-C object with a +0 retain count (non-owning reference)
       less

       2. Incorrect decrement of the reference count of an object is not owned at this point by the caller
       less

The second error is telling us that we released an object we didn't own. In fact, if you look at the applicationDidFinishLaunching: method, you'll see that when we released host we had no way of knowing that we owned it.

We'll ignore this problem for now and focus on the other issue. If you look at this code, you'll see that we own host because we created it with an alloc:

`Memory/Flashlight8/Classes/FlashlightAppDelegate.m`

```
- (Greeter *) greeterFor:(NSString *) personName {
    return [[Greeter alloc] initWithName:personName];
}
```

To highlight the problem, let's create the object and release it in two different steps like this:

`Memory/Flashlight9/Classes/FlashlightAppDelegate.m`

```
- (Greeter *) greeterFor:(NSString *) personName {
    Greeter *tempGreeter = [[Greeter alloc] initWithName:personName];
    return tempGreeter;
}
```

Where can we release tempGreeter?

You can't just release tempGreeter before you return it, or the retain count will be zero and tempGreeter will be dereferenced before you try to return it. You can't ignore the reference you hold for tempGreeter. That's the memory leak we're trying to fix. If you don't release it, you may be holding on to tempGreeter after no object is really using it because you haven't decremented its retain count.[9]

The solution is to use an autorelease pool.[10] You send tempGreeter the autorelease message, and it is marked to be released once the method that calls the greeterFor: method completes. You can also do this when you create the Greeter instance. In that case, you can eliminate the temporary variable and accomplish your needs like this:

`Memory/Flashlight10/Classes/FlashlightAppDelegate.m`

```
- (Greeter *) greeterFor:(NSString *) personName {
    return [[[Greeter alloc] initWithName:personName] autorelease];
}
```

Now we can solve our second problem by removing the call to [host release] in applicationDidFinishLaunching:. The object the host variable points to is not retained because it is now autoreleased. Since we no longer own this object, we are no longer allowed to release it.

---

9. I'll assume that it's obvious that you couldn't put the call to release the object in the line *after* the return.

10. For more information on autorelease pools and memory management, see Apple's publication *Memory Management Programming Guide for Cocoa*.

6.12 Using Convenience Constructors

We still have memory leaks in Greeter.m in the greeting and description methods. Take a look at the greeting method:

Memory/Flashlight10/Classes/Greeter.m
```
-(NSString *) greeting {
    return [[NSString alloc] initWithFormat:@"Hello, %@!", self.name];
}
```

The problem is identical to the one we just solved, and we could get rid of this memory leak by sending the object being returned an autorelease method. As it turns out, Apple provides another solution.

Here is a list of some of the methods that NSString provides for creating and initializing strings:

Creating and Initializing Strings

```
+ string
- init
- initWithBytes:length:encoding:
- initWithBytesNoCopy:length:encoding:freeWhenDone:
- initWithCharacters:length:
- initWithCharactersNoCopy:length:freeWhenDone:
- initWithString:
- initWithCString:encoding:
- initWithUTF8String:
- initWithFormat:
- initWithFormat:arguments:
- initWithFormat:locale:
- initWithFormat:locale:arguments:
- initWithData:encoding:
+ stringWithFormat:
+ localizedStringWithFormat:
+ stringWithCharacters:length:
+ stringWithString:
+ stringWithCString:encoding:
+ stringWithUTF8String:
```

The methods that are preceded by + are class methods, and the ones preceded by - are instance methods and must be used together with alloc. The class methods all have their equivalent instance method versions. For example, stringWithString: is paired with initWithString:, and string-WithUTF8String: is paired with initWithUTF8String:.

So instead of using this:

```
[[NSString alloc] initWithFormat:@"Hello, %@!", self.name]
```

we'll use the following:

```
[NSString stringWithFormat:@"Hello, %@!", self.name]
```

These two versions are *not* exactly the same. Let's review our rules.

If you create a string using the first version, then you own it and are responsible for releasing it. When we use alloc, we increase the reference count by one and need to release the string either by calling release or by using the autorelease mechanism.

On the other hand, what do the rules say about an object created using the second method? We didn't explicitly use alloc or new to create the string, and we didn't hold on to it using retain or copy. Therefore, we don't own it.

The stringWithFormat: is called a convenience constructor because it is used to create and initialize an object and give it back to us already autoreleased. In other words, the following:

```
[NSString stringWithFormat:@"Hello, %@!", self.name]
```

is equivalent to this:

```
[[[NSString alloc] initWithFormat:@"Hello, %@!", self.name] autorelease]
```

6.13 Exercise: Creating and Using a Convenience Constructor

Create your own convenience constructor for the Greeter class named greeterWithName:. You will need to declare it in Greeter.h and implement it in Greeter.m.

Refactor the applicationDidFinishLaunching: method in FlashlightAppDelegate.m to use this method to create an instance of the Greeter class. After you are done writing to the Console, the Greeter will be autoreleased, and Greeter's dealloc method will be called.

6.14 Solution: Creating and Using a Convenience Constructor

Start by declaring the class method in Greeter.h:

Memory/Flashlight11/Classes/Greeter.h

```
+(id) greeterWithName:(NSString *) newName;
```

To implement the method, create and return an autoreleased instance of the Greeter class:

Memory/Flashlight11/Classes/Greeter.m

```
+(id) greeterWithName:(NSString *) newName {
    return [[[Greeter alloc] initWithName:newName] autorelease];
}
```

The highlighted line shows you how to call this convenience method. Remember, it's a class method, so you call it on Greeter and not an instance.

Memory/Flashlight11/Classes/FlashlightAppDelegate.m

```
#import "FlashlightAppDelegate.h"
#import "Greeter.h"

@implementation FlashlightAppDelegate
@synthesize window;

- (void)applicationDidFinishLaunching:(UIApplication *)application {
    Greeter *host = [Greeter greeterWithName:@"Maggie"];
    NSLog(@"Greeter %@", host);
}

-(void) dealloc {
    [window release];
    [super dealloc];
}
@end
```

If you look at the final version in the code download, you'll see that I've also added a dealloc method to FlashlightAppDelegate.m to clean up the window variable. The dealloc is created for you in the original project template, but we removed it to help create memory leaks. If you click Build & Analyze, you'll see that we've taken care of all of our memory problems.

In this chapter, you saw the two basic types of memory errors. You learned to use reference counting in iPhone OS–based apps and to turn garbage collection on for Mac OS X–based apps available in Leopard or later. You also saw how to use the Clang Static Analyzer, Instruments, Zombies, and logging to investigate leaks.

At the beginning of this book, we started with a working browser that we created without writing any code. Now we've spent a bunch of chapters looking at the fundamentals of working with Objective-C and Cocoa. Now it's time to bring those two worlds together. Before we leave our iPhone example and head back to Mac OS X, I want to remind you that with new projects for Mac OS X, you can and should have garbage collection enabled.

Chapter 7

Outlets and Actions

Cocoa programming separates the application logic from the look and feel using Model-View-Controller (MVC). For the model, we'll create the application logic in Objective-C using Xcode. You've already seen how to create the view using Interface Builder.

The controller is the bridge between the model and the view. When the user clicks a button or types in a text field or does anything to the view, the controller responds to these actions often by sending messages on to the model. Similarly, when the model changes, the controller updates the view so that the changes are visible to the user.

The controller has to have a foot in each world. There is a class file that you use to create methods and send messages to the model or the view. We'll create an instance of the controller class in Interface Builder. This gives us a visual representation of the controller that lives in a nib that you use to wire the controller's code to the visual components you create in IB. It's sort of like having the real version of the controller living in code and its avatar living in IB.

You'll create a controller for our Simple Browser in the next chapter. In this chapter, we're going to look at how you communicate from these GUI elements created in Interface Builder to your code and how your code can make changes in the GUI. Once you have a feel for these actions and outlets, you will find yourself using them all the time.[1]

---

1. Although we're starting with this simple view of outlets and actions, we'll use them in more sophisticated ways as we progress.

7.1 The Big Picture

Imagine we have a window with a button and a text field. When the user clicks the button, we will display "Hello, World!" in the text field. We need a way to connect our button to code so that when the button is clicked, a method will be called in our code to do the work for us. We also need some connection back to the text field so we can set its text to "Hello, World!"

There are basically two ways in which the controller connects to UI elements:

- *Actions*: Controller methods used when an element such as a button wants to initiate an action performed by the controller

- *Outlets*: Controller instance variables that point to the UI elements the controller needs to send messages to

Actions and outlets are specifically designed for connections created in Interface Builder. Here's a look at the basic flow:

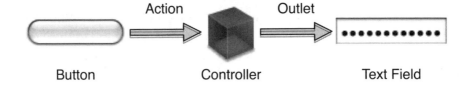

When a user clicks a button, a message is sent to a specified target to initiate a specific action. You create this target action in a controller, and you make the connection in Interface Builder. The action is just a method that will get called when the button is clicked.

There are times the controller is going to need to communicate with an object you created using IB. One way is to give the controller a handle to the object. Imagine that our controller has an outlet that is a text field. In other words, the controller has an instance variable that points to the text field. Just like a wall socket, the outlet is a place in the controller where the visual element plugs into.

7.2 Using an Outlet

Create a new project using the Cocoa Application template with all checkboxes unselected, and call it HelloWorldPro.

Add this line to HelloWorldProAppDelegate.m:

Outlets/HelloWorldPro1/HelloWorldProAppDelegate.m

```
#import "HelloWorldProAppDelegate.h"

@implementation HelloWorldProAppDelegate

@synthesize window;
- (void)applicationDidFinishLaunching:(NSNotification *)aNotification {
    self.window.backgroundColor = [NSColor greenColor];
}
@end
```

Click Build & Run, and your window should appear with the background color set to green. How did this happen? We sent a message to the window property to change its background color. How did that message get through to the actual NSWindow that is part of the nib file?

There are two important steps to making this happen. First, check out the header file for the HelloWorldProAppDelegate class:

Outlets/HelloWorldPro1/HelloWorldProAppDelegate.h

```
#import <Cocoa/Cocoa.h>

@interface HelloWorldProAppDelegate : NSObject <NSApplicationDelegate> {
    NSWindow *window;
}
@property (assign) IBOutlet NSWindow *window;
@end
```

Do you see theIBOutlet keyword tucked into the middle of the @property declaration for window? This tells Interface Builder to include window in the list of outlets for every instance of HelloWorldProAppDelegate.

Double-click the MainMenu.xib file (remember you can find it under Resources). When the nib opens in Interface Builder, look at the Document window, and select the instance of the HelloWorldProAppDelegate class.[2]

---

2. If the Document window isn't visible, you can always bring it up using ⌘0 or Window > Document.

Open its Connections inspector (Tools > Connections inspector). The window outlet has already been connected to the NSWindow object in the same nib.

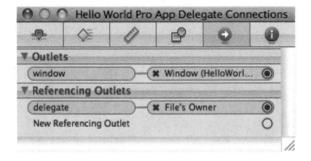

If you'd like, you can also view the connections for the NSWindow object, and you'll see the window listed as a referencing outlet.

So, you can imagine the sequence of events like this. We have a window variable and property in the HelloWorldProAppDelegate class. We have a nib that contains an instance of HelloWorldProAppDelegate and an instance of NSWindow.

App Delegate

Window

The window property is hidden away inside HelloWorldProAppDelegate. You saw in the previous chapter that we could access the property in code, but how do we connect to it in Interface Builder? The first step is to tag the property as an IBOutlet. I picture this outlet as a handle on the object that is visible in Interface Builder that I can use to connect the variable to other objects in the same nib file:

At this point, there is nothing that connects the window variable to the NSWindow object. So, we use the Connections inspector to connect the two:

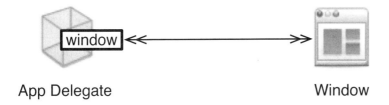

Now the two are linked. So now when we send messages to the window variable in code, the effect is that we are sending the message to the object that window is connected to in the nib file. The window variable is a proxy for the actual window. That's why when we tell the window variable to set its background color to green, the NSWindow object turns green.

7.3 Exercise: Creating and Using an Outlet

Your goal in this exercise is to use outlets to create this:

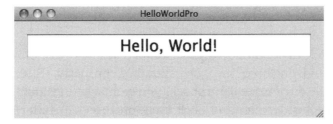

In Interface Builder, drag a text field from the Library into the window, and position it along the top using the guidelines. Go ahead and center justify the text in the text field, adjust the font size using the Attributes inspector, and save your work.

Add a new property for that text field to your header file for the Hel-loWorldProAppDelegate, and declare it to be an outlet. Use the outlet to print "Hello, World!" after the application launches.

Back in Interface Builder, connect the outlet to the text field.

Click Build & Run, and you should see a green background in your window with a text field on top displaying the message "Hello, World!"

7.4 Solution: Creating and Using an Outlet

There's a rhythm to using Xcode and Interface Builder. You'll bounce back and forth between them. You should have had no trouble drag-ging a text field and positioning it in your window in Interface Builder. Before you head back to Xcode, look at the Connections inspector for HelloWorldProAppDelegate. It should look exactly as it did before with a single outlet that is already connected.

This next part is kind of cool. Add these two highlighted lines to your header file:

```
Outlets/HelloWorldPro2/HelloWorldProAppDelegate.h

#import <Cocoa/Cocoa.h>

@interface HelloWorldProAppDelegate : NSObject <NSApplicationDelegate> {
    NSWindow *window;
▶   NSTextField *textField;
}
@property (assign) IBOutlet NSWindow *window;
▶ @property (assign) IBOutlet NSTextField *textField;
@end
```

You've added an instance variable named textField to HelloWorldProAp-pDelegate and declared the corresponding property. But even more important for our current purposes, you've marked textField as an out-let. Save the header file, and click back on the Connections inspector in Interface Builder.

Did you see that?

A new outlet has appeared. That makes me smile every time. We've added an outlet to the public interface for HelloWorldProAppDelegate to say to the world that this property is available to you. Interface Builder has picked up on this addition because you have labeled the outlet with IBOutlet.

Click inside the circle to the right of the textField outlet, and drag it to the text field you placed inside the window. Let go of the mouse, and you should have made a new connection. Save your work. You can quit Interface Builder for now if you'd like.

Back in Xcode, you have two small changes to make to the implementation file. You need to synthesize the accessors for textField, and you want to display "Hello, World!" in it. You know how to do both of these steps from before.

Outlets/HelloWorldPro2/HelloWorldProAppDelegate.m

```
#import "HelloWorldProAppDelegate.h"

@implementation HelloWorldProAppDelegate

@synthesize window, textField;

- (void)applicationDidFinishLaunching:(NSNotification *)aNotification {
    self.window.backgroundColor = [NSColor greenColor];
    [self.textField setStringValue:@"Hello, World!"];
}
@end
```

7.5 Declaring an Action

In Interface Builder, add a push button to your window, and change its title to Personalize. When the button is clicked, we'll change the greeting from "Hello, World!" to something a little more personal.

> \\// Joe Asks...
> ·?ʃ
> ⌣ **Where Do I Find the Outlet That I Just Added in Code?**
>
> If you add an outlet to a class named NSFoo, then you will find
> that outlet in IB on any object of type NSFoo. This will become
> second-nature, but many people new to Interface Builder will
> complain that they added the outlet to the class but it's not
> showing up in IB. There are usually two reasons something is
> going wrong:
>
> - Make sure you save the header file in Xcode. Files that
>   need to be saved are slightly gray in the Groups & Files
>   panel.
>
> - Make sure you are looking in the right object. In our exam-
>   ple, we added the outlet in the source file HelloWorldProAp-
>   pDelegate.h, so in Interface Builder, select the HelloWorldAp-
>   pDelegate object and look in the Connections inspector.
>
> If these steps are obvious to you, great. You understand the
> relationship between what you do in Xcode and what you do
> in Interface Builder.

We'll have to declare and implement a method in Xcode that will be
called when the button is clicked. The first step is to declare a method
using the proper syntax. For all Mac OS X Cocoa applications, your
actions have to be declared like this:

```
-(IBAction) actionSelector: (id) sender;
```

This is the same format you saw for the web view's goBack: method. The
method must be an instance method that takes a single parameter of
return type id. By convention we name the parameter sender.

The return type is IBAction. This return type signals two things at once.
First, this helps Interface Builder understand that this method is an
action so that it can be displayed in the Connections inspector. Second, IBAction is typedefed to a void, so IBAction tells you that the method
doesn't return anything.[3]

---

3. The IBAction return type is not enough to get the method to show up in Interface
Builder. IB is smart enough to make sure that there is also a single parameter of type id.

As an aside, when you are designing applications for the iPhone or the iPod touch, you can use two additional variations. You can create an action that has no arguments. The following signature will work fine in Cocoa Touch:[4]

```
- (IBAction) actionSelector
```

This version is always my first choice when working with Cocoa Touch. If I had this no argument signature available to me in Cocoa, it would be my first choice here as well. In the case that I need to pass along the sender, I love having the option to do so. But there are many times where I don't need to communicate with the sender and don't need to know anything about the sender. I'd like that to be more clearly expressed in my code by using the no-argument version.

On the other hand, sometimes I need to know more than can be communicated by just passing along the sender. Sometimes I'd like to know something about the event that triggered the message. If you are writing a Cocoa Touch application, you can use this signature for an IBAction:

```
- (IBAction)respondToButtonClick:(id)sender forEvent:(UIEvent*)event;
```

Currently, for desktop applications, we need to use the single argument form for declaring an IBAction. For Cocoa Touch applications, we are free to use the no-argument and two-argument versions as well.

Back to our current example, add this highlighted declaration to the header file, and save your work:

Outlets/HelloWorldPro3/HelloWorldProAppDelegate.h

```
#import <Cocoa/Cocoa.h>

@interface HelloWorldProAppDelegate : NSObject <NSApplicationDelegate> {
    NSWindow *window;
    NSTextField *textField;
}
@property (assign) IBOutlet NSWindow *window;
@property (assign) IBOutlet NSTextField *textField;

-(IBAction) changeGreeting:(id)sender;
@end
```

---

4. Cocoa Touch is how we describe the Cocoa APIs that target the iPhone OS.

7.6 Connecting and Implementing the Action

You've created your button and declared your action in the HelloWorld-ProAppDelegate header file. It might be helpful to picture the IBAction similar to how we pictured the IBOutlet. Imagine we started by declaring a method in HelloWorldProAppDelegate.h like this:

(void) changeGreeting

This gives us a method that we could call in code but have no way of connecting to within Interface Builder:

Change the signature of the method so that it is now an action:

(IBAction) changeGreeting:(**id**) sender

You've now exposed this method. This means that, for example, you can connect buttons to this action so that this method is performed when the button is clicked.

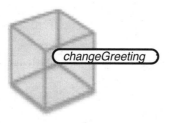

Let's take advantage of our declared action, head back to Interface Builder, and connect the action and the button. In IB select the object of type HelloWorldProAppDelegate in the Document window, and look at its connections with the Connections inspector. You should now have changeGreeting: under Received Actions.

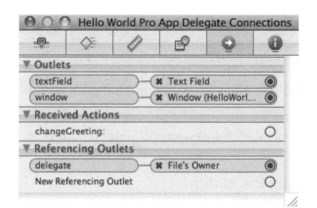

Click the circle to the right of changeGreeting:, and drag to the button you created. Release the mouse, and you will have wired up your outlet. Save your work, and quit Interface Builder.

We'll implement the action method to change the window background color to red and to greet the user personally. How can we possibly know the user's name ahead of time? We can't. But we can use the function call NSFullUserName() to retrieve the name the user entered when configuring their machine:

Outlets/HelloWorldPro3/HelloWorldProAppDelegate.m

```
-(IBAction) changeGreeting:(id)sender {
    self.window.backgroundColor = [NSColor redColor];
    [self.textField setStringValue:
        [NSString stringWithFormat:@"Hello, %@!", NSFullUserName()]];
}
```

When I run this app on my laptop, I see this:

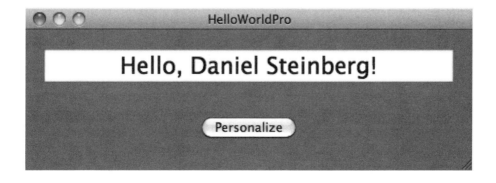

7.7 Exercise: Hiding the Button

I don't really like the current state of the application. After the user clicks Personalize and the text field displays a personal greeting, the button still says "Personalize" even though there's nothing more for the user to do.

After the user personalizes the output, hide the button.

7.8 Solution: Hiding the Button

You'll tend to write less code when you are writing Cocoa apps in Objective-C, but it will initially take you longer to find what that code is that you need to write. You'll spend a lot of time in the docs and searching the Internet. A lot of Cocoa coding requires that you not do more than you have to do.

For example, our goal here was to hide the button. We know that we have to send a message to the button, so how do we do that? We could create an outlet for an NSButton in HelloWorldProAppDelegate.h and connect the outlet to the button in the nib. This would be correct, but it would be unnecessary.

At least for now, the only place we need access to the button is inside the changeGreeting: method. And you have a handle to the button there —it's the sender that gets passed in as a parameter. All you need to do is turn around and send the right message to the button by adding this single line to your changeGreeting: implementation:

Outlets/HelloWorldPro4/HelloWorldProAppDelegate.m

```
-(IBAction) changeGreeting:(id)sender {
    self.window.backgroundColor = [NSColor redColor];
    [self.textField setStringValue:
        [NSString stringWithFormat:@"Hello, %@!", NSFullUserName()]];
    [sender setHidden:YES];
}
```

If it would make you feel better, you can cast the sender to an NSButton so that it is clearer who you are sending the message to:

```
[(NSButton *)sender setHidden:YES];
```

So, how did we know which message to send to the button? First you head to the docs for NSButton and look through the tasks for anything that has to do with hiding a button. There's nothing there. So, you go to the top of the documentation for NSButton, and you see that it inherits from NSControl : NSView : NSResponder : NSObject. This sends you up the inheritance tree. You check NSControl, and there's nothing there, so you move on to NSView.

Scanning through the tasks, there's a Hiding Views heading, and one of the methods is setHidden:. We could also have decided to remove the button entirely using this:

```
[sender removeFromSuperview];
```

From the user's point of view, there is no difference between these two approaches; however, there is an important difference between these two from a memory standpoint. When we dragged the button onto the window in Interface Builder, the button's superview (the window's content view) owned the button and increased its reference count by one. If we hide the button, it still exists; it's just not visible. If, on the other hand, we remove the button from its superview, then the only object that ever owned the button will now release the button, and the button will be freed.

Neither approach is right or wrong. You need to decide in your situation whether you are done with the button and want to release it.

7.9 Exercise: Toggling the Interface

Instead of hiding the button, let's set the button to toggle back and forth between the two views. When the app launches, the button title is "Personalize," the background is green, and the text field reads "Hello, World!"

When the user clicks the Personalize button, the button's title should change to "Generalize," the background should become red, and the text field should display the personalized greeting.

7.10 Solution: Toggling the Interface

There are so many ways to code this solution. Let's start simply and go from there. I'm going to add an instance variable of type BOOL named isPersonalized to the header file:

Outlets/HelloWorldPro5/HelloWorldProAppDelegate.h

```
NSWindow *window;
NSTextField *textField;
▶ BOOL isPersonalized;
```

Now we can make the modifications to the changeGreeting: method to set the button, text field, and background color based on whether isPersonalized is YES or NO. I've also initialized isPersonalized in the applicationDidFinishLaunching: method. The BOOL is initialized to NO by default, but I find that it helps to explicitly communicate this here:

Outlets/HelloWorldPro5/HelloWorldProAppDelegate.m

```
#import "HelloWorldProAppDelegate.h"

@implementation HelloWorldProAppDelegate

@synthesize window, textField;

- (void)applicationDidFinishLaunching:(NSNotification *)aNotification {
    self.window.backgroundColor = [NSColor greenColor];
    [self.textField setStringValue:@"Hello, World!"];
    isPersonalized = NO;
}

-(IBAction) changeGreeting:(id)sender {
    if (isPersonalized) {
        self.window.backgroundColor = [NSColor greenColor];
        [self.textField setStringValue:@"Hello, World!"];
        [sender setTitle:@"Personalize"];
        isPersonalized = NO;
    } else {
        self.window.backgroundColor = [NSColor redColor];
        [self.textField setStringValue:
            [NSString stringWithFormat:@"Hello, %@!", NSFullUserName()]];
        [sender setTitle:@"Generalize"];
        isPersonalized = YES;
    }
}
@end
```

Click Build & Run, and the application will behave the way we want it to behave.

7.11 Introducing Another Outlet

I don't like the repeated code in the applicationDidFinishLaunching: method and the true branch of the if statement in the changeGreeting:. We set the background color and the text field contents to the same values twice. I'd like to call changeGreeting: from applicationDidFinishLaunching:.

Can you see the problem with this?

Who should be the sender? How does changeGreeting: have a handle to the button if it's not called in response to a button click?

Let's introduce an outlet for our button:

Outlets/HelloWorldPro6/HelloWorldProAppDelegate.h

```
#import <Cocoa/Cocoa.h>

@interface HelloWorldProAppDelegate : NSObject <NSApplicationDelegate> {
    NSWindow *window;
    NSTextField *textField;
    NSButton *button;
    BOOL isPersonalized;
}
@property (assign) IBOutlet NSWindow *window;
@property (assign) IBOutlet NSTextField *textField;
@property (assign) IBOutlet NSButton *button;

-(IBAction) changeGreeting:(id)sender;
@end
```

Connect this new outlet to your button in Interface Builder. If you'd like, you can delete the button's title so that it is blank. Save.

In the implementation file, you'll need to synthesize button. Now you can change the use of sender to self.button inside changeGreeting:. Let's make applicationDidFinishLaunching: worse for a moment before we make it better.

Outlets/HelloWorldPro6/HelloWorldProAppDelegate.m

```
- (void)applicationDidFinishLaunching:(NSNotification *)aNotification {
    self.window.backgroundColor = [NSColor greenColor];
    [self.textField setStringValue:@"Hello, World!"];
    [self.button setTitle:@"Personalize"];
    isPersonalized = NO;
}
```

This code is now identical to the true branch of the if statement, so let's refactor. Introduce two utility methods, personalize and generalize, and use them in applicationDidFinishLaunching: and changeGreeting:.

Outlets/HelloWorldPro7/HelloWorldProAppDelegate.m

```
#import "HelloWorldProAppDelegate.h"

@implementation HelloWorldProAppDelegate

@synthesize window, textField, button;

-(void) personalize {
    self.window.backgroundColor = [NSColor redColor];
```

```
    [self.textField setStringValue:
        [NSString stringWithFormat:@"Hello, %@!", NSFullUserName()]];
    [self.button setTitle:@"Generalize"];
    isPersonalized = YES;
}
-(void) generalize {
    self.window.backgroundColor = [NSColor greenColor];
    [self.textField setStringValue:@"Hello, World!"];
    [self.button setTitle:@"Personalize"];
    isPersonalized = NO;
}
- (void)applicationDidFinishLaunching:(NSNotification *)aNotification {
    [self generalize];
}
-(IBAction) changeGreeting:(id)sender {
    if (isPersonalized) [self generalize];
    else [self personalize];
}
@end
```

The code is not really much shorter, but it is easier to read. In the next section, we'll take advantage of another feature of Objective-C to make one more change.

7.12 Creating Selectors from Strings

Let's take a step back and notice that when the button's title is "Personalize," we call the method personalize, and when the button's title is "Generalize," we call the method generalize.

It would be nice if we could take the button's title, convert it to lowercase, and use it as the method name we're calling. Because its value changes at runtime, we'll use the function NSSelectorFromString() like this:

```
NSSelectorFromString([[self.button title] lowercaseString]);
```

This returns a selector—you can think of that as the method's formal name. We then call the method with that name by sending the message performSelector: to self with the selector we just created as the argument.

In other words, the changeGreeting: can change to this:

```
Outlets/HelloWorldPro8/HelloWorldProAppDelegate.m
```

```
-(IBAction) changeGreeting:(id)sender {
    [self performSelector:
        NSSelectorFromString([[self.button title] lowercaseString])];
}
```

While we're at it, we can get rid of the BOOL named isPersonalized because we're not using it anymore. I'm not suggesting that you replace every boolean and if statement, but I did want to show you one way of using selectors for a clear path through your code without making any decisions.[5]

We began our journey by creating a web browser without writing any code. In the chapters since, you've learned a lot about the code and the connections that were created for you. In the next chapter, we'll return to our web browser and create a controller to add some functionality to what we got for free.

---

5. In this case, I've coupled our decision to the label on the button. This makes it harder when it comes time to internationalize our application. I wanted to introduce you to NSSelectorFromString(). You will learn more robust ways of using this technique.

Chapter 8

Creating a Controller

You can't accomplish everything you want your application to do just by dragging connections between the visual elements in Interface Builder. On the one hand, it's pretty amazing how easily we created a simple web browser in Chapter 2, *Using What's There*, on page 11 just using visual tools. On the other hand, the browser leaves a lot to be desired. There are some things we're just going to need to code ourselves.

In this chapter, we'll create a controller for our SimpleBrowser example. To keep things simple, we won't have a model—we'll just have a view and a controller. The main point of this example is creating a new class and instantiating it to communicate with objects you created in Interface Builder.

8.1 How We've Created Objects

We have created and connected objects in two different ways. In the SimpleBrowser example, all of our objects are created in the nib. We dragged in buttons, a text field, and a web view, and they joined the SimpleBrowserAppDelegate and all of the other objects that are created in the nib.

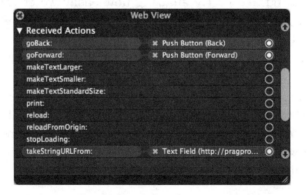

There is effectively no code for this application. All of the connections between the objects have been made in Interface Builder. Here are the actions that the web view receives. It gets the goBack: message from the Back button, the goForward: message from the Forward button, and the takeStringURLFrom: message from the text field.

Contrast this with the "Hello, World!" application we built in Chapter 4, *Classes and Objects*, on page 49. There we created a text field in code in our application delegate. We then created a custom Greeter. We instantiated it in code in our app delegate, and all of our communication among the objects we created was in code.

In Chapter 7, *Outlets and Actions*, on page 111, you learned how to connect code that you created with objects that were created in Interface Builder. If you needed to talk to a widget from your code, you created an outlet for that widget in your header file and then connected the outlet to the widget in IB.[1] If you needed a widget to trigger a method that you created in code, you declared this action in the header file and then connected the triggering widget to the action in Interface Builder.

The key to all of this is that there must be an object in your nib of the type that you are adding these outlets and actions to. For now, that will mean that we are creating an instance of our class in Interface Builder.

Let's make this more concrete. We'll create a controller class in code and then create our instance in Interface Builder.

8.2 Creating Our Controller Class

All *classes* are created in Xcode.

Reopen the SimpleBrowser project, or quickly re-create it. In Xcode, choose File > New File... or ⌘N. Choose to create a Cocoa > Objective-C class. I know this doesn't look like a controller class, and there are other options that include the word *Controller*. Don't choose them. What makes this class a controller is how you will configure and use it.

Name your class BrowserController, and make sure that the checkboxes to create BrowserController.h and to target SimpleBrowser are selected. Generally, if you accept the defaults, you should be OK. Click Finish, and save your work.

Our next step is to create an instance of the class and allow it to interact with the GUI elements you've already created. You can instantiate BrowserController using code you write in Xcode or in much the same way we instantiated the GUI elements like NSButton in Interface Builder.

Even though we always write out class code in Xcode, you've seen that we can instantiate them in code or using Interface Builder. We will create objects that belong to the model in Xcode because they don't need to directly know about or communicate with any of the GUI elements. We will create objects that are controller elements in Interface Builder so that we can drag connections between the controllers and the objects they communicate with.

---

1. I'm using widget to informally refer to one of the GUI elements like buttons, text fields, and so on.

At first, this will feel a bit odd. After all, you are creating an instance of a class that has no visual representation using a tool named *Interface Builder*. In no time, this will feel completely natural to you.

8.3 Creating an Instance of Our Controller in IB

We're now going to create an instance of the BrowserController class in Interface Builder.[2]

When we created instances of our buttons, we just looked in the Library for an NSButton that looked like the one we wanted and dragged it into our window. We can't do that with our BrowserController because there's no way that Interface Builder's Library would contain our BrowserController class—we just made it up. Fortunately, Snow Leopard and Xcode 3.2 have made this a lot easier for us.[3]

Double-click MainMenu.xib to open the nib file in IB. You aren't interested in the Window view anymore because there is no visual representation of the controller for the end user to see. Instead, bring up the Document window in Interface Builder with the key sequence ⌘ 0 or Window > Document.

Interface Builder provides us with a representation of our BrowserController object. In IB, go to the Library, and this time choose the Classes tab and look for BrowserController.

---

2. Actually, the instance isn't really created until the nib is unarchived when the application starts up. We can think of the instance being created at this point in the same way we talked about creating an object in code when we learned to use a call like this [[BrowserController alloc] init].
3. If you are running an earlier version of Xcode, you will need to adjust the directions that follow so that you drag an NSObject into the Document window and change its type using the Identity inspector.

Our BrowserController class has a simple lineage since it directly extends NSObject. If you look at the lineage for a class like the NSButton, you'll see a much deeper hierarchy.

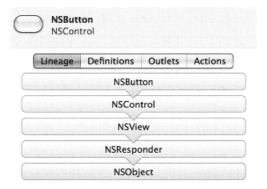

In addition to the Lineage tab, there are also tabs for looking at the class's outlets and actions and also where the class is defined. You'll notice the + and - in the bottom-left corner of both the Outlet and Action tabs. Do not add or remove outlets or actions in Interface Builder. I know it seems as if it would be easier, but changes you make in IB are not picked up by Xcode. Make your changes in the code, and let those changes be picked up in IB.

Back in our example, drag the BrowserController into the Document window, and drop it. Congratulations! You've just created an instance of

BrowserController in the nib. Here is the icon view of your Document window with the newly added instance of the BrowserController:

I prefer using the list view but wanted to show you this view in case you like it better.

8.4 Declaring an Outlet and an Action

Right now the Back button is connected to the web view's goBack: method. Let's insert the BrowserController in between. We're going to need a method in the controller that we use for loading the previous web page. It will be called by the Back button and will, in turn, have to send the message goBack: to the web view. This means we'll need an outlet for the web view and an action for the method.

Back in Xcode, add an IBAction named loadPreviousPage: to BrowserController.h. You'll also need to add an IBOutlet named myWebView using an instance variable and a property.[4] The myWebView variable is a pointer to a WebView object.

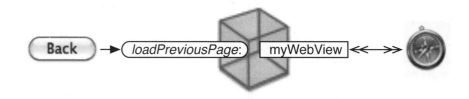

---

4. If you are using and are targeting 64-bit, you can create your property without declaring the instance variable.

With this set up, when the Back button is clicked, the loadPreviousPage: method will be called on the BrowserController object. The loadPreviousPage: method will call the goBack: method on the myWebView variable. Since the myWebView variable is also an outlet that is connected to the WebView object, this has the effect of calling the goBack: method on this WebView object. You can read more about objects and actions in Apple's *Communicating with Objects* [App08c].

Remember to synthesize myWebView in the implementation file. Here's the header:

CreatingAController/SimpleBrowser1/BrowserController.h

```
#import <Cocoa/Cocoa.h>

@interface BrowserController : NSObject {
    WebView *myWebView;
}
@property(assign) IBOutlet WebView *myWebView;

-(IBAction) loadPreviousPage: (id) sender;

@end
```

Before you hit Build & Run, can you see any problems? If you can, fix them. If not, I'll explain how in a minute. Hit Build & Run, and you should get the message "Build failed (9 errors, 6 warnings)." In the bottom right of your open window, you should see this:

⊗ Failed ⚠ 6 ❶ 9

You can click Failed, the yellow triangle with the exclamation point that indicates warnings, or the red circle with the ! that indicates errors to take you to a window that contains more details about what went wrong. These three errors and two warnings are repeated three times:

▼ ❶ Compile BrowserController.m ...in /Volumes/Data/Prags/Bo... ⚠ 2 ❶ 3
　▶ ❶ Expected specifier-qualifier-list before 'WebView'
　▶ ❶ Expected specifier-qualifier-list before 'WebView'
　　❶ No declaration of property 'myWebView' found in the interface
　　⚠ Incomplete implementation of class 'BrowserController'
　　⚠ Method definition for '-loadPreviousPage:' not found

Let's deal with the error first. Your IBOutlet uses the WebView class. But your program doesn't know anything about the WebView class. You have to import the appropriate header file. At the top of the WebView docs, you can see that it is part of the WebKit framework and is declared in

Joe Asks. . .

What's the Difference Between a Warning and an Error?

An error means that there is something that keeps your code from compiling. It's a showstopper. Your code won't compile, so there's no app to run. You don't have any choice but to fix errors.

A warning lets you know there may be a problem, but it wasn't severe enough to keep your code from compiling. This could mean that everything will be fine, or it could mean that you end up with a runtime error. A warning could be a note at compile time telling you that you've sent a message to an object that didn't declare a method with that signature. It doesn't mean that the object can't handle the message, just that the compiler can't verify that the object can.

It is easy to ignore warnings. Your code compiles—why worry? Some experienced developers think that it's too easy to ignore these warnings, so they select the option Treat Warnings as Errors.

Select the menu item Project > Edit Project Settings, go to the Build tab, and select the Treat Warnings as Errors checkbox. Search on the word *treat*.

WebView.h. One solution is to add this import to BrowserController.h below the line importing the Cocoa headers:

CreatingAController/SimpleBrowser2/BrowserController.h

```
#import <Cocoa/Cocoa.h>
#import <WebKit/WebKit.h>
@interface BrowserController : NSObject {
    WebView *myWebView;
}
@property(assign) IBOutlet WebView *myWebView;
-(IBAction) loadPreviousPage: (id) sender;
@end
```

Click Build & Run again. This time the build will succeed. There will be two unique warnings because the header file promised there would be a method named loadPreviousPage and we haven't implemented it yet. Even with this unfinished work, the program builds and launches and works the same way it did before. Stop the running application by using the red Tasks stop sign.

8.5 Forward Declaration

There's another solution to the errors we were getting in the previous section: You can use the @class directive in the header file in place of the import statement.

CreatingAController/SimpleBrowser3/BrowserController.h

```
#import <Cocoa/Cocoa.h>
@class WebView;
@interface BrowserController : NSObject {
    WebView *myWebView;
}
@property(assign) IBOutlet WebView *myWebView;
-(IBAction) loadPreviousPage: (id) sender;
@end
```

In the BrowserController.h file, the compiler only needs to know that Web-View is a legitimate class. It doesn't need to know anything about it. The @class directive does exactly that. It doesn't bring in the whole header file that tells us what an object of type WebView can do—we don't need to know that yet. It just reassures us that a class named WebView exists.

Whenever you use the @class directive in a header file, you will most likely need the corresponding import statement in the implementation file. Go ahead and add it now near the top of the implementation file. While you're at it, stub out the loadPreviousPage: action.

CreatingAController/SimpleBrowser3/BrowserController.m

```
#import "BrowserController.h"
#import <WebKit/WebKit.h>

@implementation BrowserController

@synthesize myWebView;

-(IBAction) loadPreviousPage: (id) sender{
    NSLog(@"loadPreviousPage:");
}


@end
```

Click Build & Run. There should be no warnings or errors, and your browser should run as it did before.

8.6 Wiring Up the Controller

Go back to Interface Builder; in the Document window click the Browser Controller object, and open the Connections inspector.

Under Outlets, you now find myWebView, and under Received Actions you see loadPreviousPage:. Connect the loadPreviousPage: action to the Back button. The Back button should now only be connected to the controller and not be directly connected to the web view. Also connect the myWebView outlet to the web view.

Save your work, and click Build & Run. Type in a few URLs. Try out the Back button. For now, when you click the Back button, the loadPreviousPage: message is sent to the BrowserController object, which prints the method name in the Console.

8.7 Implementing the Loading of the Previous Page

Back in Xcode, there's not much code to write. When the Back button sends the loadPreviousPage: message to the BrowserController object, the BrowserController object just turns around and sends the goBack message to myWebView.

The only decision we have to make is what to send to the web view as the sender. We can send self, or we can pass along the identity of the object calling the loadPreviousPage:. In our case, it doesn't really matter. I've decided to take the latter approach and pass on the Back button as the sender.

CreatingAController/SimpleBrowser4/BrowserController.m

```
-(IBAction) loadPreviousPage: (id) sender{
    [self.myWebView goBack:sender];
}
```

That's it! Click Build & Run, and you have a working Back button again.

8.8 Exercise: Finishing the Controller

Add another action to BrowserController named loadNextPage:, and use it to make the Forward button work through the controller.

Once that is working, add one last action to BrowserController. Name it loadURLFrom:, and use it to make the URL entry from the text field work through the controller. Remember that the text field will send a message to the controller when Enter is clicked, and then the web view is going to need to send a message back to the text field to get the text field's string value. You can do this in more than one way. You might be tempted to introduce an outlet for the text field. In this case, you don't have to do this. Use the sender to talk back to the text field.

8.9   Solution: Finishing the Controller

The first half of the exercise mirrors the step we took together. You'll need to make three changes.

First, you need to add an action to the header file BrowserController.h using Xcode and save:

```
-(IBAction) loadNextPage: (id) sender;
```

Second, go back to Interface Builder, and select the BrowserController. In the Connections inspector, drag from the circle to the right of load-NextPage: to the Forward button to make the connection. Save your work.

Finally, you need to implement the method. Looking at the web view's connections, you can see that the method you need to call is goForward:. Back in Xcode, modify BrowserController.m to add this method:

CreatingAController/SimpleBrowser5/BrowserController.m

```
-(IBAction) loadNextPage: (id) sender{
    [self.myWebView goForward:sender];
}
```

Save your work. Click Build & Run, and you should find that you now have working Back and Forward buttons. Enter a few URLs, and you should be able to use the buttons to move back and forward through your list.

For the second half of the exercise, we'll follow three similar steps. First, in Xcode add an action named loadURLFrom: to the header file and save it:

```
-(IBAction) loadURLFrom: (id) sender;
```

Select the BrowserController in your Document window in IB, and open the Connections inspector.

Drag from the circle to the right of loadURLFrom: to the text field to make the connection. We've already configured the text field to send an action to its target when the user hits the Enter key. You can check that the Action value is still set this way using the Attributes inspector for the text field. Save your work. Back in Xcode, implement your method like this:

CreatingAController/SimpleBrowser5/BrowserController.m

```
-(IBAction) loadURLFrom: (id) sender{
    [self.myWebView takeStringURLFrom:sender];
}
```

8.10 Awake from Nib

Back in Chapter 4, *Classes and Objects*, on page 49, we created and initialized our instance of the Greeter using a combination like this:

```
[[Greeter alloc] initWithName:@"Maggie"];
```

We were able to initialize our variables and do whatever customization we needed in the initWithName: method. We don't have a comparable method in BrowserController, and our BrowserController is being initialized when the nib is loaded and not with an explicit call to alloc and some form of init.

I'll go into more depth later about what happens when the nib is unarchived and loaded. For now, when the application starts up, the graph of objects archived in the nib is reconstructed. The objects are created, and the connections between them are made. Next, before anything is displayed to the end user, an awakeFromNib message is sent to all objects that have this method.[5] Just add this method to any file that needs to perform tasks just after initialization:

```
-(void) awakeFromNib {
}
```

For example, I'd like our browser to load our default web page when it launches. Now the user has to click into the text field and hit Enter to get the page to load. So in awakeFromNib, I'm going to set the text field to have the string value http://pragprog.com and then have the web view display this page.

---

5. No message is sent to objects that don't implement this message so that you don't get a runtime error.

This means I'm going to need to be able to interact with the text field in the body of awakeFromNib. We'll need to add an outlet to our header file for the NSTextField. Let's call it address.

CreatingAController/SimpleBrowser6/BrowserController.h

```
#import <Cocoa/Cocoa.h>
@class WebView;
@interface BrowserController : NSObject {
    WebView *myWebView;
    NSTextField *address;
}
@property(assign) IBOutlet WebView *myWebView;
@property(assign) IBOutlet NSTextField *address;

-(IBAction) loadPreviousPage: (id) sender;
-(IBAction) loadNextPage: (id) sender;
-(IBAction) loadURLFrom: (id) sender;
@end
```

In IB connect the address outlet to the text field. I also removed the default value for the text field using the Attributes inspector, but it doesn't really matter. Back in Xcode, synthesize address in BrowserController.m, and add this for awakeFromNib:

CreatingAController/SimpleBrowser6/BrowserController.m

```
-(void)awakeFromNib {
    [self.address setStringValue:@"http://pragprog.com"];
    [self loadURLFrom:self.address];
}
```

8.11 Disabling and Enabling the Buttons

There are still some fundamental things wrong with our web browser from a usability standpoint. For example, one problem is that the buttons are enabled all the time. This implies that the user can click them at any time. If we only look at this from the viewpoint of Objective-C programmers, we know that this is fine. We can send the goBack: method to the web view as often as we like. If there is no previous page to load, then it won't bother trying.

But one thing that distinguishes Cocoa programming is that we need to look at our application from the end user's point of view. If there's no point in clicking a button, then there should be a visual cue that lets us know that. In this section, you will write the code to enable and disable the buttons. It will mostly work.

Try implementing this on your own before reading on because the solution is included with the following code.

We'll need to send messages to the two buttons, so add two outlets to your header file:

`CreatingAController/SimpleBrowser7/BrowserController.h`

```
#import <Cocoa/Cocoa.h>
@class WebView;
@interface BrowserController : NSObject {
    WebView *myWebView;
    NSTextField *address;
▶   NSButton *backButton;
▶   NSButton *forwardButton;
}
@property(assign) IBOutlet WebView *myWebView;
▶ @property(assign) IBOutlet NSButton *backButton;
▶ @property(assign) IBOutlet NSButton *forwardButton;
@property(assign) IBOutlet NSTextField *address;


-(IBAction) loadPreviousPage: (id) sender;
-(IBAction) loadNextPage: (id) sender;
-(IBAction) loadURLFrom: (id) sender;
@end
```

Save the header file, and move back to Interface Builder's Document window. Select the Browser Controller, and open the Connections inspector. You should have new outlets labeled backButton and forwardButton. Connect them to their buttons. The Browser Controller should now have four outlets and three received actions.

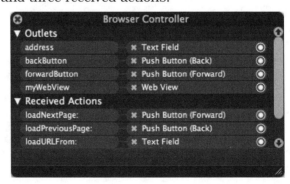

Before you move on, click the Back button, and open the Attributes inspector (click the leftmost icon at the top of the inspector window). Look most of the way down to find the Enabled checkbox in the Control group. Unselect the check box. Do the same for the Forward button. Save your work. Now your browser will start up with the two buttons disabled.

Before you write the code to reset the buttons, let's think about what you want it to do. For the Back button, you want to set it to be enabled or not enabled based on whether the web view can go back. Similarly, the state of the Forward button will depend whether the web view can go forward or not. A quick look at the docs for NSButton and WebView shows us the canGoBack and canGoForward methods we can use to reset the buttons. Here's how we'd do it:

CreatingAController/SimpleBrowser7/BrowserController.m

```
-(void) resetButtons {
    [self.backButton setEnabled:[self.myWebView canGoBack]];
    [self.forwardButton setEnabled:[self.myWebView canGoForward]];
}
```

You now need to call the resetButtons method from the action methods in BrowserController.

```
[self resetButtons];
```

We don't declare resetButtons in the header file because we aren't encouraging other objects to send a message to our controller to reset the buttons. In other words, the resetButtons method is not part of the public interface for the BrowserController. To keep the compiler happy, we move resetButtons to the top of the implementation so the other methods know about it.

Here's the complete implementation file as it now stands:

CreatingAController/SimpleBrowser7/BrowserController.m

```
#import "BrowserController.h"
#import <WebKit/WebKit.h>

@implementation BrowserController

@synthesize myWebView, address, backButton, forwardButton;

-(void) resetButtons {
    [self.backButton setEnabled:[self.myWebView canGoBack]];
    [self.forwardButton setEnabled:[self.myWebView canGoForward]];
}
-(IBAction) loadPreviousPage: (id) sender{
    [self.myWebView goBack:sender];
    [self resetButtons];
}
-(IBAction) loadNextPage: (id) sender{
    [self.myWebView goForward:sender];
    [self resetButtons];
}
```

Order Matters

Imagine you're the compiler reading your way through an Objective-C implementation file of the class SampleClass. While you are working your way through the method foo, you come across a reference to the method bar, which is also defined in SampleClass.

There are basically two ways for you to know about bar. First, bar could be declared in the header file, in which case you and anyone who imports the SampleClass header file knows about bar. The other way is for bar to be defined before foo. In that case, the compiler nods its head and says, "Oh, I've read about you."

If you haven't heard about bar, you issue a warning. But the programmer need not worry. The warning is that an object of type SampleClass may not respond to the method bar. Since Sample-Class does, in fact, implement bar, there will be no problems at runtime despite this warning at compile time.

```objc
-(IBAction) loadURLFrom: (id) sender{
    [self.myWebView takeStringURLFrom:sender];
    [self resetButtons];
}
-(void)awakeFromNib {
    [self.address setStringValue:@"http://pragprog.com"];
    [self loadURLFrom:self.address];
}
@end
```

Everything looks good. Save your work, build the application, and try it.

8.12 Still Needs Work

Uh-oh. The buttons now work worse than they did before. Before we made these latest changes, the buttons were always enabled. The problem with that was the user could sometimes click the buttons without anything happening. Now the opposite is true. Sometimes the buttons aren't enabled when they should be. There are two related problems.

To see one problem, launch the application, and enter a URL. Once the page loads, enter another URL. The Back button should be enabled, but it isn't. Once the second page loads, enter a third URL. Now the Back button is enabled, and you can use it to navigate all the way back to the first page. The problem is that it takes a while for the URL to load, and you have already set the state of the buttons based on the status just after the request to load the URL was made. It would be better if you selected canGoBack: and canGoForward: after the URL starts to load.

Quit the application, and launch it again. Enter a URL. Once the page loads, click a link. Once that page loads, follow another link. As long as you continue to use the links in the web view, the buttons are never enabled. The history is being maintained, but there's no callback to resetButtons. You can see this if you enter a URL. Once the page loads, you can use the buttons to move back and forward through the history.

All of the methods we've seen so far execute immediately. What we need is a way of delaying when a message is sent—don't ask me if I can go back or forward until I have loaded the page you requested. Fortunately, this notification mechanism is built into Cocoa with the notion of delegates. We'll look into how they work in the next chapter.

Chapter 9

Customizing with Delegates

Stuff happens.

In fact, lots of stuff is happening as your end user enters URLs and clicks buttons and links in your SimpleBrowser. The most basic type of event is target-action. The user clicks a button, and an action is sent to a target. You've learned two ways of working with these events: you can use Interface Builder to directly wire the object sending the message to the target object that will perform the action, or you can create a controller.

But once you enter a URL or use the Back or Forward button, additional events and messages are flying by that you don't even see. For example, when you load a page in Safari, you've probably noticed that the title of the new page is displayed above your toolbar before the page actually loads. Meanwhile, you can see the progress of the page being loaded by the blue bar that works its way across the text field containing your URL. There are messages being sent that Safari is able to capture and respond to. What about us?

There are plenty of messages zipping by us all the time. In this chapter, you'll learn to listen for them and how to respond to them. We'll display the title of the web page we're loading and fix the buttons and the URL while we're at it. Delegates will let us customize behavior for a class without creating a subclass.

9.1 Understanding Delegates

Before we apply delegates to our browser example, we will use the NSWindow class to explore how delegates work.

Imagine that our NSWindow object is appearing on a Cocoa game show. If you look at the documentation for NSWindow, you will see more than 200 methods listed as tasks that our window might be asked to perform.

Our window object is pretty confident that it knows how to respond to most of the messages it might be sent. For example, it knows how to respond to the message setShowsToolbarButton:. If our window has a toolbar, then passing in YES displays the toolbar button, and passing in NO hides the toolbar button. If our window doesn't have a toolbar, then calling this method doesn't do anything.

On the other hand, there are some tasks that our window doesn't know how to react to. For example, what if our window is asked this on the talk show?

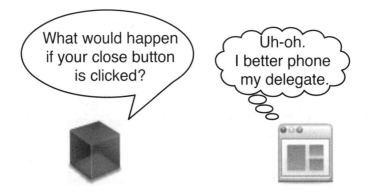

The answer is not as simple as you may think. Usually, when someone clicks the red button, the window will close, and the application will continue to run. Even though this is the default behavior, it is not the only possibility. For example, if you open System Preferences and click the red button, the window closes, and this time the application quits too.

You'll see a third type of behavior if you open a web page in Safari and then create a new tab (with tabbed browsing enabled, select File > New Tab or ⌘T). Open a web page in the new tab, and then hit the red button.

Even though you've clicked the same red button in the same application, the window doesn't automatically close when you have multiple tabs open. Instead, it asks you, "Are you sure you want to close this window?"

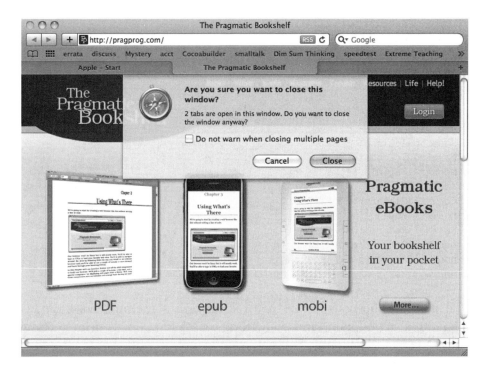

These variations present a dilemma for our window. What should it answer if it is asked by the game show host, "What would happen if I click your red button"?

The window wants to answer "It depends," but that's not an acceptable answer in a game show or in a running Cocoa application. So, the window chooses to get help answering this question by phoning a friend.

Here's the way the rules work for this game. The window identifies all the messages that it might need help with ahead of time and labels those as delegate methods.[1] In the case of the NSWindow class, here are all the delegate methods:

```
window:shouldDragDocumentWithEvent:from:withPasteboard:
window:shouldPopUpDocumentPathMenu:
window:willPositionSheet:usingRect:
windowDidBecomeKey:
windowDidBecomeMain:
windowDidChangeScreen:
windowDidChangeScreenProfile:
windowDidDeminiaturize:
```

---

1. In this chapter, we're using protocols and delegates that Apple created. We'll create our own delegate and protocol in Chapter 12, *Creating Protocols for Delegation*, on page 193.

```
windowDidEndSheet:
windowDidExpose:
windowDidMiniaturize:
windowDidMove:
windowDidResignKey:
windowDidResignMain:
windowDidResize:
windowDidUpdate:
windowShouldClose:
windowShouldZoom:toFrame:
windowWillBeginSheet:
windowWillClose:
windowWillMiniaturize:
windowWillMove:
windowWillResize:toSize:
windowWillReturnFieldEditor:toObject:
windowWillReturnUndoManager:
windowWillUseStandardFrame:defaultFrame:
```

The delegate methods come in three flavors: something will happen, something did happen, and something should happen. You implement the will version to change the behavior before an action happens and the did version to respond after the action happens. The should version returns a BOOL that allows you to cancel an action if you determine it shouldn't happen.

Just like the game shows where a contestant can "call a friend," each window object gets to designate a single friend that can be called when any of these methods is called. That friend is the delegate.

We don't really expect one friend to be able to respond to all of these messages, but our window must choose only one delegate ahead of time. Unfortunately, the window can't say, "I know who would know how to answer that question" and decide who will be called at runtime. The delegate is chosen before the question is asked.

Before the game begins, we preinterview the delegate. This way, we know which messages the delegate can handle and which ones it can't. In Cocoa terms, the delegate may implement none, any, or all of the delegate methods for an object. If a delegate has not implemented a method, it will not be called to handle that message. The window will have to come up with its own answer.

These rules might seem complicated—but a quick example should clarify the situation.

9.2 The Default Window Behavior

Create a new project in Xcode that is a Mac OS X > Application > Cocoa Application called WindowDressing. We're going to use a delegate to change the default behavior of the green and red buttons.

Click Build & Run. When you click the green button, the window should zoom up to fill most of the screen. Click it again, and the window will zoom to its original size. Click the red button and the window closes, but the application doesn't quit. Once you click the red button, there's not much more you can do. We can't create a new window so we have to quit this application anyway.

So far, we've seen the default behavior when the green or red button is clicked. This is the behavior the window provides when it isn't allowed to phone a friend. In the next section, we'll provide alternate behavior using a delegate.

9.3 Turning the Background Red

Let's change the behavior so that when the user clicks the red button, the background of the window turns red. We'll follow these steps:

1. We'll need to create a new class that we can instantiate to create the window's delegate.
2. We'll designate that object as the window's delegate.
3. We'll identify the delegate method we need to implement.
4. Finally, we'll implement the method.

The second and third steps are where people often make small, hard-to-trace mistakes. It's easy to forget to connect the window to its delegate in Interface Builder. Also, make sure that you save your nib file after you make a change. When you build your project in Xcode, you will be asked whether you want to save any source files that have been changed, but you may have unsaved changes in Interface Builder as well.

I guarantee this is going to bite you at some point. If you have been bouncing back and forth between Xcode and Interface Builder and your project isn't behaving the way you expect, take a look at your nib's Document window. If you see a dark dot in the middle of the red close button, then your file is dirty and needs to be saved.

If there are no unsaved changes, then the red close button should be clear like the yellow minimize button and green zoom button. It's a subtle hint used across Mac OS X apps and one worth watching for.

You also need to be careful to spell the delegate method name exactly as it appears in the NSWindow documentation. When we worked with buttons, we were free to assign any object as the target and make up the name of the method. Now with delegates, the name of the method is chosen for you.

In Xcode, create a new class file by selecting File > New File... or ⌘N. Choose the template Mac OS X > Cocoa Class> Objective-C class, and name it WindowHelper.

Just like the previous chapter, we'll now create a representation of this class in Interface Builder. Double-click MainMenu.xib to open it in Interface Builder. Find WindowHelper under the Classes tab in the Library, and drag it into the Document window.[2] Control-click the Window object—not the WindowHelper object—inside the Document window to bring up this connections window.

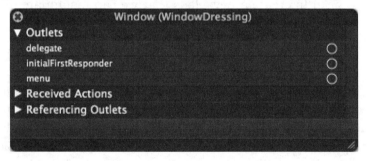

Drag from the circle next to the delegate outlet to the WindowHelper object inside the Document window. This sets the window's delegate to be an instance of the WindowHelper. Save your work, and quit Interface Builder.

Back in Xcode, you don't really have to make any changes to the WindowHelper header file. You've made the connection to the delegate in Interface Builder. As a developer, you know the signature of the methods you can implement. At runtime the system knows the messages it

2. You'll find it a lot quicker if you start typing Win into the search field at the bottom of the Library window.

can send. You can, however, make the intent of the WindowHelper clearer by indicating that it implements the NSWindowDelegate protocol.

A protocol declares a collection of methods that a class may or may not implement. You declare one or more protocols at the top of your header file between angle brackets like this:

Delegates/WindowDressing2/WindowHelper.h

```
#import <Cocoa/Cocoa.h>

@interface WindowHelper : NSObject <NSWindowDelegate> {
}
@end
```

▶

If you check the docs for the NSWindowDelegate protocol, you'll see that all of the methods are listed as *optional*. In other words, you are free to implement only the ones you need.

There are only two delegate methods that have anything to do with a window closing. There's windowShouldClose: and windowWillClose:. The windowShouldClose: method is called when the user clicks the red button and gives you an opportunity to say "Don't close the window." The windowWillClose: method is called just before the window closes. That's too late for our needs.

We'll use the windowShouldClose: method. Because it's so easy to introduce typos that are hard to detect and debug, I often go to the docs and cut and paste the method signature.

The windowShouldClose: method needs to do two things. It has to set the window's background color to red. This time, the sender is the window, so we can just tell the sender to set its background color to red.

The method also has to return NO so that the window doesn't close. If you return YES, the window will close. Here's WindowHelper.m:

Delegates/WindowDressing2/WindowHelper.m

```
#import "WindowHelper.h"

@implementation WindowHelper
- (BOOL)windowShouldClose:(id)sender {
    [sender setBackgroundColor:[NSColor redColor]];
    return NO;
}

@end
```

Click Build & Run, and the window will now turn red when you click the red button. More specifically, when you click the red button, the message windowShouldClose: message is sent to the object you've designated as the delegate for the window object. Quit WindowDressing with ⌘Q or by choosing Stop from Xcode.

9.4 Exercise: Turning the Background Green

Find the method that is called when someone clicks the green button to zoom your window to another frame size. Implement this method so that the window does not change size and so that the background of the window turns green when the green button is clicked.

9.5 Solution: Turning the Background Green

All that you need to do is implement the windowShouldZoom:toFrame: method. The body should look almost exactly like windowShouldClose:.

Delegates/WindowDressing3/WindowHelper.m

```
- (BOOL)windowShouldZoom:(NSWindow *)window toFrame:(NSRect)newFrame {
    [window setBackgroundColor:[NSColor greenColor]];
    return NO;
}
```

Click Build & Run. You can now change the window color to red and green by clicking the corresponding buttons.

9.6 Application Delegate

We've actually been using delegates since our very first project. The Cocoa Application template introduced in Xcode 3.2 includes an application delegate. Now that you understand the idea in the context of windows, you should be able to see how it applies to applications.

When an application launches, there are lots of things that must happen, and Apple takes care of that for you. But there are also things that are special to your application that Apple can't possibly know about. If there are particular things that you want to occur after the application finished launching, you implement the application delegate's applicationDidFinishLaunching: method.

Notice that your app delegate header file has the protocol declaration NSApplicationDelegate included, and the delegate outlet is connected in Interface Builder from your application to the app delegate.

If you check the NSApplicationDelegate docs, you'll find methods that help you specialize your application's behavior at dozens of different key points in your application's life. There are delegate methods that deal with launching and terminating the app, hiding the app, managing its windows, and so on.

Delegates are an important design pattern for Cocoa applications. You'll mainly find them in the modern Cocoa desktop APIs like WebKit. You'll also find delegates used throughout the iPhone APIs.

9.7 Delegates for Your Web View

During the rest of the chapter, we'll apply what we've learned about delegates to our SimpleBrowser example. Let's close the WindowDressing project and reopen our SimpleBrowser project.

In object-oriented programming, if you want to change the behavior of a class, you often create a subclass and override one or more methods. Delegation allows us to avoid creating inheritance chains every time we want to modify something in a base class. With delegation, we identify the methods that will most often need to be changed, label them delegate methods, and provide default behavior that will be executed unless we provide a delegate and implement that method with custom behavior.

An object of type NSWindow can specify a single delegate object. That is the way delegates usually work in Cocoa. Sometimes, though, you'll have a class with multiple delegates. For example, the WebView class designers looked at all of the behavior that you might want to customize and grouped them into four delegates.

These four delegates are listed in the overview section of the WebView class reference:

- WebFrameLoadDelegate
- WebPolicyDelegate
- WebResourceLoadDelegate
- WebUIDelegate

You can think of our WebView back on our Cocoa game show, but this time it can choose to call one of four friends depending on which category the question is in.

These four Delegate collections are protocols and not classes. They specify the method signatures that can be used by a class implementing the protocol. This ensures that when a message is sent to the delegate object, the corresponding method will be called. This also means that the compiler can let you know whether there's a problem.

Look in the "Tasks" section of the WebView docs under "Getting and Setting Delegates," and you will see ten methods for assigning and working with delegates. You can set delegates using outlets in Interface Builder, or you can set them programmatically using a method like setUIDelegate:.

9.8 Setting the Window Title

Next let's update the browser window's title bar with the title of the page you're loading. We'll use the webView:didReceiveTitle:forFrame: method in the WebFrameLoadDelegate.

Which object should be our delegate? We can either create a new class and instantiate it or use an instance of an existing class. In this case, the BrowserController object that we've already created is the best choice because it has connections to the GUI elements we need to access. Connect the delegate to our controller in Interface Builder like this:

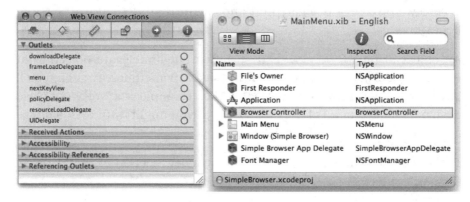

Select the web view, and open the Connections inspector. You should see the four delegate methods mixed in with the other outlets. Drag to connect frameLoadDelegate to your BrowserController. Save your work. We'll head back to Xcode to finish up.

The webView:didReceiveTitle:forFrame: method is called when the title is available. You can see that the message we receive also includes the title as a parameter. Here's how we'll use it:

- We *don't* add anything to the header file. All fifteen of the methods listed in the WebFrameLoadDelegate protocol are now available to us in BrowserController. The docs tell us that the WebFrameLoadDelegate is an informal protocol, so we don't declare it in the BrowserController header file.

- We need to implement webView:didReceiveTitle:forFrame: in BrowserController.m by filling in the body of this method:

```
-(void)webView:(WebView *)sender didReceiveTitle:(NSString *)title
                              forFrame:(WebFrame *)frame{
}
```

  We copied the signature of the method from the WebFrameLoadDelegate protocol documentation.

- We wait. The webView:didReceiveTitle:forFrame: method gets called once the title for the URL being loaded is available.

When this method is invoked, you want to set the title attribute of the application window to the title that is returned to you. Looking at the method signature, you can see that when the method is called, you will be passed a handle to the web view you are using and to the title of the new page. You can use the web view to get a pointer to the window containing the web view like this:

```
[sender window];
```

Unfortunately, you won't find the method you need in the WebView documentation. You have to look at the superclass NSView, where you will find the window method. The window method is also highlighted in the NSView as a commonly used method that "Returns the NSWindow object that contains the NSView object."

Once you have this window, you ask it to set its title to the title that you get when this delegate method is called. You need to add this method to BrowserController.m:

Delegates/SimpleBrowser8/BrowserController.m

```
- (void)webView:(WebView *)sender
didReceiveTitle:(NSString *)title
      forFrame:(WebFrame *)frame {
    [[sender window] setTitle:title];
}
```

Save your work. Click Build & Run, and now no matter how you navigate to a website in your browser, the title will appear as soon as it is available. All you had to do was find the right method, create and configure the outlets, and implement the method with a single line of code:

```
[[sender window] setTitle:title];
```

Again, we did *not* list the webView:didReceiveTitle:forFrame: method in the BrowserController header. This method is not part of the public interface for BrowserController. The only object that needs to know that BrowserController implements this method is the delegating object myWebView. The message will be sent only if the delegate is assigned and the method is implemented.

9.9 Exercise: Updating the URL and Setting Buttons

Now that you've seen how to display the page title as the window's title when it's available, you can reset the buttons and update the URL once the page is loaded. Until now, if the user clicks a link in a web page, the new page will load, but the URL won't change in the text field as the user would expect from experience with pretty much every other browser.

To reset the buttons and update the URL after the page is loaded, identify a method in the WebFrameLoadDelegate protocol that is called when the frame has completed loading. Implement the delegate method to do two things: (a) set the text field's string value to be the URL for the page's main (and only) frame and (b) call resetButtons.

Hint 1: If you look in the NSTextField class reference for a method to set the text field's string value, you won't find what you are looking for. Remember, the inherited methods do not appear in the Cocoa docs. So, you need to look at the class reference for NSTextField's superclass NSControl. You'll find setStringValue: in "Tasks" under "Setting the Control's Value."

Hint 2: WebView has a lot of methods. It's easy to miss the one you want for fetching the right URL. Look in the "Tasks" section under the heading "Getting and Setting Frame Contents."

Completing Your Thought

You can adjust Xcode's Code Sense settings in the preferences. You can adjust how quickly code completions appear. Instead of having to look up the entire hierarchy for the method you want, you can choose Edit > Completion List to see all of the available completions. In the example in the exercise, if you do that after typing [inputField, you would have seen setStringValue: in the list.

9.10 Solution: Updating the URL and Setting Buttons

Implement the webView:didFinishLoadForFrame method like this:

Delegates/SimpleBrowser9/BrowserController.m

```
- (void)webView:(WebView *)sender didFinishLoadForFrame:(WebFrame *)frame {
    [self.address setStringValue:[sender mainFrameURL]];
    [self resetButtons];
}
```

Click Build & Run. Your code should run perfectly. The window title is set at the right time, the URL changes as you navigate back and forward using the buttons, and the buttons are enabled and disabled properly. You should be feeling pretty good right now, but before you run off to the next chapter to learn something new, you've got some cleaning up to do.

The code is a mess. We have a lot of redundancy, and we could probably get rid of some of our outlets. There's nothing wrong with the path we've taken. First we got the code working, and now we're going to tidy up a bit.

9.11 Cleaning Up

You have some waste to take care of. Look at the last line of each of these methods:

Delegates/SimpleBrowser9/BrowserController.m

```
-(IBAction) loadPreviousPage: (id) sender{
    [self.myWebView goBack:sender];
▶    [self resetButtons];
}
```

```
-(IBAction) loadNextPage: (id) sender{
    [self.myWebView goForward:sender];
▶   [self resetButtons];
}
-(IBAction) loadURLFrom: (id) sender{
    [self.myWebView takeStringURLFrom:sender];
▶   [self resetButtons];
}
```

There's no need to call resetButtons in any of these methods because it's being called when the frame is done loading. Remove those three lines, and rerun your application. You'll find that it still runs fine.

Now that you have removed [self resetButtons]; from loadPreviousPage:, loadNextPage:, and loadURLFrom:, the methods don't do very much. There really isn't a need to use the controller for these actions anymore.

To make a point, I want you to leave these methods for a moment and head over to Interface Builder. Click the BrowserController in the Document window, and select the Connections inspector. Disconnect the three received actions by clicking the Xs. Now click the web view, and use the Connections inspector to reconnect the three actions you had before. Drag from goBack: to the Back button, from goForward: to the Forward button, and from takeStringURLFrom: to the text field. Save your work in Interface Builder, and then click Build & Run in Xcode. Your application runs perfectly.

That should worry you a bit.

You have just redirected your control flow entirely from IB. You have three methods in Xcode that are no longer being called. This is something you need to remember when you are working with Cocoa programs. You can't figure out the whole story merely by reading through the code. You have to look at the connections you have created elsewhere.[3]

But, you should also make it easier for people (including yourself) who will come back to this project and try to figure out what is going on. Since these three methods are not called anymore, you should eliminate them from both the header and implementation files.

---

3. If you want to use Test-Driven Development, then you should read Chris Hanson's blog posts on unit testing Cocoa user interfaces at http://eschatologist.net/blog/?p=205 and his introductory articles to unit testing Cocoa code at http://eschatologist.net/blog/?p=24 and http://chanson.livejournal.com/119303.html.

Once you've removed these, you'll need to refactor the awakeFromNib method to pass the URL to the web view without going through one of the methods we just deleted. Here's the current state of the implementation file:

Delegates/SimpleBrowser10/BrowserController.m

```objc
#import "BrowserController.h"
#import <WebKit/WebKit.h>

@implementation BrowserController

@synthesize myWebView, address, backButton, forwardButton;

- (void) resetButtons {
    [self.backButton setEnabled:[self.myWebView canGoBack]];
    [self.forwardButton setEnabled:[self.myWebView canGoForward]];
}

-(void)awakeFromNib {
    [self.address setStringValue:@"http://pragprog.com"];
    [self.myWebView takeStringURLFrom:self.address];
}

- (void)webView:(WebView *)sender
didReceiveTitle:(NSString *)title
       forFrame:(WebFrame *)frame {
    [[sender window] setTitle:title];
}

- (void)webView:(WebView *)sender
             didFinishLoadForFrame:(WebFrame *)frame {
    [self.address setStringValue:[sender mainFrameURL]];
        [self resetButtons];
}
@end
```

Here's the current header file:

Delegates/SimpleBrowser10/BrowserController.h

```objc
#import <Cocoa/Cocoa.h>
@class WebView;
@interface BrowserController : NSObject {
    NSTextField *address;
    NSButton *backButton;
    NSButton *forwardButton;
    WebView *myWebView;
}
@property(assign) IBOutlet NSButton *backButton;
@property(assign) IBOutlet NSButton *forwardButton;
@property(assign) IBOutlet NSTextField *address;
@property(assign) IBOutlet WebView *myWebView;
@end
```

Take a minute to look at how little code we need when we work *with* the existing Apple frameworks. Whenever your code gets long and complicated, you should pause and consider whether there's an easier way to accomplish what you are trying to do. Your goal is to write simple code that is clear and understandable. Cocoa programmers do not value code that is short and clever to the point of being obscure.

9.12 Exercise: Adding a Progress Indicator

A lot of what we're doing at this point is adding muscle memory as we jump back and forth between Xcode and Interface Builder. Let's take this example one step further—at least on the desktop.

Add a small circular progress indicator to the top-right side of your browser. It should be initially hidden. When a user enters a new URL or navigates to a different page, the progress indicator should appear and start to spin. We want to give the user some feedback that something is happening. Once the page has fully loaded, the progress indicator should stop spinning and should be hidden again.

Think through the steps. You need to place a progress indicator using IB. You need to add an outlet for that indicator in the BrowserController header file and then connect it in IB. You need to synthesize the property you just created and use it when the page starts and stops loading.

9.13 Solution: Adding a Progress Indicator

You can look at the solution provided in the code download to investigate the nib and header file. Here's the Attributes inspector settings for the progress indicator:

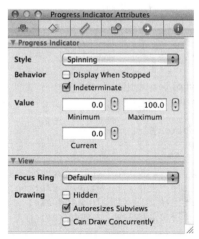

Under Behavior, I've unselected Display When Stopped, and under Drawing, I've unselected Hidden.

Here's the final version of the implementation file. We need to add a couple of lines of code to the webView:didFinishLoadForFrame: method to stop the progress bar's animation and hide it. We also need to unhide the progress indicator and start it spinning in the webView:didStartProvisional-LoadForFrame: method.

Delegates/SimpleBrowser11/BrowserController.m

```objc
#import "BrowserController.h"
#import <WebKit/WebKit.h>

@implementation BrowserController

@synthesize myWebView, address, backButton, forwardButton, progress;

- (void) resetButtons {
    [self.backButton setEnabled:[self.myWebView canGoBack]];
    [self.forwardButton setEnabled:[self.myWebView canGoForward]];
}

-(void)awakeFromNib {
    [self.address setStringValue:@"http://pragprog.com"];
    [self.myWebView takeStringURLFrom:self.address];
}
```

Sets up first page

```objc
- (void)webView:(WebView *)sender
didReceiveTitle:(NSString *)title
      forFrame:(WebFrame *)frame {
    [[sender window] setTitle:title];
}

- (void)webView:(WebView *)sender
      didFinishLoadForFrame:(WebFrame *)frame {
    [self.address setStringValue:[sender mainFrameURL]];
    [self resetButtons];
    [self.progress stopAnimation:self];
}
```

Protocol for spinner

```objc
- (void)webView:(WebView *)sender
          didStartProvisionalLoadForFrame:(WebFrame *)frame {
    [self.progress startAnimation:self];
}
@end
```

That's still not much code. In the next chapter, we'll see what needs to be changed to implement our SimpleBrowser for the iPhone.

Chapter 10

Adapting Our Browser to the iPhone

Although the Cocoa concepts you learn in this book apply to both Mac OS X and the iPhone, you will notice some differences in the APIs and in the application. You'll see that in this chapter as we re-create our browser for the iPhone and iPod touch.[1] I'm targeting the iPhone 3.x SDK in this book. Downloading the SDK is free, but first you need to agree to Apple's terms at http://developer.apple.com/iphone.

There are three reasons to port our browser to the iPhone. First, the iPhone APIs embrace the new features of Objective-C 2.0, such as properties. Second, delegates are a big part of why the iPhone APIs are cleaner. Finally, porting the browser lets you retrace your steps armed with more of an idea of where you are heading. This second pass at creating a Cocoa project should help pull everything together for you.

10.1 Creating the iPhone Project

Let's create a new project in Xcode. This time choose iPhone OS > Application > View-based Application, and name it MobileBrowser. Go ahead and run your MobileBrowser application by clicking Build & Run in Xcode. The code should compile and build, and then the iPhone Simulator should launch. The main window is filled with a single view with a gray background color.

---

1. Because these are the same, I'll talk about this target collectively as the iPhone.

More formally, when the browser application starts up, an instance of the UIApplication class is created, and the MainWindow nib is loaded.[2]

The nib contains an object that represents the application whose delegate outlet is connected to the MobileBrowserAppDelegate. The nib file also contains the MobileBrowserViewController. In the app delegate's applicationDidFinishLaunching: method, the view controller's view is added to the window.

iPhoneBrowser/MobileBrowser1/Classes/MobileBrowserAppDelegate.m

```
- (void)applicationDidFinishLaunching:(UIApplication *)application {
    // Override point for customization after app launch
    [window addSubview:viewController.view];
    [window makeKeyAndVisible];
}
```

This is the way most iPhone apps work. They have a single window for the entire application. What you think of as a screen are the contents of a view, and when you switch from one screen to another using the tab bar, nav bar, or some other means, you are replacing the window's old view with the new view by working with their view controllers.

Generally, each of these top-level views is contained in its own nib file with its view controller as the File's Owner. I'm not going to talk about the File's Owner yet. Let's just say that most of our work for this application will happen in the second nib file and in the view controller.

A view controller's job, as you might have guessed, is to control a view. While the view is all about appearance, the controller defines the

---

2. iPhone-specific classes often begin with UI and not NS as you saw in desktop applications.

behavior. To start with, as you saw in the applicationDidFinishLaunching: method, when you want to add a view to a window as its subview, you ask the view controller for the view it controls. Once everything is arranged, you can reveal the window and its contents to the user and set it to accept touches and other input.

We're not going to customize the application's behavior at launch time, so let's move our attention to the nib containing the view and its controller to create our web browser.

10.2 Creating the Look of Our Browser

Double-click MobileBrowserViewController.xib to open it in IB. We're going to transform this empty view into something that looks like this:

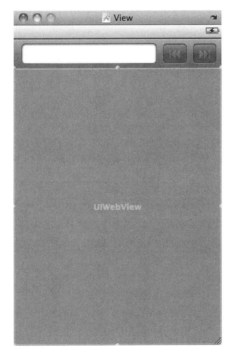

As before, you drag components out of the library and position them on the view. Place a UIToolbar at the top of the view. Drag a UITextField on top of it to the left of the UIBarButtonItem that was at the left of the UIToolbar. Drag another UIBarButtonItems and place it to the right of the text field. In our desktop version, we had room for the words *Forward* and *Back*. Here we'll borrow images provided for audio interfaces. Open the inspector.

It looks a little different than the inspector window when you are creating Mac OS X applications. You have four tabs that you'll use to inspect and change the attributes, connections, size, and identity. Choose the Attributes inspector for the Back button.

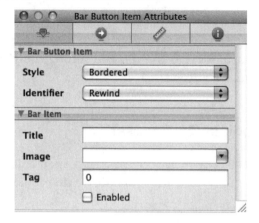

Use the pull-down menu to set Identifier to Rewind. While you're at it, unselect the Enabled checkbox so that initially the user can't click the Back button. Similarly, set the Forward button's Identifier to Fast Forward, and unselect the Enabled checkbox.

Lastly, select a UIWebView, and position it to occupy all of the view below the toolbar. Open the Attributes inspector for the web view, and check the box Web View > Scales Page to Fit. Save your work. That's our interface for now.

Let's click Build & Run and see what happens. Our app should start up fine. The Forward and Back buttons are disabled. Try to enter a URL. Click the text field. This looks promising. The text field clears, and the keypad appears. You can type in a new URL.

Now what?

You hit ↵, and nothing happens. If you click in another area of the screen, the keyboard is dismissed, but the next time you select the text field, the URL will be cleared, and you need to start all over again. How can you enter a URL and navigate to the site? It turns out, we're going to need two more delegates.

10.3 The WebView's Limitations

A UIWebView can't do as much as the WebView that we looked at before. You can see that in the Connections inspector for our UIWebView.

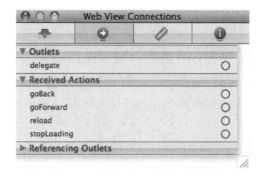

There's a lot missing, but the most immediate issue for us is that a Web-View was able to receive the message takeStringURLFrom: and a UIWebView can't. That's a problem. In the desktop version, it meant that we could wire the web view up to the text field and pass the URL without any code. Now we need to find another way.

10.4 Loading a Web Page at Launch

We can't wire the text field and the web view directly to each other, so both will need to be connected to our controller. Add two outlets to the header file for the MobileBrowserViewController.

iPhoneBrowser/MobileBrowser1/Classes/MobileBrowserViewController.h

```
#import <UIKit/UIKit.h>

@interface MobileBrowserViewController : UIViewController {
    UIWebView *webView;
    UITextField *address;
}
@property(nonatomic,retain) IBOutlet UIWebView *webView;
@property(nonatomic, retain) IBOutlet UITextField *address;

@end
```

Unlike the desktop version, the UIWebView is part of the iPhone framework that we are importing at the top of this file, so we don't have to do any special import, and we don't have to add a framework to our target as we did before.

The properties are different as well. Because we are writing for the iPhone, we'll add the nonatomic attribute to our properties as we're writing for UIKit's single-threaded, single-core model. We also don't have garbage collection available to us so we have to use retain instead of assign for the memory attribute. Don't forget to synthesize these properties in the implementation file.

Open the MobileBrowserViewController nib file, and use the Connections inspector to wire these outlets from the File's Owner to the corresponding components in the view.[3] Save and quit Interface Builder.

Back in Xcode, we want to create a method that can load a URL that we will pass in as a string. Let's head to the docs for UIWebView and see whether there's a method there that will do what we want.

Hmmm. When I look under Tasks > Loading Content, the closest thing I find is this:

```
- (void)loadRequest:(NSURLRequest *)request
```

That's pretty close, but it takes an NSURLRequest and not a string as its parameter. Let's follow the link to the NSURLRequest docs and see whether there's anything there. This time when I look at Tasks > Creating Requests, I find this:

```
+ (id)requestWithURL:(NSURL *)theURL
```

It feels as if we're getting closer, but now we have to figure out how to create an NSURL from a string. Follow the link to the NSURL docs, and look under Tasks > Creating an NSURL. There it is!

```
+ (id)URLWithString:(NSString *)URLString
```

Put these together to create our loadURLFromTextField method.[4] Add this just after the @synthesize line in MobileBrowserViewController.m:

iPhoneBrowser/MobileBrowser1/Classes/MobileBrowserViewController.m

```
-(void) loadURLFromTextField {
    NSURL *url = [NSURL URLWithString:self.address.text];
    NSURLRequest *request = [NSURLRequest requestWithURL:url];
    [self.webView loadRequest:request];
}
```

We create the URL using the text property of our text field. We create the URL request from the URL, and then we send the message to the webView outlet to have it load the URL using the request we created.

We're almost there—we just need somebody to call our loadURLFromTextField after the application launches. In the desktop version, we used the awakeFromNib method. In iPhone development, you often do this as

---

3. We know to use the File's Owner because of its type.
4. Note that we're using class methods to construct autoreleased instances of the request and the URL. We don't need to release them ourselves.

part of the viewDidLoad method.[5] If you look around in your implementation file, you should see that method commented out. Remove the comments, and add this line to load the URL:

iPhoneBrowser/MobileBrowser1/Classes/MobileBrowserViewController.m

```
- (void)viewDidLoad {
    [super viewDidLoad];
    self.address.text = @"http://pragprog.com";
    [self loadURLFromTextField];
}
```

Click Build & Run; the application should launch, and the Pragmatic home page should load scaled down so that it is viewable in the browser. You can navigate by clicking links, but you can't yet enter other URLs. Let's take care of that next.

10.5 Tweaking the Text Field in IB

As powerful and cool as the iPhone is, it is still a device with many constraints. For most of us, it is easier to enter text using our laptops than it is using an iPhone. Although the iPhone's display is beautiful and the resolution is good, we have a lot more real estate on our desktop monitors or on our laptops. When we're programming the iPhone, we need to consider the limitations of the device and make it as easy as possible for our users to interact with our application.

Let's configure the text field and keyboard to make it easier for users to enter URLs. Open the MobileBrowserViewController nib, and look at the text field using the Attributes inspector.

The first thing that I find annoying when working with this text field is that every time I click it, all of the content clears. I'd really like the option to clear it or the option to edit what's there in case I've fat-fingered a URL and am off only by a character or two. Unselect the box labeled Clear When Editing Begins, and use the pull-down menu to set the Clear Button to Appears while editing.

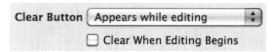

Click Build & Run, and now you will see a little x at the right of the text field when you are editing the field. The text field also no longer

---

5. Other methods we often use for this type of work is viewWillAppear and viewDidAppear.

clears when you select it, and you can double-click the text and use the iPhone's cut and paste.

Referring Outlet
backButton
↓
Fileowner

sent action
goBack → *WebView*

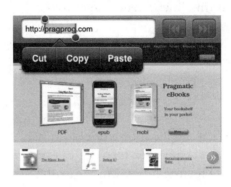

Look at the Text Input Traits listed in the Attributes inspector. Let's choose a keyboard that is more suited to web navigation. Here you can see the available choices:

Webview → Fileowner
each item
needs to connect
to Fileowner

Choose URL. This is a small but very important change to make. It exposes the keys to make URL entry easier and will vastly improve the user experience. As a final tweak, change Return Key from Default to Go. Save your work, and run the application again. Now the keyboard looks like this:

10.6 Using the Text Field Delegate

You just used the text field to set its look and the look of the keyboard associated with it. But the virtual keyboard doesn't know how to react after the user has entered data and clicks the Go button. For that we need a delegate.[6]

In Interface Builder, use the Connections inspector to connect the text field's delegate outlet to the File's Owner and save. In Xcode, add the declaration of the UITextFieldDelegate to the MobileBrowserViewController's header file in angle brackets:

iPhoneBrowser/MobileBrowser3/Classes/MobileBrowserViewController.h

```
@interface MobileBrowserViewController : UIViewController
                                      <UITextFieldDelegate> {
```

With that we've just announced to the world that our MobileBrowserView-Controller knows how to respond to any of seven optional messages for beginning and ending editing, responding to Return, clearing the field, and changing some of the characters.

For example, let's disable the web view when the user starts to edit the URL:

iPhoneBrowser/MobileBrowser3/Classes/MobileBrowserViewController.m

```
-(void)textFieldDidBeginEditing:(UITextField *)textField {
    [self disableWebView];
}
```

To disable the web view, we'll prevent the user from interacting with it, and we'll dim it by adjusting the alpha value to visually imply that it is not currently active.[7] We'll also reenable the web view by reversing the steps we took in disabling it.

iPhoneBrowser/MobileBrowser3/Classes/MobileBrowserViewController.m

```
-(void) disableWebView {
    self.webView.userInteractionEnabled = NO;
    self.webView.alpha = 0.25;
}
-(void) enableWebView {
    self.webView.userInteractionEnabled = YES;
    self.webView.alpha = 1.0;
}
```

---

6. In the case of an NSTextField, you're working with a physical keyboard and don't need a delegate.
7. Note that alpha is a property of UIView, so you can adjust this value for any subclass of UIView and not just a UIWebView.

When the user clicks Go on the keyboard, the URL is loaded, and we tell the text field to resignFirstResponder to dismiss the keyboard. We also reenable the web view. We put all of this in the delegate method textField-ShouldReturn:.

iPhoneBrowser/MobileBrowser3/Classes/MobileBrowserViewController.m

```
-(BOOL) textFieldShouldReturn:(UITextField *)textField {
    [self loadURLFromTextField];
    [textField resignFirstResponder];
    [self enableWebView];
    return YES;
}
```

Click Build & Run; you should be able to enter URLs and click Go to load the corresponding website. We have a mostly functioning browser. Let's get the buttons working next.

10.7 Using a Third Delegate to Implement the Buttons

If you look back at our BrowserController, you'll see that we need to know when the web page finished loading to reset the buttons. The only way to know when the page is finished loading is to use the UIWebView-Delegate.

We'll use our MobileBrowserViewController as the web view's delegate. We'll also add outlets for the Forward and Back buttons. Here's what our header file now looks like:

iPhoneBrowser/MobileBrowser4/Classes/MobileBrowserViewController.h

```
#import <UIKit/UIKit.h>

@interface MobileBrowserViewController : UIViewController
                                        <UITextFieldDelegate> {
    UIWebView *webView;
    UITextField *address;
    UIBarButtonItem *backButton;
    UIBarButtonItem *forwardButton;
}
@property(nonatomic,retain) IBOutlet UIWebView *webView;
@property(nonatomic, retain) IBOutlet UITextField *address;
@property(nonatomic, retain) IBOutlet UIBarButtonItem *backButton;
@property(nonatomic, retain) IBOutlet UIBarButtonItem *forwardButton;

@end
```

Open the MobileBrowserViewController nib in Interface Builder. We have five connections to make.

1. Select the File's Owner, and connect the backButton outlet to the Back button and the forwardButton outlet to the Forward button.

2. Select the web view, and connect its delegate to the File's Owner.

3. Still in the web view, connect the goBack received action to the Back button and the goForward to the Forward button.

Save your work. Now let's implement the button reset exactly as we did in the desktop browser. Don't forget to synthesize your properties. Next, we'll call a method that we create named resetButtons: from the delegate method that tells us when the web page is done loading. In the case of the iPhone, that method is webViewDidFinishLoad:.

```
iPhoneBrowser/MobileBrowser4/Classes/MobileBrowserViewController.m
-(void) resetButtons:(UIWebView *) theWebView {
    [self.backButton setEnabled:[theWebView canGoBack]];
    [self.forwardButton setEnabled:[theWebView canGoForward]];
}
-(void)webViewDidFinishLoad:(UIWebView *)theWebView {
    [self resetButtons:theWebView];
}
```

Run the browser, and navigate or enter the URL for a second web page. Once the page loads, the Back button should be enabled. Click the Back button; you will be taken to the previous page, and the Forward button will be enabled. We have a basic web browser working on the iPhone.

10.8 Exercise: Adding an Activity Indicator

Add a UIActivityIndicatorView to your application. In Interface Builder, set its Style to Large White, and select the Hide When Stopped checkbox.

Your activity indicator should spin while the website is loading. The web view should remain disabled until the page is done loading. Finally, if you navigate to a page, the text field should display the URL of this page instead of continuing to contain the last web address the user typed in.

10.9 Solution: Adding an Activity Indicator

To start with, add this outlet to your MobileBrowserViewController header file:[8]

iPhoneBrowser/MobileBrowser5/Classes/MobileBrowserViewController.h

```
#import <UIKit/UIKit.h>

@interface MobileBrowserViewController : UIViewController
                                        <UITextFieldDelegate> {
    UIWebView *webView;
    UITextField *address;
    UIBarButtonItem *backButton;
    UIBarButtonItem *forwardButton;
▶   UIActivityIndicatorView *activityView;
}
@property(nonatomic,retain) IBOutlet UIWebView *webView;
@property(nonatomic, retain) IBOutlet UITextField *address;
@property(nonatomic, retain) IBOutlet UIBarButtonItem *backButton;
@property(nonatomic, retain) IBOutlet UIBarButtonItem *forwardButton;
▶ @property(nonatomic, retain) IBOutlet UIActivityIndicatorView *activityView;
@end
```

Now open up the nib file, and drag an activity indicator view on top of the web view. Connect it to the outlet using the Connections inspector, and then use the Attributes inspector to set its Style to Large White and select the Hide When Stopped checkbox. Save your work, and return to Xcode.

We can make all of the changes we need in the webViewDidStartLoad: and webViewDidFinishLoad: methods. In addition, you can remove the call to enableWebView: in the textFieldShouldReturn: method. Let's stop and take a look back at the code we've written in this chapter. I find it striking that we've implemented a web view, text field and its keyboard, Forward and Back buttons, and an activity indicator with so little code.

iPhoneBrowser/MobileBrowser5/Classes/MobileBrowserViewController.m

```
#import "MobileBrowserViewController.h"

@implementation MobileBrowserViewController

@synthesize address, webView, backButton, forwardButton, activityView;
```

---

8. Remember that once the simulator is fixed, you can eliminate the instance variable declarations from the header file.

```objc
//View Controller Utility Methods
-(void) disableWebView {
    self.webView.userInteractionEnabled = NO;
    self.webView.alpha = 0.25;
}
-(void) enableWebView {
    self.webView.userInteractionEnabled = YES;
    self.webView.alpha = 1.0;
}
-(void) loadURLFromTextField {
    NSURL *url = [NSURL URLWithString:self.address.text];
    NSURLRequest *request = [NSURLRequest requestWithURL:url];
    [self.webView loadRequest:request];
}
-(void) resetButtons:(UIWebView *) theWebView {
    [self.backButton setEnabled:[theWebView canGoBack]];
    [self.forwardButton setEnabled:[theWebView canGoForward]];
}


//Initialization
- (void)viewDidLoad {
    [super viewDidLoad];
    self.address.text = @"http://pragprog.com";
    [self loadURLFromTextField];
}


//Web View Delegate methods
-(void)webViewDidStartLoad:(UIWebView *) theWebView {
    [self disableWebView];
    [self.activityView startAnimating];
}
-(void)webViewDidFinishLoad:(UIWebView *)theWebView {
    [self enableWebView];
    [self.activityView stopAnimating];
    [self resetButtons:theWebView];
    self.address.text = [[self.webView.request URL] absoluteString];
}


//Text Field Delegate methods
-(void)textFieldDidBeginEditing:(UITextField *)textField {
    [self disableWebView];
}
-(BOOL) textFieldShouldReturn:(UITextField *)textField {
    [self loadURLFromTextField];
    [textField resignFirstResponder];
    return YES;
}
```

```
//Memory Management
- (void)didReceiveMemoryWarning {
        // Releases the view if it doesn't have a superview.
    [super didReceiveMemoryWarning];
}
- (void)dealloc {
    self.address = nil;
    self.webView = nil;
    self.backButton = nil;
    self.forwardButton = nil;
    self.activityView = nil;
    [super dealloc];
}
@end
```

We've used three delegates and a bunch of properties, and the longest method body is four lines long. I hope with this second look at creating a web browser, this time as an iPhone app, is helping you feel the rhythm of developing a Cocoa application.

10.10 Organizing with Pragma Marks

I added comments to the last code listing to help organize the methods into categories. This helps me locate the methods I need when I'm scanning through the source code, but there is a better way.

If you look at the top of the editor window, you'll see several drop-downs. One shows you the other files that have been opened and allows you to move between them quickly. Another shows you all the method names. Select one, and you move to that spot in the source code. It currently looks like this:

✓ 🅒 @implementation MobileBrowserViewController
  🔲 *address, webView, backButton, forwardButton, activityView*
  Ⓜ –disableView
  Ⓜ –enableWebView
  Ⓜ –loadURLFromTextField
  Ⓜ –resetButtons:
  Ⓜ –viewDidLoad
  Ⓜ –webViewDidStartLoad:
  Ⓜ –webViewDidFinishLoad:
  Ⓜ –textFieldDidBeginEditing:
  Ⓜ –textFieldShouldReturn:
  Ⓜ –didReceiveMemoryWarning
  Ⓜ –dealloc

Everything is jumbled together. It's still better than searching through a long source code listing, but we can make it better using #pragma mark. Replace the following comment:

```
//Memory Management
```

with this:

```
#pragma mark -
#pragma mark Memory Management
```

Now the drop-down list of methods looks like this:

The #pragma mark - draws the horizontal line separator, and #pragma mark Memory Management produces the bold heading.[9] Introduce these headings in place of all of the sections, and your code becomes a lot more navigable, as we can see on the next page.[10]

Our desktop and iPhone web browsers have served us well. I've used them to illustrate creating classes in code and instantiating objects in code or in a nib. You've written and called methods with and without parameters.

---

9. Don't add trailing spaces after the - or #pragma mark - will render as a dash instead of a horizontal line in the drop-down list.
10. If you synthesized each property on a separate line, they will appear on separate lines and not all on one line as mine do.

✓ 🄲 @implementation MobileBrowserViewController

Synthesizers
🄜 *address,webView,backButton,forwardButton,activityView*

View Controller Utility Methods
🄜 –disableView
🄜 –enableWebView
🄜 –loadURLFromTextField
🄜 –resetButtons:

Initialization
🄜 –viewDidLoad

Web View Delegate methods
🄜 –webViewDidStartLoad:
🄜 –webViewDidFinishLoad:

Text Field Delegate methods
🄜 –textFieldDidBeginEditing:
🄜 –textFieldShouldReturn:

Memory Management
🄜 –didReceiveMemoryWarning
🄜 –dealloc

You've worked with properties and learned to manage memory. You've wired your application together with actions and outlets and learned to use delegates. These are some of the fundamental techniques that you will use all the time as a Cocoa developer.

But there's more....

Chapter 11

Posting and Listening for Notifications

There are so many things that you need to keep track of in your life. It wouldn't be practical for you to stop and check on the progress of all of them every few minutes or even once a day. For most of them, you just want to know when something has changed.

Maybe you want an alert when a stock hits a certain price. Maybe the alert should go to a broker instead with a specific set of instructions. How might you set this up?

You would have to arrange with the notification center that you are interested in knowing about a specific event. In our case, it is something like "Tell me when XXX drops to yyy." You have to tell the notification center who it should notify. Should it send the notification to you or to some agent?

Now whether the message comes to me or to someone else, we need to figure out what to do about it quickly. We get lots of notifications in a day. It's easier to parse them and figure out what to do next if the context is clear to us. In code this happens by telling the notification center what message to send us. The message might be buy: or sell:. In other words, we are telling the notification center the action it will be sending for the target we've already set.

The notification center will then send our target a notification as part of the message. In code, this means that a notification object is the parameter of the message. The notification will contain information that the recipient might need. You'll always find the name of the notification and information about who posted the notification. You will also get other information that you may need to act on the notification.[1]

11.1 Exercise: Creating a Model

Our next running example will display the name and icon of applications as they launch and terminate. As with the browser, the point of this application is not to build a full-featured application but rather to use it to learn more about aspects of Cocoa programming. In this chapter, we'll start with notifications.

Create a new Cocoa application, and name it HelloApplication. Remember, we're back in the world of Mac OS X apps, so we won't need to manage our own memory. Change the Project setting so that garbage collection is required. You'll do that for every project we create from here on out.

Add two classes that each extend NSObject. The CurrentApp class will represent your model for this application. Don't customize it in any way yet. The class ActivityController will be our controller. Instantiate it in MainMenu.xib. Create an instance of CurrentApp in the ActivityController's awakeFromNib, and store it in a property named currentApp.

11.2 Solution: Creating a Model

By now you should be building some muscle memory for creating new projects and files. You created your HelloApplication with all of the checkboxes unselected. You created a new file CurrentApp.m that was an Objective-C class that extends NSObject. You then repeated the process for ActivityController.m.

Now instantiate your classes. In Interface Builder drag an instance of ActivityController into the MainMenu.xib's Document window.

In Xcode, declare an instance variable and a property named currentApp of type CurrentApp to ActivityController.h. Remember to use @class to forward declare the CurrentApp class.

---

1. In this chapter we won't be looking at this notification object. Our example will focus on registering to receive notifications and responding to receiving a notification. We'll return to this subject and show you how to work with the notification object in Chapter 13, *Working with Dictionaries*.

> **Warning**
>
> We'll soon have a problem with this project because the ActivityController and CurrentApp objects are being released just after they are created. That's fine for now, but soon we will want them to stay around as long as the application is running. That is a subtle and significant problem that might be hard to spot. We'll retain the objects once we can see our problem in action.

Notification/HelloApplication1/ActivityController.h
```
#import <Cocoa/Cocoa.h>
@class CurrentApp;

@interface ActivityController : NSObject {
    CurrentApp *currentApp;
}
@property CurrentApp *currentApp;

@end
```

I hope that you remembered to include the forward declaration for CurrentApp just below the import statement. The property declaration may look a little naked. Without garbage collection, the memory attribute would have to be retain. With garbage collection, this is equivalent to assign, and assign is the default value, so we can leave it out altogether.[2]

In ActivityController.m, you need to synthesize currentApp and create an instance of it in awakeFromNib. Be sure to import CurrentApp.h.

Notification/HelloApplication1/ActivityController.m
```
#import "ActivityController.h"
#import "CurrentApp.h"

@implementation ActivityController

@synthesize currentApp;

-(void)awakeFromNib {
    self.currentApp = [[CurrentApp alloc] init];
}
@end
```

---

2. Of course, if you are writing on and for 64-bit machines, you can also leave out the instance variable.

11.3 Registering for Notifications

Here's how an object registers to receive notifications:

```
[[NSNotificationCenter defaultCenter]
              addObserver:observerObject
                 selector:@selector(methodName:)
                     name:NameOfNotification
                   object:notifyingObject];
```

Zero, one, or many objects can register with a notification server for the same notification, and an object can register for as many different types of notifications it wants to receive. Let's take a closer look at each of the arguments used in registration:

- You are sending the addObserver:selector:name:object: message to the default notification center.
- In our case, we will set the observerObject to self, but it can be any object interested in receiving the notification. This will be the target for the action you are setting to be triggered by the notification.
- The selector specifies the action. This is the name of the method belonging to the observer that will be called when the notification is received.
    - The name of this method ends with a colon because this method will take a single parameter.
    - This single parameter is the notification object that is passed in when the notification is sent.
- The name is the name of the notification being registered for.
- The object refers to the object whose notifications you are interested in. In our SimpleBrowser example, you may have more than one web view that is posting notifications, and you might only want to monitor a particular one. You can also pass in nil to receive this type of notification posted by any object in your application.

In the stock example, the observerObject is you or your agent. The selector is the action to be performed like buy: or sell:. The name is the notification you are registering for like "price drops to $yyy." The object could be the name of the stock to which you are listening.

The big idea is that you register to listen for a notification by passing in the name of a method that will be called on a particular object. When the method is called, it receives an NSNotification object as its only parameter.

Every notification object contains two or three pieces of information including the name of the notification and the object that initiated the notification. If a notification needs to contain more information, it stores it in a third object, an NSDictionary named userInfo.

NSNotification's three instance methods are essentially getters for these properties:

```
- (NSString *)name
- (id)object
- (NSDictionary *)userInfo
```

The name method returns the name of the notification, and the object method returns a handle to the object responsible for issuing the notification. The userInfo method returns key-value pairs of information about the specific notification. We'll look at userInfo in Chapter 13, *Working with Dictionaries*, on page 203.

In the next section, we'll make all this more concrete. We'll register to receive notifications of changes of status to our workspace.

11.4 Responding to Workspace Activity

Your application runs inside a workspace. We can track what is going on in the workspace by listening for notifications. By the end of the chapter, we'll restrict ourselves to listening for when an application launches or terminates—but let's start by listening for *any* of the notifications sent by the NSWorkspace.

We use a class method to get the singleton that represents our shared workspace and then ask it for a reference to its notification center like this:

```
NSNotificationCenter *defaultCenter = [[NSWorkspace sharedWorkspace]
                                                notificationCenter];
```

Next we register to receive the notifications we are interested in:

```
[defaultCenter addObserver:self
            selector:@selector(reportActivity:)
                name:nil
              object:nil];
```

We could have asked to be notified of a particular event by passing it as the name: parameter. But we passed a name of nil, so the notification center will inform us of all notification events. The combination of self for the observer and reportActivity: for the selector specifies the target and action that will be called when a notification is received. The notification will be sent as the parameter.

Here's the entire CurrentApp.m listing:

Notification/HelloApplication2/CurrentApp.m

```
#import "CurrentApp.h"

@implementation CurrentApp

-(void) reportActivity: (NSNotification *) notification {
    NSLog(@"%@", notification.name );
}
-(void) registerNotifications {
    NSNotificationCenter *defaultCenter = [[NSWorkspace sharedWorkspace]
                                                    notificationCenter];
    [defaultCenter addObserver:self
                    selector:@selector(reportActivity:)
                        name:nil
                      object:nil];
}
-(id) init {
    if (self = [super init]) {
        [self registerNotifications];
    }
    return self;
}
@end
```

In reportActivity:, we just write out the name of the notification to the Console window. Click Build & Run. What happens?

A window opens for the app, and I also see something like this in my Console window:

NSWorkspaceDidLaunchApplicationNotification

For kicks I start up iCal. I should see another NSWorkspaceDidLaunch-ApplicationNotification in the Console window. I don't.

I quit iCal. I should see NSWorkspaceDidTerminateApplicationNotification in the Console. I don't.[3]

Grrrrrr. This is the memory problem I was talking about. Let's pause and fix it.

---

3. If you do see these additional notifications, check your project settings, and make sure that garbage collection is set to Required.

11.5 Holding on to the Controller

We've set our instance of CurrentApp up as an observer for notifications. The only object that holds a strong reference to this object is our instance of ActivityController. The ActivityController is created in the nib file, but nothing holds on to it.[4]

Let's add an outlet in the app delegate:

`Notification/HelloApplication3/HelloApplicationAppDelegate.h`

```
#import <Cocoa/Cocoa.h>
▶ @class ActivityController;

@interface HelloApplicationAppDelegate : NSObject <NSApplicationDelegate> {
    NSWindow *window;
▶     ActivityController *ac;
}
@property IBOutlet NSWindow *window;
▶ @property IBOutlet ActivityController *ac;
@end
```

Jump over to the implementation file, and synthesize ac:

`Notification/HelloApplication3/HelloApplicationAppDelegate.m`

```
#import "HelloApplicationAppDelegate.h"

@implementation HelloApplicationAppDelegate

▶ @synthesize window, ac;

- (void)applicationDidFinishLaunching:(NSNotification *)aNotification {
}
@end
```

Save your work, and open MainMenu.xib in Interface Builder. Connect the outlet you just created to the ActivityController. Save that work, and click Build & Run.

Now when I start up and quit iCal, the Console window looks like this:

```
NSWorkspaceDidLaunchApplicationNotification
NSWorkspaceWillLaunchApplicationNotification
NSWorkspaceDidActivateApplicationNotification
NSWorkspaceDidDeactivateApplicationNotification
NSWorkspaceDidLaunchApplicationNotification
```

---

4. At great risk to my reputation, this reminds me of a scene from the *Superman* movie where Superman catches Lois Lane as she falls and says, "Don't worry, I've got you." She looks quite worried as she asks, "But who has you?"

```
NSWorkspaceDidActivateApplicationNotification
NSWorkspaceDidDeactivateApplicationNotification
NSWorkspaceDidTerminateApplicationNotification
NSWorkspaceDidActivateApplicationNotification
NSWorkspaceDidDeactivateApplicationNotification
```

There's a lot of activity going on, and now our ActivityController and CurrentApp objects live long enough to tell us about it. First our HelloApplication project launches, and we get the notification that the application did launch. When I start iCal, I get a notification that iCal will launch and that iCal did launch mixed in with notifications of the applications activating and deactivating. Next, let's alter our code to focus in on just the information we want: launching and terminating apps.

11.6 Exercise: Registering for Notifications

Modify the code to listen for NSWorkspaceDidLaunchApplicationNotification and NSWorkspaceDidTerminateApplicationNotification. Display "Launched." and "Terminated." in the Console window in response.

11.7 Solution: Registering for Notifications

Let's start by registering for and responding to the launch notifications:

Notification/HelloApplication4/CurrentApp.m
```
-(void) registerNotifications {
    NSNotificationCenter *defaultCenter = [[NSWorkspace sharedWorkspace]
                                                     notificationCenter];
    [defaultCenter addObserver:self
►               selector:@selector(applicationDidLaunch:)
►                   name:NSWorkspaceDidLaunchApplicationNotification
                    object:nil];
}
```

The main change was specifying the name of the notification we're listening for instead of getting all of them by specifying nil. I also changed the name of the callback method to applicationDidLaunch:.

If I follow the same pattern to register for and respond to the terminate notification, I'll get a lot of duplicated code.

So, I'll introduce a utility method named setUpNotification:withSelector: and refactor like this:

Notification/HelloApplication5/CurrentApp.m

```
#import "CurrentApp.h"

@implementation CurrentApp

-(void) applicationDidLaunch: (NSNotification *) notification {
    NSLog(@"Launched.");
}
-(void) applicationDidTerminate: (NSNotification *) notification {
    NSLog(@"Terminated.");
}
-(void)setUpNotification:(NSString *)notification withSelector:(SEL)methodName {
    [[[NSWorkspace sharedWorkspace] notificationCenter]
            addObserver:self
               selector:methodName
                   name:notification
                 object:nil];
}
-(void) registerNotifications {
    [self setUpNotification:NSWorkspaceDidLaunchApplicationNotification
            withSelector:@selector(applicationDidLaunch:)];
    [self setUpNotification:NSWorkspaceDidTerminateApplicationNotification
            withSelector:@selector(applicationDidTerminate:)];
}
-(id) init {
    if (self = [super init]) {
        [self registerNotifications];
    }
    return self;
}
@end
```

Now when I click Build & Run, launch, and quit iCal, I see this in the Console:

```
Launched.
Launched.
Terminated.
```

11.8 Posting Notifications

Suppose we now want to add a text field to the window and display "Launched." or "Terminated." in that text field. How might you do that?

Start by adding an outlet to the controller of type NSTextField named activityDisplay:

```
Notification/HelloApplication6/ActivityController.h
#import <Cocoa/Cocoa.h>
@class CurrentApp;

@interface ActivityController : NSObject {
    CurrentApp *currentApp;
▶   NSTextField *activityDisplay;
}
@property CurrentApp *currentApp;
▶ @property IBOutlet NSTextField *activityDisplay;
@end
```

In Interface Builder, drag a multiline text field into your application window. Unselect the Selectable checkbox in the Attributes inspector. Connect the outlet to the text field, and save.

How should we communicate the launch and terminate notifications to this view? The controller should be the object that lets the view know, but how should the controller get the news?

We could register the controller to get the launch and terminate notifications and then pass the news on to the model. The controller knows about the model (after all, it creates the model), so this would be perfectly natural. The model could contact the controller when there are changes to report. This is less natural because the model doesn't know about the controller yet. In the next chapter, we'll set the controller up as the model's delegate, and much later in the book we'll learn how to use the Key Value Observing mechanism.

Another solution is for us to post notifications of our own. Here's how to post notifications named Launched and Terminated from the applicationDidLaunch: and applicationDidTerminate: methods:

```
Notification/HelloApplication6/CurrentApp.m
-(void) applicationDidLaunch: (NSNotification *) notification {
    [[NSNotificationCenter defaultCenter]
                        postNotificationName:@"Launched" object:self];
}
-(void) applicationDidTerminate: (NSNotification *) notification {
    [[NSNotificationCenter defaultCenter]
                        postNotificationName:@"Terminated" object:self];

}
```

First we obtain our application's notification center with this call:

```
[NSNotificationCenter defaultCenter]
```

Note that this is a different call than when we were getting a handle to the notification center for our workspace. Once we have the notification center, we can post notifications using postNotificationName:object:. All that remains is for us to register for and respond to these notifications.

11.9 Exercise: Receiving the Custom Notifications

Register observers in the ActivityController for the notifications we created in the previous section. Implement methods applicationDidLaunch: and applicationDidTerminate: in ActivityController that print "Launched." or "Terminated." in the text field when the appropriate notification is received.

11.10 Solution: Receiving the Custom Notifications

You know how to do every step in this exercise; now let's put it all together. Add the registerNotifications and setUpNotification:withSelector: methods that we used in CurrentApp. Call registerNotifications from awakeFromNib.

When you receive a notification, you need to change the activeDisplay's string value to either "Launched." or "Terminated."

Notification/HelloApplication6/ActivityController.m

```
#import "ActivityController.h"
#import "CurrentApp.h"

@implementation ActivityController

@synthesize currentApp, activityDisplay;

-(void) applicationDidLaunch: (NSNotification *) notification {
    [self.activityDisplay setStringValue:@"Launched."];
}
-(void) applicationDidTerminate: (NSNotification *) notification {
    [self.activityDisplay setStringValue:@"Terminated."];
}
-(void)setUpNotification:(NSString *)notification withSelector:(SEL)methodName {
    [[NSNotificationCenter defaultCenter]
      addObserver:self
      selector:methodName
      name:notification
      object:nil];
}
```

```
-(void) registerNotifications {
    [self setUpNotification:@"Launched"
            withSelector:@selector(applicationDidLaunch:)];
    [self setUpNotification:@"Terminated"
            withSelector:@selector(applicationDidTerminate:)];
}
-(void)awakeFromNib {
    self.currentApp = [[CurrentApp alloc] init];
    [self registerNotifications];
}
@end
```

You can read more about notifications in Apple's *Notification Programming Topics for Cocoa* [App08h].

In the next chapter, we'll rearchitect this application to use delegates instead of notifications to communicate between the model and the controller. We'll need to create our own protocol and implement the delegating methods ourselves.

Chapter 12

Creating Protocols for Delegation

Notifications are great when more than one object might need to be told about a change or when you might not know ahead of time which object(s) might be interested in being notified. For example, the application we wrote in the previous chapter is listening for notifications that the NSWorkspace sends out. That's a great use of notifications in our application.

On the other hand, the communication between our model and our controller is not a very good use of notifications.[1] The CurrentApp object's applicationDidLaunch: and applicationDidTerminate: methods each do little more than call methods of essentially the same name in the ApplicationController object. This is being accomplished in a roundabout way right now. The CurrentApp methods are posting notifications that the ApplicationController has registered to observe. We'd be better off using a delegate instead of notifications.

You've used protocols and delegates before. In this chapter, we will create our own protocol and add it to the controller's header file. We'll make the controller the delegate for our model. Then comes the tricky part. The model will turn around and call the delegate methods if they exist.

---

1. If it's not a good use of notifications, then why did I show it to you? I used notifications in this way so that I could show you how to generate your own notifications. My goal is to use this example to show you a range of useful techniques.

12.1 Exercise: Creating and Setting the Delegate

Create a new property named delegate in the CurrentApp class. For now we use id as the type of delegate, so any object can be assigned to it.

Remove all the methods from ActivityController.m except for awakeFrom-Nib. We'll put some of it back before we're done, but this will help you see some of the details in declaring and implementing a protocol. Set CurrentApp's delegate to self in awakeFromNib.

12.2 Solution: Creating and Setting the Delegate

Add the delegate instance variable and property to CurrentApp.h:

Protocols/HelloApplication7/CurrentApp.h

```
#import <Cocoa/Cocoa.h>

@interface CurrentApp : NSObject {
    id delegate;
}
@property id delegate;

@end
```

We've labeled the delegate as an id so that an object of any type could be set as the CurrentApp delegate. Remember to synthesize the property in CurrentApp.m.

For now, we're doing just three things in the ActivityController's awake-FromNib method: we're creating an instance of CurrentApp, we're assigning this to our instance variable, and we're setting that object's delegate to be ourselves.

Protocols/HelloApplication7/ActivityController.m

```
#import "ActivityController.h"
#import "CurrentApp.h"

@implementation ActivityController

@synthesize currentApp, activityDisplay;

-(void)awakeFromNib {
    self.currentApp = [[CurrentApp alloc] init];
    self.currentApp.delegate = self;
}
@end
```

At this point, I checked that it was working by adding (and later removing) this simple method to ActivityController.m:

```
-(void) sayHi {
    NSLog(@"Hi");
}
```

and this call to the end of awakeFromNib:

```
[self.currentApp.delegate sayHi];
```

I ran the app and saw "Hi" in the Console window. This lets me know everything is working, so I can remove sayHi and the call to it. It was a silly exercise, but it gave me the confidence to move on.[2]

12.3 Creating and Using a Protocol

A protocol is a collection of method declarations that are made available to any class that wants to implement some or all of the methods. It's like a header file that others may freely adopt. A protocol allows you to capture common behavior in a group of classes that might not inherit from each other or be related in any way other than that they all implement the same protocol.

Objective-C is a single inheritance language. A class can extend only one class. Often you are going to want to communicate to people using your class that it extends a certain class, but it can respond to other collections of behavior. We saw this in Chapter 9, *Customizing with Delegates*, on page 147 when we had a delegate for the window. The delegate was a WindowHelper object that extended NSWindow and implemented the NSWindowDelegate protocol. You might remember that this gave us a list of methods we could implement without explicitly declaring them in the header file.[3]

By default, all of the methods you declare in the protocol are required to be implemented by any class that adopts it. However, if you add an @optional directive, the methods that follow need not be implemented in a class that adopts the protocol. The @required directive toggles back

---

2. I know many readers will object that I should be developing test first, and then I wouldn't need to depend on such hacks. That's true, but I haven't found a unit testing framework I really like enough for Objective-C to include in this book. I do use OCUnit, which comes with Xcode. You can get started with Apple's *Automated Unit Testing with Xcode 3 and Objective-C* [App09a].

3. An Objective-C protocol is similar to an interface in Java.

to listing required methods. In this code snippet, aRequiredMethod and anotherRequiredMethod are required, while anOptionalMethod is optional.

```
@protocol SomeProtocol

-(void) aRequiredMethod;

@optional
-(void) anOptionalMethod;

@required
-(void) anotherRequiredMethod;

@end
```

Let's create a protocol that we'll use to define our delegate. First create a new header file in Xcode. Select the Classes folder in Groups & Files. Create a new file, and choose the template Mac OS X > Cocoa Class > Objective-C protocol. Name the file ActivityMonitorDelegate.h, and save it.

The first line of the file is @protocol followed by the name of the protocol, which is the same as the name of the file.[4] Protocols are lists of method declarations. There are no imports, no classes, and no instance variables, so we don't need any curly braces. Here we declare applicationdidLaunch: and applicationDidTerminate: in our protocol. Notice that these methods take a parameter of type CurrentApp.

Protocols/HelloApplication7/ActivityMonitorDelegate.h

```
@class CurrentApp;

@protocol ActivityMonitorDelegate

@optional
-(void)applicationDidLaunch: (CurrentApp *) app;
-(void)applicationDidTerminate: (CurrentApp *) app;

@end
```

Now let's use this protocol in the ActivityController class. You'll need to add an import statement to the top of ActivityController.h. You'll also have to add the declaration that ActivityController conforms to the protocol by adding ActivityMonitorDelegate in angle brackets after the name of ActivityController's superclass NSObject.

---

4. The protocol and filename could have different name, but by convention they are the same.

Protocols/HelloApplication7/ActivityController.h

```
#import <Cocoa/Cocoa.h>
▶ #import "ActivityMonitorDelegate.h"
@class CurrentApp;

▶ @interface ActivityController : NSObject <ActivityMonitorDelegate> {
      CurrentApp *currentApp;
      NSTextField *activityDisplay;
}
@property CurrentApp *currentApp;
@property IBOutlet NSTextField *activityDisplay;
@end
```

Click Build & Run. There should be no warnings, but nothing much should happen when you run the application.

12.4 Requiring Methods

Remove the @optional line from the protocol, and click Build & Run. You'll get warnings like these:

⚠ Incomplete implementation of class 'ActivityController'

⚠ Method definition for '-applicationDidTerminate:' not found

⚠ Method definition for '-applicationDidLaunch:' not found

⚠ Class 'ActivityController' does not fully implement the 'ActivityMonitorDelegate' protocol

Now that applicationDidLaunch: and applicationDidTerminate: are required, we'll need to implement them in ActivityController.m:

Protocols/HelloApplication8/ActivityController.m

```
-(void) applicationDidLaunch: (CurrentApp *) app {
    [self.activityDisplay setStringValue:@"Launched"];
}
-(void) applicationDidTerminate: (CurrentApp *) app {
    [self.activityDisplay setStringValue:@"Terminated"];
}
```

Click Build & Run, and the warnings are gone again. We've set up the delegate and created a protocol that declares the methods we need. We've used the protocol and implemented the required methods. Now let's finish by replacing posting notifications in CurrentApp with sending messages to the delegate.

12.5 Responding to Selector

Here's how you'll test whether you can call the delegate method from your delegating object:

Protocols/HelloApplication8/CurrentApp.m

```
-(void) applicationDidLaunch: (NSNotification *) notification {
    if ([self.delegate
            respondsToSelector:@selector(applicationDidLaunch:)] ) {
        NSLog(@"Delegate implements applicationDidLaunch:.");
    } else {
        NSLog(@"We're on our own.");
    }

}
```

You ask the delegate whether it implements the method before you call it. You check by sending the respondsToSelector: message to the delegate and passing in the name of the method on which you are checking.

Click Build & Run. You should see the message "Delegate implements applicationDidLaunch:." in the Console window.

Let's cause a problem or two. Comment out this line in ActivityController.m:

```
self.currentApp.delegate = self;
```

Click Build & Run. This time you should see "We're on our own." in the Console.

Uncomment that last line, and comment out the applicationDidLaunch: method in ActivityController.m. Click Build & Run. Ignore the warning. Again, you'll see "We're on our own." in the Console.

Uncomment the method, and click Build & Run one more time to confirm that the delegate method can be called successfully.

12.6 Exercise: Calling the Delegate Methods

We're ready to finish our delegate. In CurrentApp's applicationDidLaunch: method, check to see that the delegate responds to a method named applicationDidLaunch:. If it does, call the method, and pass in self as the CurrentApp object.

Do the analogous thing in CurrentApp's applicationDidTerminate: method. When you click Build & Run, you should see "Launched." and "Terminated." in the text field when you start and quit applications.

12.7 Solution: Calling the Delegate Methods

This is one of those exercises that might have taken longer to describe than actually do. Here are your changes in applicationDidLaunch: and applicationDidTerminate::

Protocols/HelloApplication9/CurrentApp.m

```
-(void) applicationDidLaunch: (NSNotification *) notification {
    if ([self.delegate
            respondsToSelector:@selector(applicationDidLaunch:)] ) {
        [self.delegate applicationDidLaunch:self];
    }
}
-(void) applicationDidTerminate: (NSNotification *) notification {
    if ([self.delegate
            respondsToSelector:@selector(applicationDidTerminate:)]) {
        [self.delegate applicationDidTerminate:self];
    }
}
```

You'll also need to import ActivityMonitorDelegate.h in your CurrentApp header file. You could use a forward declaration in your header file and import in your implementation file, but I know we're going to need to move it in a minute, so I'm placing the import in the header file.

12.8 Exercise: Cleaning Up

Here's a rule of thumb for you: if you *can* do something in Interface Builder, then you *should* do it in Interface Builder.

Sure, there are exceptions, and we'll experiment with doing things in code that can be done in IB, but you'll go much further if you follow that principle.

Let's apply that to our current example to do a little cleaning up. Create your CurrentApp object in the nib, and set its delegate there as well. You'll need to hold onto this object, so let's set an outlet in the app delegate and connect it to the CurrentApp object.

12.9 Solution: Cleaning Up

We can get rid of the awakeFromNib method in ActivityController.m because we're going to create the object and set the delegate in the nib.

```
Protocols/HelloApplication10/ActivityController.m
```

```objc
#import "ActivityController.h"
#import "CurrentApp.h"

@implementation ActivityController

@synthesize activityDisplay;

-(void) applicationDidLaunch: (CurrentApp *) app {
    [self.activityDisplay setStringValue:@"Launched"];
}
-(void) applicationDidTerminate: (CurrentApp *) app {
    [self.activityDisplay setStringValue:@"Terminated"];
}
@end
```

We don't need the currentApp property anymore. Make sure you remove the variable and property declaration from the header file along with the forward declaration:

```
Protocols/HelloApplication10/ActivityController.h
```

```objc
#import <Cocoa/Cocoa.h>
#import "ActivityMonitorDelegate.h"

@interface ActivityController : NSObject <ActivityMonitorDelegate> {
    NSTextField *activityDisplay;
}
@property IBOutlet NSTextField *activityDisplay;
@end
```

We'll add an outlet to the app delegate so that the CurrentApp instance stays around as long as we need it:

```
Protocols/HelloApplication10/HelloApplicationAppDelegate.h
```

```objc
#import <Cocoa/Cocoa.h>
@class ActivityController;
@class CurrentApp;

@interface HelloApplicationAppDelegate : NSObject <NSApplicationDelegate> {
    NSWindow *window;
    ActivityController *ac;
    CurrentApp *currentApp;
}
@property IBOutlet NSWindow *window;
@property IBOutlet ActivityController *ac;
@property IBOutlet CurrentApp *currentApp;
@end
```

Remember to synthesize the currentApp property in the implementation file.

Protocols/HelloApplication10/HelloApplicationAppDelegate.m

```
#import "HelloApplicationAppDelegate.h"

@implementation HelloApplicationAppDelegate

@synthesize window, ac, currentApp;

- (void)applicationDidFinishLaunching:(NSNotification *)aNotification {
}
@end
```

Lastly, now that we'll be setting the delegate in IB, we need to more carefully specify the type. Modify CurrentApp.h like this:

Protocols/HelloApplication10/CurrentApp.h

```
#import <Cocoa/Cocoa.h>
#import "ActivityMonitorDelegate.h"

@interface CurrentApp : NSObject {
    NSObject <ActivityMonitorDelegate> *delegate;
}
@property IBOutlet NSObject <ActivityMonitorDelegate> *delegate;

@end
```

We changed id to NSObject. I've also inserted the protocol name in angle brackets. Notice that the * belongs with the variable. This won't compile if you try to keep it with NSObject. We also labeled the delegate property as an outlet.

There's a nice side effect of this change in the type declaration for the delegate property. We can now remove this guard clause from the applicationDidLaunch: method in CurrentApp.m:

```
if ([self.delegate
        respondsToSelector:@selector(applicationDidLaunch:)] )
```

We no longer need this check now that we've declared the delegate to implement the ActivityMonitorDelegate protocol, which requires the applicationDidLaunch: method. The same is true for the applicationDidTerminate: method. Here are the simplified methods in CurrentApp.m:

Protocols/HelloApplication10/CurrentApp.m

```
-(void) applicationDidLaunch: (NSNotification *) notification {
    [self.delegate applicationDidLaunch:self];
}
-(void) applicationDidTerminate: (NSNotification *) notification {
    [self.delegate applicationDidTerminate:self];
}
```

Save your work, and let's head over to Interface Builder. Find CurrentApp on the Classes tab of the Library, and drag it into the Document window. Open the Connections inspector. Select the HelloApplicationAppDelegate object, and connect its currentApp outlet to the CurrentApp object. Select the CurrentApp object, and connect its delegate outlet to the ActivityController object. Save your work, and quit IB.

Click Build & Run, and your application should run exactly as before.

We're now receiving notifications when applications launch or terminate and communicating between the model and the controller using a protocol and delegate. We haven't done much with the notification we receive, however. There's a lot of information contained inside of it that we are just ignoring. We'll fix that in the next chapter.

Chapter 13

Working with Dictionaries

In the past couple of chapters, we used notifications and delegates to output "Launched." and "Terminated." In this chapter, you'll learn to work with dictionaries to answer the questions "Launched *what*?" and "Terminated *what*?"

There is a lot of information contained in the notification that we are not yet using. Remember that an NSNotification has the name of the notification, the object sending the notification, and a dictionary named userInfo filled with key-value pairs of information about the specific notification.

In this chapter, we'll dig into the contents of that dictionary.[1] It turns out that this is an important technology to know—Cocoa frameworks use dictionaries all over the place.

13.1 Looking at the User Info

There are three basic usage patterns for notifications:

- In the first case, all that matters is that you get the notification—all you need to know is that the event you were waiting to hear about has occurred.

- In the second case, you might use the notification's name or object.

- In the third case, you need further information contained in the userInfo dictionary. For example, when you get notification that an application has launched, you may want to know the name of

---

1. Depending on which language you're coming from, you may use the term *hash* instead of *dictionary*.

the application and where it is located on your hard drive. This information would be stored as key-value pairs in an NSDictionary returned by userInfo.

Add this line to your applicationDidLaunch: method in CurrentApp.m:

Dictionaries/HelloApplication11/CurrentApp.m

```
-(void) applicationDidLaunch: (NSNotification *) notification {
    [self.delegate applicationDidLaunch:self];
    NSLog(@"%@", notification.userInfo);
}
```

Click Build & Run. You should see the userInfo dictionary in the Console window when you launch applications. For example, when I launch iCal, I see this in my Console:

```
{
    NSApplicationBundleIdentifier = "com.apple.iCal";
    NSApplicationName = iCal;
    NSApplicationPath = "/Applications/iCal.app";
    NSApplicationProcessIdentifier = 7130;
    NSApplicationProcessSerialNumberHigh = 0;
    NSApplicationProcessSerialNumberLow = 987377;
    NSWorkspaceApplicationKey = "<NSRunningApplication:
                            0x200019ae0 (com.apple.iCal - 7130)>";
}
```

You can see the name of the application and its location on the disk. You can see its bundle identifier and other identifiers. We'll start by pulling out the name.

13.2 Reading from a Dictionary

There are many ways to read from a dictionary. You can use a key enumerator to move through the dictionary entries in order and pick out values. You can get an array of all the keys or all the values. We'll use the objectForKey: method:

```
[notification.userInfo objectForKey:@"NSApplicationName"]
```

Now when we click Build & Run, we'll log the name of the applications that are launched to the Console window. That's all there is to reading from a dictionary.

13.3 Exercise: Displaying the Name

Add a property named name of type NSString to CurrentApp. Set the value of name property when you receive a notification by reading it from the userInfo dictionary. Your application window should look something like this:

In other words, when you update the text field, the message should read "Launched: iCal" or "Terminated: iCal," respectively, when you start or quit iCal.

13.4 Solution: Displaying the Name

Add the name instance variable and property to the header file. Specify the memory model as copy because NSString conforms to the NSCopying protocol.

Dictionaries/HelloApplication13/CurrentApp.h

```
#import <Cocoa/Cocoa.h>
#import "ActivityMonitorDelegate.h"

@interface CurrentApp : NSObject {
    NSObject <ActivityMonitorDelegate> *delegate;
►   NSString *name;
}
@property IBOutlet NSObject <ActivityMonitorDelegate> *delegate;
► @property(copy) NSString *name;

@end
```

Set the name in the applicationDidLaunch: and applicationDidTerminate: methods in CurrentApp.m:

Dictionaries/HelloApplication13/CurrentApp.m

```
-(void) applicationDidLaunch: (NSNotification *) notification {
►    self.name = [notification.userInfo objectForKey:@"NSApplicationName"];
     [self.delegate applicationDidLaunch:self];
}
-(void) applicationDidTerminate: (NSNotification *) notification {
►    self.name = [notification.userInfo objectForKey:@"NSApplicationName"];
     [self.delegate applicationDidTerminate:self];
}
```

The objectForKey: lets us read a particular entry from the dictionary. We pass in the key NSApplicationName and get back the name of the launching or terminating application as an NSString.

Use the fact that the app is passed in as a parameter to the applicationDidLaunch: and applicationDidTerminate: methods to create formatted strings in ActivityController.m to enhance the output.

Dictionaries/HelloApplication13/ActivityController.m

```
#import "ActivityController.h"
#import "CurrentApp.h"

@implementation ActivityController

@synthesize activityDisplay;

-(void) applicationDidLaunch: (CurrentApp *) app {
    [self.activityDisplay setStringValue:
        [NSString stringWithFormat:@"Launched: %@", app.name]];
}
-(void) applicationDidTerminate: (CurrentApp *) app {
    [self.activityDisplay setStringValue:
        [NSString stringWithFormat:@"Terminated: %@", app.name]];
}
@end
```

13.5 Reducing Redundancy

The two applicationDidXxx: method implementations in CurrentApp are nearly identical. In each case, I've reinserted the check that the delegate does respond to our selector to guard against passing a method name in that isn't implemented.

```
if ([self.delegate
        respondsToSelector:@selector(applicationDidXxx:)] ) {
    self.name = [notification.userInfo objectForKey:@"NSApplicationName"];
    [self.delegate applicationDidXxx:self];
}
```

We just need a way of making sure that Xxx is Launch in one case and Terminate in the other. We could pass the notification on to a utility method and choose the method to call based on the name of the notification like this:

Dictionaries/HelloApplication14/CurrentApp.m

```
-(void) respondToChange:(NSNotification *) notification {
    SEL methodName;
```

```
    if (notification.name == NSWorkspaceDidLaunchApplicationNotification) {
        methodName = @selector(applicationDidLaunch:);
    } else {
        methodName = @selector(applicationDidTerminate:);
    }
    if ([self.delegate respondsToSelector:methodName]) {
        self.name = [notification.userInfo objectForKey:@"NSApplicationName"];
        [self.delegate performSelector:methodName withObject:self];
    }

}
-(void) applicationDidLaunch: (NSNotification *) notification {
    [self respondToChange:notification];
}
-(void) applicationDidTerminate: (NSNotification *) notification {
    [self respondToChange:notification];
}
```

This is much nicer.[2] We've captured the common behavior in the respondToChange: method. We start by setting the method name to applicationDidLaunch: or applicationDidTerminate: based on the value of notification.name.

One difference is the way in which we call the method and pass self in as a parameter. When we have the method name, we could make a call like this:

```
[self.delegate applicationDidLaunch:self]
```

Now we need to use performSelector:withObject::

```
[self.delegate performSelector:methodName withObject:self];
```

I'm happy that we've eliminated the repeated code, but I'm bothered by the if statement. Control statements like if, for, case, and so on, are not necessarily bad, but you should consider whether there might be a more direct path through your code.

In our simple case, there are many ways of eliminating the if. I'm going to show you a technique that uses dictionaries.

---

2. As one reviewer noted, we could eliminate the applicationDidLaunch: and application-DidTerminate: methods altogether at this point and eliminate redundancy further. Unfortunately, we'd have to add them back in just a few sections, so I'm leaving them in.

13.6 Using a Dictionary for Flow Control

Let's take another look at that if statement:

Dictionaries/HelloApplication14/CurrentApp.m

```
if (notification.name == NSWorkspaceDidLaunchApplicationNotification) {
    methodName = @selector(applicationDidLaunch:);
} else {
    methodName = @selector(applicationDidTerminate:);
}
```

Let's create a dictionary that has the notification names as the keys and the names of the methods as values. Then we can replace the if statement with this:

Dictionaries/HelloApplication15/CurrentApp.m

```
SEL methodName = NSSelectorFromString(
                    [delegateMethods objectForKey:[notification name]]);
```

There's no decision to make. We just pull the method name from the dictionary.

We need to declare an instance variable named delegateMethods of type NSDictionary in CurrentApp.h. We don't need it to be a property. We'll initialize it like this:[3]

Dictionaries/HelloApplication15/CurrentApp.m

```
-(void) initializeMethodDictionary {
    delegateMethods = [[NSDictionary alloc] initWithObjectsAndKeys:
                        @"applicationDidLaunch:",
                        NSWorkspaceDidLaunchApplicationNotification,
                        @"applicationDidTerminate:",
                        NSWorkspaceDidTerminateApplicationNotification,
                        nil];
}
```

We pass in the key-value pairs as a comma-separated nil-terminated list. In each pair, we pass in the value first followed by the key. We store the method names as NSStrings because the values we put into our dictionary must be objects.

13.7 Adding and Removing Entries with a Mutable Dictionary

There are times when you want to add an entry to the dictionary or remove one or more entries from the dictionary. You can't make these

---

3. Add a call to initializeMethodDictionary to the end of the init method.

changes to an NSDictionary because it is immutable. Instead, you have to use the NSMutableDictionary. This is the subclass of NSDictionary that allows such changes.

By now you have probably found it frustrating that the Apple documentation for a class doesn't at least list all of the methods that are available for objects of a particular type. The documentation contains in-depth descriptions of methods defined for that class but doesn't show you the methods that are inherited from superclasses. You have to follow the documentation up the tree to find that a particular method is defined several levels up (often in a class you would never have thought to look at).[4]

This general inconvenience can sometimes be a benefit. For example, if you look at the documentation for NSMutableDictionary, you can quickly see how it differs from NSDictionary. Only the additional methods are listed. There are methods for creating a mutable dictionary that allow you to specify the initial capacity of the dictionary.[5] There are additional methods for adding entries to and removing entries from a mutable dictionary. In every other way, an NSMutableDictionary is just an NSDictionary, so all of those methods in the superclass are available to us in the NSMutableDictionary as well.

So, let's play with the NSMutableDictionary a bit. First declare an instance variable named runningApps in CurrentApp.h.

Dictionaries/HelloApplication16/CurrentApp.h

```
#import <Cocoa/Cocoa.h>
#import "ActivityMonitorDelegate.h"

@interface CurrentApp : NSObject {
    NSObject <ActivityMonitorDelegate> *delegate;
    NSString *name;
    NSDictionary *delegateMethods;
    NSMutableDictionary *runningApps;
}
@property IBOutlet NSObject <ActivityMonitorDelegate> *delegate;
@property(copy) NSString *name;
@end
```

---

4. You can always press Escape after typing the name of your target and a space to see all of the methods available to you. Use this in conjunction with Quick Help to quickly understand what each method does.

5. As the dictionary grows, more memory will be allocated to it as needed.

We create our mutable dictionary in the init method. Use the setObject:forKey method to add a new entry to the dictionary that has the application's name as a key and a time stamp as its value whenever an application is launched.[6]

```
[runningApps setObject:[NSDate date] forKey:appName];
```

In place of appName, we'll need to retrieve the name of the application from the userInfo dictionary for our notification. Similarly, we'll use the removeObjectForKey: method whenever an application is terminated to remove the entry with the key equal to the name of the application that is terminated.

```
[runningApps removeObjectForKey: appName];
```

Let's add logging to display the value of the runningApps variable at the end of the respondToChange: method. When I run the application and start up iCal, I see this in my Console window:

```
HelloApplication = "2009-10-03 10:45:36 -0400";
iCal = "2009-10-03 10:45:39 -0400";
```

For completeness, here is CurrentApp.m:

Dictionaries/HelloApplication16/CurrentApp.m

```
#import "CurrentApp.h"

@implementation CurrentApp

@synthesize delegate, name;

-(void) respondToChange:(NSNotification *) notification {
    SEL methodName = NSSelectorFromString(
                        [delegateMethods objectForKey:[notification name]]);
    if ([self.delegate respondsToSelector:methodName]) {
        self.name = [notification.userInfo objectForKey:@"NSApplicationName"];
        [self.delegate performSelector:methodName withObject:self];
    }
    NSLog(@"%@", runningApps);
}
-(void) applicationDidLaunch: (NSNotification *) notification {
    [runningApps setObject:[NSDate date]
                    forKey:[notification.userInfo
                                objectForKey:@"NSApplicationName"]];
    [self respondToChange:notification];
}
```

---

6. There's no real reason for doing this other than to show that we can add and remove entries to/from our dictionary.

```
    -(void) applicationDidTerminate: (NSNotification *) notification {
►       [runningApps removeObjectForKey:[notification.userInfo
►                                        objectForKey:@"NSApplicationName"]];
        [self respondToChange:notification];
    }
    -(void)setUpNotification:(NSString *)notification withSelector:(SEL)methodName {
        [[[NSWorkspace sharedWorkspace] notificationCenter]
                addObserver:self
                   selector:methodName
                       name:notification
                     object:nil];
    }
    -(void) registerNotifications {
        [self setUpNotification:NSWorkspaceDidLaunchApplicationNotification
                withSelector:@selector(applicationDidLaunch:)];
        [self setUpNotification:NSWorkspaceDidTerminateApplicationNotification
                withSelector:@selector(applicationDidTerminate:)];
    }
    -(void) initializeMethodDictionary {
        delegateMethods = [[NSDictionary alloc] initWithObjectsAndKeys:
                            @"applicationDidLaunch:",
                            NSWorkspaceDidLaunchApplicationNotification,
                            @"applicationDidTerminate:",
                            NSWorkspaceDidTerminateApplicationNotification,
                            nil];
    }
    -(id) init {
        if (self = [super init]) {
            [self registerNotifications];
            [self initializeMethodDictionary];
►           runningApps = [[NSMutableDictionary alloc] initWithCapacity:5];
        }
        return self;
    }
    @end
```

Before moving on, remove all of the lines that I highlighted in the previous code listings of the header and implementation files for CurrentApp. They don't do any harm, but they clutter up the example a bit, and now that you know how to create and work with a mutable dictionary, we don't need to keep them around.

13.8 Exercise: Adding an Icon

Now that we've tidied up our code, let's use the userInfo dictionary to add another feature to HelloApplication. Let's display the icon of the application being launched or terminated.

So, for example, when we quit iCal, our display should look something like this:

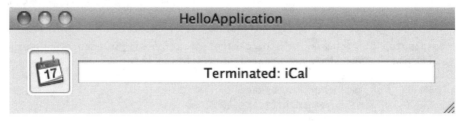

We can accomplish this change by adding an outlet to the ActivityController header file, by adding a corresponding GUI element in Interface Builder, and by reshaping our code. As is often the case with Cocoa programming, it can take a while to figure out how to accomplish this third step. Let's take care of the easier steps first.

In Xcode, add an outlet named imageView to the header file ActivityController.h. The outlet should be a pointer to an NSImageView.

In Interface Builder, find an NSImageView described as an *image well* in the Library, and drag it into your window. Adjust the window, text field, and image well so that they look like the picture you saw at the beginning of this section.

Adjust the size settings so that the user can adjust the size of the window only in the horizontal direction. When the window grows, the image well should stay where it is, and the text field should grow so that it remains the same distance from the left and right sides.

Before leaving Interface Builder, connect the imageView outlet you created in your header file to the image well. Save your work.

We'll take advantage of a new class that was added in Snow Leopard. NSRunningApplication lets you send messages and get information about a currently running user application. Look back at the last entry we saw when we displayed the userInfo dictionary in the Console window:

```
NSWorkspaceApplicationKey = "<NSRunningApplication:
                        0x200019ae0 (com.apple.iCal - 7130)>";
```

The NSRunningApplication has the following properties:

```
activationPolicy
active
bundleIdentifier
bundleURL
executableArchitecture
executableURL
```

```
finishedLaunching
hidden
icon
launchDate
localizedName
processIdentifier
terminated
```

All the information that is contained in the rest of the userInfo dictionary and more is contained in the instance of the NSRunningApplication with the key NSWorkspaceApplicationKey.

Because you are developing in Snow Leopard, you can rearchitect your application to use NSRunningApplication wherever possible. Instead of retrieving and storing the application name from the userInfo dictionary, we can retrieve and store the running application. And instead of passing an instance of CurrentApp to our delegate methods, we can pass the running application and use it to display the name and the icon.[7]

Take a few minutes to try to get this to work before moving on to read a solution.

13.9 Solution: Adding an Icon

Your header file should look like this:

Dictionaries/HelloApplication17/ActivityController.h

```
#import <Cocoa/Cocoa.h>
#import "ActivityMonitorDelegate.h"

@interface ActivityController : NSObject <ActivityMonitorDelegate> {
    NSTextField *activityDisplay;
    NSImageView *imageView;
}
@property IBOutlet NSTextField *activityDisplay;
@property IBOutlet NSImageView *imageView;
@end
```

In Interface Builder, you should have had no problem adding your image well and using the blue guidelines to arrange the image well and text field inside the window. You should have used the Size inspector to set the minimum and maximum size of the window. If the height is the same for the minimum and maximum sizes, your end user can adjust

---

7. There was no need for this overhead when we just needed the name of the application. Now it makes sense to use the NSRunningApplication instance we retrieve from the userInfo dictionary.

the size of the window horizontally only. You also should have used the Size inspector on the image well and text field so that they look right as the window is resized.

As for the code, let's start at the end. If we pass the NSRunningApplication as the parameter of the ActivityController's methods applicationDidLaunch: and applicationDidTerminate:, then we can retrieve the application name and icon from it like this:[8]

Dictionaries/HelloApplication17/ActivityController.m

```
#import "ActivityController.h"

@implementation ActivityController

@synthesize activityDisplay,imageView;

-(void) applicationDidLaunch: (NSRunningApplication *) app {
    [self.activityDisplay setStringValue:
     [NSString stringWithFormat:@"Launched: %@", app.localizedName]];
    [self.imageView setImage:app.icon];
}
-(void) applicationDidTerminate: (NSRunningApplication *) app {
    [self.activityDisplay setStringValue:
     [NSString stringWithFormat:@"Terminated: %@", app.localizedName]];
    [self.imageView setImage:app.icon];
}
@end
```

We can eliminate the redundancy by introducing a utility method displayAction:forApplication::

Dictionaries/HelloApplication18/ActivityController.m

```
#import "ActivityController.h"

@implementation ActivityController

@synthesize activityDisplay,imageView;

-(void) displayAction:(NSString *) action
         forApplication:(NSRunningApplication *) app {
    [self.activityDisplay setStringValue:
        [NSString stringWithFormat:@"%@: %@",action, app.localizedName]];
    [self.imageView setImage:app.icon];
}
```

---

8. It feels a bit strange to refer to the terminating application as a running application, but it is the NSRunningApplication instance in the userInfo dictionary included in the notification we receive.

```
-(void) applicationDidLaunch: (NSRunningApplication *) app {
    [self displayAction:@"Launched" forApplication:app];
}
-(void) applicationDidTerminate: (NSRunningApplication *) app {
    [self displayAction:@"Terminated" forApplication:app];
}
@end
```

The signature of our delegate methods has changed, so we have to update the protocol to match:

Dictionaries/HelloApplication18/ActivityMonitorDelegate.h

```
@protocol ActivityMonitorDelegate

-(void)applicationDidLaunch: (NSRunningApplication *) app;
-(void)applicationDidTerminate: (NSRunningApplication *) app;

@end
```

Another advantage of using the NSRunningApplication object is that we can remove the import and forward declarations of the CurrentApp class.

In CurrentApp.h, we replace the name property with a property named app of type NSRunningApplication:

Dictionaries/HelloApplication18/CurrentApp.h

```
#import <Cocoa/Cocoa.h>
#import "ActivityMonitorDelegate.h"

@interface CurrentApp : NSObject {
    NSObject <ActivityMonitorDelegate> *delegate;
    NSRunningApplication *app;
    NSDictionary *delegateMethods;
}
@property IBOutlet NSObject <ActivityMonitorDelegate> *delegate;
@property NSRunningApplication *app;

@end
```

Lastly, we synthesize the app property, set its value from the userInfo dictionary, and pass it in as our parameter when we call the delegate methods:

Dictionaries/HelloApplication18/CurrentApp.m

```
@synthesize delegate, app;

-(void) respondToChange:(NSNotification *) notification {
    SEL methodName = NSSelectorFromString(
                        [delegateMethods objectForKey:[notification name]]);
```

```
        if ([self.delegate respondsToSelector:methodName]) {
▶           self.app = [notification.userInfo
▶                               objectForKey:@"NSWorkspaceApplicationKey"];
▶           [self.delegate performSelector:methodName withObject:self.app];
        }
    }
```

You should notice a certain similarity between pulling objects out of dictionaries using their keys and accessing an object's properties. We'll return to this theme later.

You can now use a dictionary to pull information out of the notification you receive every time an application launches or terminates. You used this information to send text and images to standard GUI widgets. In the next chapter, you'll see how to create a custom view to display this information with more flexibility.

Chapter 14

Multiple Nibs

So far in our desktop app, everything is in a single nib. In this chapter, we're going to break the nib up into first two and then three pieces. Although we didn't worry much about it, we had two nibs files when we created our iPhone web browser. One contained our window and the view controller, and the other contained the view that the view controller controlled.

The purpose of this chapter is to show you how to work with multiple nib files. Just as you split methods or classes when they get to the point where they do too much, you'll learn to break nibs into smaller, easy-to-describe collections of objects. Just like objects and methods, when you split them into smaller pieces, you will often need to communicate among the pieces. That's the job of the File's Owner. By the end of this chapter, you'll understand how File's Owner works as well.

14.1 Methods, Objects, and Nibs

A nib is one of the organization levels for your project. A nib is a collection of objects and their connections to each other.

Zooming in, each object is a cohesive collection of functionality. An object might include variables, properties, functions, and methods. Of course, this means that objects are state plus behavior, but I like to think of objects in terms of what they can do. This means that to me an object is characterized by its methods.

Methods are the smallest organizational level that I want to think of right now. We create a method when we want to accomplish a task or implement an action or perform a calculation. Methods that belong together are collected in a class. Objects are instances of these classes. We often collect objects that need to communicate with each other in a nib file.

In other words, a nib is a cohesive collection of objects, their initial state, and their connections to each other in the same way that an object is a collection of variables, their initial state, and the messages the object understands. Over the next few chapters, I will help you see that one nib is seldom enough for your application any more than a single object is.

Before we start splitting this nib into smaller pieces, let's consider the advantages and disadvantages that you've seen when refactoring methods or classes. Shorter methods can be more easily described, and what they do is more easily understood. For example, when we create a new instance of CurrentApp, we currently do this:

Dictionaries/HelloApplication18/CurrentApp.m

```
-(id) init {
    if (self = [super init]) {
        [self registerNotifications];
        [self initializeMethodDictionary];
    }
    return self;
}
```

Our customization is to register the notifications for this object and to initialize the method dictionary. This method reads like prose. The registerNotifications method looks like this:

Dictionaries/HelloApplication18/CurrentApp.m

```
-(void) registerNotifications {
    [self setUpNotification:NSWorkspaceDidLaunchApplicationNotification
            withSelector:@selector(applicationDidLaunch:)];
    [self setUpNotification:NSWorkspaceDidTerminateApplicationNotification
            withSelector:@selector(applicationDidTerminate:)];
}
```

Again, once you've wrapped your head around Objective-C syntax, this reads clearly. It says that we are setting up the "did launch" application notification with the callback method applicationDidLaunch: and the "did terminate" application notification with the callback method applicationDidTerminate:. How we actually do that is captured in the setUpNotification:withSelector: method.

Dictionaries/HelloApplication18/CurrentApp.m

```
-(void)setUpNotification:(NSString *)notification withSelector:(SEL)methodName {
    [[[NSWorkspace sharedWorkspace] notificationCenter]
            addObserver:self
              selector:methodName
                  name:notification
                object:nil];
}
```

This method is just a wrapper around a call to the shared workspace's notification center to register our notification.

Breaking down the process into these smaller pieces makes each piece easier to understand. We understand immediately *what* is being done in the init method even though we don't have all the details of *how*. We could have written one long init method that replaced each piece with the code that it calls. There would be no need to make up new names for our own methods and pass information around. Everything would have been in one location.

The same tension applies when we design classes and objects. We've isolated the model behavior in CurrentApp and the controller behavior in ActivityController. Each piece is now easier to understand, but we spent the past three chapters exploring different ways to communicate between them. We could have combined them into one harder to understand object that might have been easier to implement.

In this case, I chose to separate them because I get flexibility I wouldn't otherwise have. I'm going to be able to use this same model for an entirely different controller and view without rewriting a line of code in CurrentApp.m. Later when I need to make further adjustments to the code, I will know whether the change needs to be to the model or the controller. In other words, in this case the simplicity of the objects is more important than the difficulty of communicating between them.

14.2 Splitting Nibs

We have a single nib file named MainMenu.xib that contains a lot of objects.

MainMenu

NSApplication	Activity Controller
Main Menu	View
Window	Image Well
Current App	Text Field
App Delegate	

The ActivityController is a bridge between two worlds. It needs to communicate with the components of the view to display the icon in the image well and a message in the text field. We'll put these components into one nib. The ActivityController object also needs to communicate with the model. We're going to split the nib into these two pieces with the same instance of the ActivityController living in each:

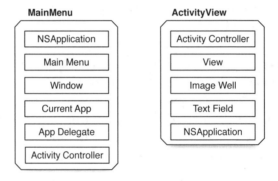

The ActivityView is a cohesive collection of objects. It's the components of the view along with the view controller. The MainMenu.xib can be further split to move the NSWindow into its own nib. We'll need to introduce a window controller to manage our window the same way we use a view controller to manage our view.

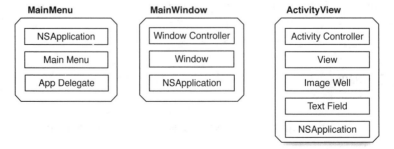

The object I've positioned at the top of each nib is the File's Owner. You'll soon see that the File's Owner is the object that will connect the new nib file to the rest of the application. So, we've broken our single nib into three smaller pieces that are connected via their File's Owners. Let's start splitting off our first nib.

14.3 Preparing to Split Out the View

Let's start by splitting out the view. The whole key to this operation is the view controller. We're going to move the text field and the image well that the view controller controls into a new nib that contains a view. We'll add this view to the window, *but* we're not going to move the window, the model, or the app delegate. Here are the ActivityController's current connections:

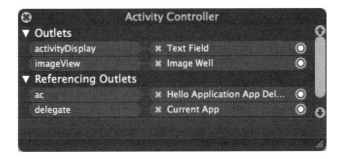

Notice that our ActivityController is connected to four objects that will soon be contained in two different nibs. The trick is to make sure that the same instance of ActivityController will be able to communicate with both nibs. We'll create the ActivityController in the MainMenu nib and use it as our File's Owner in our new nib. One of my goals in this exercise is to help you understand the role of the File's Owner.

We've been using the ActivityController as a view controller, but so far it hasn't extended the NSViewController class. Let's fix that by changing the superclass in the ActivityController header file:

MultipleNibs/HelloApplication19/ActivityController.h

```
@interface ActivityController : NSViewController <ActivityMonitorDelegate> {
```

Now if you check out the ActivityController's outlets in the Connections inspector, you'll see a new view outlet. We'll use that in the next section when we split this nib in two.

14.4 Creating the View Nib

Next, create the new nib file. This will hold our text field and image well. Select the Resources folder in Groups & Files, and create a new file. This time choose Mac OS X > User Interface > View XIB.

Application XIB   Empty XIB   Main Menu XIB

View XIB   Window XIB

Name the nib file ActivityView.xib, and click the Finish button.

Now we're going to do some surgery. We're going to move two elements from the MainMenu nib to the ActivityView nib. Look inside the Main-Menu.xib's Document window, and find your text field and image well.

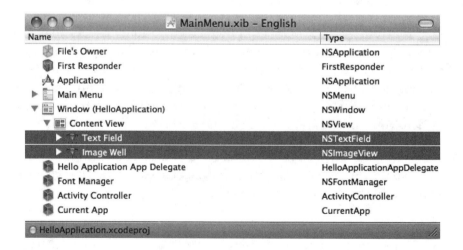

Drag these two items from MainMenu.xib into ActivityView.xib, and position them so that they are children of the custom view.

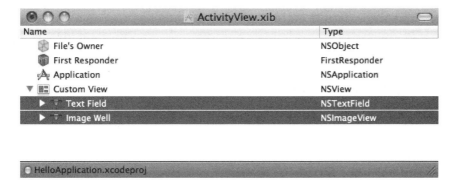

Delete them from the MainMenu.xib. Back in ActivityView.xib, double-click Custom View, reposition the image well and text field, and resize the custom view.

We have a few more steps to connect everything back up. First, let's take some time to better understand the nib and the File's Owner.

14.5 Integrating a Nib File

Remember that a nib is a frozen graph of objects. For the nib files that you will create and bring to life, there will need to be an object that sends the message to load the nib file, and there needs to be an object that is responsible for connecting the objects in the nib file to objects in the already running application. There is no formal name for this first role. Any object can send the message to load the nib file. The object that is responsible for connecting the nib to the running application is called the *File's Owner.*

Every nib needs an object called the File's Owner. This object must exist before the nib is loaded. In fact, as you'll see in the examples in this chapter, the File's Owner can also be the object that loads the nib. With the MainMenu nib the File's Owner is the application object. It is instantiated before the nib is loaded. At some point, our new ActivityView nib will be loaded. We're going to set its File's Owner to be the ActivityController object created in the MainMenu nib.

To understand the role of the File's Owner, imagine there's a party that you and a group of your friends want to attend. You have no idea where the party is, and you don't know anyone there. A voice on the phone tells you to just to hang out and wait until someone comes to get you. You'll be taken to the party and be introduced to your *Connection*.

"How will I know this Connection?" you ask.

"You'll recognize the type," you're told.

And so you and your friends hang out much like a graph of objects frozen in a nib file. Hours pass. While you hang out in your nib, the application is like the party going on without you. At the party there are objects interacting and sending messages back and forth.

There's a knock at the door. You and your friends stretch and start chatting among yourselves. The door bursts open.

"C'mon," says a gruff voice, "all of you get in the car." Ahhh, this is the object whose job it is to load the nib.

You arrive at the party and get out of the car. You and your friends look around feeling lost. You look back at the driver, and he points to a man dressed in black. It's *the guy*. You've never met him before, but the voice on the phone was right. You *do* recognize the type. It's your connection—your File's Owner. He shows you and your group around and helps make introductions.

Alternate Ending

You arrive at the party and get out of the car. You and your friends look around feeling lost. You look back at the driver. He smiles back at you in a quirky way, and you realize he's *the guy*. The voice on the phone was right. Now that you're taking a good look you *do* recognize the type. It's your connection—your File's Owner. He shows you and your group around and helps make introductions.

Why are there two endings? In the first ending, the File's Owner is different from the object that loads the nib, and in the second ending, they are the same object. In both cases, the nib knows what type to expect, but it is up to the object that loads the nib to point out the object of that type who is actually the File's Owner.

14.6 The File's Owner

One advantage of having small focused nib files like ActivityView.xib is that we can choose a File's Owner that better fits. Here the nib file is currently the view that we'll be displaying in the main window, so our File's Owner will be in charge of managing the view and its contents. The natural choice for the File's Owner is the ActivityController object we created in MainMenu.xib.

To set the File's Owner, select File's Owner in the ActivityView.xib's Document window. Use the Identity inspector to change the class name of the File's Owner to ActivityController, and save your work.

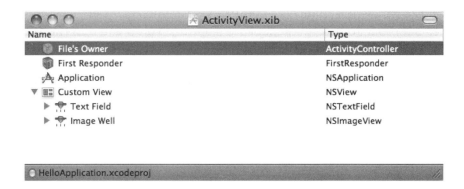

Let's connect up the ActivityController. There are five possible connections. The two reference outlets are connected in MainMenu.xib.

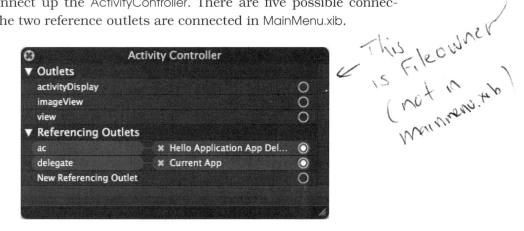

activity controller

← This is Fileowner (not in mainmenu.xib)

We need to connect the three outlets in ActivityView.xib. Connect the view outlet to the Custom View, the imageView outlet to the NSImageView, and the activityDisplay outlet to the NSTextView.

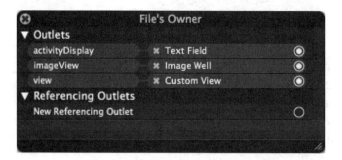

Your ActivityController object has a foot in both nibs so you can make some of the connections in the first nib and other connections in the second nib. The ActivityController object is the link between these two worlds.

I want to stress an important point here. The File's Owner ActivityController is a proxy to the ActivityController instance you created in the Main-Menu nib. It is the same object.

If instead you had dragged an ActivityController into the ActivityView nib, you would have been creating a new instance of the ActivityController. These would have been two separate objects, so the connections in one nib and the connections in the other nib would not have helped communicate at all.

14.7 Exercise: Loading the View

Click Build & Run, and the code should compile, build, and run, and an empty window should appear.

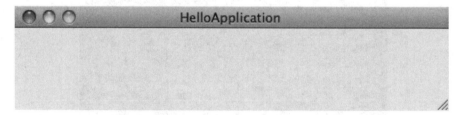

We need to fix this. Which object can communicate with the window and the view controller? Use that object to set the window's content view to be the view controller's view. We could do this in IB, but let's do it in code.

You'll know you've gotten it right when you click Build & Run and the text field and image well are visible again and filled in.

14.8 Solution: Loading the View

Your application delegate is the object with properties for the window and the view controller. All you need to do is import the ActivityController header file and set the content view to be the view controller's view like this:

MultipleNibs/HelloApplication19/HelloApplicationAppDelegate.m

```
#import "HelloApplicationAppDelegate.h"
▶ #import "ActivityController.h"

@implementation HelloApplicationAppDelegate

@synthesize window, ac, currentApp;

- (void)applicationDidFinishLaunching:(NSNotification *)aNotification {
▶     self.window.contentView = ac.view;
}
@end
```

Why is this View? (remember we made ac an activity controller which is child of NSViewController

Click Build & Run, and our application should run just as it did at the end of the previous chapter.[1]

14.9 Creating the Window Nib

We're going to split the MainMenu nib into two pieces again. We'll create a new nib that contains the window. Let's create a window controller that we can use as the File's Owner. In Xcode, select the Classes folder in Groups & Files, create a new file of type Mac OS X > Cocoa Class > Objective-C Class, and use the drop-down list to select NSWindow-Controller. Name your class MyWindowController.

---

1. There were a lot of steps used to create and use the new nib. Remember, you can look at the downloadable code to compare this version with the previous one.

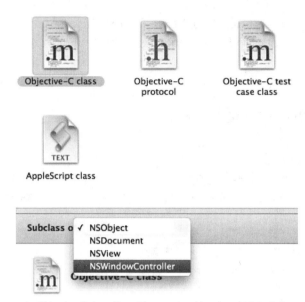

An Objective-C class file, with an optional header which includes the <Cocoa/Cocoa.h> header.

Now select the Resources folder, and create a new file using the Mac OS X > User Interface > Window XIB template. Name the nib MainWindow.xib. Use the Identity inspector to change the type of the File's Owner to MyWindowController.

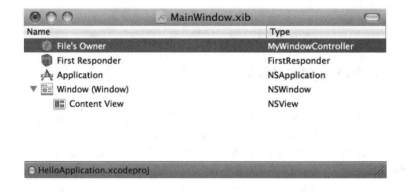

Use the Attributes inspector to change the window's title to Hello Application. Connect your File's Owner's window outlet to your window, and save your work. We'll come back to this nib in a little bit, but first let's back up and clean out the MainMenu nib.

14.10 Loading the Window Nib

Open MainMenu.xib. Delete the CurrentApp object, the ActivityController object, and the NSWindow object along with the ContentView inside of it. There's not much left—just the app delegate, the menu, and a couple of stock items.

The app delegate no longer has a connection to the model, the window, or the view controller. We'll figure out where to reconnect all of these objects in a bit. Right now we can clear out the header file for our app delegate:

MultipleNibs/HelloApplication20/HelloApplicationAppDelegate.h

```
#import <Cocoa/Cocoa.h>

@interface HelloApplicationAppDelegate : NSObject <NSApplicationDelegate> {
}

@end
```

In the implementation file, we'll instantiate the window controller and load its nib file:

MultipleNibs/HelloApplication20/HelloApplicationAppDelegate.m

```
#import "HelloApplicationAppDelegate.h"
► #import "MyWindowController.h"

@implementation HelloApplicationAppDelegate

- (void)applicationDidFinishLaunching:(NSNotification *)aNotification {
►    [[MyWindowController alloc] initWithWindowNibName:@"MainWindow"];
}
@end
```

The initWithWindowNibName: takes the name of the nib as an NSString. This means there can't be any compile-time checking that you've typed the name correctly. You type in the name of the nib but not the suffix

(.nib or .xib). If you click Build & Run, your app will compile, build, and launch, but the application's window won't appear. Let's fix that next.

14.11 Presenting the Window

Override the initWithWindowNibName: method in MyWindowController.m. Click Build & Run, and you will now see your application window once the app launches. We still have some work to do to connect the view and the model so that we see the applications as they launch and terminate.

MultipleNibs/HelloApplication20/MyWindowController.m

```
#import "MyWindowController.h"

@implementation MyWindowController

-(id) initWithWindowNibName:(NSString *)windowNibName {
    if (self = [super initWithWindowNibName:windowNibName]) {
        [self showWindow:self];
    }
    return self;
}

@end
```

14.12 Exercise: Connecting the View and the Model

You already know one way to connect the view and the model. You can add an ActivityController and a CurrentApp object to MainWindow.xib, create corresponding outlets in the window controller header file, and set the window's content view in the window controller implementation file.

We're going to try a different approach. There really isn't any need to add the view controller and the model to our nib file, so we're going to do it all in code. This should feel a lot like what we just did when creating the window controller and specifying the nib in code.

Add properties for the view controller and the model to MyWindowController.h. In the implementation file, create your ActivityController object, and initialize it using initWithNibName:bundle:. The nib name is ActivityView, and you should pass in nil for the bundle. Create an instance of CurrentApp as well, and set the ActivityController to be its delegate. Set the window's content view to be the ActivityController's view. If you want, see whether you can figure out how to resize the window to exactly fit around your view.

Click Build & Run. Don't panic. It doesn't look as if anything is happening. The window should launch, and you should see the image well and the text field, but they will be empty. HelloApplication finished launching before your model registered to listen for notifications. Start up iCal, and you'll see the icon and message appear as expected. Try to fix this problem so that the HelloApplication's icon and launch method appear when we start up.

14.13 Solution: Connecting the View and the Model

We added the properties to the header file:

MultipleNibs/HelloApplication21/MyWindowController.h

```
#import <Cocoa/Cocoa.h>
@class CurrentApp;
@class ActivityController;

@interface MyWindowController : NSWindowController {
    CurrentApp *currentApp;
    ActivityController *ac;
}
@property CurrentApp *currentApp;
@property ActivityController *ac;

@end
```

Let's take a more careful look at the implementation file:

MultipleNibs/HelloApplication21/MyWindowController.m

```
Line 1  #import "MyWindowController.h"
   -    #import "ActivityController.h"
   -    #import "CurrentApp.h"
   -
   5    @implementation MyWindowController
   -
   -    @synthesize ac, currentApp;
   -
   -    -(void) setUpView {
  10        self.ac = [[ActivityController alloc]
   -                    initWithNibName:@"ActivityView" bundle:nil];
   -        self.currentApp = [[CurrentApp alloc] init];
   -        self.currentApp.delegate = self.ac;
   -        [self.window setContentSize:[self.ac.view bounds].size];
  15        self.window.contentView = self.ac.view;
   -        [self.ac applicationDidLaunch:[NSRunningApplication currentApplication]];
   -    }
   -
```

```
   -    -(id) initWithWindowNibName:(NSString *)windowNibName {
   20       if (self = [super initWithWindowNibName:windowNibName]) {
   -           [self setUpView];
   -           [self showWindow:self];
   -       }
   -       return self;
   25    }
   -    @end
```

- We instantiate the ActivityController and load the nib it will control in lines 10 and 11.

- We instantiate the CurrentApp object on the next line and then set the ActivityController to be its delegate.

- On line 14, we resize the window so that its content size exactly matches the size of the view.

- Once its properly sized, we then set the content view to be replaced by the view controller's view.

- Finally on line 16, we initialize the view controller to use the icon and app name for our HelloApplication app.

We now have three separate nibs that are cohesive and easy to understand. The first, MainMenu.xib, consists of the app, the app delegate, and the (unused) menu. The second nib is loaded, and its File's Owner is created by the app delegate. The second nib, MainWindow.xib, contains the window and has the window controller as its File's Owner. The window controller loads the third nib and creates its File's Owner—the ActivityController along with the model. This third nib, ActivityView.xib, contains the view and has the view controller as its File's Owner.

There were a lot of steps in this chapter. The techniques are important. Keep your eye on your nib files the same way you do on your classes. When they get too big and lose focus, then consider splitting them. There are two main reasons to split a nib file. First, you want to keep them cohesive and single-purpose. Second, as you'll see in Chapter 17, *Saving Data to Disk*, on page 261, you can manage your memory better by loading the nib when you need it and releasing the memory when you aren't using it.

Chapter 15

Creating Custom Views

Until now, we've used Interface Builder to build our entire view. In this chapter, we're taking the first step toward a more complicated UI. You're going to have to supplement the information entered in Interface Builder with code. You are going to subclass NSView to create your own custom views.

We'll start by drawing the launched or terminated application's icon into an NSImageView. Then we will create a custom view and learn how to draw shapes and text on it. Finally, we'll move your icon display onto the custom view so that you will see how to draw images in a custom view.

15.1 Creating a Custom View

Create a new view-based nib file to use for our drawing, and call it IconView.xib. We'll need a view controller for this nib, so create a new NSObject named IconViewController. Change the header file so that it extends NSViewController and implements the ActivityMonitorDelegate protocol.

CustomView/HelloApplication22/IconViewController.h

```
#import <Cocoa/Cocoa.h>
#import "ActivityMonitorDelegate.h"

@interface IconViewController :NSViewController <ActivityMonitorDelegate>{
}
@end
```

The ActivityMonitorDelegate protocol has two required methods, so we have to stub them out in IconViewController.m:

```objc
#import "IconViewController.h"

@implementation IconViewController

-(void) applicationDidLaunch: (NSRunningApplication *) app {}
-(void) applicationDidTerminate: (NSRunningApplication *) app {}

@end
```

Now, here's the part that's different.

We're going to create a custom class for the view. Create a new class of type NSView, and name it IconView.[1] We'll spend much of this chapter working with the IconView class, but first let's set up the infrastructure around it.

In IconView.xib, use the Identity inspector to change the File's Owner's class to IconViewController and the view's class to IconView. Use the Connections inspector to connect the IconViewController's view outlet to the IconView. Also use the Size inspector to set the IconView's width to be 216 and height to be 240. Save your work, and quit IB.

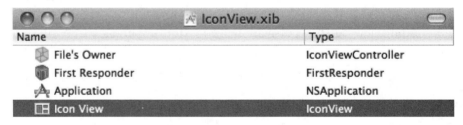

We also need to change MyWindowController to create an IconViewController and load the IconView nib. In the MyWindowController header file, we can just change all of the instances of ActivityController to IconViewController.

---

1. Select the Objective-C class template, and use the drop-down list to find the NSView option.

CustomView/HelloApplication22/MyWindowController.h

```
#import <Cocoa/Cocoa.h>
@class CurrentApp;
@class IconViewController;

@interface MyWindowController : NSWindowController {
    CurrentApp *currentApp;
    IconViewController *ac;
}
@property CurrentApp *currentApp;
@property IconViewController *ac;

@end
```

The only two changes to the implementation are to add the import of IconViewController.h and to change the line where we create the view controller and load the nib to this:

CustomView/HelloApplication22/MyWindowController.m

```
self.ac = [[IconViewController alloc]
        initWithNibName:@"IconView" bundle:nil];
```

Click Build & Run, and you should see an empty window proudly displaying our new view. In a minute, we'll fill this window with something.

15.2 Drawing Shapes into a Custom View

Before we draw shapes or text into a custom view, you need to understand how an NSView draws itself. It's different from what you've seen so far.

In the previous chapter, when you drew an icon onto an image view, you sent the message setImage: to an instance of NSImageView. Also, when you wanted to display text in a text field, you sent the message setStringValue: to an instance of NSTextField. This is probably a model you are used to from other platforms. You call the various configuring and drawing methods on the object you are drawing.

Drawing into an NSView is completely different. You set all of the parameters and instructions for the drawing inside the NSView's drawRect: method. You don't call drawRect: directly. It will be called when your view first needs to be drawn, and soon I'll show you how you signal that it needs to be called again to redraw a view.

For now, here's how we would create a blue rectangle inside the view:

CustomView/HelloApplication23/IconView.m

```
#import "IconView.h"

@implementation IconView

- (void)drawRect:(NSRect)dirtyRect {
▶      NSRect innerRect = NSMakeRect(18, 42, 180, 180);
▶      [[NSColor blueColor] set];
▶      [NSBezierPath fillRect:innerRect];
}

@end
```

At first this looks weird. You are sending the set message to the NSColor object. It may seem at first that you *should* be telling the NSView to set its color to blue. With views, you need to keep in mind that they draw themselves. When they need to be redrawn, the focus is locked on the view being drawn, its drawRect: method is called, and then the focus is unlocked.

Here's how you have to think about the drawing that goes on within the drawRect: method. When you send set to [NSColor blueColor], you are saying, "Blue crayon you are selected. Put yourself in my hand." Then in the next line when you fill in the rectangle, the blue crayon is in your hand, so that's what you use.

Suppose you now want to draw a black boundary around your blue rectangle. If we use the same dimensions for the rectangle and choose a stroke width of 12, our framed rectangle will look like this:

Notice there's more room below the rectangle than there is above it. That's because the coordinate system is anchored in the lower-left corner of our view. The x-axis increases to the right, and the y-axis increases from bottom to top. So, we've constructed a rectangle that starts at the point (18, 42) with width and height 180. The stroke, unless we specify otherwise, will straddle the line, so really the bottom-left corner of the black frame is at the point (12, 36).

A lot of our work with graphics objects will feel more like C than Objective-C. For example, this NSRect is a struct that represents a rectangle. It consists of two other structs: an NSPoint that is used to specify the position of the rectangle and an NSSize that is used to specify the width and height of the rectangle.

Also note that NSMakeRect() is a standard C function and not an Objective-C method. You'll find these constructor functions for most of the structs that you will use.

Once you've created your rectangle, you'll use it for the blue fill and for the black stroke. After you've finished filling in your blue rectangle, you then say [[NSColor blackColor] set] and draw something different with your black crayon. Instead of the fillRect:, this time you'll use strokeRect: to draw a black border around the blue rectangle.

CustomView/HelloApplication24/IconView.m

```
- (void)drawRect:(NSRect)dirtyRect {
    NSRect innerRect = NSMakeRect(18, 42, 180, 180);
    [[NSColor blueColor] set];
    [NSBezierPath fillRect:innerRect];
    [[NSColor blackColor] set];
    [NSBezierPath setDefaultLineWidth:12];
    [NSBezierPath strokeRect:innerRect];
}
```

Check out the documentation for NSBezierPath, and you can see that you can use it to draw all sorts of shapes. We'll stick with rectangles when we create a custom view for HelloApplication.

So far, we're drawing the rectangle only when the view is first instantiated. Next let's redraw the view whenever an application launches or terminates.

15.3   Exercise: Changing the Stroke Color

I want you to draw a red frame when an application quits and a green frame when one launches. Don't bother filling in the rectangle.

Add a property named alertColor of type NSColor to your IconView. Change the drawRect: code to set the pen color to the alertColor and stroke the rectangle.

Implement the applicationDidLaunch: in the IconViewController to set the IconView's alertColor to green. The IconView instance is the IconViewController's view. Unfortunately, you need to cast the type of the variable view to be an IconView in order to set the alertColor property.

There is one more step. You need to mark the IconView as dirty so that it will be redrawn. You signal that the view needs to be redrawn by sending it the following message:

```
[self.view setNeedsDisplay:YES]
```

Implement the applicationDidTerminate: method, and set the alertColor to red. Click Build & Run. When the application finishes launching, you should see a green frame. When you quit another application, the frame should turn to red.

15.4   Solution: Changing the Stroke Color

When you add the alertColor property, you need to specify the memory attribute as copy because NSColor conforms to the NSCopying protocol. I've also added an NSRect named frameRect as an instance variable.

```
CustomView/HelloApplication25/IconView.h
#import <Cocoa/Cocoa.h>

@interface IconView : NSView {
    NSColor *alertColor;
    NSRect frameRect;
}
@property(copy) NSColor *alertColor;
@end
```

In the view's implementation file, we send the set method to the alert-Color and stroke the boundary of the rectangle. I've created the rectangle and set the line width to 12 in awakeFromNib to avoid doing so every time drawRect: is called.

CustomView/HelloApplication25/IconView.m

```objc
#import "IconView.h"

@implementation IconView

@synthesize alertColor;

- (void)drawRect:(NSRect)dirtyRect {
    [self.alertColor set];
    [NSBezierPath strokeRect:frameRect];
}

-(void) awakeFromNib {
    frameRect = NSMakeRect(18, 42, 180, 180);
    [NSBezierPath setDefaultLineWidth:12];
}
@end
```

In the IconViewController, we set the view's frame color and tell the view it needs to redraw itself.

CustomView/HelloApplication25/IconViewController.m

```objc
#import "IconViewController.h"
#import "IconView.h"

@implementation IconViewController

-(void) applicationDidLaunch: (NSRunningApplication *) app {
    ((IconView *)self.view).alertColor = [NSColor greenColor];
    [self.view setNeedsDisplay:YES];
}
-(void) applicationDidTerminate: (NSRunningApplication *) app {
    ((IconView *)self.view).alertColor = [NSColor redColor];
    [self.view setNeedsDisplay:YES];
}
@end
```

Of course, this sort of drawing can become arbitrarily complex. You can build very complicated paths up from a small array of primitives and adjust many drawing parameters as you did the line width and color. When you're ready for that, you should curl up with a good book on Quartz. Two good ones are *Programming with Quartz, 2D and PDF Graphics in Mac OS X* [GL06] and *Quartz 2D graphics for Mac OS X developers* [Tho06].

Part of what makes MVC difficult to understand is that the controller and the model or the controller and the view are often mixed. You'll even see some aspects of the controller mixed into what we think of as view components such as buttons. Here you can see a clean split in responsibilities between the IconViewController and the IconView.

15.5 Drawing Images

We're going to draw the application icon in a subview of our custom view so that it appears inside our frame. This turns out to be surprisingly straightforward. We'll create an image view, size it, and set it to be a subview of the custom view.

CustomView/HelloApplication26/IconView.m

```
-(void) awakeFromNib {
    frameRect = NSMakeRect(18, 42, 180, 180);
    [NSBezierPath setDefaultLineWidth:12];
▶   imageRect = NSMakeRect(36, 66, 144, 144);
▶   self.imageView = [[NSImageView alloc] initWithFrame:imageRect];
▶   [self addSubview:self.imageView];
}
```

You can see that we need to declare a property named imageView and an instance variable named imageRect.

CustomView/HelloApplication26/IconView.h

```
#import <Cocoa/Cocoa.h>

@interface IconView : NSView {
    NSColor *alertColor;
    NSRect frameRect;
▶   NSRect imageRect;
▶   NSImageView *imageView;
}
@property(copy) NSColor *alertColor;
▶ @property NSImageView *imageView;
@end
```

As before, I've factored out the repeated code in our two delegate methods and added this highlighted line to set the contents of our imageView property's image to be the active application's icon.

CustomView/HelloApplication26/IconViewController.m

```
#import "IconViewController.h"
#import "IconView.h"

@implementation IconViewController

-(void) displayColor:(NSColor *) color for:(NSRunningApplication *) app {
    ((IconView *)self.view).alertColor = color;
```

```
        ((IconView *)self.view).imageView.image = app.icon;
        [self.view setNeedsDisplay:YES];
}
-(void) applicationDidLaunch: (NSRunningApplication *) app {
        [self displayColor:[NSColor greenColor] for:app];
}
-(void) applicationDidTerminate: (NSRunningApplication *) app {
        [self displayColor:[NSColor redColor] for:app];
}
@end
```

Unfortunately, the actual image is too small. When it comes time for drawRect: to be called, the image will be redrawn at its default size. I'd like it to fill most of the frame, so I've added a line to resize the image to the drawRect: method.

CustomView/HelloApplication26/IconView.m

```
- (void)drawRect:(NSRect)dirtyRect {
    [self.alertColor set];
    [NSBezierPath strokeRect:frameRect];
    [self.imageView.image setSize:imageRect.size];
}
```

Click Build & Run. As you launch and quit applications, you should see something like this:

Step back a minute, and think about what you've done to draw an image. You've instantiated a container for that image and set its location and dimensions. You've then filled the container with the image. The process is that straightforward.

15.6 Drawing Text

You should use a text field or a text view when you are displaying a lot of text. We aren't. We are displaying a simple and short message, so we can draw text into our custom view. This section shows you the techniques you'll use when you need to draw text into a custom view.

To draw a string into the custom view, we'll send the message drawin-Rect:withAttributes: to that string inside the drawRect: method. This method takes two parameters. The first is the location and dimensions of the rectangle into which the string will be drawn. The second is a dictionary containing any special attributes you want to set.

Add an instance variable for the rectangle and for the string that will hold the name of the application to IconView.h. Create a property for the appName variable:

CustomView/HelloApplication27/IconView.h

```
#import <Cocoa/Cocoa.h>

@interface IconView : NSView {
    NSColor *alertColor;
    NSRect frameRect;
    NSImageView *imageView;
    NSRect imageRect;
▶    NSString *appName;
▶    NSRect textRect;
}
@property(copy) NSColor *alertColor;
@property NSImageView *imageView;
▶ @property(copy) NSString *appName;
@end
```

In IconView.m, add this line to create this rectangle to the end of the awakeFromNib method:

CustomView/HelloApplication27/IconView.m

```
textRect = NSMakeRect(36, 10, 144, 20);
```

That way, you create the rectangle once, and you write different text in it every time the drawRect: method is called. In this version, we'll use the default look, so we'll pass in nil in place of the dictionary. Add this line to the end of the drawRect: method:

CustomView/HelloApplication27/IconView.m

```
[self.appName drawInRect:textRect withAttributes:nil];
```

You should see this "default" look:

You can change the look of this string by entering attributes in a mutable dictionary. For example, we can fill a dictionary with the following attributes to make the string blue, bold, and centered.[2]

CustomView/HelloApplication28/IconView.m

```
NSMutableParagraphStyle *par = [[NSMutableParagraphStyle alloc] init];
[par setAlignment:NSCenterTextAlignment];
textAttributes = [[NSMutableDictionary alloc] initWithObjectsAndKeys:
                [NSColor blueColor], NSForegroundColorAttributeName,
                par, NSParagraphStyleAttributeName,
                [NSFont boldSystemFontOfSize:12], NSFontAttributeName,
                nil];
```

It took us remarkably little code to implement this effect with our custom view and its controller. Here's the final implementation of the view controller:

CustomView/HelloApplication28/IconViewController.m

```
#import "IconViewController.h"
#import "IconView.h"

@implementation IconViewController

-(void) displayColor:(NSColor *) color for:(NSRunningApplication *) app {
    ((IconView *)self.view).alertColor = color;
    ((IconView *)self.view).imageView.image = app.icon;
    ((IconView *)self.view).appName = app.localizedName;
    [self.view setNeedsDisplay:YES];
}
```

---

2. For a list of the standard attributes for displaying strings, see http://developer.apple. com/documentation/Cocoa/Reference/ApplicationKit/Classes/NSAttributedString_AppKitAdditions/ Reference/Reference.html#//apple_ref/doc/uid/20000167-BAJJCCFC. You can also just search on NSAttributedString(AppKitAdditions) in the developer documentation.

```objc
-(void) applicationDidLaunch: (NSRunningApplication *) app {
    [self displayColor:[NSColor greenColor] for:app];
}
-(void) applicationDidTerminate: (NSRunningApplication *) app {
    [self displayColor:[NSColor redColor] for:app];
}
@end
```

The result should look like this:

The header file for our IconView has grown. We've introduced a lot of instance variables, but only the three that need to be set by the view controller have been exposed as properties.

CustomView/HelloApplication28/IconView.h

```objc
#import <Cocoa/Cocoa.h>

@interface IconView : NSView {
    NSColor *alertColor;
    NSRect frameRect;
    NSImageView *imageView;
    NSRect imageRect;
    NSString *appName;
    NSRect textRect;
    NSMutableDictionary *textAttributes;
}
@property(copy) NSColor *alertColor;
@property NSImageView *imageView;
@property(copy) NSString *appName;
@end
```

I've refactored IconView.m to separate out the initialization of the three different pieces. We've also managed to keep the drawRect: method small and straightforward.

```
#import "IconView.h"

@implementation IconView

@synthesize alertColor, imageView, appName;

- (void)drawRect:(NSRect)dirtyRect {
    [self.alertColor set];
    [NSBezierPath strokeRect:frameRect];
    [self.imageView.image setSize:imageRect.size];
    [self.appName drawInRect:textRect withAttributes:textAttributes];
}
-(void) setUpFrameRect {
    frameRect = NSMakeRect(18, 42, 180, 180);
    [NSBezierPath setDefaultLineWidth:12];
}
-(void) setUpImageView {
    imageRect = NSMakeRect(36, 66, 144, 144);
    self.imageView = [[NSImageView alloc] initWithFrame:imageRect];
    [self addSubview:self.imageView];
}
-(void) setUpTextView {
    textRect = NSMakeRect(36, 10, 144, 20);
    NSMutableParagraphStyle *par = [[NSMutableParagraphStyle alloc] init];
    [par setAlignment:NSCenterTextAlignment];
    textAttributes = [[NSMutableDictionary alloc] initWithObjectsAndKeys:
                        [NSColor blueColor], NSForegroundColorAttributeName,
                        par, NSParagraphStyleAttributeName,
                        [NSFont boldSystemFontOfSize:12], NSFontAttributeName,
                        nil];
}
-(void) awakeFromNib {
    [self setUpFrameRect];
    [self setUpImageView];
    [self setUpTextView];
}
@end
```

So, now you have created a custom view where you draw shapes, text, and images. You've seen how to create and configure visual objects in code. In this chapter, we focused on the view. In the next chapter, we'll create a table to hold the list of all running applications.

Chapter 16

Displaying Data in a Table

We're going to work with successively cooler and more powerful ways to interact with data between now and the end of the book. In this chapter, you'll learn a fairly basic way to display data in a table view.

We'll use an array as the data source for our table view. Each entry in the array will consist of an NSRunningApplication instance that will be used to populate a row in our displayed table. The object properties will correspond to the table columns. This correspondence between column identifiers and properties will be your first step on our journey through Key Value Coding, Key Value Observing, and the rest of Bindings on our way to Core Data.

By the end of this chapter, your table view will respond to updates to the underlying data, and you will be able to update your data from the table view. To get going, we'll create a table view and tie it to a simulated data source.

16.1 Tables and Data Sources

Let's start by setting up your table view and its corresponding data source. In this first example, you'll just fill each cell in the table with its row and column numbers. We can reuse the ActivityView nib and the ActivityController for this example.

First, clean out the ActivityController.m file like this:

Tables/HelloApplication29/ActivityController.m

```
#import "ActivityController.h"

@implementation ActivityController

-(void) applicationDidLaunch: (NSRunningApplication *) app {}
-(void) applicationDidTerminate: (NSRunningApplication *) app {}
@end
```

Remove the properties and the instance variables from the header file as well:

Tables/HelloApplication29/ActivityController.h

```
#import <Cocoa/Cocoa.h>
#import "ActivityMonitorDelegate.h"

@interface ActivityController : NSViewController <ActivityMonitorDelegate> {
}
@end
```

We have to swap the view controller and nib loaded by MyWindowController, so let's change the header file to make this swapping back and forth a little easier. We're changing the type of the variable ac so that it is neither ActivityController nor IconViewController. Instead, we're declaring it to be of type NSViewController and specifying that it implements the ActivityMonitorDelegate protocol.

Tables/HelloApplication29/MyWindowController.h

```
#import <Cocoa/Cocoa.h>
#import "ActivityMonitorDelegate.h"
@class CurrentApp;

@interface MyWindowController : NSWindowController {
    CurrentApp *currentApp;
    NSViewController <ActivityMonitorDelegate> *ac;
}
@property CurrentApp *currentApp;
@property NSViewController <ActivityMonitorDelegate> *ac;

@end
```

(handwritten note in left margin: Current App is the Model)

In the implementation file, change your instantiation of ac to this, and add the appropriate import to the top of the file:

Tables/HelloApplication29/MyWindowController.m

```
self.ac = [[ActivityController alloc]
        initWithNibName:@"ActivityView" bundle:nil];
```

(handwritten note: part of Activity Monitor Delegate)

Double-click ActivityView.xib. When Interface Builder opens the nib file, delete the text field and image well from the view. Resize the view to be big enough to hold a two-column table with half a dozen rows or so. Drag a table view from the Library, drop it on the view, and position it using the guidelines. This component is actually an NSTableView contained in an NSScrollView. The table comes configured with two columns—you can adjust this number up or down using the Attributes inspector for the table view. Double-click the header at the top of each column, and label the left column Column 1 and the right column Column 2.

Select the table view, and connect both the dataSource and delegate outlets to the ActivityController.[1]

Unfortunately, clicking the table view is a pain. You think you're clicking it but find you have the scroll view selected instead.[2] So, you try double-clicking and find that you have a column selected. Not what you wanted. Instead, navigate the hierarchy in the document window, or hold down the Shift and Control keys and click the table. You should see something like this:

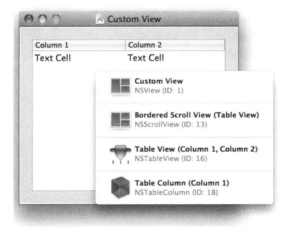

Now you can quickly select the table view and make your connections. Save your work. You have created part of the scaffolding for the table view and its data source. There are two gaping holes we need to fill. Let's explore them in a quick exercise.

---

1. The ActivityController is the File's Owner.
2. You almost never want the scroll view.

16.2 Exercise: Implementing a Basic Data Source

Click Build & Run, and you should get this error:

```
Illegal NSTableView data source (<ActivityController: 0x200053b60>).
Must implement numberOfRowsInTableView: and
         tableView:objectValueForTableColumn:row:
```

This is as helpful as an error message could possibly be. It tells us which methods to implement in ActivityController so that it can act as the data source for our table view. I'm going to let you try it first as an exercise.

The rows in a table represent different records in your data source, and the columns are various attributes for each record. So, for example, we could display a roster of people in your local CocoaHeads group. The first column might contain their first name, and the second column might contain their last name. You might even have more information in your data source (email addresses, phone numbers, ...) than you want to display in your table.

You set up the columns in Interface Builder when you created your table view, but usually you won't know the number of records in the data source until runtime. In fact, if you create an application where you can add and delete records, then this number will change at runtime. So, your data source must be able to tell the table how many rows are in the table view. The table view can then fill itself by looping through the number of visible rows and columns and asking the data source what belongs in each cell by calling the tableView:objectValueForTableColumn:row: method for each cell.

The data source records are often stored in an array, but actually they can be stored any way you want as long as the data source can respond to the two methods numberOfRowsInTableView: and tableView:objectValueForTableColumn:row:. What this amounts to is that the records must be able to be indexed by integers.

Implement these methods in the most simplistic way possible. Return a fixed integer from numberOfRowsInTableView:. Choose a large enough number like 100 so that the scroll view is engaged as well. Return the row number (as a string) from tableView:objectValueForTableColumn:row:. Both columns of the row will show the row number.

Use the documentation to get the method signatures right. Search the docs on the name of the method. Once you locate the method, copy the method signature from the documentation and paste it into your code. Whatever you do, don't type all of that in yourself!

Uh-oh. We have another problem. You should have an easy enough time returning the row number, but how do you find the column number? Search through the NSTableColumn docs, and you'll see methods like identifier, dataCellForRow:, and headerCell. It doesn't look as if the column knows its index number. You'll soon see why. For now, just fill each cell with the row number.

16.3 Solution: Implementing a Basic Data Source

You shouldn't have made any changes to the ActivityController header file. If you stop to think a moment, that may actually be surprising. You didn't have to declare that ActivityController is implementing the NSTableViewDataSource or NSTableViewDelegate protocol. You are free to add them if you want—in fact, that might better communicate the purpose of the ActivityController to others reading your source code. You aren't required to because only the table view will be calling the methods declared in the protocol, so no warnings will appear.

As for the implementation file, you should have added these methods:

Tables/HelloApplication30/ActivityController.m

```
- (NSInteger)numberOfRowsInTableView:(NSTableView *)aTableView {
    return 100;
}
- (id)          tableView:(NSTableView *)aTableView
objectValueForTableColumn:(NSTableColumn *)aTableColumn
                      row:(NSInteger)rowIndex {
    return [NSString stringWithFormat:@"Row = %d", rowIndex];
}
```

Click Build & Run. With the application running, double-click the first column to select it. Drag that column to the right until the two columns switch places like the picture on the following page.

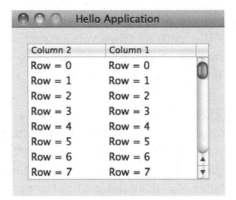

So, we can't and shouldn't identify columns by their position because this position could change. We ordinarily would not have used a number in the header for each column either, but I wanted it to be visually clear that the two had switched places.

16.4 Exercise: Introducing a Data Source

Right now we don't have any real data backing our table. Let's create an array of the applications that are running when our application first launches and display that in the table. For now you'll display the same information in both columns.

Declare a mutable array called runningApps to be a property of Activity-Controller. Override initWithNibName:Bundle: to set the value of this array to runningApplications for the shared instance of the NSWorkspace.[3]

Your table view is going to display the contents of the runningApps array. How many rows are there in the table? The answer to that question is the value you will return from numberOfRowsInTableView.

All that remains is for you to fill each cell with the application name for each record. The runningApps array is filled with objects of type NSRunningApplication. You know how to retrieve the application name. You'll need to get the object from the runningApps array that has the same index as the rowIndex.

---

3. This is marked as a class method in the docs, but at the time of this writing is implemented as an instance method.

Your application should look something like this:

16.5   Solution: Introducing a Data Source

Add the runningApps property to your header file. It looks odd, but we have to specify the memory attribute as retain. Usually we get that for free by not specifying any attribute. This would give us the default attribute of assign, which under garbage collection is equivalent to retain. The problem here is that NSMutableArray extends NSArray, which uses copy, so we need to explicitly specify retain so that the compiler is confident we know what we're doing:

Tables/HelloApplication31/ActivityController.h

```
#import <Cocoa/Cocoa.h>
#import "ActivityMonitorDelegate.h"

@interface ActivityController : NSViewController <ActivityMonitorDelegate,
                                    NSTableViewDelegate, NSTableViewDataSource> {
    NSMutableArray *runningApps;
}
@property(retain) NSMutableArray *runningApps;
@end
```

Next we hop over to the implementation file. How many rows should our table have? It should have as many rows as there are running applications. When your table is backed by an array, then the number of rows in the table view at any time should be equal to the current count for the array.

Tables/HelloApplication31/ActivityController.m

```
- (NSInteger)numberOfRowsInTableView:(NSTableView *)aTableView {
    return [runningApps count];
}
```

What should get returned for the cells in a particular row? The local-izedName of the RunningApplication object at that same index should be returned.

Tables/HelloApplication31/ActivityController.m

```
- (id)tableView:(NSTableView *)aTableView
      objectValueForTableColumn:(NSTableColumn *)aTableColumn
                          row:(NSInteger)rowIndex {
    return [[runningApps objectAtIndex:rowIndex] localizedName];
}
```

The hard part of this exercise is initializing runningApps. We can't just cast the runningApplications array to a mutable array. Instead, we create a mutable array and then add the contents of runningApplications to it.

Tables/HelloApplication31/ActivityController.m

```
- (id)initWithNibName:(NSString *)nibName bundle:(NSBundle *)nibBundle{
    if (self = [super initWithNibName:nibName  bundle:nibBundle] ) {
        self.runningApps = [NSMutableArray arrayWithCapacity:20];
        [self.runningApps addObjectsFromArray:[[NSWorkspace sharedWorkspace]
                                              runningApplications]];
    }
    return self;
}
```

Next, let's take this to the next stage and display something different in each column.

16.6 Filling Cells Based on Table Column Titles

It's easy for the body of the tableView:objectValueForTableColumn:row: method to get ugly. How, for example, would you display the application's icon in the first column and its name in the second?

To start, we have to modify the nib file so that you can display images in the first column. Open ActivityView.xib in Interface Builder. Look in the Library for NSImageCell. Drag it on top of the first column. The word *TextCell* should be replaced with the generic application icon.

Change the title of the first column to Icon and the second to Name:

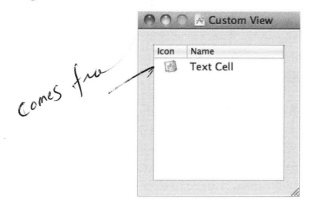

comes fro [handwritten annotation]

Icon View Controller In your Sample Code was not Used yet [handwritten annotation]

You might be tempted to use something like this if/else construction:

`Tables/HelloApplication32/ActivityController.m`

```
//don't even think of doing it this way
- (id)tableView:(NSTableView *)aTableView
      objectValueForTableColumn:(NSTableColumn *)aTableColumn
                        row:(NSInteger)rowIndex {
    if([[[aTableColumn headerCell] title] isEqualToString:@"Icon"]){
        return [[self.runningApps objectAtIndex:rowIndex] icon];
    } else {
    return [[self.runningApps objectAtIndex:rowIndex] localizedName];
    }
}
```

The good news is that the code does exactly what we want it to do.
We see the application icons in the left column and their names in the
right.

The bad news is that this is tremendously ugly code. We don't want to
have to use an if statement every time we fill a table cell. We used a

dictionary to eliminate an if in another part of our code. This time we'll use another technique.

16.7 Table Column Identifiers as Keys

Instead of using the column header titles in our if statement, we can use another property of table columns called the *identifier*. The title is text that is visible at the top of the column in the header cell. That text is meant to communicate with the application user. The identifier is invisible to the end user. The data source uses it to identify the column. We can use the identifier as a key in a dictionary or as a name of a property or method.

So, select the table's first column in Interface Builder, and use the Attributes inspector to set the Identifier to icon. Similarly, set the Identifier in the second column to localizedName. I haven't chosen those names at random; these are the names of the properties in the NSRunning-Application class that I want to appear in each of the columns.

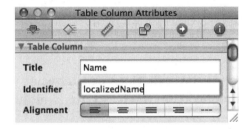

Now we can call the method with the same name as the identifier. It is just the getter for the property with that name.

Tables/HelloApplication33/ActivityController.m

```
- (id)tableView:(NSTableView *)aTableView
      objectValueForTableColumn:(NSTableColumn *)aTableColumn
                           row:(NSInteger)rowIndex {
▶    return [[self.runningApps objectAtIndex:rowIndex]
▶        performSelector:NSSelectorFromString([aTableColumn identifier])];
}
```

Here's roughly what has to happen to fill the table with icons and names. First the table view asks its data source how many rows are in this table. The data source replies [runningApps count]. Then for each cell in the table, the table view asks its data source, "What goes here?"

The data source now answers with the information for the application whose index in the array matches the row number.[4] And in each cell the data source responds with the value of the property that matches the cell's column's identifier. Pretty nifty.

Look how this simplifies the code—there are no choices to make. Better yet, we don't have to change this code if we introduce new columns.

16.8 Previews of Coming Attractions

It turns out that one advantage of properties is that they follow a certain naming convention that allows us to treat objects as if they were dictionaries. In other words, we can pass in the name of the property whose value we want the same way we pass in keys to a dictionary. You'll learn a lot more about this in Chapter 19, *Key Value Coding*, on page 291.

This is such a great place to apply the technique that I just can't wait until we get there. You don't need to understand KVC to appreciate this application. Instead of converting the identifier to a SEL and then performing that selector, we use the valueForKey: method and pass in the identifier as the key.

```
Tables/HelloApplication34/ActivityController.m
- (id)tableView:(NSTableView *)aTableView
      objectValueForTableColumn:(NSTableColumn *)aTableColumn
                        row:(NSInteger)rowIndex {
    return [[self.runningApps objectAtIndex:rowIndex]
                    valueForKey:[aTableColumn identifier]];
}
```

This is yet another thing about programming with Cocoa that makes me smile.

16.9 Exercise: Adding and Removing Rows

Our mini-Dock now shows a snapshot of the icons and names of the applications that are running when our application launches. Next, let's update the list by adding launching apps and removing terminating apps.

---

4. Fortunately, the count for each of them begins with 0.

We could just regenerate the list each time an application launches or terminates from NSWorkspace's runningApplications array. My goal here, though, is to show you how to add to and remove from the underlying data source of a table view and then update the view.

You already have delegate methods that respond when an application is launched or terminates. Implement one to add the launching application to the bottom of the table view by adding an entry to the end of runningApps and updating the table view. Similarly, implement the other to remove the terminating application from the table view by removing the appropriate entry from runningApps and updating the table view.

16.10 Solution: Adding and Removing Rows

We are going to need to contact the table view from our ActivityController. Add an outlet to the header file:

Tables/HelloApplication35/ActivityController.h

```
#import <Cocoa/Cocoa.h>
#import "ActivityMonitorDelegate.h"

@interface ActivityController : NSViewController <ActivityMonitorDelegate,
NSTableViewDelegate, NSTableViewDataSource> {
    NSMutableArray *runningApps;
    NSTableView *table;
}
@property(retain) NSMutableArray *runningApps;
@property IBOutlet NSTableView *table;
@end
```

In Interface Builder, connect this outlet to your table view.

Back in Xcode, you should have added these two methods to your implementation file for ActivityController. Then add and remove the appropriate entry to the runningApps array, and tell the table view to reload.[5]

Tables/HelloApplication35/ActivityController.m

```
-(void) applicationDidLaunch: (NSRunningApplication *) app {
    [self.runningApps addObject:app];
    [self.table reloadData];
}
```

---

5. Also, you should remember that every time we add a property in a header file that you need to synthesize it in the corresponding implementation file.

```
-(void) applicationDidTerminate: (NSRunningApplication *) app {
    [self.runningApps removeObject:app];
    [self.table reloadData];
}
```

16.11 Manually Removing Rows

So far, we have initiated changes in the data source that are reflected in the table. In this section, we're also going to take advantage of the fact that we set the ActivityController to also be the delegate for the table view.

Let's add a Remove button to our application. This will allow the user to remove applications from the list. The button will become visible only when the user selects an application in the table view. Then if the user clicks the button, the selected application will disappear from the list, and we'll hide the button again.

Start by adding an outlet and an action to your ActivityController header file. The outlet will connect to the new button, and the action will be the method that gets called when the button is clicked.

Tables/HelloApplication36/ActivityController.h

```
#import <Cocoa/Cocoa.h>
#import "ActivityMonitorDelegate.h"

@interface ActivityController : NSViewController <ActivityMonitorDelegate,
NSTableViewDelegate, NSTableViewDataSource> {
    NSMutableArray *runningApps;
    NSTableView *table;
►   NSButton *deleteButton;
}
@property(retain) NSMutableArray *runningApps;
@property IBOutlet NSTableView *table;
► @property IBOutlet NSButton *deleteButton;
► -(IBAction)removeRow:(id)sender;
@end
```

In Interface Builder, add a little square button below the table view. Instead of giving it a title, we'll display a minus sign on it. To do this, open the Attributes inspector, and set the button's image to NSRemove-Template. Also select the Hidden checkbox.

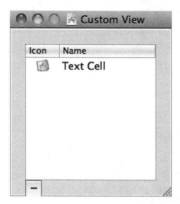

Connect the ActivityController's deleteButton outlet to the button, and wire up the removeRow: action as well. Save.

You now have two methods to implement in ActivityController. The first is a delegate method that is called when the user selects a row. All we want to do is make the button visible when a row is selected.

Tables/HelloApplication36/ActivityController.m

```
-(void)tableViewSelectionDidChange:(NSNotification *)notification {
    [self.deleteButton setHidden:NO];
}
```

When the user clicks the Delete button, we remove the selected row from the runningApps array and reload the table view. We also make sure no row is selected in the table view anymore and hide the button.

Tables/HelloApplication36/ActivityController.m

```
-(IBAction)removeRow:(id)sender{
    [self.runningApps removeObjectAtIndex:[self.table selectedRow]];
    [self.table deselectAll:nil];
    [self.table reloadData];
    [self.deleteButton setHidden:YES];
}
```

Again, I love that the code reads pretty much like the description of what we're trying to accomplish.

Click Build & Run, and you will be able to select rows and remove them from the list. Unfortunately, if you quit HelloApplication and start it up again, the items you removed are back again. In the next chapter, we'll add persistence and preferences to this example.

Chapter 17

Saving Data to Disk

At the end of the previous chapter, we added the ability for your users to remove applications from the table view. If you're playing a game at work or surfing the Net, you might not want the game or your web browser to be in your visible list of running applications.

But, as we've coded things now, the next time you run HelloApplication, the banished items will pop up on the list again. In this chapter, you'll persist the list of removed items in two different ways. You'll also learn how to work with preferences to allow the user to choose whether to use the saved list of removed items.

As always, the example is just a vehicle. We'll look at creating, saving, and reading property lists. We'll learn to archive, save, and unarchive object graphs. Finally, we'll learn how to create and read two types of defaults.

First, we'll work with saving the list of banished apps in our running application.

17.1 Saving in Your Running Application

Before we worry about remembering the removed items from previous times we ran HelloApplication, we need to remember the removed items while our application is running. Start up HelloApplication, and I'll show you what I mean.

Remove one of the applications from your list—I'll use iCal as an example. iCal is still running, but it's not on your list. So, quit iCal. Now start iCal. See? There it is again at the end of your list of running applications. I don't want you to have to remove iCal from the list every time you restart it.

To solve this problem, we'll create a helper class for keeping track of which apps we've removed. Create a new class named BanishedApps using the NSObject template. We'll keep a list of the names of the banished applications in an NSMutableArray. We'll also need methods for adding apps to this array and for checking whether an app is already a member.

Persistence/HelloApplication37/BanishedApps.h

```objc
#import <Cocoa/Cocoa.h>

@interface BanishedApps : NSObject {
    NSMutableArray *apps;
}
@property(retain) NSMutableArray *apps;
-(void)add:(NSRunningApplication *) app;
-(BOOL)contains:(NSRunningApplication *) app;
@end
```

There's not much to our implementation. We'll initialize the mutable array in the init method. The add: and contains: methods are light wrappers that allow us to pass in objects of type NSRunningApplication but store the information as a string using the application's localizedName.

Persistence/HelloApplication37/BanishedApps.m

```objc
#import "BanishedApps.h"

@implementation BanishedApps

@synthesize apps;

-(BOOL)contains:(NSRunningApplication *) app {
    return [self.apps containsObject:app.localizedName];
}
-(void)add:(NSRunningApplication *) app {
    if ([self contains:app]) return;
    [self.apps addObject:app.localizedName];
}
-(id)init {
    if (self = [super init]) {
        self.apps = [NSMutableArray arrayWithCapacity:5];
    }
    return self;
}
@end
```

The first line of the add: method might look a little odd.

You might be more used to writing this method like this:

```
-(void) add: (NSRunningApplication *) app {
    if (![self contains:app]) {
        [self.apps addObject:app.localizedName];
    }
}
```

That version reads something like this: "If this app is not contained in our list of banished apps, then add it to the list." The approach I used instead was an early exit. If the app is already contained in our list of banished apps, then we're done here.

We have to make a few modifications to ActivityController.m. Add this line to initWithNibName:bundle: to initialize the BanishedApps object.[1]

Persistence/HelloApplication37/ActivityController.m

```
self.banishedApps = [[BanishedApps alloc] init];
```

When an application launches, you need to add this check before adding it to runningApps:

Persistence/HelloApplication37/ActivityController.m

```
-(void) applicationDidLaunch: (NSRunningApplication *) app {
    if ([self.banishedApps contains:app]) return;
    [self.runningApps addObject:app];
    [self.table reloadData];
}
```

When the user removes an application from the table, we need to add this line to add it to the banished applications:

Persistence/HelloApplication37/ActivityController.m

```
-(void) removeRow:(id) sender{
    [self.banishedApps add:[self.runningApps
                            objectAtIndex:[self.table selectedRow]]];
    [self.runningApps removeObjectAtIndex:[self.table selectedRow]];
    [self.table deselectAll:nil];
    [self.table reloadData];
    [self.deleteButton setHidden:YES];
}
```

---

1. By now you know that this line implies a lot of other code changes. You'll need to have declared the banishedApps instance variable and the corresponding property. You will have needed to synthesize the property. Finally, you would have used a forward declaration for the BanishedApps class in the ActivityController header file and the corresponding import statement at the top of the implementation file.

Click Build & Run. Remove an application. Quit that application, and restart it; this time it's not added to the table view. Cool.

We haven't made a lot of changes, but now we have everything working while HelloApplication is running. Next we will add persistence so that we don't have to remove the same applications the next time we run HelloApplication.

17.2 Where to Put Application Support

Let's save the names of the removed applications to disk every time one is added and retrieve the contents of the file when we instantiate BanishedApps. In this section, we'll work with a property list that we create from the NSMutableArray. This technique is great when you are working with a single collection that contains a small amount of data consisting of strings and numbers.

You store your application support files in a folder named for your application or company inside ~/Library/Application Support. The ~ is shorthand for your home directory. We'll use the function NSSearchPathForDirectoriesInDomains() to get the path to your application support directory like this:

```
NSSearchPathForDirectoriesInDomains(NSApplicationSupportDirectory,
                                    NSUserDomainMask, YES)
```

*code for User App Support direct_*

The first parameter is a constant indicating we want the application support directory. The second parameter is filled by a constant that indicates we want to use the user's Library directory as opposed to the system's. The third parameter is a boolean we've set to YES so that ~ is expanded to the full path to the user directory. This call will result in an array containing the path we want as its only member. We'll pull this value out of the array as a string and append the string /HelloApplication to get our full path to where we'll be storing our application data.

We'll do our work in BanishedApps.m. It's pretty ugly-looking code, but it is essentially boilerplate that you'll use to locate your application support files.

Persistence/HelloApplication38/BanishedApps.m

```
-(void) setSupportFile {
    NSFileManager *fileManager = [NSFileManager defaultManager];
    NSString *appSupport =
        [NSSearchPathForDirectoriesInDomains(
                                    NSApplicationSupportDirectory,
                                    NSUserDomainMask, YES)
            objectAtIndex:0];
```

```
NSString *dir =
    [NSString stringWithFormat:@"%@/HelloApplication", appSupport];      OK
[fileManager createDirectoryAtPath:dir
     withIntermediateDirectories:YES
                      attributes:nil
                           error: nil];
self.dataFile =
    [dir stringByAppendingPathComponent:@"removedApps.plist"];
}
```

Add the property NSString *dataFile to the BanishedApps header file. By now you may have noticed that you always need to specify the copy attribute for NSString properties. If you forget, you will be prompted to do so by a compiler warning.

You also need to add the call [self setSupportFile]; to the init method.

Click Build & Run. Navigate into ~/Library/Application Support/, and you should see a newly created directory named HelloApplication.

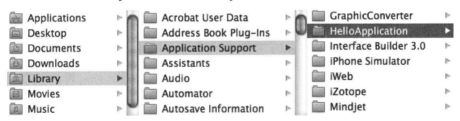

17.3   Saving to a Plist

Objects of type NSArray know how to write themselves to a plist file. In fact, any collection that consists of objects of type NSDictionary, NSArray, NSString, NSDate, NSData, or NSNumber can easily write itself to disk as a plist. You can make other objects fit by converting them to NSData and stuffing them inside an array or dictionary.

We want to save the contents of the apps array whenever we add an application to it. Add the highlighted line to your add: method.

Persistence/HelloApplication38/BanishedApps.m

```
-(void)add:(NSRunningApplication *) app {
    if ([self contains:app]) return;
    [self.apps addObject:app.localizedName];
    [self.apps writeToFile:self.dataFile atomically:YES];
}
```

This is pretty amazing. All you have to do is tell the array to save itself to a file and provide the path to that file. Arrays, dictionaries, strings,

Things that write to plist (like xml

numbers, dates, and data know how to save themselves to disk and how to reconstitute themselves later.

Click Build & Run. Remove some of your running applications. I've removed the loginwindow, AppleSpell.service, iChatAgent, and iTunes Helper. After you've removed some apps, you will have created a plist. Open it, and you should see something like this:

Key	Type	Value
▼ Root	Array	(4 items)
Item 0	String	loginwindow
Item 1	String	AppleSpell.service
Item 2	String	iChatAgent
Item 3	String	iTunes Helper

17.4 Reading a Plist

Let's move in the other direction. Now we want to be able to read our stored information and populate BanishedApps' apps array with it. In the init method, we'll check to make sure the plist file exists. If it does, we'll initialize apps with the stored values.

```
Persistence/HelloApplication38/BanishedApps.m
-(id)init {
  if (self = [super init]) {
    [self setSupportFile];
    if([[NSFileManager defaultManager] fileExistsAtPath:self.dataFile]){
      self.apps = [NSMutableArray arrayWithContentsOfFile:self.dataFile];
    } else {
      self.apps = [NSMutableArray arrayWithCapacity:5];
    }
  }
  return self;
}
```

We still have a problem. Applications that have been removed will be displayed even though they shouldn't be if they are running when we first launch HelloApplication. To prevent this, we have to modify initWithNibName:bundle: in ActivityController.m. We'll use fast enumeration to check each application in the workspace's runningApplications array. We'll only add the ones that are not on the banished list to our runningApps array.

```
- (id)initWithNibName:(NSString *)nibName bundle:(NSBundle *)nibBundle{
    if (self = [super initWithNibName:nibName  bundle:nibBundle] ) {
        self.banishedApps = [[BanishedApps alloc] init];
        self.runningApps = [NSMutableArray arrayWithCapacity:20];
▶       for (NSRunningApplication *app in
▶               [[NSWorkspace sharedWorkspace] runningApplications]) {
▶           if (![self.banishedApps contains:app]) {
▶               [self.runningApps addObject:app];
▶           }
▶       }
    }
    return self;
}
```

Click Build & Run. Applications you remove should not appear in your table view even if you quit and relaunch either HelloApplication or the applications you remove.

17.5   Saving an Archive to Disk

You'll normally use plists to persist relatively small amounts of application data (often configuration related). But what if you want to store large amounts of data or if you want to persist an object tree? For the most part, you'll want to use the techniques I'll describe in Chapter 22, *Core Data*, on page 343. There are, however, in-between times when you need to write your data as an archive.

There are essentially two levels to saving an object graph to disk. At the top level, you need to create an archive of all the objects that need to be saved and later retrieved. These actions are handled by methods in instances of the NSKeyedArchiver and NSKeyedUnarchiver classes. You pass in the object at the root of the tree, and each object will be asked to encode or decode itself.

At this object level, each object is responsible for knowing what part of its state needs to be persisted using the encodeWithCoder: method. Loading the data from disk is the inverse operation and uses each object's initWithCoder: method.

I'm not going to have you build a new application to illustrate this concept. For the most part, you should either be able to use the plist approach, or you should look to use Core Data. But imagine that the apps is an NSMutableSet instead of an NSMutableArray.[2]

Suppose you want to persist the current state of your BanishedApps object to disk. There are only two variables that we could think of persisting: apps and dataFile. It makes no sense to persist dataFile because it is the path to the directory where I would be persisting it—we'd never have any use for the saved value. So when it is time to save our BanishedApps object, we just need to encode the contents of apps. Implement the encodeWithCoder: method.

```
-(void) encodeWithCoder: (NSCoder *) coder {
    [coder encodeObject:self.apps forKey:@"bannedApps"];
}
```

You don't call encodeWithCoder:. It is called by the keyed archiver when it is saving the object tree. Our BanishedApps object is part of the tree that has an ActivityController object above it. So, we might create the archive in the window controller with a call like this:

```
[NSKeyedArchiver archiveRootObject:ac toFile:self.dataFile];
```

Here ac is the instance of the ActivityController that will be at the root of our tree, and dataFile points to the file where we are writing the data.

We reverse this process with a call like this:

```
self.ac = [NSKeyedUnarchiver unarchiveObjectWithFile:self.dataFile];
```

During the unarchiving process, each object must know how to unencode itself. We do this in a variant on the init method named initWithCoder:. For example, somewhere inside the initWithCoder: method for BanishedApps will have this line:

```
self.apps = [coder decodeObjectForKey:@"bannedApps"];
```

Those are the four steps to creating archives when your objects are comprised of types that don't know how to write themselves to files. Now let's get back to our running example and allow the user to set preferences for your application.

---

2. It is easy enough to convert an NSSet to an NSArray and back again that in practice we would do the conversion and persist as a plist. The purpose here is to show you how to use an NSCoder.

17.6   Reading and Using Preferences

We'll create a very basic preference panel that allows the user to choose whether to use the stored list of removed applications or to instead start from scratch when we launch HelloApplication. In this section, we assume the preference exists and has been set.

Currently we ask whether the data file exists before we try to restore apps from disk. Modify this check to make sure that the user wants us to restore from disk and that the data file exists.

Persistence/HelloApplication39/BanishedApps.m

```
-(id)init {
  if (self = [super init]) {
    [self setSupportFile];
    if([self shouldLoadSavedRemovedApps] &&
       [[NSFileManager defaultManager] fileExistsAtPath:self.dataFile]){
      self.apps = [NSMutableArray arrayWithContentsOfFile:self.dataFile];
    } else {
      self.apps = [NSMutableArray arrayWithCapacity:5];
    }
  }
  return self;
}
```

The method shouldLoadSavedRemovedApps returns a value based on what is stored in the preferences.

Persistence/HelloApplication39/BanishedApps.m

```
-(BOOL) shouldLoadSavedRemovedApps {
    return[[NSUserDefaults standardUserDefaults]
                          boolForKey:@"LoadSavedRemovedApps"];
}
```

This is a familiar pattern by now. You ask for the standard user defaults the same way you've asked for the default workspace or the file manager. Once you have the instance you need, you ask it for the value that corresponds to the key LoadSavedRemovedApps and return that value as a BOOL.

17.7   Setting the Factory Defaults

Let's set a default value for shouldLoadSavedRemovedApps.

There are five levels of defaults that you can set in a Cocoa application. We'll just worry about two of them: the factory defaults and the user defaults. We'll ignore defaults that are passed in on the command line, those that are set for the entire system, and the ones that depend on localization. We'll load the factory defaults right away and then check to see whether the user has used a preference panel to change any values.

In this section, we'll look at the defaults set in the registration domain. You can think of these as the factory settings—these are the values before the user makes any adjustments. Let's set the value of should-LoadSavedRemovedApps to NO.

The best place to set the registration domain defaults is in an initialize method. The reason is that the initialize method is a class method that is called before any other method is called on HelloApplicationAppDelegate or a subclass. Anything in the initialize method will be done before anything else using our app delegate—even before the applicationDidFinishLaunching: method executes.

Let's create the initialize method in our application delegate:

Persistence/HelloApplication39/HelloApplicationAppDelegate.m

```
+(void)initialize {
    NSDictionary *defaults =
      [NSDictionary dictionaryWithObject:[NSNumber numberWithBool:NO]
                                  forKey:@"LoadSavedRemovedApps"];
    [[NSUserDefaults standardUserDefaults] registerDefaults:defaults];
}
```

Click Build & Run. Each time you run the app, you'll be starting with an empty array of removed applications. Change the NO to a YES, and you will now launch with the saved list of removed applications.

Actually, you don't need to be so explicit when you place the BOOL in the dictionary. You could pass in the value YES or NO as a string and still create a BOOL from this value when you read from the preferences.

Persistence/HelloApplication40/HelloApplicationAppDelegate.m

```
+(void)initialize {
    NSDictionary *defaults =
      [NSDictionary dictionaryWithObject:@"NO"
                                  forKey:@"LoadSavedRemovedApps"];
    [[NSUserDefaults standardUserDefaults] registerDefaults:defaults];
}
```

A common example of storing a more complicated object in the preferences file is saving a color. We don't have a need for this in our application, but let's take a quick look at how you would do it. You need to store the color object as data. Use the technique we learned for creating an archive earlier in this chapter.

Don't actually make these changes to our project—I just want to show you how it's done.

To store a color in the preferences, I create a new color object named myColor and set its value to red. Now use an NSArchiver to encode the color into a data object. The rest is as before. Put the data in a dictionary, and register your defaults.

```
+ (void)initialize{
    NSColor *myColor = [NSColor redColor];
    NSData *colorData=[NSArchiver archivedDataWithRootObject:myColor];
    NSDictionary *defaults = [NSDictionary dictionaryWithObject:colorData
                                            forKey:@"BackgroundColor"];
    [[NSUserDefaults standardUserDefaults] registerDefaults:defaults];
}
```

To reverse the process, we'll pull a data object out of the standard defaults and then use an NSUnarchiver to convert the data to a color object.

```
NSData *colorData = [[NSUserDefaults standardUserDefaults]
                                  dataForKey:@"BackgroundColor"];
NSColor *myBackgroundColor =
        (NSColor *)[NSUnarchiver unarchiveObjectWithData:colorData];
```

You can use this technique to save or retrieve any nonstandard type with a preferences file. Notice that we are able to read from the standard user defaults from anywhere in our application. The objects that write to the defaults and the objects that read from them don't need to know anything about each other.

17.8 Preparing to Set User Defaults

Let's configure your app to put the defaults in the right place. User preference files for your application should go in ~/Library/Preferences in a file named com.your company name.your application name.plist. In our case, we will call the file com.pragprog.HelloApplication.plist.

You can set this by editing the HelloApplication-Info.plist file for your application. You'll find it under Resources in the Groups & Files section of your project window. Edit the Bundle identifier to have the value com. pragprog.HelloApplication, and save.

Key	Value
▼ Information Property List	(13 items)
Localization native development re	English
Executable file	${EXECUTABLE_NAME}
Icon file	
Bundle identifier	com.pragprog.HelloApplication
InfoDictionary version	6.0
Bundle name	${PRODUCT_NAME}
Bundle OS Type code	APPL
Bundle creator OS Type code	????
Bundle versions string, short	1.0
Minimum system version	${MACOSX_DEPLOYMENT_TARGET}
Bundle version	1
Main nib file base name	MainMenu
Principal class	NSApplication

17.9 The Preference Window Nib

Next, let's create a nib file we'll use as our Preferences window. Add a new file to the Resources folder. When prompted, select the Mac OS X > User Interface > Window XIB template. Save it as Preferences.xib.

Double-click Preferences.xib to open it in Interface Builder. Unselect the Visible At Launch checkbox for the window, and change the window title to Preferences. Drag in a checkbox, and add descriptive text like this:

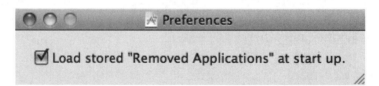

One of the nice things about creating all of these small focused nibs is that our path forward is much clearer. When we created nibs that contained a view, we knew we needed to create a view controller and set it to be the File's Owner. Similarly, when a nib contains little more than a window, we will tend to create a window controller and set it to be the File's Owner.

Create a new class named PreferencesController using the NSWindowController template. Add an outlet to the header file to connect to the checkbox and an action that is called when the user selects or unselects the checkbox.

Persistence/HelloApplication40/PreferencesController.h

```
#import <Cocoa/Cocoa.h>

@interface PreferencesController : NSWindowController {
    NSButton *loadSavedRemovedAppsCheckbox;
}
@property IBOutlet NSButton *loadSavedRemovedAppsCheckbox;
-(IBAction) toggleLoadSavedRemovedApps: (id)sender;

@end
```

The PreferencesController doesn't need to do very much. When the preference window appears, we want to set the checkbox to the state that is stored in the user preferences:

Persistence/HelloApplication40/PreferencesController.m

```
-(void) awakeFromNib {
    [self.loadSavedRemovedAppsCheckbox
            setState:[[NSUserDefaults standardUserDefaults]
        boolForKey:@"LoadSavedRemovedApps"]];
}
```

And when the user selects or unselects the checkbox, we need to store the new value in the user preferences:

Persistence/HelloApplication40/PreferencesController.m

```
-(IBAction) toggleLoadSavedRemovedApps: (id) sender {
    [[NSUserDefaults standardUserDefaults]
            setBool:[self.loadSavedRemovedAppsCheckbox state]
                forKey:@"LoadSavedRemovedApps"];
}
```

Let's connect the PreferencesController to the nib it manages. Double-click Preferences.xib. Set the File's Owner class to be PreferencesController. Connect its window outlet to the Window. Connect its loadSavedRemovedAppsCheckbox outlet and toggleLoadSavedRemovedApps action to the Checkbox. Select the Window, and connect its delegate to the File's Owner.

Save your work. We've created the preference window and its controller. We've implemented the controller and wired up everything in our new nib. Meanwhile, we also have set the ActivityController to use these preferences. All that remains is to pop open the Preferences window when the user selects HelloApplication > Preferences.

17.10 Enabling the Preferences Window

Our last step is to integrate the preferences window into our running application. A simple solution is to add an action named openPreferences: to the HelloApplicationAppDelegate class that is called when the user selects the Preferences menu item. We'll also add a property to hang onto our preference controller.

Persistence/HelloApplication40/HelloApplicationAppDelegate.h

```
#import <Cocoa/Cocoa.h>

@interface HelloApplicationAppDelegate:NSObject<NSApplicationDelegate> {
}
-(IBAction) openPreferences:(id) sender;
@end
```

The openPreferences: method will initialize the preference controller, load the preferences nib file, and then ask the preferencesController to showWindow:.

Persistence/HelloApplication40/HelloApplicationAppDelegate.m

```
-(IBAction) openPreferences: (id)sender {
    PreferencesController *prefController = [[PreferencesController alloc]
                         initWithWindowNibName:@"Preferences"];

    [prefController showWindow:self];
}
```

Double-click MainMenu.xib. Find the Preferences... menu item.

Use the Connections inspector to connect the HelloApplicationDelegate's openPreference: action to the Preferences… menu item.

So, we now initialize the PreferencesController and load the Preferences nib file when the user selects Preferences…. We also need to clean up these resources when the user dismisses the preference window. There's no need for the window to exist when it isn't visible, so we'll destroy it and create a new one if the user decides to modify the preferences later.

The PreferencesController is the delegate for its window, so we can implement this delegate method:

`Persistence/HelloApplication40/PreferencesController.m`

```
-(void)windowWillClose: (NSNotification *) notification {
    [self autorelease];
}
```

This is yet another advantage of using many small focused nibs. We can load resources when we need them and clean them up afterward.

At this point, if you click Build & Run, you can bring up the Preferences window either using the menu item or using the ⌘ , keyboard shortcut. Everything is positioned for you to set and retrieve settings. Play around with changing the preferences and quitting and restarting.

You can even open your preference file (the plist not the window) and look at the value you've set.

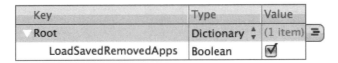

In this chapter, you've learned techniques for saving small amounts of data. You've seen how to create plists from basic types like NSArrays and how to archive more complex data. You've also seen how to work with user preferences. When we need to store either a greater amount or a more complex arrangement of data, we'll turn to Core Data. In the next chapter, we'll swap different views, and then we'll begin the journey to understanding Core Data.

Chapter 18

Changing Views

Back in Chapter 16, *Displaying Data in a Table*, on page 247, we made it easy to swap which view controller and view were used by the window controller. The good news is that you can switch back and forth by changing the name of the view controller class and the nib name and recompiling. The bad news is that your user can't make that same change at runtime.

In this chapter, we'll create a new preference that the user can set to specify which view should be visible when the application launches. We'll then use that preference to display the view that the user chose at launch time. We'll then extend the example to allow the user to switch back and forth as often as they'd like while the application is running.

We wrapped up the first act of our story by re-creating our simple web browser for the iPhone. There wasn't a lot of new material, but the point was to take another quick pass through what you've learned so far in a new context.

As the curtain falls on our second act, let's look back on some of the techniques you've learned while working with this example. Although you'll learn new things here and there, the main goal is for you to see the advantages of working with multiple nibs and small well-defined classes and methods.

18.1 Working with Radio Buttons

Let's add a group of radio buttons to the preference panel. Double-click Preferences.xib, and search in the Library for *Radio*.

You should find this widget:

Drag it onto the preference window. Resize your widget and window, and add text to the right of the two radio buttons so it looks something like this:

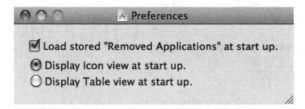

Take a look at the hierarchy of GUI elements in the Preferences.xib Document window:

We could connect to and interact with each NSButtonCell object in the radio button group individually. Instead, we're going to work with the group as a whole by using the NSMatrix object.

To set which radio button is selected from the PreferencesController object, add a property named viewGroup of type NSMatrix to the PreferencesController class. You also need to add an action to PreferencesController that is called whenever a radio button is selected. Name your action chooseView:, and save PreferencesController.h. In IB, use the Connections inspector to wire this outlet and action to the NSMatrix.

If we're going to connect the controller to the NSMatrix and not the individual buttons, we need a way to tell the two buttons apart so that we can figure out which one is selected. When we worked with tables, we used the column's identifier. NSButtonCells don't have identifiers, but they do have tags.

In Interface Builder, select the button you've labeled Display Icon view at startup. Look at the bottom of the Attributes inspector, and you should see the attribute Tag with the value 1. Similarly, the Tag attribute for the other button cell has the value 0.[1]

18.2 Adding Preferences for View at Launch

We need to do four things to get the preferences working:

1. Choose a name for the preference and a format for it.

2. Create a default value that will be used before the user sets their own preferences.

3. Read from the preference when our PreferencesController awakes from nib.

4. Write to the preference when the user selects a radio button.

We could store our preference as a boolean like we did for the checkbox. This would work fine for now because either we are using the Icon view or we're not. We've done that already. Let's do something different.

Let's store the tag of the currently selected button as the value of the preference. The tag is an int. We need to convert it to and from an NSNumber when writing to or reading from preferences. We create an NSNumber from an int with the class method numberWithInt:. Going the other way, we extract the int from the NSNumber with the method int-Value.

Now that we have a format for our preference, we can name it to communicate what it is. Let's call it TagForView. We can register the default value in HelloApplicationAppDelegate.m just below where we registered the default value for LoadSavedRemovedApps.

ChangingViews/HelloApplication41/HelloApplicationAppDelegate.m
```
+(void)initialize {
    NSDictionary *defaults =
        [NSDictionary dictionaryWithObjectsAndKeys:
        @"NO", @"LoadSavedRemovedApps",
        [NSNumber numberWithInt:1], @"TagForView",
        nil];
    [[NSUserDefaults standardUserDefaults] registerDefaults:defaults];
}
```

---

1. If the values of these tags are different, please change them to 1 and 0.

In the previous chapter, we selected or unselected the checkbox based on the value stored in the preferences. Do the same thing for the radio buttons. Pull the NSNumber from preferences, and convert it to an int. Tell the NSMatrix object to select the cell with that tag.

ChangingViews/HelloApplication41/PreferencesController.m

```
-(void) awakeFromNib {
    [self.loadSavedRemovedAppsCheckbox
                setState:[[NSUserDefaults standardUserDefaults]
                        boolForKey:@"LoadSavedRemovedApps"]];
    [self.viewGroup selectCellWithTag:
                [[[NSUserDefaults standardUserDefaults]
                                objectForKey:@"TagForView"] intValue]];
}
```

The chooseView: action is called whenever a user selects a radio button. We take the tag of the cell the user selected, convert it to an NSNumber, and update the value of the TagForView preference.

ChangingViews/HelloApplication41/PreferencesController.m

```
-(IBAction) chooseView: (id) sender {
    [[NSUserDefaults standardUserDefaults]
        setObject:[NSNumber numberWithInt:[[sender selectedCell] tag]]
            forKey:@"TagForView"];
}
```

Click Build & Run. You can now toggle which view should load at launch time. Close the preference window, and reopen it. Quit the application, and restart. It doesn't matter. Your preference is saved each time it is set. Next let's use this setting to load the correct view.

18.3 Exercise: Launching with the Right View

Modify MyWindowController.m to read the value stored in the TagForView preference. You should launch with the Icon view loaded if the value is 1 and with the table view loaded if the value is 0.

18.4 Solution: Launching with the Right View

We've been specifying the view controller and the nib name in the first two lines of setUpView. Let's split those lines out into methods loadIcon-View and loadTableView so that we can call these methods to load the view we want.

ChangingViews/HelloApplication42/MyWindowController.m

```
-(void) setUpView {
    self.currentApp = [[CurrentApp alloc] init];
    self.currentApp.delegate = self.ac;
    [self.window setContentSize:[self.ac.view bounds].size];
    self.window.contentView = self.ac.view;
    [self.ac applicationDidLaunch:
                    [NSRunningApplication currentApplication]];
}
-(void) loadIconView {
    self.ac = [[IconViewController alloc]
            initWithNibName:@"IconView" bundle:nil];
    [self setUpView];
}
-(void) loadTableView {
    self.ac = [[ActivityController alloc]
            initWithNibName:@"ActivityView" bundle:nil];
    [self setUpView];
}
```

Create a new method named shouldLoadIconView to read the value stored in the preference:

ChangingViews/HelloApplication42/MyWindowController.m

```
-(BOOL) shouldLoadIconView{
    return (1 == [[[NSUserDefaults standardUserDefaults]
                objectForKey:@"TagForView"] intValue]);
}
```

The shouldLoadIconView method is short, and you might be tempted to do without it. I introduced it because it makes the logic in initWithWindowNibName: easier to read than if we inlined retrieving the preference value.

ChangingViews/HelloApplication42/MyWindowController.m

```
-(id) initWithWindowNibName:(NSString *)windowNibName {
    if (self = [super initWithWindowNibName:windowNibName]) {
►       if ([self shouldLoadIconView])[self loadIconView];
►       else [self loadTableView];
        [self showWindow:self];
    }
    return self;
}
@end
```

Click Build & Run, and your app will launch with the preferred view displayed. For the rest of this chapter, we'll work toward allowing switching between views any time.

18.5 Eliminating Magic Numbers

I'm going to take a brief side trip for those of you disturbed by the use of a magic number in our solution. Make a copy of our project because we're going to return to this stage of the code in the next section. You can safely skip this section and pick up the story in the next section.

The problem is the use of the number 1 here:

ChangingViews/HelloApplication42/MyWindowController.m

```
-(BOOL) shouldLoadIconView{
    return (1 == [[[NSUserDefaults standardUserDefaults]
                    objectForKey:@"TagForView"] intValue]);
}
```

The 1 is a magic number that is tied to the tag of our radio buttons used to select which view to load. You can place #define ICON_VIEW_ID 1 just below @implementation and use ICON_VIEW_ID in place of 1. That certainly makes the intent of the code clearer to other developers. You can also declare and define a public constant in the application delegate.

Let's create and use a property list named Views:

ChangingViews/HelloApplication42alt/Views

```
<?xml version="1.0" encoding="UTF-8"?>
<!DOCTYPE plist PUBLIC "-//Apple//DTD PLIST 1.0//EN"
"http://www.apple.com/DTDs/PropertyList-1.0.dtd">
<plist version="1.0">
<array>
        <dict>
                <key>class</key>
                <string>ActivityController</string>
                <key>nib</key>
                <string>ActivityView</string>
        </dict>
        <dict>
                <key>class</key>
                <string>IconViewController</string>
                <key>nib</key>
                <string>IconView</string>
        </dict>
</array>
</plist>
```

This is short enough to enter by hand. It is an array of dictionaries. The dictionary at index 0 represents the table view, and the dictionary at index 1 represents the Icon view. If we add more views, then we would just add entries to this array. Each dictionary has a string with key "class" whose corresponding value is the class name of the view controller. The value with key "nib" is a string with the name of the nib for our view.

If you'd rather not write this file by hand, you can write it in code. Add this to your app delegate's applicationDidFinishLaunching: method, click Build & Run, and then remove this code. This will create a file named Views in your build directory.

```
NSDictionary *tableView = [NSDictionary dictionaryWithObjectsAndKeys:
        @"ActivityView", @"nib", @"ActivityController", @"class", nil];
NSDictionary *iconView =  [NSDictionary dictionaryWithObjectsAndKeys:
        @"IconView", @"nib", @"IconViewController", @"class", nil];
NSArray *viewArray =
            [NSArray arrayWithObjects:tableView, iconView, nil];
[viewArray writeToFile:@"Views" atomically:YES];
```

Whichever way you created the Views file, you now need to add it to your project. Control-click Folder under Groups & Files, and choose Add > Existing Files…. Navigate to your Views file, and click the Add button. When this list drops down, check the "Copy items into destination group's folder (if needed)" checkbox, and set Reference Type to Relative to Project using the drop-down menu. This will enable us to access the file by its name without providing a long path. Click the Add button to finish.

Up until now your code is unchanged. We've moved both the magic number and the decision making into this new configuration file we've created. Now let's use it in MyWindowController.m. We can replace both the loadIconView and loadTableView methods with this method:

ChangingViews/HelloApplication42alt/MyWindowController.m

```
-(void)loadView {
    NSArray *viewArray = [NSArray arrayWithContentsOfFile:
                        [[NSBundle mainBundle] pathForResource:@"Views"
                                                        ofType:nil]];
    NSDictionary *view = [viewArray objectAtIndex:
                        [[[NSUserDefaults standardUserDefaults]
                            objectForKey:@"TagForView"] intValue]];
    self.ac =
        [[NSClassFromString([view objectForKey:@"class"]) alloc]
        initWithNibName:[view objectForKey:@"nib"] bundle:nil];
    [self setUpView];
}
```

We start by creating our array of dictionaries from the Views file. Then we use the value of the TagForView preference to select which dictionary we want. Then we create a new view controller using the class name and nib name stored in the dictionary.

We can delete the shouldLoadIconView method and remove the if statement from the initWithWindowNibName: method:

`ChangingViews/HelloApplication42alt/MyWindowController.m`

```
-(id) initWithWindowNibName:(NSString *)windowNibName {
    if (self = [super initWithWindowNibName:windowNibName]) {
        [self loadView];
        [self showWindow:self];
    }
    return self;
}
@end
```

Click Build & Run, and the application works the same as our solution. We've eliminated the magic number and the decision making. I'm not sure whether the code is easier to understand. I'm going to continue with the version of the code we had before this section.[2]

18.6 Customizing the Menu Bar

When you run our app, you see a menu bar that is mostly filled with items that are irrelevant to the user. There's nothing in the File, Edit, or Format menus that anyone would ever need. Let's get rid of them.

Double-click the MainMenu.xib file. In the Document window, select and delete one at a time the NSMenuItems labeled File, Edit, Format, Window, and Help.[3] Your main menu should look like this is the Document window:

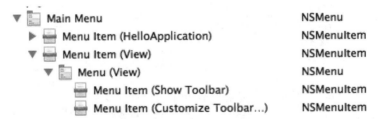

Change the two bottom items. Select the one labeled Show Toolbar, and open the Attributes inspector. Change the title to Show Table View, and leave its keyboard equivalent as ⌥⌘T (Option-Command-T). Similarly,

---

2. You can continue with this version of the code for the remainder of the chapter. I haven't detailed the changes that are required, but my background as a mathematician compels me to say at this point, "It is left as an exercise for the reader."
3. We could have kept the Window menu for the Minimize command, but I want to focus on the View menu.

select the Customize Toolbar... menu item, and change its title to Show Icon View. Set its keyboard equivalent to ⌥⌘I (Option-Command-I).

Save, and then click Build & Run. Our new menu bar looks pretty good:

The items and their keyboard shortcuts are there. They're grayed out because they currently can't be selected by the user. They don't do anything yet.

18.7 Moving the Main Window

When a user selects one of the two menu items, the obvious object to respond is the window controller. The window controller is set up to swap one view for another. Unfortunately, the menu items and the window controller are in separate nibs, so we can't just create an action in the window controller and wire it to a menu item.

Open MainMenu.xib in Interface Builder. Drag an instance of MyWindow-Controller from the Classes tab of the Library into the Document window. Now we have to adjust how we load our window controller and MainWindow nib.

The applicationDidFinishLaunching: method in HelloApplicationAppDelegate contains this single line:

```
[[MyWindowController alloc] initWithWindowNibName:@"MainWindow"];
```

We need to remove it. By dragging MyWindowController into the Main-Menu, we are instantiating it there. We shouldn't create a separate instance of it in the app delegate, or we will be looking at one instance and sending messages to another instance. Get rid of this line so that the applicationDidFinishLaunching: method is empty.

If you click Build & Run at this point, the application will launch, but you won't see a window. Take a look at MyWindowController.m. It has the method initWithWindowNibName:, but there's nothing left to tell it what its nib name is.

Add this implementation of init just below the initWithWindowNibName: method:

ChangingViews/HelloApplication43/MyWindowController.m

```
-(id) init {
    return [self initWithWindowNibName:@"MainWindow"];
}

@end
```

This simple call provides all the help we need. It says that when it's time to create a new instance of MyWindowController, then the nib containing the window it controls is MainWindow.

Click Build & Run, and the window should again be visible at launch.

18.8 Exercise: Switching Views (Mostly)

Change the loadIconView and loadTableView methods in MyWindowController.m to actions, and connect them to your menu items. Our application should mostly work. I say "mostly" because every time you switch back to the Icon view, the first application that will be displayed is HelloApplication. We'll have to fix that next.

18.9 Solution: Switching Views (Mostly)

Add declarations for the two actions to MyWindowController.h:

ChangingViews/HelloApplication44/MyWindowController.h

```
#import <Cocoa/Cocoa.h>
#import "ActivityMonitorDelegate.h"
@class CurrentApp;

@interface MyWindowController : NSWindowController {
    CurrentApp *currentApp;
    NSViewController <ActivityMonitorDelegate> *ac;
}
@property CurrentApp *currentApp;
@property NSViewController <ActivityMonitorDelegate> *ac;
```
▶ `-(IBAction) loadIconView:(id) sender;`
▶ `-(IBAction) loadTableView: (id) sender;`
```
@end
```

Make the corresponding changes to the method signatures in the implementation file:

ChangingViews/HelloApplication44/MyWindowController.m

```
▶ -(IBAction) loadIconView:(id) sender {
       self.ac = [[IconViewController alloc]
                   initWithNibName:@"IconView" bundle:nil];
       [self setUpView];
   }
▶ -(IBAction) loadTableView: (id) sender {
       self.ac = [[ActivityController alloc]
                   initWithNibName:@"ActivityView" bundle:nil];
       [self setUpView];
   }
```

You'll also need to add self as a parameter when you call these methods from inside initWithWindowNibName::

ChangingViews/HelloApplication44/MyWindowController.m

```
if ([self shouldLoadIconView])[self loadIconView:self];
else [self loadTableView:self];
```

Save your work, and open MainMenu.xib in Interface Builder. Use the Connections inspector to connect these actions to their corresponding menu items. Save.

Click Build & Run, and you should be able to toggle back and forth between the two views using the menu items or the keyboard equivalents. Every time we toggle back to the Icon view, it displays the launch notification for HelloApplication. The problem is in the setUpView method.

ChangingViews/HelloApplication44/MyWindowController.m

```
-(void) setUpView {
▶      self.currentApp = [[CurrentApp alloc] init];
       self.currentApp.delegate = self.ac;
       [self.window setContentSize:[self.ac.view bounds].size];
       self.window.contentView = self.ac.view;
▶      [self.ac applicationDidLaunch:
▶                          [NSRunningApplication currentApplication]];
   }
```

The setUpView method was meant to be called only once when the application first launches. Now it is called every time we switch views. There's no reason to create a fresh instance of CurrentApp every time we switch views. We also only want to hard-code the fact that we are launching the current application the first time through.

We'll solve the first problem with lazy initialization and the second problem by figuring out whether the current app is running.

18.10 Lazy Initialization

We don't want to create a CurrentApp instance every time we switch views. We want to instantiate CurrentApp only the first time we need it.

Even though our getter and setter for the currentApp property are generated for us, we are free to override them. We'll override the getter method currentApp like this:

`ChangingViews/HelloApplication45/MyWindowController.m`

```
-(CurrentApp *) currentApp {
    if (!currentApp) {
        self.currentApp = [[CurrentApp alloc] init];
    }
    return currentApp;
}
```

If the currentApp instance variable is not nil, then we just return it. If it doesn't exist yet, then we create an instance of CurrentApp and assign it to our property using the setter.

Update the init method in CurrentApp.m to set its app property to be the current application:

`ChangingViews/HelloApplication45/CurrentApp.m`

```
-(id) init {
    if (self = [super init]) {
        [self registerNotifications];
        [self initializeMethodDictionary];
        self.app = [NSRunningApplication currentApplication];
    }
    return self;
}
```

Now we have a single instance of CurrentApp throughout the lifetime of our application, and it always knows what the launching or terminating application is.

There are many ways to figure out whether our current application is launching or terminating. For example, we could add a property to CurrentApp to hold this information. We could save the notification in the view controller and key off of its type. I've taken a simpler approach. Since we know what the app is that just launched or terminated, we can check to see whether it is in the array of running applications.

ChangingViews/HelloApplication45/MyWindowController.m

```
-(void)launchOrTerminate {
    if ([[[NSWorkspace sharedWorkspace] runningApplications]
                    containsObject:self.currentApp.app]) {
        [self.ac applicationDidLaunch:self.currentApp.app];
    } else [self.ac applicationDidTerminate:self.currentApp.app];
}
```

Finally—and I do mean *finally*—we need to revise the setUpView method. Remove the lines at the top and bottom that created a new CurrentApp object every time through and called the applicationDidLaunch: with the current running application as its parameter. Also, insert this high-lighted line that calls out launchOrTerminate:

ChangingViews/HelloApplication45/MyWindowController.m

```
-(void) setUpView {
    self.currentApp.delegate = self.ac;
    [self.window setContentSize:[self.ac.view bounds].size];
    [self launchOrTerminate];
    self.window.contentView = self.ac.view;
}
```

Click Build & Run. You can now switch between the views as often as you want, and the latest activity will be displayed in the Icon view, and the list of all running applications that you haven't banished will be displayed in the table view.

There's so much more we could do. If this were a shipping application, I'd probably remove the preference to set your view on startup and replace it by remembering the view the user displayed the last time they quit the application. I might add animation to the Icon view as applications launch and terminate. There's no end to the little touches we could add, but it's time to say goodbye to this example.

We've used it to cover a lot. We responded to notifications and created some of our own. We created and used our own protocol and delegate. We worked with dictionaries and tables. We saved data and worked with preferences. We split our nib into small pieces, created a custom view, and swapped nibs in and out for our preference window and for switching views.

The example has served us well, but it's time to move on to our next running example that will carry us through various aspects of Bindings and Core Data.

Chapter 19

Key Value Coding

It's so easy to miss the point of Key Value Coding. Most people focus on the mechanism and not on what it allows you to do. Let's get some of the *how* out of the way so that we can think a bit more about the *why* and *when*.

Suppose you have a class named PragBook, and it has a property title. Then if jrport is an instance of PragBook, you would get its title like this:

```
NSString *bookTitle = [jrport title];
```

You might also use this dot syntax to access the property.

```
NSString *bookTitle = jrport.title;
```

With Key Value Coding, which we'll call KVC from now on, you would write something more like this:

```
NSString *bookTitle = [jrport valueForKey:@"title"];
```

That looks horrible. There are so many ways in which that is clearly worse than the direct approach. First, it's more typing. Second, we're passing the name of the variable in as a string, so there is no compile-time checking. Third, why would anyone come up with such a stupid way of accessing variables?

KVC is the first step in our path to understanding Key Value Observing, Bindings, and Core Data. In this chapter, you'll get a feel for what it is, how you'll use it, and why you'll want to use it.

19.1 Treating Objects Like Dictionaries

Once we calm down, we remember that we've seen notation like valueForKey: before. This looks a lot like the objectForKey: method we used when we worked with dictionaries.

We started out by pulling out specific entries from the dictionary using hard-coded keys. When we got to Chapter 16, *Displaying Data in a Table*, everything changed. We were filling tables by keying off the column identifier. This meant that we filled the table with the contents of these dictionaries without writing a lot of conditional code. With KVC, we can pull the same tricks with objects and their variables.[1]

We're going to build an application that lets you type *author* or *title* into one text field, and the author's name or the book's title will appear in the other text field. The GUI will look like this:

Create a new Cocoa application named Bookshelf, and add an Objective-C class to it named PragBook with this header:

```
KVC/Bookshelf1/PragBook.h
```

```
#import <Cocoa/Cocoa.h>

@interface PragBook : NSObject {
    NSString *title;
    NSString *author;
}
@property (copy) NSString *title, *author;

@end
```

While you're at it, synthesize the accessors title, setTitle:, author, and setAuthor: in the implementation file.

---

1. You saw the valueForKey: method briefly in Section 16.8, *Previews of Coming Attractions*, on page 257.

KVC/Bookshelf1/PragBook.m

```
#import "PragBook.h"

@implementation PragBook
@synthesize title, author;
@end
```

These give us the class PragBook with two instance variables, title and author, and their corresponding accessor methods. We should be able to key on those variable names somehow. We should be able to ask the value of title in the same way we returned an object from a dictionary.

That's what KVC gives us. It allows us to use valueForKey: to return the value that corresponds to a variable's name passed in as a string.[2] It's kind of ingenious how it works. Say your code calls this:

```
[jrport valueForKey:@"title"];
```

The runtime searches the PragBook class for an instance method named getTitle, title, or isTitle in that order. The first one it finds is invoked. If none of these exists, the next step is to search for methods that correspond to collections—we'll skip that step for now since title is not a collection.

So, if none of the simple accessor methods exists, the next step is to try to directly find the value of the ivar.[3] If the object's method accessInstanceVariablesDirectly returns YES, then the runtime searches for an instance variable named _title, _isTitle, title, and isTitle, in that order, and returns the value of the variable.

You should know two more things. First, I've skimped on some of the details. If the variable is not a pointer to an object, then there's some conversion to either an NSNumber if that's appropriate or an NSValue if it's not. Second, if no method or variable is found, then the method valueForUndefinedKey: is invoked.

Notice that by using properties we've written almost no code and still satisfied the conditions needed to provide the support for KVC. Now let's use this class in a simple application.

---

2. We've already done something similar for methods. We've specified the name of methods we want invoked under certain circumstances by passing in their names as strings.
3. You'll hear "i-var" pronounced to rhyme with "my car" for instance variable.

19.2 Getting Variables Using KVC

Add another Objective-C class named BookshelfController that extends NSViewController. For now, BookshelfController will contain a single Prag-Book instance. We'll need an action that is called when the user has finished entering *author* or *title*. We'll also need an outlet so we can write the title or author's name in the second text field. You'll see all this in the header file for BookshelfController.

KVC/Bookshelf1/BookshelfController.h

```objc
#import <Cocoa/Cocoa.h>
@class PragBook;

@interface BookshelfController : NSViewController {
    NSTextField *valueField;
    PragBook *book;
}
@property IBOutlet NSTextField *valueField;
@property PragBook *book;

-(IBAction) getValue:(id) sender;
@end
```

The implementation will create a single book instance and respond to the user typing *author* or *title* in the top text field by filling the bottom text field with the author's name or the title of the book.

KVC/Bookshelf1/BookshelfController.m

```objc
#import "BookshelfController.h"
#import "PragBook.h"

@implementation BookshelfController
@synthesize book, valueField;

-(IBAction) getValue:(id) sender {
    [self.valueField setStringValue:
                        [self.book valueForKey:[sender stringValue]]];
}

-(PragBook *) book {
    if (!book) {
        self.book = [[PragBook alloc] init];
        self.book.title = @"Manage Your Project Portfolio";
        self.book.author = @"Johanna Rothman";
    }
    return book;
}
@end
```

I'm going to take a minute to finish describing the plumbing you need to add to make this app work, and then I'll come back and make a huge deal out of the getValue: action.

Create a new view-based nib file, and name it Bookshelf. To create your GUI, arrange a label and two text fields like the picture you just saw. Use the Attributes inspector to make the second field not selectable and to have the action on the first text field sent on Enter only.

Use the Identity inspector to set your File's Owner's type to be BookshelfController. Next use the Connections inspector to connect the valueField outlet to the bottom text field and the getValue: action to the top text field. Connect the view outlet to the Custom View. Save.

Create an instance of our view controller, and load the Bookshelf nib in your app delegate's applicationDidFinishLaunching: method. Resize the window, and set its content view to be our view controller's view.

KVC/Bookshelf1/BookshelfAppDelegate.m

```
#import "BookshelfAppDelegate.h"
#import "BookshelfController.h"

@implementation BookshelfAppDelegate

@synthesize window;

- (void)applicationDidFinishLaunching:(NSNotification *)aNotification {
    BookshelfController * bc = [[BookshelfController alloc]
                                initWithNibName:@"Bookshelf" bundle:nil];
    [self.window setContentSize:[bc.view bounds].size];
    self.window.contentView = bc.view;
}

@end
```

Click Build & Run. Type *title* into the top text field, and when you hit ↵, you'll see "Manage Your Project Portfolio" in the bottom text field. Type *author* instead, and you'll see "Johanna Rothman" instead. We've used KVC to get the value of a variable. I love the simplicity and flexibility contained in this one call in the getValue: method.

KVC/Bookshelf1/BookshelfController.m

```
[self.valueField setStringValue:
                [self.book valueForKey:[sender stringValue]]];
```

Let's work our way from the inside out. The getValue: method is called when the user presses Enter after typing *author* or *title*. The first text field passes a pointer to itself along as the sender argument, and we use that to get the string that the user typed in. Next, we use that string as the key and look for the value of a property with that name in book. Finally, we pass this value on to the second text field to be displayed as a string.

Suppose you add a property to PragBook for the subtitle or another for a praise quote like "I laughed, I cried, it moved me." You don't have to make any change to the nib file, and you don't have to make any change to the getValue: method. You only need to change the PragBook class.

19.3 Undefined Keys

There's a fundamental problem with our application. Though we've prompted the user to type *author* or *title* into that first text field, they can type anything they want. Try it. Type *asdf* into the first text field.

The user won't get any feedback in the window. They don't know that they've done anything wrong. On the other hand, we, as developers, can see this in the debugger console:

```
Exception detected while handling key input.
[<PragBook 0x1001068f0> valueForUndefinedKey:]:
          this class is not key value coding-compliant for the key asdf.
```

To fix this, our PragBook has to implement the method valueForUndefined-Key:. In this case, we'll return an error message as a string. If need be, you can return different objects based on which keys the user typed in. In this case, we're returning the same string for all errors.

KVC/Bookshelf2/PragBook.m

```
#import "PragBook.h"

@implementation PragBook
@synthesize title, author;

▶  -(id) valueForUndefinedKey:(NSString *)key {
▶      return [NSString stringWithFormat:@"No property with key %@.", key];
▶  }
   @end
```

With this simple change, we display the error in the second text field.

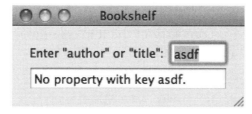

Although it's nice to have this facility for dealing with unwanted input, you're better off designing an interface that doesn't allow the user to enter undefined keys. You could do this with a prepopulated drop-down list, or you could use an interface with fixed fields—one for each property you want to display.

19.4 Exercise: Setting Variables Using KVC

There is the setter method setValue:forKey: paired with the getter method valueForKey:. Add an action to BookshelfController named setValue:.

In this method, you set whichever property's name appears in the top text field to be the value that is entered in the bottom text field. In other words, the user is entering a key-value pair where the key (either author or title) is the contents of the top text field, and the value you are assigning that key is entered in the bottom text field.

19.5 Solution: Setting Variables Using KVC

Granted, this is a silly example, but it illustrates getting and setting properties using KVC. You'll need to add an outlet and an action to the BookshelfController header file:

```
KVC/Bookshelf3/BookshelfController.h
#import <Cocoa/Cocoa.h>
@class PragBook;

@interface BookshelfController : NSViewController {
▶    NSTextField *keyField;
    NSTextField *valueField;
    PragBook *book;
}
▶ @property IBOutlet NSTextField *valueField, *keyField;
@property PragBook *book;

-(IBAction) getValue:(id) sender;
▶ -(IBAction) setValue:(id) sender;
@end
```

Connect your new outlet and action in the nib file. Set your bottom text field to be selectable and editable and to send its value on Enter.

Synthesize the keyField property in the implementation file, and implement the setValue: action like this:

KVC/Bookshelf3/BookshelfController.m

```
-(IBAction) setValue:(id) sender {
    [self.book setValue:[sender stringValue]
                forKey:[self.keyField stringValue]];
}
```

Now you can get and set the value of any defined property as if you were using keys and values in a dictionary. Let's take that a step further.

19.6 KVC and Dictionaries

So, we've seen that Key Value Coding lets us treat properties and their values as if they were entries in a dictionary. Let's take that a step further—it turns out to be trivial to use a dictionary to fill an object's properties or to create a dictionary from a class so long as the keys match the names of the properties.

Let's transform our running Bookshelf example to instantiate our Prag-Book and fill it with values pulled from a dictionary. This time, instead of initializing the properties in book, we create a dictionary named bookInfo with the keys title and author. We now set the values of book's properties all at once from the bookInfo dictionary like this:

KVC/Bookshelf4/BookshelfController.m

```
-(PragBook *) book {
    if (!book) {
        self.book = [[PragBook alloc] init];
►       NSDictionary *bookInfo =
►                       [NSDictionary dictionaryWithObjectsAndKeys:
►                       @"Manage Your Project Portfolio", @"title",
►                       @"Johanna Rothman", @"author", nil];
►       [self.book setValuesForKeysWithDictionary: bookInfo];
    }
    return book;
}
```

That's it.

Going the other way is only slightly more involved. We need to pass in an array that is filled with the new dictionary's keys. These are the same as the object properties we want to capture in this dictionary. In our case, we'll capture both of them. Add this line to setValue: to create our dictionary and log it whenever the user changes the value of the title or author:

KVC/Bookshelf5/BookshelfController.m

```
-(IBAction) setValue:(id) sender {
    [self.book setValue:[sender stringValue]
                forKey:[self.keyField stringValue]];
▶   NSLog(@"%@", [self.book dictionaryWithValuesForKeys:
▶             [NSArray arrayWithObjects:@"author", @"title", nil]]);
}
```

Here I've changed the value of the author variable from Johanna Rothman to JR:

```
Bookshelf[6388:a0f] {
    author = JR;
    title = "Manage Your Project Portfolio";
}
```

Again, this example seems a little silly in this simple form, but you could easily think of cases where this facility would be useful. Imagine, for example, that you want to save your book information to disk whenever the value is changed. You already know how to read and write dictionaries to disk, and now you know how to convert a KVC-compliant class to and from a dictionary. This allows you to store and retrieve any KVC-compliant class.

19.7 Keypaths for Navigating a Class Hierarchy

For now our bookshelf has a single book. Now let's add a single chapter to the book. The Chapter object will have variables for storing the title and the number of pages. My goal is to show you how to traverse a hierarchy with KVC by using keypaths in place of keys.

Create a new Objective-C class named Chapter. Here's the header file:

KVC/Bookshelf6/Chapter.h

```
#import <Cocoa/Cocoa.h>

@interface Chapter : NSObject {
    NSString *chapterTitle;
    NSNumber *pageCount;
}
@property(copy) NSString *chapterTitle;
@property(copy) NSNumber *pageCount;
@end
```

Again, we'll do nothing more than synthesize the properties in the implementation file:

KVC/Bookshelf6/Chapter.m

```
#import "Chapter.h"

@implementation Chapter
@synthesize chapterTitle, pageCount;

@end
```

Now pop up a level and add an instance of Chapter to PragBook:

KVC/Bookshelf6/PragBook.h

```
#import <Cocoa/Cocoa.h>
▶ @class Chapter;

@interface PragBook : NSObject {
    NSString *title;
    NSString *author;
▶    Chapter *chapter;
}
@property (copy) NSString *title, *author;
▶ @property Chapter *chapter;
@end
```

Synthesize the accessors for chapter. Create and initialize chapter in PragBook's init method:

KVC/Bookshelf6/PragBook.m

```
#import "PragBook.h"
▶ #import "Chapter.h"

@implementation PragBook
▶ @synthesize title, author, chapter;

▶ -(id)init {
▶     if (self=[super init]) {
▶         self.chapter = [[Chapter alloc] init];
▶     }
▶     return self;
▶ }

-(id) valueForUndefinedKey:(NSString *)key {
    return [NSString stringWithFormat:@"No property with key %@.", key];
}
@end
```

Now our BookshelfController object has a single PragBook instance, which in turn now has a single instance of Chapter that has properties named chapterTitle and pageCount. Let's use KVC to set the values of the chapter's title and page count in the book method in BookshelfController.m. I've used setValue:forKeyPath: twice in the highlighted lines.

```
-(PragBook *) book {
    if (!book) {
        self.book = [[PragBook alloc] init];
        NSDictionary *bookInfo =
                        [NSDictionary dictionaryWithObjectsAndKeys:
                         @"Manage Your Project Portfolio", @"title",
                         @"Johanna Rothman", @"author", nil];
        [self.book setValuesForKeysWithDictionary: bookInfo];
▶       [self.book setValue:@"Preface"
▶               forKeyPath:@"chapter.chapterTitle"];
▶       [self setValue:[NSNumber numberWithInt:4]
▶           forKeyPath:@"book.chapter.pageCount"];
    }
    return book;
}
```

I've used two different paths just for illustration. When I start at book, I use the keypath chapter.chapterTitle. When I start at self (in other words at the BookshelfController level), the keypath is book.chapter.pageCount.

Notice that we use the method setValue:forKeyPath: where we used to use the method setValue:forKey:. You can actually view the keys as a very short keypath and use setValue:forKeyPath: in our setValue: action.

```
-(IBAction) setValue:(id) sender {
▶   [self.book setValue:[sender stringValue]
▶           forKeyPath:[self.keyField stringValue]];
}
```

Similarly, the getter valueForKeyPath: is used where we used to use valueForKey:. This will let us enter keys or keypaths where before we could only enter keys.

```
-(IBAction) getValue:(id) sender {
▶   [self.valueField setStringValue:
▶                       [self.book valueForKeyPath:[sender stringValue]]];
}
```

So now, in addition to entering the author and title keys in the top text field, we can safely use the keypaths "chapter.chapterTitle" and "chapter.pageCount" to get and set those values as well.

Keypaths are a lot less mysterious now that we have properties and dot notation. Key Value Coding works even when we don't have properties so long as your class is Key Value Coding–compliant for that key. The Apple docs explain that in the case of an attribute named "key," that means you either need a getter named key or isKey or have an ivar named key or _key. If you need a setter, its name should be setKey:, which is a method that does not perform validation. We haven't validated our input, but if you need to, the validation belongs in the validateKey:error: method.

19.8 Exercise: Filling Tables Using KVC

KVC allows us to fill a table as easily as we filled one from a dictionary earlier.

Populate the table from an array of chapters that you add to the Prag-Book class in place of the chapter property we have there now. The BookshelfController will be the table view's data source and delegate. Which methods do you need to implement? How should you implement them?

19.9 Solution: Filling Tables Using KVC

Let's start with the Bookshelf nib file. Drag a table view into your Document window. You can delete your custom view along with its label and text fields. Use the Attributes inspector to set the first column's identifier to chapterTitle and the second column's identifier to pageCount. Be

sure to set the table view's delegate and data source to the BookshelfController, and connect the BookshelfController's view outlet to the bordered
scroll view. Save.

If you click Build & Run, your application should launch, and the window should appear with your table view inside, but you will see this
error in the Console:

```
Illegal NSTableView data source (<BookshelfController: 0x200092c60>).
Must implement numberOfRowsInTableView: and
            tableView:objectValueForTableColumn:row:
```

Assume that PragBook has a property named chapters that is an NSArray
filled with Chapter objects. Then we implement numberOfRowsInTable-
View: by returning the number of elements in the chapters array. There
is no benefit in using KVC for this:

KVC/Bookshelf7/BookshelfController.m

```
-(NSInteger) numberOfRowsInTableView:(NSTableView *) aTableView {
    return [self.book.chapters count];
}
```

Use KVC to fill each cell of the table view:

KVC/Bookshelf7/BookshelfController.m

```
- (id)tableView:(NSTableView *)aTableView
            objectValueForTableColumn:(NSTableColumn *)aTableColumn
                              row:(NSInteger)rowIndex {
    return [[self.book.chapters objectAtIndex:rowIndex]
                        valueForKey:[aTableColumn identifier]];
}
```

To round out this application, add these convenience methods to Chapter for creating new objects:

KVC/Bookshelf7/Chapter.m

```
-(id) initWithTitle:(NSString *) title pageCount: (int) count {
    if (self=[super init]) {
        self.chapterTitle = title;
        self.pageCount = [NSNumber numberWithInt:count];
    }
    return self;
}
+(id) chapterWithTitle:(NSString *) title pageCount: (int)count {
    return [[Chapter alloc ] initWithTitle:title
                                pageCount:count];
}
```

Add an array named chapters to PragBook. You can remove the chapter variable of type Chapter. Fill the chapters array with a bunch of chapters in the init method of PragBook.[4]

`KVC/Bookshelf7/PragBook.m`

```
-(id)init {
    if (self=[super init]) {
        self.chapters = [[NSArray alloc] initWithObjects:
            [Chapter chapterWithTitle:@"Preface"
                            pageCount:3],
            [Chapter chapterWithTitle:@"Meet Your Project Portfolio"
                            pageCount:12],
            [Chapter chapterWithTitle:@"Create Your First Draft"
                            pageCount:10],
            [Chapter chapterWithTitle:@"Evaluate Your Projects"
                            pageCount:14],
            [Chapter chapterWithTitle:@"Rank the Portfolio"
                            pageCount:20], nil];
    }
    return self;
}
```

This should be enough information for you to get this project up and working. You'll need to add the appropriate declarations to the header files and fill out some of the methods. You also should remove the outlets and actions from BookshelfController. [5] If you get stuck, remember you can consult KVC/Bookshelf7 in the code download.

19.10 Arrays and KVC

In the previous section, we picked off specific elements in our array of chapters like this:

```
[[self.book.chapters objectAtIndex:rowIndex]
                        valueForKey:[aTableColumn identifier]];
```

This first part of the code picks off a particular chapter, and the second selects one of its properties. We can do more. For example, we can create an array that consists of all the chapter titles at once using this call:

```
[self.book.chapters valueForKey:@"chapterTitle"]
```

---

4. Remove the code for setting up a single chapter title and page count from the book method.
5. Watch for the easily made mistake of using book.chapter instead of book.chapters. You should have removed the variable named chapter and so can search to make sure you're using the plural version chapters only.

There's more to this than first might appear. We have an array named chapters whose entries are all objects of type Chapter. Each chapter has two properties: chapterTitle and pageCount. Imagine the steps you would have to go through to create this array in the past. You would have to create the new array and copy the elements over from the old array. It's not a huge deal, but KVC makes it cleaner and easier.

But that's not all.

You can operate on these new collections and perform all sorts of calculations. The pageCount property, for example, is a number, so you can calculate the sum or the average of all the page counts in chapters. Here's how you would calculate the sum:

```
[self.book valueForKeyPath:@"chapters.@sum.pageCount"]
```

Isn't that cool? You just insert @sum before pageCount in the keypath. In general, you insert the operator between the keypath to the array and the keypath to the property.

There are two types of operators. The first type operates on a collection of numbers and returns the average, maximum, minimum, or sum (respectively, @avg, @max, @min, and @sum). The second type operates on collections and returns their @count, @distinctUnionOfArrays, @distinctUnionOfObjects, @distinctUnionOfSets, @unionOfArrays, @unionOfObjects, and @unionOfSets.

We can take some of these for a ride in our application. Declare an instance method named createReport in the BookshelfController's header file, and implement it like this:

KVC/Bookshelf8/BookshelfController.m

```
-(void)createReport {
    NSLog(@"There are %@ chapters.",
        [self valueForKeyPath:@"book.chapters.@count.chapterTitle"]);
    NSLog(@"The titles are: %@",
        [self.book.chapters valueForKey:@"chapterTitle"]);
    NSLog(@"This book has %@ pages so far.",
        [self.book valueForKeyPath:@"chapters.@sum.pageCount"]);
    NSLog(@"The longest chapter is %@ pages long.",
        [self valueForKeyPath:@"book.chapters.@max.pageCount"]);
    NSLog(@"The average chapter length is %@.",
        [self.book.chapters valueForKeyPath:@"@avg.pageCount"]);
}
```

You might notice that again I've used different anchors for the keypaths to show you where to insert the operator. Call this method from the end of the applicationDidFinishLaunching: method in your app delegate.

KVC/Bookshelf8/BookshelfAppDelegate.m

```
- (void)applicationDidFinishLaunching:(NSNotification *)aNotification {
    BookshelfController * bc = [[BookshelfController alloc]
                                initWithNibName:@"Bookshelf" bundle:nil];
    [self.window setContentSize:[bc.view bounds].size];
    self.window.contentView = bc.view;
    [bc createReport];
}
```

Click Build & Run, and you should see something like this in your Console:

```
There are 5 chapters.
The titles are: (
    "Preface",
    "Meet Your Project Portfolio",
    "Create Your First Draft",
    "Evaluate Your Projects",
    "Rank the Portfolio"
)
This book has 59 pages so far.
The longest chapter is 20 pages long.
The average chapter length is 11.8.
```

So, have I convinced you? Can you see that KVC is about much more than replacing [foo bar] with [foo valueForKey:@"bar"]? You can read more about KVC in Apple's *Key-Value Coding Programming Guide* [App08g].

KVC brings you a lot of flexibility, but that's only the half of it. The real power of KVC is in the other technologies that it enables. In the next chapter, we'll look at the other foundational piece of this puzzle: Key Value Observing.

Chapter 20

Key Value Observing

When I was a kid, we'd hope for snow days. These were days when it snowed so much that school was canceled and we could spend the day playing outside in the snow. Back then when it snowed, we'd listen to the radio or watch television for the list of school closings. We had to pick our school out of the list—the radio personality or TV weather man didn't know about us or which school we were listening for.

Now, with my daughter, things are different. We can still listen for school closings on radio and television, but we can also register with a local television channel's website. Each year I go to the site and enter my email address and the specific school I'm interested in.

I'm registering as an observer. My email is on a list that is notified when the value of Cocoa Valley Schools changes from open to any other value. In this chapter, we'll look at Key Value Observing (KVO), which is your Cocoa application's version of the Observer pattern.

20.1 Codeless Connections

Let's start this chapter with a basic application.

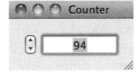

On the left you have a stepper, and on the right you have a text field. As you click the top part of the stepper, the number in the text field increases by one at a time, and if you click the bottom part of the stepper, the number in the text field decreases.

How would you code this? Actually, let's start with no code at all.

Create a new Cocoa project named Counter. We'll use a single nib for this example, so double-click MainMenu.xib. Drag an NSStepper and a text field into the window, and resize them so they look like our picture. An NSStepper contains the value you will want to display in the text field. All you need to do is set the limits and make the connection.

For the limits to the stepper, let's just use the default values. You can click the stepper and use the Attributes inspector to see that the stepper values start at 0 and go between 0 and 100 in steps of size 1. Select the Behavior checkbox so that the value will wrap.

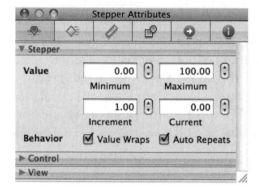

Now let's make the connection. Select the stepper. Control-click the circle to the right of selector in Sent Actions in the Connections inspector. Drag the connection to the text field and release, and you should see these options:

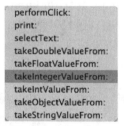

Choose takeIntegerValueFrom:. As a final step, click the text field, and use the Attributes inspector to set its title to 0. This way, when the user runs your application, the initial value will appear. Save your work, and return to Xcode. Click Build & Run. You have a working counter with no code.

So far, there is no observing going on. Right now when the user clicks the stepper, the stepper sends a message to the text field. This is the traditional target-action approach. In the next section, we'll make this even more explicit with code so you can see the direction of the message being sent. Then we'll turn the model on its head and introduce an observer.

20.2 A Target-Action Counter

Before we set up an observer, I'm going to have you expand this example by inserting two objects between the stepper and the text field to illustrate that we are currently using target action. The stepper will send a message to an UpOrDown object, which will send a message to a Display object, which will send a message to the text field. The flow is something like this:

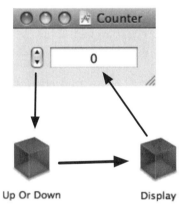

This might feel like a step in the wrong direction, but I think it will help you better see what KVO gives you when we get there in the next section.

Create a new Objective-C class, and name it Display. This class will need an outlet that you'll connect to the text field, and it will need a method that can be called by the UpOrDown object to pass in the new value for the text field.

Notice that there is no property for the displayField, so we indicate that it is an IBOutlet when we declare the variable. If there was a corresponding property, we technically could leave the IBOutlet label with the declaration of the instance variable, but it is better form to move it to the property declaration as we've done before.

```
KVO/Counter2/Display.h
```

```objc
#import <Cocoa/Cocoa.h>

@interface Display : NSObject {
    IBOutlet NSTextField *displayField;
}
-(void)updateDisplay: (NSNumber *) newValue;
@end
```

The implementation of Display contains nothing more than the method that updates the text field:

```
KVO/Counter2/Display.m
```

```objc
#import "Display.h"

@implementation Display

-(void)updateDisplay: (NSNumber *) value{
    [displayField setIntegerValue:[value integerValue]];
}

@end
```

Also, create a new Objective-C class named UpOrDown to receive the action from the stepper and pass it along to the Display object. UpOrDown will need an outlet to connect to the Display and an action method:

```
KVO/Counter2/UpOrDown.h
```

```objc
#import <Cocoa/Cocoa.h>
@class Display;

@interface UpOrDown : NSObject {
    IBOutlet Display *display;
}
-(IBAction) step:(id) sender;
@end
```

Implement the action to call the Display's updateDisplay: method:

```
KVO/Counter2/UpOrDown.m
```

```objc
#import "UpOrDown.h"
#import "Display.h"

@implementation UpOrDown

-(IBAction) step: (id) sender {
    [display updateDisplay:
            [NSNumber numberWithInteger:[sender integerValue]]];
}
@end
```

Save your work, and head over to Interface Builder to wire everything up.

Add an object of type Display and an object of type UpOrDown to your Document window. In the Connections inspector, first break the direct connection between the stepper and the text field. Click UpOrDown, and connect the display outlet to the Display object. Connect the step: received action to the stepper. Click the Display. Connect the displayField outlet to the text field. Save, and click Build & Run.

From a user's standpoint, there is no difference between this version and the codeless version.

Notice that the Display object doesn't have to know anything about the UpOrDown object, but the UpOrDown object needs to know about the Display object. Coming up next, we'll turn this on its head when we make the Display object an observer.

20.3 Introducing an Observer

With the traditional target-action approach, the UpOrDown object had a handle to the Display object and sent the message updateDisplay: to that object. With KVO, the observer knows who it is watching. The observed object just sends out a message when the state has changed—all registered observers will get the notification.

In our example, the Display object will need to send a message to the UpOrDown object to register as an observer. This means that our Display object will need a handle to the UpOrDown object. At this point, you have a relationship that looks like this:

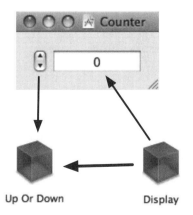

Up Or Down   Display

In other words, you haven't changed the relationship between UpOr-
Down and the stepper or between Display and the text field. But now
Display needs to know about UpOrDown, whereas before it was the other
way around.

Our diagram points out a problem that we have now that we didn't
before. Nothing holds on to the Display object. We're running our applications with garbage collection on. The Display object will register itself
as an observer and then be garbage collected unless we hold on to it.

Add a property to the app delegate:

KVO/Counter3/CounterAppDelegate.h

```
#import <Cocoa/Cocoa.h>
▶ @class Display;

@interface CounterAppDelegate : NSObject <NSApplicationDelegate> {
    NSWindow *window;
▶    Display *display;
}
@property (assign) IBOutlet NSWindow *window;
▶ @property IBOutlet Display *display;
@end
```

Synthesize the property in the implementation file, and connect this
outlet in Interface Builder to the Display object.

Next we connect the Display object to the UpOrDown object and prepare
the objects for adding an observer. First, add an IBOutlet to the Display
header:

KVO/Counter3/Display.h

```
#import <Cocoa/Cocoa.h>
▶ @class UpOrDown;

@interface Display : NSObject {
    IBOutlet NSTextField *displayField;
▶    IBOutlet UpOrDown *counter;
}
@end
```

I've removed the declaration for the updateDisplay: method. We'll still
implement this method, but it no longer is part of the Display's public
interface.

Next, let's move over to the object it's observing. The UpOrDown header
file can be altered a bit. We'll remove all references to Display and add
an ivar of type NSNumber named count.

KVO/Counter3/UpOrDown.h

```
#import <Cocoa/Cocoa.h>

@interface UpOrDown : NSObject {
    NSNumber *count;
}
-(IBAction) step:(id) sender;
@end
```

Let's go fix the nib file and then come back and implement these two classes. In Interface Builder, break the connection between UpOrDown's display outlet and Display. Select Display, and connect its counter outlet to UpOrDown. Save your work.

Now we're ready to set up our observer. There are three basic steps:

1. The observer needs to register with the object that contains a property it wants to observe.

2. The observed object must update its property in such a way that observers will be notified of the change.

3. The observer must respond to notifications it receives.

Let's look at each of these in turn.

20.4 Registering an Observer

Registering as an observer is easy. You just send this message to the object you want to observe:

```
addObserver:forKeyPath:options:context:
```

Pass in a pointer to the observer as the first parameter. In this case, we'll pass in self, but you can use any object. The keypath is the path to the property we're interested in. This is the same form that you saw when learning about KVC. Four options are available to you, and you can combine them using |.

The four NSKeyValueObservingOptions are NSKeyValueObservingOptionNew, NSKeyValueObservingOptionOld, NSKeyValueObservingOptionInitial, and NS-KeyValueObservingOptionPrior. The first two control whether you get the new or old value of the attribute you're watching. The third sends a notification when you are first setting up the observer. The last indicates you want a message sent before and after each change instead of just after.

Here's how we register our Display to listen for changes in the count property of the UpOrDown object. We'll register when the Display object awakes from nib.

`KVO/Counter3/Display.m`

```
-(void) awakeFromNib {
    [counter addObserver:self
                forKeyPath:@"count"
                    options:NSKeyValueObservingOptionNew
                    context:NULL];
}
```

All objects inherit addObserver:forKeyPath:options:context: from NSObject so the Display object can send that message to the UpOrDown object to register itself as an observer of the count property.

Don't forget to clean up after yourself. You need to unregister your observers when the observer is being released. When we managed memory by reference counting, we released resources in the dealloc method. Now, with automatic garbage collection turned on, we instead use the finalize method as dealloc is never called.

`KVO/Counter3/Display.m`

```
-(void) finalize {
    [counter removeObserver:self forKeyPath:@"count"];
    [super finalize];
}
```

That's all there is to responsibly registering an observer.

20.5 Making Changes Observable

We've seen so much magic in Cocoa that it seems as if you should just be able to set the value of UpOrDown's ivar count like this and have the change get picked up by Display.

```
-(void) step: (id) sender {
    //not good enough
    count = [NSNumber numberWithInteger:[sender integerValue]];
}
```

Unfortunately, when you set a variable directly, you need to bracket the change with a signal that an observed value is about to change and another signal that the observed value did change.

The corrected code looks like this:

KVO/Counter3/UpOrDown.m

```
-(IBAction) step: (id) sender {
▶       [self willChangeValueForKey:@"count"];
        count = [NSNumber numberWithInteger:[sender integerValue]];
▶       [self didChangeValueForKey:@"count"];
}
```

This is a pain in the neck. There are two other less painful ways. One is to use Key Value Coding. When you use setValue:forKey:, the observers are notified. KVC and KVO are made to work together. Here's how you would modify UpOrDown to use KVC:

KVO/Counter4/UpOrDown.m

```
-(IBAction) step: (id) sender {
▶       [self setValue:[NSNumber numberWithInteger:[sender integerValue]]
▶               forKey:@"count"];
}
```

I don't know if that went by too quickly for you to notice how slick it was. count is an instance variable and not a property, and we just used KVC to change its value. I know I said we could in the previous chapter, but now you can see an added benefit of doing so. You change the value of the variable, and you send notifications of that change to observers that have registered using KVO.

Another solution is to declare and use a property for the variable count. Add your property to the header file:

KVO/Counter5/UpOrDown.h

```
#import <Cocoa/Cocoa.h>

@interface UpOrDown : NSObject {
    NSNumber *count;
}
▶ @property(copy) NSNumber *count;
-(IBAction) step:(id) sender;
@end
```

Set the property value directly. The observer will be notified of the change:

KVO/Counter5/UpOrDown.m

```
#import "UpOrDown.h"

@implementation UpOrDown
▶ @synthesize count;
```

```
-(IBAction) step: (id) sender {
    self.count = [NSNumber numberWithInteger:[sender integerValue]];
}
@end
```

In this section, you've seen three methods of changing the value of a variable in such a way that observers can be notified. First, you can directly change the value of the variable, but you have to wrap it in calls to willChangeValueForKey: and didChangeValueForKey:. Second, you can use KVC to change the value of the variable using setValue:ForKey:. Finally, you can create a property and change the value of the property instead of the underlying instance variable.

20.6 Observing the Changes

Now the observer is registered, and the attribute it is watching is set up to be observed and to notify the observer of changes. The last step is for the observer to respond to the changes. I have to warn you, this is the part that gets a lot of complaints. Here's what it might look like in our application:

KVO/Counter5/Display.m

```
Line 1  - (void)observeValueForKeyPath:(NSString *)keyPath
     2                       ofObject:(id)object
     3                         change:(NSDictionary *)change
     4                        context:(void *)context {
     5        [self updateDisplay:[object valueForKeyPath:keyPath]];
     6  }
```

The method signature is four lines long while the method body is a single line. In line 5, I've chosen to update the display with the new value that I pull off the change dictionary.

So, what's the complaint?

This method gets called for every property this object is observing. You might be listening for changes in multiple properties in the same object, or you might be listening for changes in properties that belong to different objects. If you are registered to be notified of updates to a property, then this is the method that gets called, and it's up to you to figure out who called you and what to do about it.

This isn't a big deal, but this differs from the way notifications work. With notifications, you get to specify which method in which object would be called for any given notification. This is a different mechanism, and people who want to interact with it the same way they worked with notifications complain loudly.

There are many ways to handle this limitation. One is to check that the keypath is to the count property. You'll soon see that this can get ugly and out of hand if we are listening for changes in more than one property. The easiest way to get around this limitation is to create small focused observers that each only listen for changes in a single property. We'll come back to that approach later in this chapter.

20.7 Exercise: Adding a Second Observer

One advantage of KVO is that the object containing the attribute being observed doesn't need to know anything about the observer. You can add as many observers as you want.

Let's do that. Add a second observer for the count property in UpOrDown. Create a class named Logger that outputs the counter's new value to the Console. You shouldn't have to make any changes to UpOrDown or to Display.

20.8 Solution: Adding a Second Observer

Add a new Objective-C class named Logger to your project. Logger will need an outlet to connect to the UpOrDown instance, so your header should look something like this:

KVO/Counter6/Logger.h

```
#import <Cocoa/Cocoa.h>
@class UpOrDown;

@interface Logger : NSObject {
    IBOutlet UpOrDown *counter;
}
@end
```

Add an outlet for your Logger object in CounterAppDelegate.h. Create an instance of Logger in Interface Builder, and connect its counter outlet to UpOrDown. Connect CounterAppDelegate's logger outlet to your Logger outlet. Save.

The implementation of Logger is almost identical to Display. The differences are highlighted here. I'm showing you all of Logger since you've only seen Display in bits and pieces.

KVO/Counter6/Logger.m

```
#import "Logger.h"


@implementation Logger
►  -(void)logValue: (NSNumber *) value{
►      NSLog(@"%@", value);
►  }
   -(void) awakeFromNib {
       [counter addObserver:self
                 forKeyPath:@"count"
                    options:NSKeyValueObservingOptionNew
                    context:NULL];
   }
   - (void)observeValueForKeyPath:(NSString *)keyPath
                         ofObject:(id)object
                           change:(NSDictionary *)change
                          context:(void *)context {
►      [self logValue:[object valueForKeyPath:keyPath]];
   }
   -(void) finalize {
       [counter removeObserver:self forKeyPath:@"count"];
       [super finalize];
   }
@end
```

So, it's easy to add as many observers as you'd like. They don't affect the object they're observing, and they don't need to know about other observers.

On the other hand, things get complicated when you have one object observe more than one attribute in one or more objects.

20.9 The Ugly Way to Observe More Than One Attribute

Let's double our fun with two steppers and two displays. Each display is tied to just one of the steppers. We're going to use UpOrDown to interact with both steppers. Display will register as an observer for the current counts for both steppers.

This means the same object will be an observer for two different attributes. We'll handle this in two ways—but first we need to do a little prep work.

Our interface looks like this:

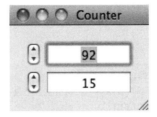

Let's get rid of the Logger files. They don't do any harm, but they clutter up this example a bit. You'll need to delete Logger.h and Logger.m. Don't forget to delete the Logger object from Interface Builder's Document window and remove the logger property from CounterAppDelegate.

UpOrDown will now need two outlets and two properties:

`KVO/Counter7/UpOrDown.h`

```
#import <Cocoa/Cocoa.h>

@interface UpOrDown : NSObject {
    NSNumber *countOne, *countTwo;
}
@property(copy) NSNumber *countOne, *countTwo;
-(IBAction) stepOne:(id) sender;
-(IBAction) stepTwo:(id) sender;
@end
```

In UpOrDown.m, you need to synthesize both variables and implement the actions to set the properties using the current counter value:

`KVO/Counter7/UpOrDown.m`

```
#import "UpOrDown.h"

@implementation UpOrDown

@synthesize countOne, countTwo;

-(IBAction) stepOne: (id) sender {
    self.countOne = [NSNumber numberWithInteger:[sender integerValue]];
}
-(IBAction) stepTwo: (id) sender {
    self.countTwo = [NSNumber numberWithInteger:[sender integerValue]];
}
@end
```

Add a second outlet for the additional text field in Display.h:

`KVO/Counter7/Display.h`

```
#import <Cocoa/Cocoa.h>
@class UpOrDown;

@interface Display : NSObject {
    IBOutlet NSTextField *displayFieldOne, *displayFieldTwo;
    IBOutlet UpOrDown *counter;
}
@end
```

Wire up your actions and outlets in Interface Builder, and remove the stale links.

Back in Xcode, finish up with Display.m. For the most part, we are doing everything twice. We could have gotten clever with KVC, but that would have obscured the point of this example, which is how one object observes more than one attribute.

The Display object is listening for changes both to countOne and to countTwo. If either changes, then the observeValueForKeyPath: method is called. That means we have to figure out why this method is being called. One solution, highlighted here, is to examine the keypath, and if need be, the object that is being observed to see who issued the notification and why.

`KVO/Counter7/Display.m`

```
#import "Display.h"

@implementation Display

-(void) updateDisplayOne: (NSNumber *) newValue{
    [displayFieldOne setIntegerValue:[newValue integerValue]];
}
-(void) updateDisplayTwo: (NSNumber *) newValue{
    [displayFieldTwo setIntegerValue:[newValue integerValue]];
}
-(void) awakeFromNib {
    [counter addObserver:self
            forKeyPath:@"countOne"
                options:NSKeyValueObservingOptionNew
                context:NULL];
    [counter addObserver:self
            forKeyPath:@"countTwo"
                options:NSKeyValueObservingOptionNew
                context:NULL];
}
```

```
- (void)observeValueForKeyPath:(NSString *)keyPath
                      ofObject:(id)object
                       change:(NSDictionary *)change
                      context:(void *)context {
▶      if ([keyPath isEqualToString:@"countOne"]){
▶          [self updateDisplayOne:[object valueForKeyPath:keyPath]];
▶      } else if ([keyPath isEqualToString:@"countTwo"]){
▶          [self updateDisplayTwo:[object valueForKeyPath:keyPath]] ;
▶      }
    }
    -(void) finalize {
        [counter removeObserver:self forKeyPath:@"countOne"];
        [counter removeObserver:self forKeyPath:@"countTwo"];
        [super finalize];
    }
    @end
```

I'm not particularly proud of code like this. For the most part, you've
seen that we can wiggle out of a lot of conditionals when we code in
Cocoa using Objective-C. This gives us a cleaner path through the code.

In the next two sections I'll show you two different approaches. First,
we'll use KVC to call the correct method depending on the key of the
notification we are sent. Second, we'll introduce dedicated observer
objects. The difference between these two approaches comes down to
making the decision at the time you register as an observer or when
you receive the notification. I prefer using dedicated observers, but I'm
not religious about it.

20.10 Selecting Methods Using KVC

When we receive a notification, it is because of changes either to countOne or to countTwo. So, one approach we could take is to rename the
methods for updating the two displays:

KVO/Counter8/Display.m

```
-(void) updateDisplayForcountOne: (NSNumber *) newValue{
    [displayFieldOne setIntegerValue:[newValue integerValue]];
}
-(void) updateDisplayForcountTwo: (NSNumber *) newValue{
    [displayFieldTwo setIntegerValue:[newValue integerValue]];
}
```

Now we can call the right method by appending countOne or countTwo to the end of updateDisplayFor and passing in the value of the appropriate counter as a parameter:

KVO/Counter8/Display.m

```
- (void)observeValueForKeyPath:(NSString *)keyPath
                    ofObject:(id)object
                      change:(NSDictionary *)change
                     context:(void *)context {
▶    [self performSelector:NSSelectorFromString(
▶          [NSString stringWithFormat:@"updateDisplayFor%@:",keyPath])
▶                      withObject: [object valueForKeyPath:keyPath]];
}
```

Code like this always feels a bit slick to me. It's clever, it works, and it's a nice example of using KVC, but I don't think the intent of the code is clear. Let's restore the method names to updateDisplayOne: and updateDisplayTwo: and set up independent observers.

20.11 Implementing an Observer Object

We can easily create an Observer that is a helper object. We'll set it up and tell it who to call and what method to invoke when the notification is sent.

Create an Observer class, and add properties to hold a pointer to the target object and action. Also, declare a special init method that allows you to pass this information in.

KVO/Counter9/Observer.h

```
#import <Cocoa/Cocoa.h>

@interface Observer : NSObject {
    id targetObject;
    SEL targetAction;
}
@property id targetObject;
@property SEL targetAction;
-(id) initWithTarget:(id)object action: (SEL)action;

@end
```

The observeValueForKeyPath:ofObject:change:context: method invokes the action that we've captured in the targetAction property on an object we've captured in the targetObject property. It passes in the current value of the counter as a parameter.

KVO/Counter9/Observer.m

```objc
#import "Observer.h"

@implementation Observer

@synthesize targetObject, targetAction;

- (void)observeValueForKeyPath:(NSString *)keyPath
                      ofObject:(id)object
                        change:(NSDictionary *)change
                       context:(void *)context {
    [self.targetObject performSelector:self.targetAction
                            withObject:[object valueForKeyPath:keyPath]];
}
-(id) initWithTarget:(id)object action: (SEL)action {
    if (self = [super init]) {
        self.targetObject = object;
        self.targetAction = action;
    }
    return self;
}
@end
```

Now our Display class can be simplified. Declare the instance variables observerOne and observerTwo of type Observer in the Display header file:

KVO/Counter9/Display.h

```objc
#import <Cocoa/Cocoa.h>
@class UpOrDown;
@class Observer;

@interface Display : NSObject {
    IBOutlet NSTextField *displayFieldOne, *displayFieldTwo;
    IBOutlet UpOrDown *counter;
    Observer *observerOne, *observerTwo;
}
@end
```

Register the new observers in awakeFromNib. Remove the observeValue-ForKeyPath:ofObject:change:context: method. It's now implemented in the observer. Release the observers in the finalize method.

KVO/Counter9/Display.m

```objc
#import "Display.h"
#import "Observer.h"

@implementation Display

-(void) updateDisplayOne: (NSNumber *) newValue{
    [displayFieldOne setIntegerValue:[newValue integerValue]];
}
```

```
-(void) updateDisplayTwo: (NSNumber *) newValue{
    [displayFieldTwo setIntegerValue:[newValue integerValue]];
}
-(void) awakeFromNib {
    observerOne = [[Observer alloc]
                    initWithTarget:self
                        action:@selector(updateDisplayOne:)];
    observerTwo = [[Observer alloc]
                    initWithTarget:self
                        action:@selector(updateDisplayTwo:)];
    [counter addObserver:observerOne
            forKeyPath:@"countOne"
                options:NSKeyValueObservingOptionNew
                context:NULL];
    [counter addObserver:observerTwo
            forKeyPath:@"countTwo"
                options:NSKeyValueObservingOptionNew
                context:NULL];
}
-(void) finalize {
    [counter removeObserver:observerOne forKeyPath:@"countOne"];
    [counter removeObserver:observerTwo forKeyPath:@"countTwo"];
    [super finalize];
}
@end
```

Small, single-purpose classes like Observer can unclutter your code. Each instance of the Observer knows which object to send which method when it gets called.

20.12 Updating Dependent Variables

Sometimes within a class you have variables that depend on the values of other variables. The dependent variables can always be recalculated from the independent variables. Suppose, for example, we want to introduce a new variable called totalCount in UpOrDown that represents the sum of countOne and countTwo. Any time a user clicks either of the steppers, the value of totalCount will change.

We need to be able to do the following:

- Register that totalCount depends on both countOne and countTwo.
- Add an observer that listens for changes in totalCount. It actually will listen for changes in any of the attributes that we registered in the previous step.
- Specify what we want to have happen when we receive a notification of a change in totalCount.

There are two forms for registering totalCount's dependencies. One is to use this method:

```
+ (NSSet *)keyPathsForValuesAffectingValueForKey:(NSString *)key
```

This class method can be used for registering dependencies for any number of variables. You just return different NSSets for each key. An alternate form of the method involves concatenating the variable name to the end of keyPathsForValuesAffecting. So, for the variable totalCount, we have this method that registers its dependence on countOne and countTwo:

```
+(NSSet *)keyPathsForValuesAffectingTotalCount {
    return [NSSet setWithObjects:@"countOne",@"countTwo",nil];
}
```

In the header file for UpOrDown, add a declaration for a pointer to an NSNumber named totalCount:

`KVO/Counter10/UpOrDown.h`

```
#import <Cocoa/Cocoa.h>

@interface UpOrDown : NSObject {
    NSNumber *countOne, *countTwo, *totalCount;
}
@property(copy) NSNumber *countOne, *countTwo, *totalCount;
-(IBAction) stepOne:(id) sender;
-(IBAction) stepTwo:(id) sender;
@end
```

Here's the implementation for UpOrDown:

`KVO/Counter10/UpOrDown.m`

```
#import "UpOrDown.h"

@implementation UpOrDown

@synthesize countOne, countTwo, totalCount;

-(IBAction) stepOne: (id) sender {
    self.countOne = [NSNumber numberWithInteger:[sender integerValue]];
}
-(IBAction) stepTwo: (id) sender {
    self.countTwo = [NSNumber numberWithInteger:[sender integerValue]];
}
+(NSSet *)keyPathsForValuesAffectingTotalCount {
    return [NSSet setWithObjects:@"countOne", @"countTwo", nil];
}
-(NSNumber *) totalCount {
    return [NSNumber numberWithInt:
            [self.countOne intValue] + [self.countTwo intValue]];
}
```

```
-(void)awakeFromNib{
    [self addObserver:self
           forKeyPath:@"totalCount"
              options:NSKeyValueObservingOptionNew
              context:NULL];
}
-(void)observeValueForKeyPath:(NSString *)keyPath
                     ofObject:(id)object
                       change:(NSDictionary *)change
                      context:(void *)context {
    NSLog(@"%@", self.totalCount);
}
@end
```

In addition to keyPathsForValuesAffectingTotalCount:, we register the observer in the awakeFromNib method. We also have a getter method for totalCount that returns the sum of countOne and countTwo. This is called from the observeValueForKeyPath:ofObject:change:context: method whenever either value is changed. In response, we just log the total to the Console.[1]

This chapter took you through the fundamentals of observing.[2] You register an object and wait until it is called back. This is like a notification without a notification center. This is just a relationship between two objects, and only the observer needs to know about the observed. You've seen how to register multiple observers to one attribute and how to register a single observer to multiple attributes. Finally, you saw how to set up a dependent variable so its observers were updated when the variables it depends on change.

As cool as KVO and KVC are both individually and together, their real power is in the technologies they enable. We'll strip out code from the controller layer with Bindings and from the model layer with Core Data.

You can use KVO and KVC whether you're developing for Mac OS X or for iPhone OS. If you are mainly interested in developing for Mac OS X, you're going to love where we're headed next. We're going to see how these technologies enable bindings, which let you write less code for the controller layer. Unfortunately, there currently isn't any support for bindings for iPhone OS.

---

1. See KVO/Counter11 in the code zip file to see that you can remove the totalCount instance variable and property and still get this same behavior.
2. You can find more information in Apple's *Key-Value Observing Guide* [App08f].

Chapter 21

Cocoa Bindings

So far, we've used Interface Builder to create our GUI and to connect buttons, labels, tables, and more to controllers and models. This eliminates a lot of boilerplate code. You don't need to inherit from an NSButton and configure its look and placement in code. You know from our work with custom views that you can write that code—you just don't have to this.

Cocoa Bindings looks at the controller layer and asks how much of the repetitive code can be removed. It turns out, if you are careful to work with KVO- and KVC-compliant classes, the answer is "most of it." Much of this chapter will find us back in Interface Builder making connections and typing in keypaths. We'll have a little bit of code to write but not much.

We'll start this chapter by creating a new Cocoa application named CounterWithBindings. You will add a new Objective-C class named Counter, declare a property named count of type NSNumber, and synthesize it. That's all the code you're going to need to write to create your model.

As for the view, you'll drag a stepper and a text field into the window. We'll add more as the chapter progresses, but that will be good enough to begin with.

That leaves us with the controller. In this chapter, you won't be implementing the controller in code. You'll use Cocoa Bindings and the fact that your model is KVC and KVO compliant to create your controller using Interface Builder. Cocoa Bindings will let the view and model communicate without us writing a lot of boilerplate glue code. We'll start by revisiting our example from the previous chapter.

21.1 The Model and View for Our Counter with Bindings

Create a new project named CounterWithBindings. Add a new Objective-C class named Counter that contains the property count. In other words, you add two lines of code to the header file template:

Bindings/CounterWithBindings1/Counter.h

```
#import <Cocoa/Cocoa.h>

@interface Counter : NSObject {
    NSNumber *count;
}
@property(copy) NSNumber *count;

@end
```

You also need to add one line of code to the implementation to synthesize the property count:

Bindings/CounterWithBindings1/Counter.m

```
#import "Counter.h"

@implementation Counter

@synthesize count;

@end
```

We have a single class with a single property defined. There will be no other code in this application for the first part of this chapter.

Now let's create the view. Drag a stepper and a text field into the main window. As before, use the Attributes inspector so that the stepper's behavior is set to Value Wraps. Resize the window to look like this:

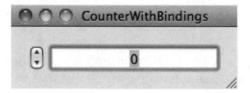

OK. Now we have our model and our view. Let's create the controller.

21.2 Creating and Connecting the NSObjectController

In Interface Builder, drag a Counter object from the Library, and drop it on the Document window. This is the instance of your model.

\\// Joe Asks...

Wouldn't Code Be Better?

Depending on your background, it sure can feel like that. A lot of the logic now moves to files you set up with Interface Builder. When you have a problem, you can't use the techniques you've been using forever. Initially, it *is* harder to locate problems. On the other hand, you're less likely to create these problems by making mistakes in what should be boilerplate code.

Cocoa Bindings can be scary. But soon you'll get a feel for where you should look when things go wrong. If you think back to your early days coding, the same thing was true there. You had to learn where to look for problems. You probably stared long and hard before you found that you typed = when you meant to type ==. So, this isn't a new frustration so much as a new frontier for an old one.

Next, drag an NSObjectController from your Library to the Document window. Remember back to our early examples in this book. The controller sits between the model and the view. The controller insists on being an intermediary. You will need to configure your controller by following these three steps:

1. Connect to the object that the object controller is controlling.

2. Specify which keys the object controller is responsible for.

3. Bind each element to a property that the object controller is controlling.

Connecting the Controller

The object controller needs to know which object it is controlling. Click the object controller, and look in the Connections inspector for its content outlet. Connect this content connection to the Counter object. You can (and soon will) have more than one object of the same type. This is the step where you are specifying which one the object controller is responsible for.

Selecting the Keys

Next you'll need to make the count key available to objects that bind to the NSObjectController. Select the object controller, and use the Attributes inspector to set the class name to Counter. Notice that there are two modes. We are using the class mode here because Counter is a class. When we build data models with Core Data, we will use the entity mode.

You have to explicitly specify which keys the object controller will make available for binding. Here there is only one possible choice. Use the plus sign to add the key count.

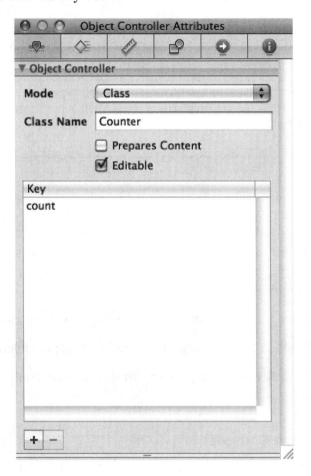

Binding a Component

Click the text field to select it, and open its Bindings inspector using ⌘4 or just by clicking the inspector's fourth tab.

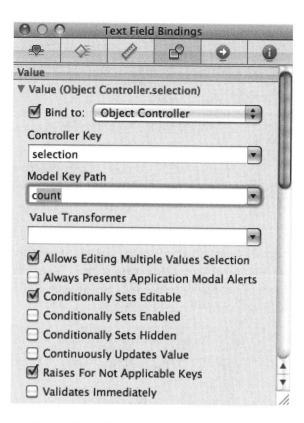

In the Value section, select the "Bind to" checkbox, and use the drop-down list to select Object Controller. The controller key is selection, and the model key path is count. Do the same for the stepper.

Both the stepper and the text field are bound to the value of count. Click Build & Run. Click the stepper, and you can see the values of the text field are changed. So far, this doesn't seem like a very big win. But it is.

When you click the stepper, its value is bound to the value of count, so count is updated automatically. Similarly, the text field is bound to the value of count. Whenever the value of count changes, the text field is automatically updated. The connections are made through the controller. There is a lot of activity going on here. In the next section, we'll add more widgets to make this clearer.

21.3 Binding More Objects

Add a circular slider and a horizontal slider to the view. Bind each to the count by using the object controller.

Configure your sliders to look like this:

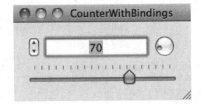

As you click the stepper, the value of count is updated, and all of the bound elements are notified of the change. So, you can see in the figure that when I entered 70 in the text field, the two sliders moved to the corresponding value.

Drag the horizontal slider all the way to the right so the value is 100. Use the stepper to bump the value up by one. The horizontal slider should have moved all the way to the left. Rotate the circular slider and let go. You should see something like this:

I'm not really happy with the way the sliders work right now. I just want integer values for my count, but, as you can see, it's too easy for my sliders to result in a value with many digits to the right of the decimal point.

We could select a slider and use the Attributes inspector to specify that we want the slider to "Only stop on tick marks." I've set up my horizontal slider with twenty tick marks, so this would allow me to choose multiples of five. So, I restrict my values to integers, but I can't select any integer that is not a multiple of five.

We'll use a number formatter to get what we want.

21.4 Number Formatters

Look in your Interface Builder Library for an NSNumberFormatter. Drag it from the Library, and drop it on your text field. You should see the number formatter icon below your text field when your text field is selected. You may have to select another element and then select your text field to see the icon appear the first time. You can also find the number formatter in the Document window.

Select the number formatter, and then take a look at the Attributes inspector:

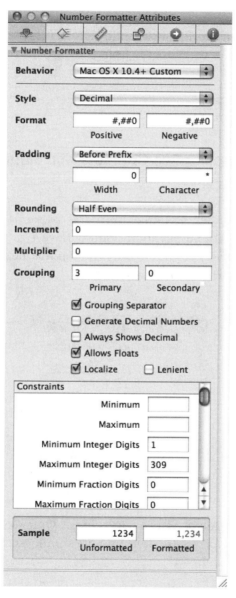

You have an amazing range of parameters you can set. We will adjust only a couple of them. Notice the drop-down at the top of the inspector. Two styles of number formatting are available to you. We are targeting the more modern version, so make sure Mac OS X 10.4+ Custom is selected. You can think of an integer as a decimal with nothing after the decimal point. So, first, set the style to Decimal. Now skip down to the "Constraints" section and set the value of Maximum Fraction Digits to 0.

That's it. Save your work. Click Build & Run, and your sliders will be able to choose any of the integers from 0 to 100 and nothing else.[1]

21.5   Exercise: Connecting Two Counters with Bindings

Let's re-create another example from the previous chapter without adding any code. The application should have two steppers and two text fields. The top stepper alters only the top text field, and the bottom stepper alters only the bottom text field.

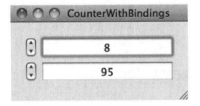

Again, you should be able to accomplish this entirely in Interface Builder without changing or adding a line of code.

Here's one tip you might find useful. Select your Counter, and look at the Identity inspector. At the bottom you should see a section labeled "Interface Builder Identity."

---

1. This solution corresponds to what you'll find in Bindings/CounterWithBindings3 in the code samples.

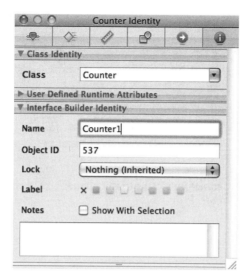

You can see that I've changed the name from the blank text field you see to Counter1. Do that, and take a look at your Document window.

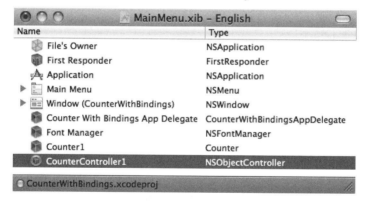

We've changed the object's name to Counter1 without changing its associated class. This will make it easier for you to distinguish between the two counters. You can see that I've also changed the name of the NSObjectController. We don't need to worry so much about the visible elements because we can click one text field or the other and know which one we mean. For the nonvisual elements, the ability to give them distinct names is really helpful.

21.6 Solution: Connecting Two Counters with Bindings

You just need to build a second parallel system to the one you have. You'll end up with two steppers, two text fields, two controllers, and two model objects.

The Family of NSControllers

NSObjectController extends from the abstract classNSController. Here is a family portrait of the NSObjectController and its siblings:

 Object Controller – A Cocoa bindings–compatible controller class. Properties of the content object of an instance of this class...

 Array Controller – A Cocoa bindings compatible class that manages a collection of objects.

 Tree Controller – A Cocoa bindings compatible controller that manages a tree of objects.

 User Defaults Controller – A Cocoa bindings compatible controller class. Properties of the shared instance of this class can be bound to...

 Dictionary Controller – A Cocoa bindings compatible class that manages display and editing of the contents of an NSDictionary...

Start with a little cleanup. Remove the two sliders from the interface, and add another stepper and text field. I removed the number formatter, but you don't need to do so. You can speed this step by selecting the existing stepper and text field, duplicating them using ⌘D, and placing the new items where you want them.

Use the Identity inspector to change the names of the Counter and NSObjectController to Counter1 and CounterController1, respectively.

Drag a Counter object from the Library to the Document window, and change its and its name to Counter2. Drag a new object controller in from the Library, and change its name to CounterController2.

Now just follow the steps you did before. Select the CounterController2, and use the Connections inspector to connect the content outlet to Counter2. Switch to the Attributes inspector, set the class to Counter, and add the count key.

Your final step is to bind the bottom stepper and text field. Select them in turn, and use the Bindings inspector to bind to CounterController2. Set the value of Controller Key to selection and Model Key Path to count.[2]

21.7 The Model for Our Bookshelf Example

We're going to revisit our example of a bookshelf that contains books. The goal is to move from working with bindings and object controllers to bindings with array controllers.

Create a new Cocoa project called BookshelfWithBindings, and add the PragBook class with two properties, title and author, that are both strings:

Bindings/BookshelfWithBindings/PragBook.h

```
#import <Cocoa/Cocoa.h>

@interface PragBook : NSObject {
    NSString *author, *title;
}
@property (copy) NSString *author, *title;
@end
```

Synthesize the properties in the implementation:

Bindings/BookshelfWithBindings/PragBook.m

```
#import "PragBook.h"

@implementation PragBook
@synthesize author, title;
@end
```

Create a Bookshelf class to contain one or more PragBooks. The Bookshelf class contains an NSMutableArray named bookList as its only property:

Bindings/BookshelfWithBindings/Bookshelf.h

```
#import <Cocoa/Cocoa.h>

@interface Bookshelf : NSObject {
    NSMutableArray *bookList;
}
@property(retain) NSMutableArray *bookList;
@end
```

---

2. The solution is in the code download in Bindings/CounterWithBindings4.

We need to initialize the bookList before we work with it. Let's do that in our awakeFromNib method:

`Bindings/BookshelfWithBindings/Bookshelf.m`

```
#import "Bookshelf.h"

@implementation Bookshelf
@synthesize bookList;
-(void) awakeFromNib {
    self.bookList = [NSMutableArray arrayWithCapacity:1];
}
@end
```

Bookshelf doesn't know about PragBook. We'll use Bindings later to specify that PragBook is the type of object contained in the bookList.

That's it. That's all the code we need to write for this example.[3] Once you see what our finished project can do, I think you'll be convinced of the power of Bindings and the NSArrayController.

21.8 Creating the View for the Bookshelf

Add a table view and two square buttons to your window, and adjust the various headings so you have something like this:

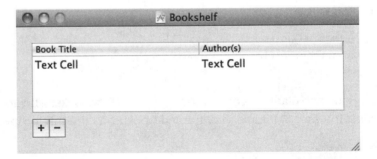

The trickiest part may be setting the + and - signs on the square buttons. Your first impulse may be to just type + or - in for the button titles. This will work, but it won't look nearly as nice. Apple has provided a set of images that you can select with the image drop-down list.

---

3. The word *need* is not quite correct. We can write less code and will once we get to Core Data.

SelectNSAddTemplate for the + and NSRemoveTemplate for the - like this:

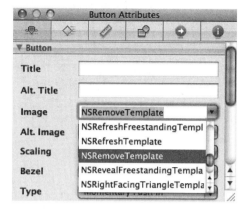

This time you don't need to create identifiers for the table columns. We'll do all of that work using Bindings.

21.9 Binding with the NSArrayController

Add an array controller and a Bookshelf object to your Document window so that we have all of our ingredients available to us in Interface Builder.

We'll follow these steps to set up the bindings:

1. Specify the object contained in the array, and specify the keys we want to bind to.

2. Bind the array controller to the array it contains.

3. Bind the table columns.

We'll then need to wire up the + and - buttons.

Setting the Array's Contents

When the user presses the + button, an object will be added to the book-List array. We need to specify that this object should be an instance of PragBook. Select the array controller, and open the Attributes inspector.

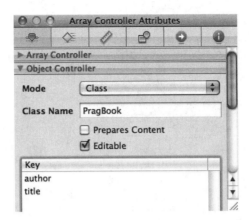

Set Class Name to PragBook. Add the keys author and title.

Connect the Controller to Its Array

You connected the object controller to its object using the content out-let. This time you'll bind the array controller to the array using the content array. Select the array controller, and open the Bindings inspector.

Under Controller Content, find Content Array. Select the "Bind to" checkbox, and choose Bookshelf in the drop-down list. Set the Model Key Path to bookList.

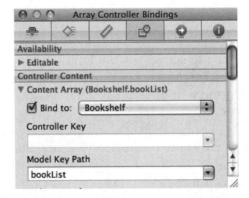

You've configured the array controller. Next we'll bind elements of the view to our array controller to finish wiring up our application.

Configure the Table Columns

Now you are going to bind the table columns so that the first column is filled with the name of the title and the second is filled with the name of the author. Select the first table column, and open the Bindings inspector.

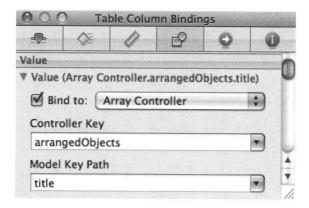

Bind to the array controller. Notice this time Controller Key is arrange-dObjects and not selection because the column is associated with this slice of the entire array. Set Model Key Path to title. Repeat the process for the second column, but this time set Model Key Path to author.

Wiring Up the Buttons

Use the Connections inspector to wire up the buttons. Drag from the + button's sent action to the array controller. You should get a list of possible actions. Choose add:. Do the same for the - button, but this time choose remove:.

Before we call it a day, we'll make sure that the - button is enabled only when there are items in the array that can be removed. Select the - button, and open the Bindings inspector.

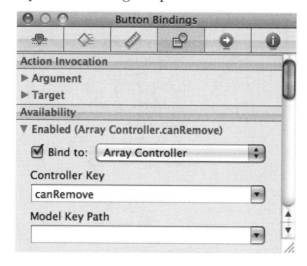

So far we've only used selection and arrangedObjects for Controller Key. There are a lot of other options that correspond to situations that arise when working with arrays. One of them is canRemove:. That's what we bind the - button to in the button's Bindings inspector under Availability > Enabled.

21.10 The Big Finish

Click Build & Run. Click the + button, and add books to your list. Click the - button, and remove some.

I know this isn't magic, but it feels pretty close. With a minimal amount of code, we've created an application that allows us to add entries to a table and remove them.

This should be enough to get you started with controllers. You can use the user defaults controller to bind GUI elements to your stored defaults. The dictionary and tree controllers are similar to the array controller, but they manage (obviously) dictionaries and trees. For more information, have a look at Apple's *Cocoa Bindings Programming Topics* [App08a] and Apple's *Cocoa Bindings Reference* [App08b].

You can add code to customize your controllers in much the same way that we customized the view to do things that weren't easy in Interface Builder. I'm not suggesting that you don't code—I'm saying that you should take advantage of what you get for free and only write code when you need to write. We'll push this one step further in our next chapter on Core Data.

Chapter 22

Core Data

We've been pretty successful at separating our model, view, and controller. You've seen from our work in custom views that we can write code to describe our views, but you've also seen the power and flexibility we get by creating as much of our views as we can using Interface Builder. You've also seen that the controller layer provides the glue between the model and the view. We've written much of the controller logic in code, but you've seen the power of using Cocoa Bindings to wire up our view and model again in Interface Builder.

But if you look back at the past couple of chapters, there hasn't been a lot to our model. We've created a couple of classes that contain a couple of properties. Core Data lets us build models like this using GUI tools. Entities and attributes will be the Core Data analog for classes and properties.

Core Data provides you with a tool for designing the elements of your model and how they interact with each other. It automatically creates the classes and objects your program will need to work with these model objects, and it takes care of persistence for you. If you are writing data to or reading data from disk in your Cocoa app, you should be using Core Data.

In this chapter, we'll revisit the book example we've worked with and create an entity relationship diagram with Xcode's data modeling tool. We'll re-create and extend this entire example without writing any code. Each book will have a title, one or more authors, and a collection of chapters. We'll allow the user to add, remove, or alter this information for any book they select. We'll also look at how Bindings and Core Data work together to fill these tables, to save and retrieve the information from disk, and to support sorting and searching.

22.1 Entities and Attributes

Let's start by re-creating the model for our bookshelf using Core Data. Flip back a few pages to Section 21.7, *The Model for Our Bookshelf Example*, on page 337. There's not a lot to that model. The PragBook header file declares two properties, author and title, and the implementation synthesizes their accessor methods.

Instead of having a class named PragBook, we will use terms more familiar from working with databases. So, now we'll create an entity named PragBook in our data model. We'll also use attributes in our data model where we used properties.

Create a new project in Xcode using the Mac OS X > Application > Cocoa Application template, but this time make sure you select the "Use Core Data for storage" checkbox.

Name it CDBookshelf. Under Groups & Files, you should see a new group named Models. It contains a single file with the name CDBookshelf_DataModel.xcdatamodel. Double-click this file, and once we add our first entity, you should see something like this:

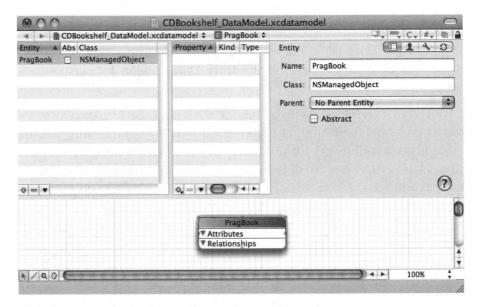

Across the top you'll see subviews for adding entities and properties. I've already added an entity, and you should do the same. Click the +

at the lower left of the Entity area. Type *PragBook* in the Name field.[1] The bottom of the window holds a graphical representation of your data model. You should see PragBook with no attributes or relationships.

Now let's add attributes for the book's title and author's name. With PragBook selected in the entity view, click the + button at the bottom of the properties view. A pop-up list appears with the options Add Attribute, Add Fetched Property, Add Relationship, and Add Fetch Request.

Choose Add Attribute, or use the menu item Design > Data Model > Add Attribute or the keyboard shortcut ⌃ ⌘ A . Name the attribute title, and configure it so it is not optional and so that it is of type String. Because this attribute is not optional, you should add a default value like "Book's title." Add another attribute named author, and also set it to not be optional and to be of type String. Your data model should look like this:

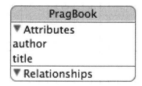

We're done with the data model for now. We'll do the rest of our work in the nib file.

22.2 Using the Core Data Widget

Make a copy of your project because we're going to finish the application in two different ways. First we'll use the widget that Apple has provided that will create both the controller and the view at the same time.

Double-click MainMenu.xib to open the nib in IB. Drag a Core Data Entity from the Library onto your Window object. A wizard will allow you to select the PragBook entity. To do so, you first select the current Xcode project, and then you select the data model contained in the project. Projects can contain more than one data model. In our case, there is only one. Within the data model there are usually multiple entities.

---

1. You need to tab out of the Name field for *PragBook* to appear in the entity view as well.

Ours contains only the PragBook entity. Select it, and click the Next button.

The next panel allows you to choose from three views—I chose Master/Detail view. I've also selected the Add/Remove checkbox so that I can let the user add and remove book entries at runtime. I've also selected the Search Field option to allow users to narrow the set of books displayed based on search criteria. I've left the Detail Fields checkbox unselected. You don't get more information by selecting it in our case; you just get the same information contained in the table called out below. Click Next.

The final panel allows you to select the properties that are included in this interface. I've chosen to display both author and title.

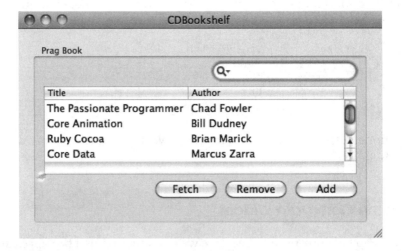

Click Build & Run, and you have a working application that allows you to add and remove books and to search for the entries you want.[2]

Enter some books, and quit your application. Start it up again, and you should see that they are still there. Test that you can remove one or more of your book entries and that you can filter the list by typing into the search field. You have a fully functional Core Data app without really knowing much about what's going on.

---

2. See CoreData/InstantBookshelf in the code download.

Now, let's put this instant bookshelf aside; we'll start again from the data model and add the controller and view by hand. This will help you understand the various layers involved in a Core Data application.

22.3 The Managed Object Context

Go back to a fresh copy of the project, and let's pick it up after you have created the data model with a single entity named PragBook that contains the two required string attributes named title and author. Open your nib file.

Add an array controller to the nib's Document window. Use the Identity inspector to set the name of the array controller to BookController. Note that we are changing the name but not the class. We need to make only two small changes to set up the array controller.

First, open the Attributes inspector for the BookController. This time set the mode to Entity, and type in *PragBook* for the entity name.

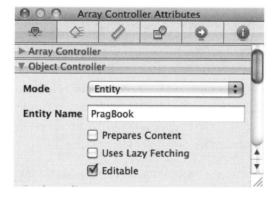

Next, open the Bindings inspector for the array controller. Way down at the bottom under the "Parameters" heading, open the disclosure triangle for the Managed Object Context. I'll tell you what to set, and then I'll explain what you've done.

Select the "Bind to" checkbox, and select CDBookshelf_AppDelegate from the drop-down list. You'll leave the Controller Key and Value Transformer entries blank. Set Model Key Path to managedObjectContext.

You should have something that looks like this:

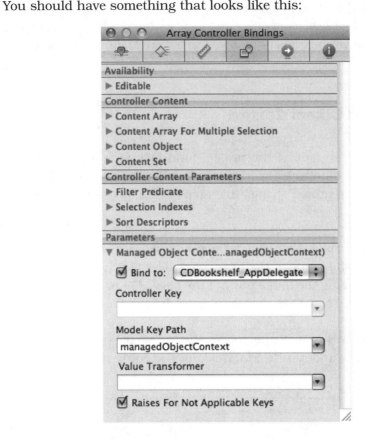

The managed object context is the dividing line between your running application and the mechanism that saves and retrieves data from disk. Your running application will interact with the managed object context using objects (actually managed objects) that are created at runtime from your data model.

An NSManagedObject or a subclass of NSManagedObject will be created to represent each entity in your data model. The actual objects are created as needed.

So, you've wired up the controller to the model in two steps. You had to bind the controller to its managed object context through the application delegate. You also had to use the Attributes inspector to indicate which entity this controller is responsible for.

You have your model and controller set. Now re-create the view exactly as you did in Section 21.8, *Creating the View for the Bookshelf*, on page 338. This is one of the advantages of using MVC. We have completely changed the model and don't need to make any changes to the view.

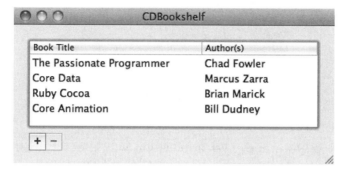

You don't even need to modify the connections and bindings between the view and controller. As before, you bind the table columns to the controller using the Controller Key setting of arrangedObjects with the Model Key Path setting of title for the first column and author for the second. You need to connect the buttons to the controller's add: and remove: methods.

22.4 The Persistence Layer

Click Build & Run. Add some books to your application, and quit. Restart. Hey, wait a minute. What happened to your data? Why are you greeted by an empty table?

Remember from Chapter 17, *Saving Data to Disk*, on page 261 that your application data is stored in your home directory at ~/Library/Application Support. The directory is named the same as your application, so I look inside CDBookshelf and find the file storedata. Open storedata in your favorite text editor, and you should see that your data has been stored and looks something like this:

```
<object type="PRAGBOOK" id="z106">
  <attribute name="title" type="string">
                              The Passionate Programmer</attribute>
  <attribute name="author" type="string">Chad Fowler</attribute>
</object>
```

So, the data is saved to disk without any effort on your part. You need to make one simple change to have it read from disk when your application starts back up. In the Book Controller's Attributes inspector, select the Prepares Content checkbox.

Click Build & Run, and your application will start up with the table populated with the values you entered before.[3] All of this is taken care of for you on the back end by the persistent store coordinator. Your managed object context interacts with your running application to create the objects you need based on your data model. It also interacts with the persistent store coordinator to store and retrieve the data.

If you look at the template code that was generated for you, you'll find that you've created an NSPersistentStoreCoordinator in your application delegate. Here's a snippet from the persistentStoreCoordinator method:

```
CoreData/CDBookshelf1/CDBookshelf_AppDelegate.m
NSURL *url = [NSURL fileURLWithPath: [applicationSupportDirectory
                   stringByAppendingPathComponent: @"storedata"]];
persistentStoreCoordinator = [[NSPersistentStoreCoordinator alloc]
                          initWithManagedObjectModel: mom];
if (![persistentStoreCoordinator
      addPersistentStoreWithType:NSXMLStoreType
      configuration:nil URL:url options:nil error:&error]){
```

In the first highlighted line, we complete the path to where we are storing the data on disk by appending storedata to the path to the CDBookshelf folder in the Application Support directory. In the second highlighted line, we add the persistent store to the persistent store coordinator and set its type to be NSXMLStoreType. So, we've specified that we want to store the data as XML, and we've named the file that will contain the data.

You'll often do your development work using XML as your persistence format and decide whether to switch to SQLite or some custom format

---

3. This is the project CDBookshelf1 in your code download.

as you get close to deploy time. Working in XML lets you open up the stored data and read what was written to disk.[4]

When it's time to ship your app, you can switch the persistent store type to be NSSQLiteStoreType and change the name of the file you're storing the data in if you'd like.

For now, let's continue to work with XML.

22.5 Introducing Relationships

Let's change our data model a bit. A book can have more than one author, and an author might be an entity all on its own containing its own attributes. We'll keep things simple and let an author consist of a first name, middle initial, and last name.

We're about to introduce a bit of complexity into the data model, so you should also delete the entire directory CDBookshelf from your Application Support folder.[5]

Now open your data model, and select the author attribute in the Prag-Book entity. Delete it either by using the menu item Edit > Delete or by hitting your Delete key.

Create a new entity named Author, and give it three attributes: firstName, middleInitial, and lastName. Make them all strings, and make sure that only the middleInitial is optional. Also, set the middleInitial's minimum and maximum length to be one.

This gives you two entities with nothing to connect them in any way. We have books. We have authors.

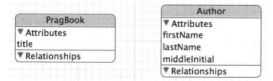

We're going to create a relationship in PragBook that points to the Author entity. Every PragBook will have one or more Authors. Select PragBook; in

---

4. Sure, if you're already someone who loves using SQLite, you are probably comfortable issuing commands from the terminal to look at your tables, but it still feels easier to me to start with XML and switch to SQLite.

5. There are ways to migrate from one version of your schema to another, but those will take us too far afield.

the properties area, click the +, and choose to add a relationship. You can also use the menu item Design > Data Model > Add Relationship or the keyboard shortcut ^ ⌘ R.

Name the relationship authors, and set its destination to be the entity Author. The relationship should be a to-many relationship and not be optional, and the minimum count should be one. Every book needs at least one author, but there may be more than one.

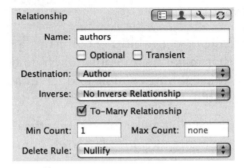

Similarly, every author could have written or helped to write more than one book. So, we need a relationship in the other direction as well. Select Author, and add an optional to-many relationship named books with destination PragBook. This time, click the inverse relationship pull-down, and select authors.

You now have these two inverse relationships between your entities. When you are working with Core Data, you always want to have two-way relationships even if you don't think you need to connect in both directions.

A book also has chapters, so let's add a Chapter entity that has the required attribute title of type string. Of course, a real model would have a great deal more complexity, but including them would get in the way of explaining the basics of working with Core Data.

Since a book has one or more chapters, select PragBook, and create a new relationship named chapters. It is a required to-many relationship with target entity Chapter. Select Chapter, and create the inverse relationship named book. Although other publishers may repurpose chapters, for now each chapter belongs to only one book, so this is not a to-many relationship. It is, however, nonoptional and has target entity PragBook and inverse relationship chapters.

Our entity relationship diagram now looks like this:

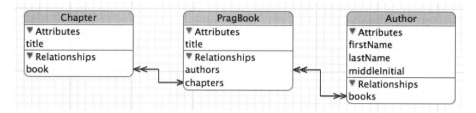

We have a simple data model with three entities, a handful of attributes, and a relationship between each pair of entities. We have one more step before our model is ready for prime time.

22.6 Choosing a Relationship's Delete Rule

Before we wrap up this data model, we need to consider what happens when the user deletes data. For instance, when the user deletes a book, then the book's chapters should disappear as well. But when the user deletes a chapter, the book shouldn't disappear. When the user deletes a book, what should happen to the authors?

We have several options when the user deletes an entry: Deny, Nullify, Cascade, and No Action. These delete rules are part of defining a relationship. Let's look at some examples in our current model.

To start with, how should we set the delete rule for the chapters relationship? We want to make sure that if there are any chapters left in a book, then the user can't delete the book that currently contains the chapters.

In other words, we choose the Deny option so that when a user tries to delete the book, their request will be denied if there are still chapters that would be orphaned without the book they belong to. The Deny option won't let you delete the entity if there is at least one item at the relationship's destination.

Authors are different. One author may have written more than one book, so we don't want to delete the authors when we delete a book. In this case, we choose Nullify as the option. With Nullify, we are not prevented from deleting the book if one or more author still exists. We will set the book relationship in each of the authors to be null. We nullify that relationship because that book no longer exists, so the author couldn't have written it.

We have another option for the chapters relationship. When we delete the book, we could delete all of the chapters for that book as well. In other words, we want the delete to cascade down. We are still enforcing the idea that it doesn't make sense for the chapters to survive if the book doesn't—we've just chosen a different result.

So, set the Delete rule for chapters to Cascade. The inverse relationship book should have the Delete rule Nullify. When we delete a chapter, we don't delete the book it belongs to, but we make sure the book no longer has a reference to this deleted chapter. Similarly, the rule for authors and books should be Nullify.[6]

22.7 Updating the View

By this point, you should be comfortable using Interface Builder without a lot of direction. Open your nib file, select your table view, and reduce the number of columns to one. Select all of the components inside your content view, and choose Layout > Embed Objects In > Box. Change the box's title to Prag Books. Copy that box, paste it twice, and customize the contents to look like this:

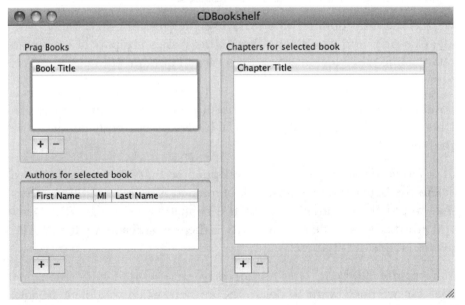

The contents of the chapter and authors boxes need to depend on which book is selected. That's a job for the controller layer.

---

6. You can compare your work with the data model in CDBookshelf2 in the code download.

22.8 Managing Dependencies

To let your users add chapters to a book, start by following the same steps we followed for the Book Controller. Drag an array controller from the Library to your Document window. In the Identity inspector, change its name to Chapter Controller. In the Attributes inspector, change the mode to Entity and Entity Name to Chapter. This time leave Prepares Content unselected. In the Bindings inspector, bind Managed Object Context to the CDBookshelf_AppDelegate with the Model Key Path setting of managedObjectContext.

Now we'll do something dramatically different. Each book has its own set of chapters. The Chapter Controller will manage the chapters for whatever book is currently selected. As you'll soon see, if you switch books, the chapters should switch as well. In the Bindings inspector, you'll need to bind Content Set for the Chapter Controller to the appropriate keypath in the Book Controller. To do this, Controller Key should be selection, and Model Key Path should be chapters.

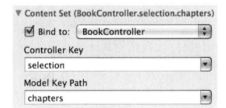

All that remains is to wire up the view. If you created the chapter table and buttons by duplicating the book table, the elements are probably connected to the BookController. Let's move everything to the Chapter-Controller.

Select the + button in the Chapter section. In the Connections inspector, connect the selector: to the Chapter Controller. When you get a pop-up of available connections, choose add:. Similarly, connect the - button's selector: to the Chapter Controller's remove: method.

We also need to set the bindings on the buttons. Select the + button again, and use the Bindings inspector to bind Enabled to the Chapter Controller with Controller Key canAdd. Similarly, bind Enabled for the - button with the Controller Key canRemove.

Finally, you need to bind the table column to the Chapter Controller. As before, you'll bind Value with the Controller Key setting of arrangedObjects because you are binding a column to the contents of an array. You'll use the Model Key Path setting of title. I'll pause while you retrace these steps for the author table in the following exercise.

22.9 Exercise: Enabling Author Addition and Removal

Add an Author Controller to your nib file. It should connect to the managed object context and work with Author entities associated with the selected book. Connect and bind the visual elements to the Author Controller much as you did for the Chapter Controller.[7]

Click Build & Run. Without writing any code, you have a fully functional app that allows you to add and remove book titles and their chapter titles. Your buttons will be enabled or disabled appropriately, and the information will be saved to and retrieved from disk. We even got Undo for free. Add some books and their corresponding chapters. Now use Edit > Undo or ⌘Z, and you can undo your work a step at a time.

22.10 Sorting

You might have noticed that there's a slight problem—if you quit and restart the application, undo a chapter entry, or just move from book to book, the chapter order may change. The reason is that the content sets are sets. In other words, there is no built-in order. You can enter the chapters for a book in order, but there's no way to guarantee they will come up in that same order the next time you select the book or restart the app. There has been discussion on the Apple *cocoa-dev* list about this over the years.[8] People like Tim Isted[9] and Brian Webster[10] have created useful workarounds that are beyond the scope of this book.

We'll take a simpler approach and create another attribute to store the chapter numbers and allow the chapter table to be sorted on this list. Before we start, delete the CDBookshelf directory from Application Support.

---

7. You can find the solution in CDBookshelf3 in the code download.
8. For example, see this thread: http://www.cocoabuilder.com/archive/message/cocoa/2005/6/14/138793.
9. http://www.timisted.net/blog/archive/core-data-drag-drop/.
10. http://www.fatcatsoftware.com/blog/2008/per-object-ordered-relationships-using-core-data.

Open your data model in Xcode. Select the Chapter entity, and add a new attribute named chapterNumber of type Integer 16. Save your work, and head to your nib.

In Interface Builder, add a second column to the table in the Chapters area. Rearrange the two columns so that the new column is on the left and is fairly narrow, with only # as the column's title. Bind the column's value to the Chapter Controller with the Controller Key setting of arrangedObjects and the Model Key Path setting of chapterNumber.

We have a small adjustment to make. The column expects to get input as an NSNumber, but when you type into the available field, it will be read as an NSString. To fix this, grab a number formatter from the Library, and drop it on the table cell. Use the Attributes inspector to set the number formatter to support a Decimal style with a maximum of 0 fraction digits. Your formatter should be set to support Mac OS X 10.4+ Custom. You'll know that you have this set up if you see "123" where you used to see "Text Cell."

Chapters for selected book	
#	Chapter Title
123	Text Cell

Now we'll set both columns to sort on the chapter number. Select the first column, and open the Attributes inspector. Set Sort Key to chapterNumber, and set Selector to compare:. Do the same in the second column—make sure that you are still sorting on chapterNumber.

Click Build & Run. Enter the chapter numbers and titles for a book. If the chapters get out of order, you can reorder the table by clicking the title bar of either column. I'm still not happy with this behavior. I'd like to be able to start up the application and have the Chapters table sorted by default. Unfortunately, we're going to need just a little bit of code to make that work so it will have to wait.

Before we move on, I want you to pause and take a look back at how far we've come in this chapter without writing any code. We have an application that can persist its data on disk and allow the user to create and modify information on books, authors, and chapters.[11] Up next we'll let the user filter which books are displayed.

---

11. Compare your version with CDBookshelf4 in the code download.

22.11 Filtering Items

Once your book list grows, you're going to want to filter it to narrow the list based on some criteria. As a first step, let's filter by the name of the book. I want to have a search box that allows me to start typing some part of a title and immediately restrict the displayed list to book titles containing the string I've entered so far. It should work just like the search field at the bottom of your Library window in Interface Builder.

We're going to be able to do all our work in the nib file. Grab a search field from the Library, and place it inside your window. You may want to add a label to let the user know what they can search for.

Select the search field, and use the Bindings inspector to set the search criteria. In the Search group, open the Predicate disclosure triangle. We're going to bind this search to the Book Controller with a Controller Key of filterPredicate.

You search by constructing a predicate and passing this predicate in. Predicates can be quite complicated and can be constructed in code if you find they grow too much to be comfortably entered in the provided space.[12] In our case, you are searching for books whose title contains the text the user is typing in. We'll also make this a case-insensitive search like this:

```
title contains[c] $value
```

In short, you should have modified the search field's Bindings inspector like this:

---

12. See Apple's *Predicate Programming Guide*.

Now, when I type *Core* into the search field, my list of all the Pragmatic Bookshelf books is narrowed to *Core Animation* and *Core Data*. Compare your results to CDBookshelf5.

This search isn't interesting or exceptionally useful. I could have scanned the list of books to find the book titles that included *Core* myself. What if I want to turn the hierarchy on its head? Let's search for all books written by a particular author. This would be a pain to do by hand. We'd have to select each book title, look at the author names that appear, and see whether any match our criteria. Automating this search is a great idea and doesn't take much work.

We still bind our search to the Book Controller. This time we'll search through all the authors for each book to see whether their last name contains the string the user has entered. To do this, replace the Predicate Format setting with this:

```
any authors.lastName contains[c] $value
```

Now when I type in *Dudney*, my book list displays the *Core Animation* book that Bill wrote and the *iPhone SDK* book that he coauthored. This is pretty powerful. Otherwise, you would have had to select each book title in turn and then look through the list of authors that came up.[13]

22.12 Coding the Sort Descriptor

Anything you can do in Interface Builder you can also do in code. In fact, some of the things we've done in Interface Builder are very thin layers on method calls. For example, when you added sorting to the table columns, you specified the method name when you entered compare: for the selector.

Remember that we didn't quite get the behavior we wanted. I'd like the chapter table to be sorted the moment it displays. We're going to need a little bit of code. Declare an instance variable named sortDescriptors of type NSArray and a corresponding property of the same name in the CDBookShelf_AppDelegate header file.

---

13. This version of the search is CDBookshelf6 in the code download.

Synthesize the sort descriptor and initialize to key off the chapterNumber attribute by implementing the app delegate's applicationDidFinishLaunching: method like this:

CoreData/CDBookshelf7/CDBookshelf_AppDelegate.m

```
@synthesize window, sortDescriptors;

-(void) applicationDidFinishLaunching: (NSNotification *) notification {
    self.sortDescriptors = [NSArray arrayWithObject:
            [[NSSortDescriptor alloc] initWithKey:@"chapterNumber"
                                        ascending:YES]];
}
```

Now that we've created and initialized the sortDescriptors, we can bind the Chapter Controller's sort descriptors to it:

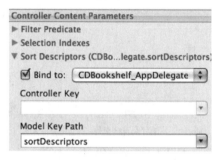

Click Build & Run, and now the chapters remain ordered according to their chapter number from launch time to quit time.

In this chapter, I've described how you work with Core Data in apps that target Mac OS X. Remember that we don't have bindings yet in iPhone OS, so the details of how you work with Core Data are a little bit different. You still define your data in the same way, but you fetch the data a bit differently.

There's no way to completely cover Core Data in a chapter or two. Marcus Zarra's *Core Data* [Zar09] book looks at some of the more advanced ideas. You should also look at Apple's *Introduction to Core Data Programming* [App09d].

Much of the code you will need or want to write will fit nicely into the controller layer or into your app delegate. There are times, however, when you'd really like to make changes or additions to a class that represents an entity. In the next chapter, you'll learn a technique that makes it easier to make changes to classes outside of the class itself using a powerful technique called *categories*.

Chapter 23

Categories

Way back on Section 17.5, *Saving an Archive to Disk*, on page 267, we wanted to save an NSSet to disk and then read it back later. This would have been easy if we had an NSArray. An NSArray has built-in methods for writing itself to a file and for creating an array from a file. NSSet doesn't have this ability.

Categories let us scoff at these limitations. We use categories to declare and implement new methods for existing classes. These can be classes that we create, or they can be classes for which we don't even have access to the source code.

In this chapter, we will use categories to teach a set to save itself to and retrieve itself from disk. Then we'll use a variant of categories to declare private methods in our code. Finally, we'll use categories with Core Data to modify the behavior of objects in two different ways.

23.1 Overcoming Limitations

Let's start with a simple application that can read and write an array to disk. Create a new Cocoa application named Bounce. Make sure that the Use Core Data for Storage checkbox is unselected. Our application will create an array, save it to disk, create a second array from what is saved on disk, and log the new array.

The simplest way is to put this code in the applicationDidFinishLaunching: method in the file BounceAppDelegate.m:

Categories/Bounce1/BounceAppDelegate.m

```
- (void)applicationDidFinishLaunching:(NSNotification *)aNotification {
    NSArray *source = [NSArray arrayWithObjects:@"One", @"Two", nil];
    [source writeToFile:@"savedArray" atomically:YES];
    NSArray *fromDisk = [NSArray arrayWithContentsOfFile:@"savedArray"];
    NSLog(@"Array from disk: %@",fromDisk);
}
```

Click Build & Run, and everything works fine. Our first array is created and saved to disk. Our second array is created with the contents of what was saved, and the following is logged to the Console window:

```
Array from disk: (
    One,
    Two
)
```

I'd like to do the same thing with an NSSet instead of an NSArray. In other words, I'd like to change the applicationDidFinishLaunching: method implementation to the following and have it just work:

Categories/Bounce2/BounceAppDelegate.m

```
- (void)applicationDidFinishLaunching:(NSNotification *)aNotification {
▶   NSSet *source = [NSSet setWithObjects:@"One", @"Two", nil];
    [source writeToFile:@"savedSet" atomically:YES];
▶   NSSet *fromDisk = [NSSet setWithContentsOfFile:@"savedSet"];
    NSLog(@"Set from disk: %@",fromDisk);
}
```

The compiler complains that NSSet may not respond to the methods writeToFile:atomically: and setWithContentsOfFile:. Even worse, if we ignore these warnings and run our application, we get a runtime exception because the selector writeToFile:atomically: doesn't exist.

Let's fix that. An NSSet doesn't know how to write itself to a file location. We're going to create a category for NSSet named Persistence to add this ability.

23.2 Creating a Category

Create a new Objective-C class that extends NSObject. I know we are really creating a category and not a class, but there currently isn't a template for a category. The convention is to name the file by combining the name of the category with the name of the class it is a category on. We will name our category Persistence. It will add functionality to the NSSet class, so the category's implementation file is named NSSet+Persistence.m.

A category cannot contain any instance variables. You are essentially decorating a class after the memory has been allocated and the variables have been initialized. You can add new methods to the class you're decorating, but that's all.

This may seem a little bit like protocols. There's a huge difference. As you saw back in Chapter 12, *Creating Protocols for Delegation*, on page 193, a protocol is a collection of method declarations that can be optional or required. Any class is free to adopt a protocol. A class that promises in its header file to conform to a protocol is promising to implement the required methods somehow.

A category, on the other hand, is tied to a specific class, which it must name in both the interface and implementation. The category also has to implement the methods it declares. The methods you declare and implement in a category are just like the ones you declare and implement in the class' header and implementation file.

Doctor up your header file to look like this:

Categories/Bounce3/NSSet+Persistence.h

```
#import <Cocoa/Cocoa.h>

@interface NSSet(Persistence)

- (BOOL)writeToFile:(NSString *)path atomically:(BOOL)flag;
+ (id)setWithContentsOfFile:(NSString *)aPath;

@end
```

There's a lot to notice in this small file. You can see how you specify that this is the interface of the Persistence category that you're defining on NSSet. We got rid of the curly brackets since we can't have any instance variables. As for the methods we're declaring, I've copied the signature of the method writeToFile:atomically: from the NSArray class and adapted the signature of arrayWithContentsOfFile:.

Here's the shell of the corresponding implementation file:

Categories/Bounce3/NSSet+Persistence.m

```
#import "NSSet+Persistence.h"

@implementation NSSet(Persistence)

@end
```

We just need to implement the two methods we declared in the header file. Remember, the strategy is to convert our set to and from an array and then use the array's methods to write to and read from disk. Fortunately, NSSet has a class method setWithArray: that creates a new NSSet from an NSArray. We can chain that with NSArray's arrayWithContentsOfFile: like this:

Categories/Bounce3/NSSet+Persistence.m

```
+ (id)setWithContentsOfFile:(NSString *)aPath {
    return [NSSet setWithArray:[NSArray arrayWithContentsOfFile:aPath]];
}
```

It's slightly trickier to write to disk because NSArray doesn't have a convenience constructor for creating an array from a set. Create an NSMutableArray of the same size as our NSSet, and iterate through all elements of the set, adding them one at a time to the array. Once you're done, the array can write itself to disk.

Categories/Bounce3/NSSet+Persistence.m

```
- (BOOL)writeToFile:(NSString *)path atomically:(BOOL)flag {
    NSMutableArray *temp = [NSMutableArray arrayWithCapacity:self.count];
    for (id element in self) {
        [temp addObject:element];
    }
    return [temp writeToFile:path atomically:YES];
}
```

Notice we can call methods and access instance variables from the class we're decorating. We're using count and iterating over all of the elements of the underlying NSSet object.

Click Build & Run. You should still get the two compiler warnings that NSSet may not respond to the methods writeToFile:atomically: and setWithContentsOfFile:. This time, however, there are no runtime errors. The application runs perfectly. The set is created, and the methods added in the category take care of writing it to and reading it from disk.

23.3 Category Cautions

Did you notice what just happened?

We wrote some client code that called two methods that didn't exist in the NSSet class. The compiler complained, and we got a runtime exception. We fixed our problem without ever touching this code again and without having access to the NSSet source code.

We added a category for NSSet and added the methods we needed to this category, and everything worked fine. Sure, the compiler still complained, but our app worked fine.

How do you feel about that?

Your answer will probably reveal more about your programming background than anything else. Rubyists don't see what the big deal is—this is just mix-ins. They've been wondering for a dozen or more chapters when we were going to get to them. If you were raised in a statically typed language, your head is reeling. How do you ever know what to depend on? The foundations on which you are building your code could be changed by someone else creating categories.

It's true that they could, but in practice they don't. Don't use categories to redefine existing methods. In fact, if there is any possibility of a name collision, you should prepend the method name with something that sets it apart. For example, I might use PP for Pragmatic Programmers and name the methods PP_writeToFile: and PP_setWithContentsOfFile:.

I also want to be explicit when my code *uses* a category. Add this import to the top of BounceAppDelegate.m:

```
#import "NSSet+Persistence.h"
```

Once you add this, the compiler warning will go away. This class now knows about the additional methods.

Soon we'll apply categories to our Core Data example, but first let's look at a special kind of category—one with no name.

23.4 Private Methods in Class Extensions

Suppose we want to refactor the BounceAppDelegate's applicationDidFinishLaunching: method. Remember that right now everything is jumbled together.

Categories/Bounce3/BounceAppDelegate.m

```
- (void)applicationDidFinishLaunching:(NSNotification *)aNotification {
    NSSet *source = [NSSet setWithObjects:@"One", @"Two", nil];
    [source writeToFile:@"savedSet" atomically:YES];
    NSSet *fromDisk = [NSSet setWithContentsOfFile:@"savedSet"];
    NSLog(@"Set from disk: %@",fromDisk);
}
```

> ## ⊻⁄ Joe Asks...
> ### Why Couldn't You Give the Category a Name?
>
> We could have. Let's name it Private and declare it like this:
>
> `@interface BounceAppDelegate(Private)`
>
> at the top of BounceAppDelegate.m. This is a different construct called an *informal protocol*. To create an informal protocol, you declare the interface for a named category with no corresponding implementation. The class or any subclass of the class to which the category is attached is free to implement or not implement the methods that are declared.
>
> I don't spend much time on informal protocols since you will most likely never declare any yourself. In fact, now that methods in protocols can be declared to be optional, Apple is phasing out some of the informal protocols for formal. Look at the description of numberOfRowsInTableView: in the NSTableViewDataSource protocol reference. Under Availability you'll see that until Snow Leopard, this method was part of an informal protocol. Now it is part of a formal protocol—what I've been referring to as *protocol* throughout this book.

Let's create a new method named createSetOnDisk that contains the first two lines and a new method named setFromDisk that contains the last two lines. Here's your refactored applicationDidFinishLaunching: method:

Categories/Bounce4/BounceAppDelegate.m

```
- (void)applicationDidFinishLaunching:(NSNotification *)aNotification {
    [self createSetOnDisk];
    [self setFromDisk];
}
```

Where should I put these new methods createSetOnDisk and setFromDisk?

So far I have only two choices. One option is to put the methods in source code before applicationDidFinishLaunching: so that the compiler doesn't complain that the BounceAppDelegate class might not implement the methods. The other option is to declare the methods in the header file. Then I am free to put them anywhere I want.

It's not really a big deal in this little toy example, but there are times that I don't like either one of these choices. My source file could be getting long, so I want to group my methods logically for a human reader unconstrained by a compiler that reads through the source code linearly. On the other hand, these methods are not part of the public interface. I don't want to declare them in the header file. What I really want is a way of declaring them privately.

The class extension is created for exactly this situation. Add this to the top of your implementation file just under your imports:

```
@interface BounceAppDelegate()
@end
```

A class extension looks just like a category with no name. Because the extension is defined in our implementation file, we aren't sharing these method declarations with anyone else. These are private functions just for our own use. Declare our new methods in the class extension, and then you are free to put the methods anywhere in the class implementation.

Categories/Bounce4/BounceAppDelegate.m

```
#import "BounceAppDelegate.h"
#import "NSSet+Persistence.h"

@interface BounceAppDelegate()
-(void)createSetOnDisk;
-(void)setFromDisk;
@end

@implementation BounceAppDelegate
@synthesize window;
- (void)applicationDidFinishLaunching:(NSNotification *)aNotification {
    [self createSetOnDisk];
    [self setFromDisk];
}
-(void) createSetOnDisk {
    NSSet *source = [NSSet setWithObjects:@"One", @"Two", nil];
    [source writeToFile:@"savedSet" atomically:YES];
}
-(void) setFromDisk {
    NSSet *fromDisk = [NSSet setWithContentsOfFile:@"savedSet"];
    NSLog(@"Set from disk: %@",fromDisk);
}
@end
```

Our class extension is treated as an extension of the methods declared in the class' interface, and the compiler will enforce that you implement the methods declared there.[1]

23.5 Exercise: Extending Properties with Class Extensions

Here's another fun trick you can do with class extensions. You can create a property that is read-only to the outside world and yet is read-write for you. This lets you take advantage of all the memory management goodness you get for free in properties while restricting client code to only get the value of your property.

Add a read-only property of type NSSet to BounceAppDelegate named retrievedSet. Add a line to the end of your implementation of application-DidFinishLaunching: to write the value of the retrievedSet to the Console window. Here you are using the property's getter method.

Modify the setFromDisk method so that it sets the value of retrievedSet to the contents of the file savedSet. Here you are using the setter, so when you build the project, you should get the compiler error.

```
Object cannot be set - either readonly property or no setter found
```

Fix this error by adding a property declaration to the class extension. You will get a compiler warning that this definition doesn't agree with the property definition in the class interface. The warning is correct, and it is good to be warned of such things so you don't accidentally change the behavior you declared in the header file. The build succeeds, and you can successfully run your app.

23.6 Solution: Extending Properties with Class Extensions

Add your instance variable and read-only property to BounceAppDelegate.h:

`Categories/Bounce5/BounceAppDelegate.h`

```
#import <Cocoa/Cocoa.h>

@interface BounceAppDelegate : NSObject <NSApplicationDelegate> {
    NSWindow *window;
▶    NSSet *retrievedSet;
}
```

---

1. Bill Bumgarner has blogged on the implementation issues and the intent of the class extension at http://www.friday.com/bbum/2009/09/11/class-extensions-explained/.

▶
```
@property (readonly) NSSet *retrievedSet;
@property (assign) IBOutlet NSWindow *window;
@end
```

Synthesize your property in the implementation file, and add this line to the applicationDidFinishLaunching: method:

Categories/Bounce5/BounceAppDelegate.m

```
- (void)applicationDidFinishLaunching:(NSNotification *)aNotification {
    [self createSetOnDisk];
    [self setFromDisk];
    NSLog(@"Set from disk: %@", self.retrievedSet);
}
```

The additional line uses the property's getter, and this change to set-FromDisk uses the property's setter:

Categories/Bounce5/BounceAppDelegate.m

```
-(void) setFromDisk {
    self.retrievedSet = [NSSet setWithContentsOfFile:@"savedSet"];
}
```

Make the property writable by overriding the declaration of the retrieved-Set property:

Categories/Bounce5/BounceAppDelegate.m

```
@interface BounceAppDelegate()
-(void)createSetOnDisk;
-(void)setFromDisk;
```
▶
```
@property(copy) NSSet *retrievedSet;
@end
```

Now any client code that imports the header will see this property as read-only while internally we have redefined the property as read-write before synthesizing the methods. You can't add a new property in the class extension unless there is already an underlying instance variable. Here we've just modified the attributes of an existing property.

23.7 Categories and Core Data

Suppose I want to add behavior to my Core Data entities. Suppose I want to log some sort of report to the Console window. We can add an action to CDBookshelf_AppDelegate.h:

```
- (IBAction)createReport:(id) sender;
```

Add a button to the user interface, and connect it to this action. Let's enumerate through all of the managed objects in memory and ask the ones that know how to report to do so.

Categories/CDBookshelf8/CDBookshelf_AppDelegate.m

```
- (IBAction)createReport:(id) sender {
    for(NSManagedObject* element in
                    [[self managedObjectContext] registeredObjects]){
        if ([element respondsToSelector:@selector(PP_report)]) {
            [element PP_report];
        }
    }
}
```

Where should we define the PP_report method? In this first example, let's add a category to NSManagedObject and create it there. Declare it in the header.

Categories/CDBookshelf8/NSManagedObject+Report.h

```
#import <Cocoa/Cocoa.h>

@interface NSManagedObject(Report)
-(void) PP_report;
@end
```

To implement it, just log the description to the Console:

Categories/CDBookshelf8/NSManagedObject+Report.m

```
#import "NSManagedObject+Report.h"

@implementation NSManagedObject(Report)
-(void)PP_report {
    NSLog(@"%@",[self description]);
}
@end
```

You can add the import for the category to your app delegate and click Build & Run. Click the report button, and you should see a bunch of entries that look something like this in the Console:

```
<NSManagedObject: 0x2000a9f60> (entity: Author;
id: 0x20008cb80 <x-coredata://44E-0D0D-46A2-9497-182BB3C/Author/p103> ;
data: {
    books = "<relationship fault: 0x2000c44e0 'books'>";
    firstName = Chad;
    lastName = Fowler;
    middleInitial = nil;
})
```

That was pretty straightforward if we want to report on all objects regardless of which entity they come from. What if we want to report on books only? Let's get rid of this category on NSManagedObject and introduce one on PragBook instead.

23.8 Generated Classes in Core Data

Create a new category named Report on the class PragBook. The implementation file should look like this:

Categories/CDBookshelf9/PragBook+Report.m

```objc
#import "PragBook+Report.h"

@implementation PragBook(Report)
-(void)PP_report {
    NSLog(@"%@",[self description]);
}
@end
```

The header file needs to import PragBook, and that's something we're not able to do.

Categories/CDBookshelf9/PragBook+Report.h

```objc
#import <Cocoa/Cocoa.h>
#import "PragBook.h"

@interface PragBook(Report)
-(void)PP_report;
@end
```

PragBook.h doesn't exist. Currently the class associated with the PragBook entity is NSManagedObject. We need to generate the PragBook class source code.

Select your data model, and choose the menu item File > New File.... If you have the data model selected, when you do this, then you'll see a new option listed under Mac OS X > Cocoa Class. Choose the Managed Object Class, and click the Next button. The wizard will let you select the location, project, and targets. Stick with the defaults, and click the Next button again.

The next panel lets you choose which entities you are generating classes for. Select the PragBook entity. You have three options at the bottom of the panel. Select the Generate Obj-C 2.0 Properties box, and leave the "Generate accessors" and "Generate validation methods" checkboxes unselected. Click the Finish button.

The data model shows that the PragBook entity is now tied to the Prag-Book class we just generated and not the generic NSManagedObject:

Entity	Abs	Class
Author	☐	NSManagedObject
Chapter	☐	NSManagedObject
PragBook	☐	PragBook

Next, take a look at the generated header file PragBook.h:

Categories/CDBookshelf9/PragBook.h

```
#import <CoreData/CoreData.h>

@interface PragBook : NSManagedObject{}

@end
```

There's nothing there except that the PragBook class extends NS-ManagedObject and not just NSObject. The implementation file is empty as well. That's all we need to get our revised application to compile and run.

Click Build & Run; you will get a report as before, but this time it only includes PragBook objects and not Chapter or Author objects.

PragBook is a subclass of NSManagedObject. You should carefully read the overview section of the docs for notes on subclassing NSManaged-Object. The bottom line is that you absolutely shouldn't override most of the methods, and you should have little need to override the others. In addition, the documentation lets you know there is little reason to write custom accessor methods.

Mostly you will need to add functionality to your classes and not modify existing behavior. You should make these modifications in a category like we just did and not in the generated file. Categories allow you to split your functionality for a class across multiple source files. In the case of Core Data, this is particularly convenient because if you change your data model and need to regenerate class files, you would overwrite any local modifications.

23.9 Accessing Properties

OK, here's something pretty cool. Let's change the report to display only the book's title and not all the other stuff that is returned by description.

Change the implementation of PP_report to this:

Categories/CDBookshelf10/PragBook+Report.m

```
#import "PragBook+Report.h"

@implementation PragBook(Report)
-(void)PP_report {
    NSLog(@"%@", [self title]);
}
@end
```

Now when I click Build & Run and create a report, I see something like this in the Console:

```
Core Animation
The Passionate Programmer
Core Data
iPhone SDK Development
```

This makes me pretty happy. I can access the property title by calling its getter because the attributes in Core Data support KVC. I'd prefer to access the property using dot notation. To do this, I need to regenerate the PragBook class with different options selected.[2]

23.10 Regenerating Class Files from Entities

Select your data model again, create a new Mac OS X > Cocoa Class, and again choose Managed Object Class. We're going to again generate files for PragBook, but this time you will leave both the "Generate accessors" and "Generate Obj-C 2.0 Properties" checkboxes selected.

When you click Finish, you will be warned that the template files exist. Choose to remove the old files and create new ones. This highlights a great reason for us declaring and implementing PP_report in a category as opposed to in the PragBook source files. Our work in the source files would have been blown away by this process. Categories allows us to write our custom code in a separate location than where the generator is placing its code. This is another reason to split our code for one class over several locations.

---

2. I wouldn't bother doing all of this if I just wanted to enable dot notation. I want to show you a few more things about Core Data and categories.

Take a look at the new header file for PragBook:

Categories/CDBookshelf11/PragBook.h

```
#import <CoreData/CoreData.h>

@interface PragBook : NSManagedObject {}

@property (nonatomic, retain) NSString * title;
@property (nonatomic, retain) NSSet* authors;
@property (nonatomic, retain) NSSet* chapters;
@end

@interface PragBook (CoreDataGeneratedAccessors)
- (void)addAuthorsObject:(NSManagedObject *)value;
- (void)removeAuthorsObject:(NSManagedObject *)value;
- (void)addAuthors:(NSSet *)value;
- (void)removeAuthors:(NSSet *)value;

- (void)addChaptersObject:(NSManagedObject *)value;
- (void)removeChaptersObject:(NSManagedObject *)value;
- (void)addChapters:(NSSet *)value;
- (void)removeChapters:(NSSet *)value;
@end
```

Wow, there's a lot of added code. At the top there are three properties. One corresponds to the title attribute, and the two others correspond to the authors and chapters relationships.

The bottom consists of an informal protocol—a category interface without the corresponding implementation. We're not going to implement any of these methods, so we can delete the entire informal protocol.

The implementation file contains a keyword we haven't seen before:

Categories/CDBookshelf11/PragBook.m

```
#import "PragBook.h"

@implementation PragBook
@dynamic title;
@dynamic authors;
@dynamic chapters;
@end
```

Instead of synthesizing the properties, the template uses the @dynamic keyword. This tells the compiler not to synthesize the getters and setters. In this case, it indicates that the method implementations will be provided at runtime.[3]

These three properties are now available to us, so we can revise the PP_report method to use dot notation to access the title property.

Categories/CDBookshelf11/PragBook+Report.m

```
#import "PragBook+Report.h"

@implementation PragBook(Report)
-(void)PP_report {
    NSLog(@"%@", self.title);
}
@end
```

Click Build & Run, and when you click the button to generate the report, the book titles will be logged to the Console.

In this chapter, we've used categories to add code to classes you create, to classes Apple creates, and to classes that are created from Core Data entities. We've also worked with a variation of categories, class extensions, to add private methods to a class. There's a lot of power and freedom available to you—it should not be the first option you consider.

---

3. You can also use @dynamic if you are providing the implementations of the getter and setter yourself.

Chapter 24

Blocks

Usually when we have work to do, we call a method that knows how to do the work and send it the data it needs. In this chapter, we'll look at three cases where we also send the method some of the work that needs to be done. This work is passed in as a special Objective-C object known as a *block*. A block is a chunk of executable code that can be passed around along with data that is copied from the scope containing the block.

We're going to look at three uses of blocks. First we'll look at wrappers—code that performs some specific setup, invokes the code in a block, and then possibly does some tidying up after the block finishes. Next we'll look at how well blocks work with collections of objects—they allow you to specify code that applies to each element of the collection independent of the way you access the collection. And finally we'll look at callbacks—the ability to have a chunk of code run when some event occurs.[1]

If you have used blocks, closures, lambdas, or even function pointers in other languages, much of what you know applies here as well. The syntax and specifics may be different, but the big ideas and general strategies are the same.

---

1.   In addition, we'll look at applications of blocks to concurrency in Chapter 26, *Dispatch Queues*, on page 407.

> **Official Support for Blocks**
>
> Blocks are currently available only on Mac OS X Snow Leopard and newer. You won't use blocks if you are targeting the iPhone or earlier releases of Mac OS X.

24.1 The Need for Blocks in Wrappers

Suppose we want to add two integers that I've stored as NSNumbers. Create a new Cocoa application named SimpleCalc, and create this add:to: method in SimpleCalcAppDelegate.m.[2]

`Blocks/SimpleCalc1/SimpleCalcAppDelegate.m`

```
-(NSNumber *) add: (NSNumber *)x to:(NSNumber *) y {
    NSInteger xAsInt = [x integerValue];
    NSInteger yASInt = [y integerValue];
    NSInteger result = xAsInt + yASInt;
    return [NSNumber numberWithInteger:result];
}
```

The two NSNumbers are converted to NSIntegers and added together, and then the sum is converted back to an NSNumber and returned.

Very little of this code has anything to do with the actual calculation. To see this, we can create a new method named multiply:by: that multiplies two NSNumbers. There's a lot of repeated code between this method and add:to:. We still have to convert the NSNumbers to NSIntegers, and we still have to return the result. The only thing that changes is the method name and the operation on the two NSIntegers.

`Blocks/SimpleCalc2/SimpleCalcAppDelegate.m`

```
-(NSNumber *) multiply: (NSNumber *)x by:(NSNumber *) y {
    NSInteger xAsInt = [x integerValue];
    NSInteger yASInt = [y integerValue];
    NSInteger result = xAsInt * yASInt;
    return [NSNumber numberWithInteger:result];
}
```

What I really want is a method that allows me to pass in the two NSNumbers and the operation to be performed on them. This new method will take the two NSNumbers as its first two parameters and will begin

---

2. I've removed the window property from the app delegate. Make sure you edit the project settings so that garbage collection is required.

by converting them to NSIntegers the same way we did in both add:to: and multiply:by:. Our new method will have a third parameter that will accept the operation that will act on the two NSIntegers. This information is captured in a block.

24.2 Declaring a Block

Here's the signature for the method we'll use to replace add:to: and multiply:by::

`Blocks/SimpleCalc4/SimpleCalcAppDelegate.m`

```
-(NSNumber *) combine:(NSNumber *) x
            with:(NSNumber *) y
      usingBlock:(NSInteger (^)(NSInteger,NSInteger)) block
```

Before we look at the block declaration, take another look at how we declare the first parameter of the combine:with:usingBlock: method:

```
(NSNumber *) x
```

We put the type for x in parentheses before the variable. This type is a pointer to an NSNumber.

The third parameter declares a special kind of object called a *block*. A block is essentially a function that captures and copies data at the moment that execution passes over the point of declaration of the block. A block may take one or more inputs, and it might have a return value. The format for specifying a block as a method parameter looks generally like this:

```
(return_type (^) (parameterType1, parameterType2)) block_name
```

The ^ indicates a block. It is preceded by the type returned by the block and followed by the types of the block's parameters.

In our specific case, the block is declared like this:

```
( NSInteger (^) (NSInteger, NSInteger)) block
```

In words, our block will be referred to by the name block. It is a function that takes two NSIntegers and returns an NSInteger. This lets the compiler check to make sure the block being passed in has the right signature.

Later in the chapter we'll declare a block as a variable. That form looks slightly different. Here is what our example block would look like:

```
NSInteger (^block) (NSInteger, NSInteger) = // block definition
```

We use that same form if our block is a parameter in a C function:

```
(NSInteger *) combineUsingBlock (NSNumber *x, NSNumber *y,
                          NSInteger (^block)(NSInteger,NSInteger)){
//function body
}
```

We're going to continue with the method parameter version. Next, let's see how you would implement and call this particular block.

24.3 Using Blocks in Wrappers

You use the block inside the combine:with:usingBlock: method as you would a function.

Blocks/SimpleCalc4/SimpleCalcAppDelegate.m

```
-(NSNumber *) combine:(NSNumber *) x
              with:(NSNumber *) y
        usingBlock:(NSInteger (^)(NSInteger,NSInteger)) block
{
    NSInteger xAsInt = [x integerValue];
    NSInteger yASInt = [y integerValue];
    NSInteger result = block(xAsInt, yASInt);
    return [NSNumber numberWithInteger:result];
}
```

We're all set up to accept and use a block in the combine:with:usingBlock: method. Here's the block we're going to pass to this method to add two numbers. In this case, the return type of the block can be inferred and doesn't need to be specified.

```
^(NSInteger x, NSInteger y) {
    return x+y;
}
```

This type of expression is called a *block literal*. The body can contain multiple statements and declared variables. Ours happens to be very simple. It is a block that takes two NSIntegers as arguments. We need to name these arguments so that we can use them inside the body of the block. We'll name them x and y, and the block will do nothing more than return their sum.

So when you call block(xAsInt,yAsInt); in combine:with:usingBlock:, it's as if you are calling this function:

```
(NSInteger) block(NSInteger x, NSInteger y) {
    return x+y;
}
```

The power of blocks is that you can change the body of this function to return the product instead just by passing in a different block. Here is the complete applicationDidFinishLaunching: method. I've highlighted passing in the two different blocks.

```
Blocks/SimpleCalc4/SimpleCalcAppDelegate.m
```

```
Line 1  - (void)applicationDidFinishLaunching:(NSNotification *)aNotification {
   -        NSNumber *firstNumber = [NSNumber numberWithInteger:7];
   -        NSNumber *secondNumber = [NSNumber numberWithInteger:5];
   -        NSNumber *sum = [self combine:firstNumber
   5                             with:secondNumber
   ▶                        usingBlock:^(NSInteger x,NSInteger y){return x+y;}];
   -        NSLog(@"The sum of %@ and %@ is %@.",
   -              firstNumber, secondNumber, sum);
   -        NSNumber *product = [self combine:firstNumber
  10                                 with:secondNumber
   ▶                            usingBlock:^(NSInteger x,NSInteger y){return x*y;}];
   -        NSLog(@"The product of %@ and %@ is %@.",
   -              firstNumber, secondNumber, product);
   -    }
```

You already know how to provide a block as a parameter. We pass in blocks for addition and multiplication in lines 6 and 11.

This was sort of a silly example of using wrappers, but it illustrated the technique. A more typical situation might be performing actions on a file that is stored remotely. No matter what your action, you need to perform a set of steps to access the file before your action, and you need to perform another set of steps to clean up your resource after your action. It would make sense to write a method that includes that protocol with the action accepted in the middle as a block. In fact, any time you have more than one action that is preceded and/or followed by the same steps, consider using this wrapper technique with blocks.

What about iterating through an array and performing an action on each one of the elements? It turns out that this is such a common situation that Apple has built in the ability to send a block to each element of a collection into arrays, sets, and dictionaries. We'll look at that after we look at how blocks work with variables defined in the same scope.

24.4 Capturing Values

So far, I've ignored a major feature of blocks: they include a snapshot of the values of variables that are in scope at the time the block is declared. I'm going to simplify our example in a couple of ways. First, I'm going to replace the NSNumbers with NSIntegers to eliminate the converting back and forth. That was useful to show you how and why we would use blocks to pass an operation into a wrapper, but it now muddies things a bit. Second, instead of multiplying two numbers together, I will triple a number that is defined in a local variable in the same scope as where the block is defined.

Blocks/SimpleCalc5/SimpleCalcAppDelegate.m

```
Line 1   #import "SimpleCalcAppDelegate.h"

         @implementation SimpleCalcAppDelegate

5        -(NSInteger) tripleUsingBlock:(NSInteger (^)(NSInteger)) block
         {
             return block(3);
         }
         - (void)applicationDidFinishLaunching:(NSNotification *)aNotification {
10           NSInteger multiplicand = 5;
             NSInteger product = [self tripleUsingBlock:^(NSInteger multiplier){
                 return multiplier * multiplicand;
             }];
             NSLog(@"Triple %d is %d.", multiplicand, product);
15       }
         @end
```

There's a lot going on in this short listing. Start with the declaration of the tripleUsingBlock: method in line 5. We aren't passing in the value of the multiplicand. The only parameter is the block itself.

The multiplicand is declared in applicationDidFinishLaunching: just before we declare the block on line 11. Here's the actual block definition:

```
^(NSInteger multiplier){ return multiplier * multiplicand; }
```

The block takes a single argument, an NSInteger named multiplier. Now here's the point of this example. The block returns the result of multiplying this multiplier by a second variable named multiplicand. The value of the multiplicand is 5 at the point that the execution hits the ^, so that value travels with the block. The result is that when the block is called in line 10, the value of multiplicand is still frozen at 5, so that's the value that 3 is multiplied by.

Now that you understand what's going on, take another look back at the code. Initially, blocks look a bit strange. As you look back at the code listing with greater understanding, they will start to look more natural to you. Next, let's extend this example by passing blocks to a collection.

24.5 Blocks and Collections

Apple has added dozens of methods to let you pass blocks into collections for sorting or transforming the elements in Snow Leopard. As an example of how to use them, let's put a handful of integers into an NSArray and then iterate through the array and multiply each element by 3.

Create a new Cocoa project named CollectionCalc. In applicationDidFinishLaunching:, we'll create and display our initial array, multiply each of the elements by 3, and display the result.

Blocks/CollectionCalc1/CollectionCalcAppDelegate.m

```
- (void)applicationDidFinishLaunching:(NSNotification *)aNotification {
    NSArray *numbers = [self createArray];
    NSLog(@"Elements in the initial array:%@", numbers);
    NSArray *transformedNumbers = [self tripleElementsIn: numbers];
    NSLog(@"Elements in the tripled array:%@", transformedNumbers);
}
```

There's not much to the createArray method. You just need to remember that arrays can contain only objects, not primitives, so we have to convert our NSIntegers to NSNumbers.

Blocks/CollectionCalc1/CollectionCalcAppDelegate.m

```
-(NSArray *) createArray {
    return [NSArray arrayWithObjects:[NSNumber numberWithInt:5],
            [NSNumber numberWithInt:2],
            [NSNumber numberWithInt:17],
            [NSNumber numberWithInt:-3],
            [NSNumber numberWithInt:14],nil];
}
```

We will transform the array in the tripleElementsIn: method. If we weren't using blocks, we'd just use the for in fast enumeration introduced in Objective-C 2.0. In this case, we would be responsible for enumerating through the array. After the enumerator moves to the next element, it asks us what work needs to be done.

```
for (NSNumber *element in originalArray) {
  // do some work
}
```

With Snow Leopard, we can call this method on an array:

```
- (void)enumerateObjectsUsingBlock:
              (void (^)(id obj, NSUInteger idx, BOOL *stop))block
```

Now we're telling the array to apply the work we pass in to each of its elements. We aren't calling out the enumeration as a separate activity. Here's how we use this technique to triple each value in the array:

Blocks/CollectionCalc1/CollectionCalcAppDelegate.m

```
-(NSArray *) tripleElementsIn:(NSArray *) originalArray {
    NSMutableArray *tempArray =
    [[NSMutableArray alloc] initWithCapacity:[originalArray count]];
▶   [originalArray enumerateObjectsUsingBlock:
▶                            ^(id obj, NSUInteger idx, BOOL *stop) {
▶       [tempArray addObject:[NSNumber numberWithInt: 3 * [obj intValue]]];
▶   }];
    return tempArray;
}
```

Notice in this array example that the block is passed three parameters. The first parameter, obj, is the pointer to the current element. That gives us a handle to the object whose value we're tripling. The second parameter is the index of the current element. We don't have any need for it in our current application. The final parameter acts as a break. It is a BOOL that allows you to stop iterating through the array when you set its value to YES. You might, for example, want to traverse an array until you find the first occurrence of something. At that point, you would set stop to YES.

At this point, there's probably a "What's the big deal?" welling up inside you. Good question. Let's dig a little deeper. Remember, blocks are objects. We can declare and initialize them and pass them around instead of just declaring them in place. Let's see how that changes our code.

24.6 Declaring, Defining, and Using Blocks

So far, we've described our blocks *inline*. When blocks are very short, this is a convenient way to capture the work that needs to be done. But blocks are also objects, so we can declare them and use them as we would other objects. For example, let's declare a block that multiplies an NSNumber and an NSInteger and returns their product as an NSNumber. We'll create both an instance variable and the corresponding property in CollectionCalcAppDelegate.h.

Blocks/CollectionCalc2/CollectionCalcAppDelegate.h

```
#import <Cocoa/Cocoa.h>

@interface CollectionCalcAppDelegate : NSObject <NSApplicationDelegate> {
        NSNumber *(^multiply)(NSNumber *, NSInteger);
}
@property(copy) NSNumber *(^multiply)(NSNumber *, NSInteger);
@end
```

Don't forget to synthesize this property at the top of CollectionCalcAppDelegate.m:

Blocks/CollectionCalc2/CollectionCalcAppDelegate.m

```
@synthesize multiply;
```

Add the block initialization to the applicationDidFinishLaunching: method:

Blocks/CollectionCalc2/CollectionCalcAppDelegate.m

```
- (void)applicationDidFinishLaunching:(NSNotification *)aNotification {
    NSArray *numbers = [self createArray];
►       self.multiply = ^(NSNumber *x, NSInteger y) {
►               return [NSNumber numberWithInt:[x intValue] * y];
►       };
    NSLog(@"Elements in the initial array:%@", numbers);
    NSArray *transformedNumbers = [self tripleElementsIn: numbers];
    NSLog(@"Elements in the tripled array:%@", transformedNumbers);
}
```

If you're passing a block out of the scope where it was created, you need to copy it. Otherwise, the block may be destroyed when the method containing the block initialization returns. This is why we are using the property for multiply. We are taking advantage of the copy memory attribute that we set on multiply.

Now use this block from inside the block we are using when enumerating the array:

Blocks/CollectionCalc2/CollectionCalcAppDelegate.m

```
-(NSArray *) tripleElementsIn:(NSArray *) originalArray {
    NSMutableArray *tempArray =
    [[NSMutableArray alloc] initWithCapacity:[originalArray count]];
    [originalArray enumerateObjectsUsingBlock:
                            ^(id obj, NSUInteger idx, BOOL *stop) {
►       [tempArray addObject:multiply(obj,3)];
    }];
    return tempArray;
}
```

Isn't that nice? If I didn't have to shorten the lines to fit in this book, we'd have the entire array transformation on a single line.

24.7 Using __block

We are going to push this example in several different directions to explore variables. In this section, let's create a new method named squareElementsIn: to return an array containing the square of each element in the original array.

Blocks/CollectionCalc3/CollectionCalcAppDelegate.m

```
-(NSArray *) squareElementsIn:(NSArray *) originalArray {
    NSMutableArray *tempArray =
    [[NSMutableArray alloc] initWithCapacity:[originalArray count]];
    [originalArray enumerateObjectsUsingBlock:
        ^(id obj, NSUInteger idx, BOOL *stop) {
            [tempArray addObject:multiply(obj,[obj intValue])];
        }];
    return tempArray;
}
```

Call this method in applicationDidFinishLaunching:, and display the results. When you click Build & Run, everything runs fine, and you should get an array containing the squares of the original array.

Now, introduce a temporary variable for [obj integerValue] outside the block so you can see what can go wrong.

Blocks/CollectionCalc4/CollectionCalcAppDelegate.m

```
-(NSArray *) squareElementsIn:(NSArray *) originalArray {
    NSMutableArray *tempArray =
    [[NSMutableArray alloc] initWithCapacity:[originalArray count]];
        NSInteger multiplier;
    [originalArray enumerateObjectsUsingBlock:
        ^(id obj, NSUInteger idx, BOOL *stop) {
            multiplier = [obj intValue];
            [tempArray addObject:multiply(obj,multiplier)];
        }];
    return tempArray;
}
```

This won't even compile. We've declared an NSInteger outside the block and tried to update it. The error message is "Assignment of read-only variable 'multiplier'." We could have avoided this problem by declaring the variable inside the block, but the point is for us to understand why multiplier is read-only.

This is a very important point. When you enter the block, the runtime takes a snapshot of the accessible variables at that time. That's how we were able to use the multiplicand variable in the block we used back in Section 24.4, *Capturing Values*, on page 381. Unless you indicate otherwise, these variables are treated as if they were constants—code in the block can read their values but not alter them. This helps with performance and multithreading.

More precisely, when we enter the block, execution passes over to the block literal. Nonobject types have their values set at that point. If instead of an NSInteger, multiplier was an object, then the object the variable points to would be mutable by the block.

So, how do you indicate otherwise? If you need the block to change the value of a nonobject variable that is declared outside the block, then you need to use __block when you declare the variable.[3] With this single change, the application now builds and runs fine.

Blocks/CollectionCalc5/CollectionCalcAppDelegate.m
```
-(NSArray *) squareElementsIn:(NSArray *) originalArray {
    NSMutableArray *tempArray =
    [[NSMutableArray alloc] initWithCapacity:[originalArray count]];
        __block NSInteger multiplier;
    [originalArray enumerateObjectsUsingBlock:
        ^(id obj, NSUInteger idx, BOOL *stop) {
                multiplier = [obj intValue];
                [tempArray addObject:multiply(obj,multiplier)];
        }];
    return tempArray;
}
```

There are a lot of subtleties with blocks and variables. You should definitely read Apple's *Blocks Programming Topics* [App09b], particularly the section titled "Blocks and Variables."

24.8 Cleaning Up with typedef

Let's declare a second block named add with the same signature as multiply. Declare it to be a property and synthesize it. We aren't going to use this block; I'm only introducing it to show you a way to clean up your declarations.

---

3. That is two underscores followed by the word block.

```
Blocks/CollectionCalc6/CollectionCalcAppDelegate.h
```
```objc
#import <Cocoa/Cocoa.h>

@interface CollectionCalcAppDelegate : NSObject <NSApplicationDelegate> {
        NSNumber *(^multiply)(NSNumber *, NSInteger);
        NSNumber *(^add)(NSNumber *, NSInteger);
}
@property(copy) NSNumber *(^multiply)(NSNumber *, NSInteger);
@property(copy) NSNumber *(^add)(NSNumber *, NSInteger);
@end
```

The add and multiply blocks have the same type—they both take an NSNumber and an NSInteger and return an NSNumber. Let's formalize that concept by using typedef to define this new type that we'll call ArithmeticOperation.

```
Blocks/CollectionCalc7/CollectionCalcAppDelegate.h
```
```objc
#import <Cocoa/Cocoa.h>

typedef NSNumber *(^ArithmeticOperation)(NSNumber *, NSInteger);

@interface CollectionCalcAppDelegate : NSObject <NSApplicationDelegate> {
        ArithmeticOperation multiply;
        ArithmeticOperation add;
}
@property(copy) ArithmeticOperation multiply;
@property(copy) ArithmeticOperation add;
@end
```

There are positives and negatives to this approach. On the plus side, you can certainly see that the code is much cleaner. On the negative side, it can be a pain in larger programs for people to locate the typedefs and figure out what is going on underneath.

24.9 Exercise: Using Blocks in Callbacks

Let's round out this introduction to blocks with an example of a callback. Our application will listen for all notifications issued from the notification center and log them to the Console. We need to send a message to the notification center and specify the object and method that should be called by the notification center whenever this type of notification is posted. Once we've set this up in the traditional way, you'll replace the callback mechanism with a block.

Create a new Cocoa application that doesn't use Core Data. Name it Callback, and change the CallbackAppDelegate.m file to this:

Blocks/Callback1/CallbackAppDelegate.m

```
#import "CallbackAppDelegate.h"

@implementation CallbackAppDelegate

@synthesize window;

-(void) response:(NSNotification *) notification {
    NSLog(@"Received: %@.", [notification name]);
}
-(void)registerWithoutBlocks {
    [[NSNotificationCenter defaultCenter]
                        addObserver:self
                           selector:@selector(response:)
                               name:nil
                             object:nil];
}
- (void)applicationDidFinishLaunching:(NSNotification *)aNotification {
        [self registerWithoutBlocks];
}
@end
```

Look at the registerWithoutBlocks method where we register to receive notifications. In this case, we pass in nil for the notification name to receive every notification. We also specify which object is to be notified and which method will be called back when the notification is received.

You can see that the callback method response: doesn't do very much.[4]

The Snow Leopard APIs adds a new method for registering a block to receive notifications. You eliminate the need for the callback method by passing in what you want done when the notification is received as a block. This one method combines both the registration for notifications and the callback.

```
addObserverForName:(NSString *)name
            object:(id)obj
                queue:(NSOperationQueue *)queue
            usingBlock:(void (^)(NSNotification *arg1))block
```

Revise CallbackAppDelegate.m to use this method and a block.

---

4. I do find it a bit disturbing that we just have to know that the callback method needs to accept a single parameter of type NSNotification. You'll see that this requirement is clearer in the blocks version.

24.10 Solution: Using Blocks in Callbacks

You can eliminate the response: method and replace the registerWithout-Blocks method with this method:

Blocks/Callback2/CallbackAppDelegate.m

```
-(void)registerWithBlocks {
    [[NSNotificationCenter defaultCenter]
                    addObserverForName:nil
                                object:nil
                                 queue:nil
▶                            usingBlock:^(NSNotification *notification) {
▶                            NSLog(@"Received: %@.", [notification name]);
▶                            }];
}
```

The body of the block is the body of the old response:. For clarity, I've changed the name of the NSNotification from arg1 to notification. One advantage of using blocks is that you are expressing what needs to be done where it needs to be done. Your logic isn't split all over the place.

Click Build & Run, and your Console should be filled with notifications like these:

```
Received: NSMenuDidChangeItemNotification.
Received: NSWindowDidBecomeKeyNotification.
Received: NSWindowDidBecomeMainNotification.
```

There is a big problem with this code. The problem isn't block-specific, but it trips people up enough that we should talk a bit about it. After a few seconds, the notifications stop. Even if you resize the application window, you won't see an NSWindowDidResizeNotification or other related event notifications.

You may remember this problem from when we worked with KVO. With automatic garbage collection, we have to explicitly hold on to the observer, or it is garbage collected, and there is no object there to receive the notification. Add an instance variable to the header file.

Blocks/Callback3/CallbackAppDelegate.h

```
#import <Cocoa/Cocoa.h>
@interface CallbackAppDelegate : NSObject <NSApplicationDelegate> {
    NSWindow *window;
▶   NSObject *observer;
}
@property (assign) IBOutlet NSWindow *window;
@end
```

Set observer to be the object returned when we register to listen for notifications and retain this object.

`Blocks/Callback3/CallbackAppDelegate.m`

```
-(void)registerWithBlocks {
    observer = [[[NSNotificationCenter defaultCenter]
                 addObserverForName:nil object:nil queue:nil
                 usingBlock:^(NSNotification *notification) {
                     NSLog(@"Received: %@.", [notification name]);
                 }] retain];
}
```

Now everything works perfectly. Notifications are sent and received until we quit the application.

Blocks turn the way you think about code on its head. Instead of passing a lot of parameters to a method that knows what to do with them, you are passing in an action to the object along with a snapshot of some of the data that needs to be acted upon. With practice, you'll get a feel for whether you are in a situation that would benefit from blocks.

There is a lot of good online material on blocks. BBum has an essential series of posts that you should read on his weblog-o-mat. In particular, read Basic Blocks[5] and Blocks Tips & Tricks.[6] Mike Ash posted two very good entries in his Friday Q&A series on blocks.[7,8] Joachim Bengtsson has an online introduction to blocks,[9] and Drew McCormack wrote an excellent guide to "10 Uses for Blocks" in his Cocoa for Scientists series.[10]

In this chapter, you got a feel for various ways to use blocks when you need to wrap some behavior, use a callback, or work with collections. Next we'll look at concurrency and how blocks are built to make your code perform better.

---

5.   http://www.friday.com/bbum/2009/08/29/basic-blocks/
6.   http://www.friday.com/bbum/2009/08/29/blocks-tips-tricks/
7.   http://mikeash.com/pyblog/friday-qa-2008-12-26.html
8.   http://mikeash.com/pyblog/friday-qa-2009-08-14-practical-blocks.html
9.   http://thirdcog.eu/pwcblocks/
10. http://www.macresearch.org/cocoa-scientists-xxxii-10-uses-blocks-cobjective-c

Chapter 25

Operations and Their Queues

Concurrency is difficult. Computers are not particularly good at mediating access to shared resources (in particular memory). The good news is that folks are working hard to make things easier so that we can take advantage of the additional processors on our machines.

One technique is to carve larger tasks into discrete units of work that can be either performed in order or run in parallel in separate threads. When that work completes, our original program collects the results.

Mac OS X Leopard introduced this idea of operation queues to coordinate the distribution of work between multiple threads. Snow Leopard takes this further with dispatch queues, which we'll cover in the next chapter.

Let's start by creating a bad application that makes its users wait (the infamous spinning beach ball effect), and then we'll fix it up using operation queues.

25.1 Making the Beach Ball Spin

In this first example, we'll spin twenty-five progress indicators for one second each, one at a time. This application should be unresponsive, and you should see the spinning beach ball while the progress indicators are displayed.

Create a new Cocoa application named Spinner. When the application runs, it will first create and configure an array of twenty-five progress indicators, and then it will tell each of them to spin for one second.

`Operations/Spinner1/SpinnerAppDelegate.m`

```
- (void)applicationDidFinishLaunching:(NSNotification *)aNotification {
    NSArray *arrayOfSpinners = [self arrayOfSpinners];
    for (NSProgressIndicator *spinner in arrayOfSpinners) {
        [self spin:spinner];
    }
}
```

I'm going to size the window and place the progress indicators so that
if all were visible at once, they would look like this:

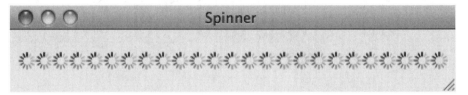

To do this, resize the window in Interface Builder so that its width is
415 and its height is 56. Create and place the progress indicators using
Xcode in the arrayOfSpinners method.

`Operations/Spinner1/SpinnerAppDelegate.m`

```
-(NSArray *) arrayOfSpinners {
    NSMutableArray *array = [[NSMutableArray alloc] initWithCapacity:25];
    for (int i = 0; i < 25; i++){
        NSProgressIndicator *spinner = [[NSProgressIndicator alloc]
                    initWithFrame: NSMakeRect(16 * i + 8, 20, 16, 16)];
        [spinner setStyle:NSProgressIndicatorSpinningStyle];
        [spinner setControlSize:NSSmallControlSize];
        [spinner setDisplayedWhenStopped:NO];
        [window.contentView addSubview:spinner];
        [array addObject:spinner];
    }
    return array;
}
```

The arrayOfSpinners method returns an array filled with the progress
indicators. We iterate through this array and tell each one to start animating, sleep for one second, and then stop animating.

`Operations/Spinner1/SpinnerAppDelegate.m`

```
-(void) spin:(NSProgressIndicator *) spinner {
    [spinner startAnimation:self];
    sleep(1);
    [spinner stopAnimation:self];
}
```

Click Build & Run. The application will start up, and the progress indicators will appear and spin one at a time. If you hover your mouse

pointer over the window, you will see the spinning beach ball. You might notice that the window is not the active window. If you try to click the window, it will be unresponsive.

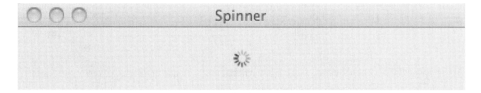

You can also see this if you create a release version of the application and run it as a stand-alone application. It will be reported as "not responding" in your window for force-quitting applications.

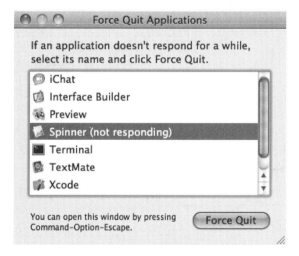

The app is nonresponsive because its main event processing thread is blocked waiting on the spin method to complete. We'll fix this lack of responsiveness with operations and queues. There are three basic types of operations. We'll begin with a type that allows us to turn a method call into an operation.

25.2 Invocation Operations

Right now we just call the spin: method directly:

```
Operations/Spinner1/SpinnerAppDelegate.m
```
```
for (NSProgressIndicator *spinner in arrayOfSpinners) {
    [self spin:spinner];
}
```

An NSInvocationOperation allows us to create an object from this method call by specifying the method, the target for the method, and the parameter to be passed to the method.

```
NSInvocationOperation *op =
        [[NSInvocationOperation alloc] initWithTarget:self
                                            selector:@selector(spin:)
                                              object:spinner];
```

Once you have some sort of an operation, you add it to an operation queue that manages the operations in it.

Operations/Spinner2/SpinnerAppDelegate.m

```
- (void)applicationDidFinishLaunching:(NSNotification *)aNotification {
    NSArray *arrayOfSpinners = [self arrayOfSpinners];
▶   NSOperationQueue *queue = [[NSOperationQueue alloc] init];
    for (NSProgressIndicator *spinner in arrayOfSpinners) {
▶       [queue addOperation:[[NSInvocationOperation alloc]
                             initWithTarget:self
                                   selector:@selector(spin:)
                                     object:spinner]];
    }
}
```

Click Build & Run, and things are quite a bit different.[1] All of the spinners spin at once, and you can select the application window. There's no spinning beach ball. The window will become the active window.

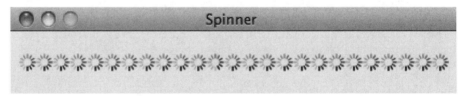

So, how do we get the spinners to spin one at a time? We can cap the number operations that can be performed concurrently. We can set this value to three and watch three progress indicators spin at a time. As a special case, we can set this value to one and turn the queue into a serial queue. The operations will be performed one at a time.

Operations/Spinner3/SpinnerAppDelegate.m

```
- (void)applicationDidFinishLaunching:(NSNotification *)aNotification {
    NSArray *arrayOfSpinners = [self arrayOfSpinners];
    NSOperationQueue *queue = [[NSOperationQueue alloc] init];
▶   [queue setMaxConcurrentOperationCount:1];
```

---

1. If this goes by too quickly, you may want to increase the sleep time from one second to ten seconds.

```
    for (NSProgressIndicator *spinner in arrayOfSpinners) {
        [queue addOperation:[[NSInvocationOperation alloc]
                        initWithTarget:self
                            selector:@selector(spin:)
                                object:spinner]];
    }
}
```

Now the progress indicators spin one at a time, and the application is responsive. No spinning beach balls; we can select the window, and it becomes the active window.

I know I'm making a big deal out of this. This is a big deal. Even when you have serial tasks to perform, you can make your application more responsive and performant by using NSOperation. You are pushing tasks to background threads and reserving the main thread for user interaction.

25.3 Block Operations

If you are targeting Mac OS X 10.6 or newer, then you can use blocks instead of methods.[2] You create an NSBlockOperation object with this convenience constructor:

```
+ (id)blockOperationWithBlock:(void (^)(void))block
```

This signature means that the block doesn't take any parameters and doesn't return anything. This fits our needs perfectly. Create a block inline with the same body as the spin: method:

Operations/Spinner4/SpinnerAppDelegate.m

```
- (void)applicationDidFinishLaunching:(NSNotification *)aNotification {
    NSArray *arrayOfSpinners = [self arrayOfSpinners];
    NSOperationQueue *queue = [[NSOperationQueue alloc] init];
    [queue setMaxConcurrentOperationCount:1];
    for (NSProgressIndicator *spinner in arrayOfSpinners) {
        [queue addOperation:[NSBlockOperation blockOperationWithBlock:^{
            [spinner startAnimation:self];
```

---

2. You may want to take a look back at Chapter 24, *Blocks*, on page 377 to refamiliarize yourself with the block syntax.

```
▶           sleep(1);
▶           [spinner stopAnimation:self];
▶       }]];
      }
}
```

Eliminate the spin: method. Click Build & Run, and the application should run as before with the progress indicators spinning one at a time and with the application being responsive to mouse clicks.

In this case, we can also use the addOperationWithBlock: method that was added to NSOperationQueue in Snow Leopard. Replace the following:

```
[queue addOperation:[NSBlockOperation blockOperationWithBlock:^{
```

with this:

```
[queue addOperationWithBlock:^{
```

Also remove one of the closing square braces that follows the curly brace that closes the block:

```
Operations/Spinner5/SpinnerAppDelegate.m
```

```
- (void)applicationDidFinishLaunching:(NSNotification *)aNotification {
      NSArray *arrayOfSpinners = [self arrayOfSpinners];
      NSOperationQueue *queue = [[NSOperationQueue alloc] init];
      [queue setMaxConcurrentOperationCount:1];
      for (NSProgressIndicator *spinner in arrayOfSpinners) {
▶         [queue addOperationWithBlock:^{
              [spinner startAnimation:self];
              sleep(1);
              [spinner stopAnimation:self];
▶         }];
      }
}
```

That's it. Click Build & Run, and everything runs as before.

25.4 Interacting with the Queue and Operations

You can get information from and send messages to your NSOperations and your NSOperationQueue. For instance, we can get an array of all current operations in a queue or just get a count of how many there are. We can cancel them all or just suspend or resume the queue. We can ask an operation if it is canceled, executing, finished, ready, or concurrent. We can cancel an operation before it starts.

To explore these a little bit, add three actions to the header file. We'll also move the declaration of the NSOperationQueue to the header file so that it can be accessed from more than one method.

Operations/Spinner6/SpinnerAppDelegate.h

```
#import <Cocoa/Cocoa.h>

@interface SpinnerAppDelegate : NSObject <NSApplicationDelegate> {
    NSWindow *window;
▶   NSOperationQueue *queue;
}
@property (assign) IBOutlet NSWindow *window;
▶ -(IBAction)toggleIsSuspended:(id)sender;
▶ -(IBAction)cancelAllOperations:(id)sender;
▶ -(IBAction)queueStatus:(id)sender;
@end
```

You'll need to remove the declaration of the NSOperationQueue from the applicationDidFinishLaunching: method. While we're there, I'm going to change the maximum number of concurrent threads to three just for fun.

Operations/Spinner6/SpinnerAppDelegate.m

```
queue = [[NSOperationQueue alloc] init];
[queue setMaxConcurrentOperationCount:3];
```

Let's implement the action to cancel all operations in the queue.

Operations/Spinner6/SpinnerAppDelegate.m

```
-(IBAction)cancelAllOperations:(id)sender {
    [queue cancelAllOperations];
}
```

When you tell a queue to cancel all of its operations, it will send each operation in its queue the cancel message. If an operation hasn't started yet, then it will be canceled and won't be run. If an operation has already started, then it's up to you to respond to cancel or not. By default cancel doesn't force the task to quit. You need to check to see whether isCancelled returns YES or NO and respond accordingly. You'll see how this works at the end of the next section.

In our example, any NSProgressIndicator that is spinning when we cancel all operations will continue to spin. Any that have not yet begun spinning will be canceled.

Next let's allow users to pause and resume the spinning:

Operations/Spinner6/SpinnerAppDelegate.m

```
-(IBAction)toggleIsSuspended:(id)sender {
    [queue setSuspended:![queue isSuspended]];
}
```

When you send the queue the message setSuspended:YES, the queue will be paused. As with cancel, the progress indicators that are currently spinning will continue to spin until they have finished, but no further indicators will spin until you send the queue the message setSuspended:NO.

Finally, we can create an array of the operations in the queue and ask each one if it is executing or in a ready state. Operations that are executing are also considered to be ready.

Operations/Spinner6/SpinnerAppDelegate.m

```
-(IBAction)queueStatus:(id)sender {
    NSArray *ops =[queue operations];
    int  executing =0;
    int ready=0;
    for (NSOperation *operation in ops) {
        if ([operation isExecuting]) executing++;
        if ([operation isReady]) ready++;
    }
    NSLog(@"Status for %d operations: executing %d and %d are waiting.",
        [queue operationCount], executing, ready - executing);
}
```

This will generate reports like the following in the Console. After nine operations have completed, this is the report that I get:

```
Status for 16 operations: executing 3 and 13 are waiting.
```

Head over to Interface Builder, and add these three buttons to the top of the window:

Wire your actions to these buttons. Save, and click Build & Run. The buttons should work just as I've described them.

25.5 Custom NSOperations

Block operations and invocation operations are going to meet most of your needs. When they don't, you can create your own subclass of NSOperation to create custom operations that you add to a queue.

Add a new file to your project, a class of type NSObject named Spinner-Operation. We need to make some changes to the header file. The SpinnerOperation class must subclass the NSOperation class. We also need to declare an instance variable for the spinner and a custom init method to set the spinner when we initialize the SpinnerOperation object.

Operations/Spinner7/SpinnerOperation.h

```
#import <Foundation/Foundation.h>

@interface SpinnerOperation : NSOperation {
    NSProgressIndicator *spinner;
}
-(id) initWithSpinner:(NSProgressIndicator *) newSpinner;

@end
```

Implement the custom init like this:

Operations/Spinner7/SpinnerOperation.m

```
-(id) initWithSpinner:(NSProgressIndicator *) newSpinner {
    if (self = [super init]) {
        spinner = newSpinner;
    }
    return self;
}
```

When you subclass NSOperation and you don't have to worry about concurrency, put work that needs to be performed by this operation in the main method.[3]

Operations/Spinner7/SpinnerOperation.m

```
-(void) main {
    [spinner startAnimation:self];
    sleep(4);
    [spinner stopAnimation:self];
}
```

---

3. The NSOperation docs specify a lot of extra work that needs to be done if you are making your operations concurrent. We aren't, and you never have to if you use your operations with an operation queue. The NSOperation docs make it clear that when you use an operation queue, there is no reason to make your operation concurrent.

The rest of the changes are in the SpinnerAppDelegate.m file. After adding an import for our new header file, we'll change the arrayOfSpinners method to this arrayOfSpinnerOperations method:

Operations/Spinner7/SpinnerAppDelegate.m

```
-(NSArray *) arrayOfSpinnerOperations {
    NSMutableArray *array = [[NSMutableArray alloc] initWithCapacity:25];
    for (int i = 0; i < 25; i++){
        NSProgressIndicator *spinner = [[NSProgressIndicator alloc]
                    initWithFrame: NSMakeRect(16 * i + 8, 20, 16, 16)];
        [spinner setStyle:NSProgressIndicatorSpinningStyle];
        [spinner setControlSize:NSSmallControlSize];
        [spinner setDisplayedWhenStopped:NO];
        [window.contentView addSubview:spinner];
        SpinnerOperation *op = [[SpinnerOperation alloc]
                                    initWithSpinner:spinner];
        [array addObject:op];
    }
    return array;
}
```

The two methods are very similar. In addition to changing the name of the method, we pass in the progress indicator we create and configure to the SpinnerOperation's initWithSpinner: method and add the SpinnerOperation object to the array instead of the NSProgressIndicator.

The applicationDidFinishLaunching: method is much cleaner now. It is focused on the operation queue and not on the work the operations perform.

Operations/Spinner7/SpinnerAppDelegate.m

```
- (void)applicationDidFinishLaunching:(NSNotification *)aNotification {
    NSArray *arrayOfSpinnerOperations = [self arrayOfSpinnerOperations];
    queue = [[NSOperationQueue alloc] init];
    [queue setMaxConcurrentOperationCount:1];
    for (SpinnerOperation *spinnerOp in arrayOfSpinnerOperations) {
        [queue addOperation:spinnerOp];
    }
}
```

I'd like to make one more change to make this application more responsive. In our case the work is trivial—the thread sleeps for some amount of time. We can split this time into smaller bits and check the status of the cancelled flag.

Operations/Spinner8/SpinnerOperation.m

```
-(void) main {
    [spinner startAnimation:self];
    for (int i = 0; i<4; i++){
        if ([self isCancelled]) break;
```

```
►        sleep(1);
►    }
     [spinner stopAnimation:self];
}
```

Click Build & Run. Now you can cancel all operations in the middle of a running operation.

25.6 From Operation Queues to Dispatch Queues

Concurrency can be difficult. But, as you've seen even in the contrived example in this chapter, judicious use of concurrency is how you give your users the feeling that their computers and your application are responsive.

The techniques for using operation queues are a lot easier than the techniques I'll show you in the next chapter for using dispatch queues. Operation queues are straightforward and fairly easy to use. Dispatch queues are a lower-level C-based API that require you to know more of the details of what's going on. You should always start with the higher-level abstractions, in this case operation queues, before you start using the C-level APIs for dispatch queues.

Also, if you are targeting Snow Leopard or higher, the classes you've worked with in this chapter have been reengineered to work on top of Grand Central Dispatch (the marketing term for the infrastructure that manages the dispatch queues).

Don't believe me? I'll show you.

Open Xcode, and build the Spinner app you've just created. Once you have a successful build, choose Run > Run with Performance Tool > Multicore. This will start up Instruments with two instruments loaded: the Thread States instrument is on top, and the Dispatch instrument is on the bottom. The Spinner app will then run while Instruments records the activity.

Here's the graphical summary from the Dispatch instrument:

The text is a bit hard to read, but the writing at the left side identifies the four global dispatch queues that you'll explicitly use in the next chapter. The main thread is at the top. It is where items submitted to the main queue happen. The main queue and the associated main thread are where all of UI occurs.

You can see that the bottom three queues are kept pretty busy so that the main thread is available for user input. The bottom three queues are all global queues designed to accept work at three different priority levels. From top to bottom in the image these are default priority, high priority, and low priority. You can see that the workload has been spread around pretty evenly.

Contrast that with a run of the first version of the Spinner before we used any queues.

You can see that things get underway in much the same way as our concurrent version. But after the work is divided up, nothing else happens until just after twenty-five seconds when the final spinner is finished spinning. You can poke around in Instruments if you want more of the details of what's going on, but even a quick glance at these two reports shows you that something is different.

Take a look at the reports from the Thread States instrument, and you'll see even more of the story. We aren't explicitly creating and using threads, but underneath this is being done for us. First here's the report for the original nonresponsive version of Spinner:

Compare that with this bottom part of the report for our concurrent version. The diagonal pattern of threads continues up and to the right.

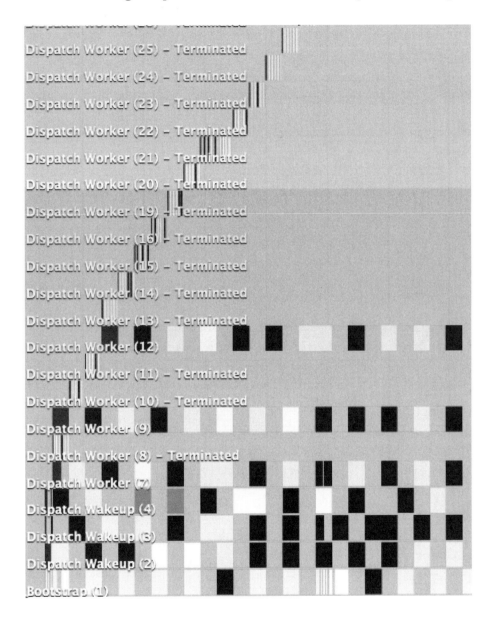

You can see the contents of Dispatch Worker 7 in the first version is distributed over all of those threads near the top of the image and beyond in the second version. Again, even without delving into the details, you can see that the concurrent version is likely to be more performant and responsive.

The next chapter will dig into the details of explicitly using Grand Central Dispatch. There's a good chance that you'll never need to do anything more than use operation queues to get the behavior you want.

Chapter 26

Dispatch Queues

As computers ship with more cores, one way to make your application faster and more responsive is to keep those processors busy. In the previous chapter, you learned the easiest way for your application to take advantage of concurrency is to use operation queues.

Sometimes you need finer control or need to integrate with system-level activities. If you're writing an iPhone app or a desktop app that targets Leopard or earlier, you're out of luck. You have to use threads. It's hard to write and schedule threads. It's easy to make a mistake when you're using threads and actually make your app worse.

Apple introduced Grand Central Dispatch (GCD) in Snow Leopard. GCD puts the operating system in charge of managing the tasks in the threads. You add tasks to dispatch queues, and GCD takes care of when to send the tasks in the various queues off to a processor.

In this chapter, you'll learn how and when to use the different types of dispatch queues. We're just skimming the surface of a deep and difficult topic, but you'll get an idea of what is possible and how to integrate dispatch queues in your application.

26.1 When to Use Dispatch Queues

Imagine you've written a program that searches different websites for the least expensive flights to a particular location on a particular day. Your program would ask the user where they want their trip to begin and end and when they want to travel. You wouldn't think of searching one site at a time. The user could do that themselves. You would send off all of the queries one after another asynchronously, and you would gather and begin to present the results as you get them.

This is an example of the type of problem that is well suited for dispatch queues. You have a collection of tasks that can be performed concurrently, and each task takes enough time that you don't want to block the program to wait until it finishes.

Once you start looking for tasks that could benefit from using dispatch queues, you'll find them everywhere. Suppose you have a bunch of images to which you want to apply a filter. If you have multiple cores available, you could easily have the same filter being applied to different images at the same time and finish the batch much more quickly. For some filters, the task might be accelerated even more by breaking an image into smaller pieces and applying the filter to each of the pieces and reassembling at the end.

Our example in this chapter centers around a long series of calculations that we apply to hundreds of thousands of square regions of a grid to determine the color to use to fill the square.

The details of the fractal I'm drawing aren't important. What makes this a good candidate for dispatch queues is that the calculations for each of the more than quarter million squares is independent of each other, and the calculations are nontrivial. In our case, thousands of calculations are required to determine the color of each square. So, we're doing significant work that is easily parallelized.

26.2 Quick Queue Overview

There are three basic types of dispatch queues:

- Concurrent queues
- The main dispatch queue
- Private dispatch queues

We looked briefly at concurrent and main queue at the end of the previous chapter.

You'll use global concurrent queues for parallelizable operations. There are actually three different concurrent queues with low, medium, and high priorities. Even though the tasks in each queue are available to be run concurrently, all dispatch queues are first-in, first-out, so the tasks will be started in the same order that they are added to the queue. Tasks in the high-priority queue are run before those in the default priority queue, and so on.

Sometimes you want to run a set of tasks in a set order. In that case, you'll pass the tasks to a serial queue. The main dispatch queue is a global serial queue. You often use it for GUI operations and to synchronize with the event loop. You can also use it to synchronize access to a shared resource across your application.

If you are just looking to synchronize tasks, you can create a serial queue to ensure that the tasks submitted to a queue are executed in order. You could use the main queue to synchronize tasks because it is a serial queue as well, but the goal is to get increased performance and responsiveness by pushing tasks off the main queue.

You can submit either a block or a function to a queue. In this book, we'll use blocks. You can add blocks to the queues either synchronously or asynchronously. Mostly you will prefer to use the dispatch_asynch() function to add a block to a queue and return immediately. That's right—we need to use C syntax as we're working with plain old C functions and variables.

If you need to wait until a task finishes before executing the next line in your program, then you'll add the block to a queue using the dispatch_synch() function. There are other techniques, such as groups, that you can use to coordinate what work gets done when. We won't be covering them in this book. Once you get your head around how to work with these basic options, you'll want to read Apple's *Concurrency Programming Guide* [App09c].

26.3 Drawing Our Fractal

Start with the Newton project you'll find in the Dispatch/Newton1 directory in the code download. It contains two classes in addition to the application delegate. The Grid class is an NSView that we use to display the results. The Grid will create an instance of the Tile class that represents a rectangle to be colored. The Tile object will calculate its color and spawn four subrectangles that need to be colored. We'll repeat this cycle of coloring the rectangle and splitting into four subrectangles until we have covered our 512 by 512 Grid with 262,144 one-by-one squares.

The Grid class has a property of type NSMutableArray named tiles that holds the rectangles and their color. You can see in the code that follows that we initialize the array in the initWithFrame: method. For the drawing, we copy over the array and iterate through the tiles that are contained in the dirty rectangle and draw any one that needs to be redrawn. The startTiling method creates the initial Tile and starts things off.

```
Dispatch/Newton1/Grid.m
#import "Grid.h"
#import "Tile.h"

@implementation Grid
@synthesize tiles;

- (id)initWithFrame:(NSRect)frame {
    if (self= [super initWithFrame:frame]) {
        self.tiles = [[NSMutableArray alloc] initWithCapacity:1000];
    }
    return self;
}
-(void)startTiling {
    [[[Tile alloc] initWithFrame:self.frame view:self] cycle];
}
- (void)drawRect:(NSRect)dirtyRect {
    for (Tile *tile in [NSArray arrayWithArray:tiles]){
        if(NSContainsRect(dirtyRect, tile.frame)) {
```

```
            [tile.color set];
            [NSBezierPath fillRect:tile.frame];
        }
    }//NSLog( @"here");
}
@end
```

For the most part, we aren't going to touch any of these files as we introduce dispatch queues. In the next section, I'll show you the areas of the Tile class that we'll optimize with queues.

26.4 Working Without Dispatch Queues

In this application, the bulk of the work is performed in the Tile class. At the top level, the life of a Tile object looks like this:

Dispatch/Newton1/Tile.m

```
-(void) cycle {
    [self calculateColor];
        [self.grid.tiles addObject:self];
    [self.grid setNeedsDisplayInRect:self.frame];
    if (self.frame.size.width > 2) {
        [self split];
    }
}
```

We call the calculateColor method, which iterates 2,000 times using Newton's method and sets the color of the current Tile object. We can improve on this algorithm, but in this chapter we'll explore how much we can improve the performance and responsiveness using dispatch queues.

The rest of the cycle method adds the current tile to the grid's tiles array and then tests to see whether we should continue subdividing. The split method creates four equal subtiles that cover the current tile.

Dispatch/Newton1/Tile.m

```
-(void) split {
    CGFloat size = (self.frame.size.width)/2;
    CGFloat x = self.frame.origin.x;
    CGFloat y = self.frame.origin.y;
    [self tileWithX:x Y:y size:size];
    [self tileWithX:x Y:y+size size:size];
    [self tileWithX:x+size Y:y size:size];
    [self tileWithX:x+size Y:y+size size:size];
    [self.grid.tiles removeObject:self];
}
```

I've chosen to start with a square with sides of length 512. Each time I subdivide the squares and then determine their color. Once we add threads, we can set the minimum size of the squares at one, but for now I've chosen to stop when the width of the square is 8.

Click Build & Run with various values for the minimum width. On my laptop, I see results almost immediately when the minimum width is eight. Here's the final image when the minimum size of the tiles is eight:

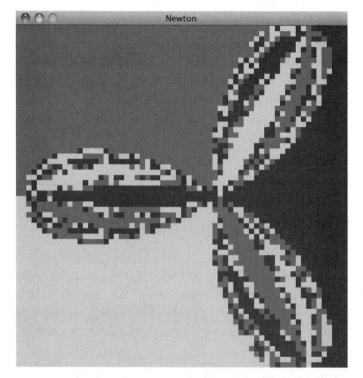

At four there is a slight pause before the results show up. When the minimum width is two, there is a long pause where I see nothing but the proverbial spinning beach ball. There's nothing else but a white screen for just under twenty seconds, and then the final image appears all at once.

Log a message from the drawRect: method in Grid.m to see that the method is called only once.

Suppose that you call the drawRect: method directly instead of using setNeedsDisplayInRect:. Don't do it. Just suppose. If you did, then the Grid's drawRect: method would be called every time through the loop, but nothing would be displayed until the calculations have finished. In addition, this direct call increases the running time of the application. Leave the call as setNeedsDisplayInRect: and not drawRect:.

Next let's add some multithreading goodness.

26.5 The Main Queue

Remember that several global queues are available to you and that the one associated with the main thread is a serial queue known as the *main queue*. Events and changes to your GUI happen on the main thread, so as you start to use asynchronous threads to get better performance in your app, you'll push updates to the main thread so that your users aren't sitting there watching the spinning beach ball. This is going to take us a couple of sections to get right.

You don't create the main queue or any of the global queues yourself. You will call a function that returns a reference to the queue you are requesting. In the case of the main queue, you use the functiondispatch_get_main_queue() to get a reference to it. Here's how you get and store a handle to the main queue. Note the type is dispatch_queue_t.

```
dispatch_queue_t main = dispatch_get_main_queue();
```

We'll be passing blocks to queues using either the dispatch_async() or dispatch_sync() function. Mostly we'll use dispatch_async() so that we don't have to wait for the task to complete. Both methods take two arguments. The first is the queue, and the second is the block describing the task to be performed.

```
dispatch_async(main, ^{
  //code to be executed
});
```

Revise the cycle method to push our requests both to add the tile to the Grid's array and to display the results to the main thread.

Dispatch/Newton2/Tile.m

```
-(void) cycle {
    [self calculateColor];
    dispatch_async(dispatch_get_main_queue(), ^{
        [self.grid.tiles addObject:self];
        [self.grid setNeedsDisplayInRect:self.frame];
    });
    if (self.frame.size.width > 2 ) {
        [self split];
    }
}
```

On my laptop the performance is even better than before. The time for the minimum width of two has gone from around twenty seconds to less than five. The time for a width of one is now around twenty seconds. Next, we'll start to wrap the calculations in queues that don't execute on the main thread.

26.6 Global Concurrent Queues

This next change is striking. You'll get a little performance improvement, but the main difference is that the drawing will begin right away, and the image will update until it is finished.

When you don't need to integrate with the main GUI thread, you should look to see whether you can safely spin off an operation to another thread. When you can, you should use a global concurrent queue. You get a handle to one by calling the function dispatch_get_global_queue(). The first argument specifies the priority of the queue. Your choices are DISPATCH_QUEUE_PRIORITY_DEFAULT, DISPATCH_QUEUE_PRIORITY_LOW, and DISPATCH_QUEUE_PRIORITY_HIGH. The docs explain that the second argument should be 0 for now because that slot is being reserved for future expansion.

Soon we'll use lots of these concurrent queues. For now we'll just send the calls to spawn off the four subtiles to a concurrent queue inside the split method. Use the default priority level.

`Dispatch/Newton3/Tile.m`

```
-(void) split {
    CGFloat size = (self.frame.size.width)/2;
    CGFloat x = self.frame.origin.x;
    CGFloat y = self.frame.origin.y;
    dispatch_async(
        dispatch_get_global_queue(DISPATCH_QUEUE_PRIORITY_DEFAULT, 0), ^{
        [self tileWithX:x Y:y size:size];
        [self tileWithX:x Y:y+size size:size];
        [self tileWithX:x+size Y:y size:size];
        [self tileWithX:x+size Y:y+size size:size];
    });
    [self.grid.tiles removeObject:self];
}
```

The result is much more satisfying. You should quickly see some of the larger squares displayed, and then you should see the fractal animate a bit as the image is refined. Try this with different values for the minimum width of a tile. The program should run slightly faster than before, but more importantly, it's kind of fun to watch.

26.7 Synchronizing on the Main Queue

We've sped up the application—it now looks and feels better—but we've also introduced a problem. Because this is a concurrent application, you may see this message in your Console each time you run the application. When the minimum size is small enough, I fairly consistently see this warning:

```
*** -[NSCFArray initWithObjects:count:]:
            attempt to insert nil object at objects[5733]
```

The problem is that we are adding objects to and removing objects from the tiles property, an array belonging to our Grid object. We are adding the objects to the array from the main queue, which is a global serial queue, but not removing them from that queue, so the program may be checking whether the tile needs to be drawn after it has been removed from the array. We can fix the problem by dispatching the call to remove objects from the tile array to the main queue.

```
Dispatch/Newton4/Tile.m
```
```
-(void) split {
    CGFloat size = (self.frame.size.width)/2;
    CGFloat x = self.frame.origin.x;
    CGFloat y = self.frame.origin.y;
►   dispatch_async(
►       dispatch_get_global_queue(DISPATCH_QUEUE_PRIORITY_DEFAULT, 0), ^{
        [self tileWithX:x Y:y size:size];
        [self tileWithX:x Y:y+size size:size];
        [self tileWithX:x+size Y:y size:size];
        [self tileWithX:x+size Y:y+size size:size];
►   });
►   dispatch_async(dispatch_get_main_queue(), ^{
    [self.grid.tiles removeObject:self];
    });
}
```

The main queue is a serial queue, so by accessing the array only from the main queue, we can ensure that there will be no resource contention. The main queue is also where events are processed, so that is where you can do any other UI tasks you need to do.

You might also notice that the animation is a bit different. I preferred the way it was before with an initial coloring of the entire view and then a refinement as further calculations are made. Now the animation begins in the bottom-left corner and mostly works its way up and to the right.

26.8 Private Dispatch Queues

It makes sense to use the main queue to synchronize access to the tiles array because we're using it for the drawing we're doing on the main thread. We're also synchronizing these calls among thousands of Tile objects.

Sometimes, however, you want to organize a small collection of tasks over a short span of time or in a small portion of code. You can do this with serial queues that you create and release yourself. The serial queues are not global; you have to create them yourselves using a call like this:

```
dispatch_queue_t myQ = dispatch_queue_create("com.pragprog.myQ",NULL);
```

The first parameter is a label for your queue that is used for debugging. Use a reverse DNS scheme, and give your queues a unique name so you can figure out where things went wrong. The second parameter is currently unused, and the docs tell you to just past NULL.

This is a serial queue so that each task we add to the queue is performed before the next one begins. Here we'll add two tasks to the queue. In fact, each task is a dispatch to a queue. In the first we spawn the four subtiles, and in the second we remove the parent tile from the tiles array.

Dispatch/Newton5/Tile.m

```
-(void) split {
    CGFloat size = (self.frame.size.width)/2;
    CGFloat x = self.frame.origin.x;
    CGFloat y = self.frame.origin.y;
►   dispatch_queue_t myQ =
►                       dispatch_queue_create("com.pragprog.myQ", NULL);
►   dispatch_async(myQ, ^{
        dispatch_async(
            dispatch_get_global_queue(
                            DISPATCH_QUEUE_PRIORITY_DEFAULT, 0), ^{
            [self tileWithX:x Y:y size:size];
            [self tileWithX:x Y:y+size size:size];
            [self tileWithX:x+size Y:y size:size];
            [self tileWithX:x+size Y:y+size size:size];
►       });
►   });
```

```
►       dispatch_async(myQ, ^{
            dispatch_async(dispatch_get_main_queue(), ^{
                [self.grid.tiles removeObject:self];
            });
►       });
►       dispatch_release(myQ);
    }
```

These private dispatch queues are reference counted and are not currently cleaned up by the automatic garbage collection. You can see in the last highlighted line above that we had to explicitly release the queue like this:

```
dispatch_release(myQ)
```

Similarly, if you had to pass one of these queues around, any object that needed to own the queue would have to explicitly retain it and later release it. When you create a serial queue using dispatch_queue_create(), the reference count for the returned queue is one. That's why we needed to manually release it once we're done with it.

Click Build & Run, and this works fine. There's a lot of overhead here, though. You're creating and destroying a lot of dispatch queue objects. You can see this by running Instruments against this version of the project using the Dispatch instrument. You can see that a ton of queues are created and used for a very short time.

In general, when you create or use a queue, you want to make sure that it's doing enough work to justify its use. Unfortunately, sometimes you can't avoid this overhead. Next we'll consider a situation where we don't need to use the main queue or these private dispatch queues.

26.9 Synchronous Tasks

Everything is running so much faster and better that you're going to be tempted to use dispatch queues everywhere. For example, let's push the calculation of the color of the tile into a concurrent queue:

Dispatch/Newton6/Tile.m

```
-(void) cycle {
►   dispatch_async(
        dispatch_get_global_queue(
                            DISPATCH_QUEUE_PRIORITY_DEFAULT, 0), ^{
            [self calculateColor];
►       });
        dispatch_async(dispatch_get_main_queue(), ^{
            [self.grid.tiles addObject:self];
```

```
        [self.grid setNeedsDisplayInRect:self.frame];
    });
    if (self.frame.size.width > 1 ) {
        [self split];
    }
}
```

It's easier to see the problem with this approach if we take out the serial queue we added in the previous section:

```
Dispatch/Newton6/Tile.m
```

```
-(void) split {
    CGFloat size = (self.frame.size.width)/2;
    CGFloat x = self.frame.origin.x;
    CGFloat y = self.frame.origin.y;
    dispatch_async(
        dispatch_get_global_queue(DISPATCH_QUEUE_PRIORITY_DEFAULT,0),^{
            [self tileWithX:x Y:y size:size];
            [self tileWithX:x Y:y+size size:size];
            [self tileWithX:x+size Y:y size:size];
            [self tileWithX:x+size Y:y+size size:size];
        });
}
```

Click Build & Run. I see splotches of color on a black background. The code to draw the rectangles to the screen is being called before the color has been calculated. You can see varying amounts of black by changing the number of iterations in Newton's method from 2,000 to 200 to 20 if you'd like.

We have a race condition. There is no guarantee that calculateColor will be executed before self is drawn in the main queue. This illustrates the problem that we avoided in the previous section by using serial dispatch queues. In this code, we send the calculation of the tile's color to a global concurrent thread using dispatch_async(). We don't wait for the color calculation to complete when we send an asynchronous request to the main queue to draw the tile.

Let's make one tiny change to the code. Change the first call to the function dispatch_async() in the cycle todispatch_sync().

```
Dispatch/Newton7/Tile.m
-(void) cycle {
    dispatch_sync(
        dispatch_get_global_queue(DISPATCH_QUEUE_PRIORITY_DEFAULT, 0), ^{
            [self calculateColor];
        });
    dispatch_async(dispatch_get_main_queue(), ^{
        [self.grid.tiles addObject:self];
        [self.grid setNeedsDisplayInRect:self.frame];
    });
    if (self.frame.size.width > 1 ) {
        [self split];
    }
}
```

Now the calculation of the tile's color completes before we push the request to draw the tile to the main thread. This version runs in the same way as the version using the serial queues without the overhead of creating those queues.

In this quick introduction to dispatch queues, we looked at the three basic types of queues and how to send tasks to them using the functions dispatch_async() and dispatch_sync(). If this example program were the ends and not the means, we would have a lot of tuning left to do. We could streamline the drawing routine so that we don't redraw cells where nothing is changing. We would also speed up the algorithm without losing accuracy.

You can gain a lot of speed and responsiveness usingqueues, but there are costs. You need to make sure you don't accidentally introduce unintended behavior, and you have to make sure that adding the complexity that queues require really results in perceivable improvements.

Read Mike Ash's four-part series on Grand Central Dispatch and his other related posts.[1] Drew McCormack also has a nice introduction to GCD.[2]

1. http://mikeash.com/pyblog/?tag=gcd
2. http://www.macresearch.org/cocoa-scientists-xxxi-all-aboard-grand-central

Chapter 27

Up and Out

So now you've gotten a solid introduction to the Mac and iPhone developers' neighborhood. You know the programming equivalent of where to go for coffee and where to catch the bus that takes you downtown. I didn't list the entire menu and prices for the local coffeehouse nor did I give you the entire bus schedule. These details will change, and you can look them up when you need them.

You've been on quite a journey. You've learned how to use the fundamental development tools for Mac OS X and iPhone apps. You've learned the ins and outs of Cocoa and Objective-C. Most importantly, you've learned how to get the most out of this platform using the techniques and design patterns central to Cocoa development.

27.1 But What About...

There are a ton of topics I considered including but didn't. I wanted to keep the focus of the book on the skills you needed for programming and not on the APIs. You will have pet topics that you hoped would be covered but weren't.

For instance, I developed a web services example where you would have created a simple Twitter client. When I stepped back and looked at the example, it was way too API focused. You learned how to send synchronous and asynchronous requests, parse the XML that you received in response, and even respond to an authentication challenge. This is similar to an example used in our iPhone SDK book and to a sequence we teach in our iPhone Studio course, but it didn't fit this book. Other than introducing you to a few more classes and methods, the main technique used in this example was delegates.

Similarly, at one point I ported the Core Data example to the iPhone. There are no bindings on the iPhone, so you have to fetch the data yourself and present it in the table views. Although this is a difference in the specific settings of Core Data, it uses techniques that you used to fill tables long before we got to Core Data, so there was no justification for including this material.

And so it went. This book could have easily been twice as long as it is, but in each case I asked the material to justify its existence. Do you really add something new here? Often the candidate chapters shrugged their shoulders and said, "I guess not."

There was one exception. I wrestled with whether to end with a chapter on OpenCL for months. I finally decided that it was a niche topic. In fact, this decision made me scale back the chapter on Grand Central Dispatch to cover the basics.

So when you say, "You could have included a chapter on...," I agree with you. I could have. In many cases, I considered doing so but decided the book would not have been made stronger with this additional material. I wanted to minimize the side trips that we'd take on this journey through Cocoa development techniques.

27.2 What's Next

It's time to stop reading books and to start writing a real application.

Before you sit down and write a line of code, make sure you nail what it is you are writing and who it's for. Can you picture someone using your app? What are they doing with it? When do they use it? What itch are they scratching, or what problem are they solving? How will you explain to someone why they should download or pay money for your app?

This sounds small, but if you look at the previous section, you can see how useful it was. I knew exactly who I intended this book for and what it was I was providing for you in this book. It made the hard decisions easier. Identify your audience and what they will get from your application.

You still aren't ready to write any code. Sketch your screens, and imagine the user navigating from screen to screen and interacting with your application. This paper prototyping step might feel unnecessary, but it helps you think through the flow of your application. It's a lot easier to fix problems before you start writing code and creating nibs than after.

During these initial steps, make sure that you don't use words that programmers use. Don't talk about using a delegate or describe your model or talk about separate nibs. All of your thoughts at this point should be in terms of the person using your application. This is the hardest rule to follow, but the idea is that you should not be worried about implementation at this point. For now, you're making sure that you have something worth implementing.

Now you are ready to open up Xcode and start coding. When you have something you can get into the hands of testers, do so. You are too close to the application. You know that you have to go to some particular submenu to find just what you need—if this isn't clear to your testers, then you need to address it. For the most part, you want your app to behave consistently with other Mac or iPhone applications.

Along the way, you will run into dead ends. You won't be able to find what you need in the docs. You'll need some special case that isn't covered in this book or in any of the other books you own. Arm yourself with Mike Ash's post on "Getting Answers," and head to Apple and third-party forums and mailing lists.[1]

Keep pushing and polishing, but remember Steve Jobs' famous admonition that "Real artists ship."[2]

I can't wait to see what you come up with.

27.3 Acknowledgments

I couldn't figure out where to put the acknowledgments in this book. I know they usually go up front, but this book is about your journey, not mine. I couldn't see starting you on this journey and then stopping to talk about me. If this were a GCD-enabled program and not a book, I would have kept the book on the main queue and sent the thanks to a concurrent high-priority thread. Please understand that these acknowledgments have not been left to the end because they aren't important.

First, thanks to Kimberli Diemert and Margaret Steinberg. No one is more important to me than my wife, Kim, and my daughter, Maggie.

---

1. http://www.mikeash.com/getting_answers.html
2. http://www.folklore.org/StoryView.py?story=Pirate_Flag.txt

Nothing gets done without their help and support and daily doses of reality.

Second, thanks to Dave Thomas for agreeing to edit this book. That was a gift that I have benefited on every page of this book. He made suggestions to the prose and the code. Anything that you don't like about the book is definitely his fault.

Of course, I'm kidding. It's probably Andy Hunt's fault.

Yes, kidding again. Beyond editing the book, I'd like to thank Dave and Andy for giving me a home as an author and editor and for providing a great set of tools that support the writing and life cycle of a technology book.

Thanks to Mike and Nicole Clark for letting me teach Cocoa programming and iPhone programming at the Pragmatic Studios. Thanks to the many students in the studios who gave me great feedback on the material. Thanks to friends and colleagues Craig Castelaz, Chris Adamson, Bill Dudney, Eric Freeman, Scott Kovatch, and Dee Wu for their helpful comments throughout the life of this project.

Thanks also to the tech reviewers and the readers who submitted errata over the year that this book was in beta. Thanks to folks at Apple who I'm not allowed to name or it would get them in trouble. Two in particular took me out to lunch several years ago to make sure I understood that I needed to move from Java to Objective-C if I wanted to continue to write code for this platform. Finally, thanks to the folks at Apple who have created such a wonderful platform. Writing Cocoa and Objective-C is a pleasure.

27.4 Dedication

This book is dedicated to my friend James Duncan Davidson.

I met Duncan at an Apple Worldwide Developer Conference (WWDC) back when they were held in San Jose. He was researching his book *Learning Cocoa* [DA02]. Honestly, if I'd had my druthers, he would have written this book, and I would have edited it. I've tried to be true to the spirit of his book.

Duncan met Kim, my wife, on a Mac geek cruise and quickly became a family friend. He first met my daughters while visiting before the two of us drove up to Mac Hack. In other words, all of my family's first interactions with this man were tied up in Mac events.

My daughter Maggie would tell her friends in a hushed voice, "He's very famous. He created Ant and Tomcat." She also messed up his name on purpose and called him James David Duncanson.

I loved his relationship with my youngest daughter. Both in our house and when we visited him in Portland or met him in San Francisco, they had a special give-and-take. She would tease him and flirt with him, and in return he would talk to her in a way that was both age appropriate and respectful of who she was. Yes, was. After Elena died, Duncan came out and took care of us. He dropped everything and stayed with us after the funeral was over and made sure we had what we needed.

A couple of years ago I approached Duncan about writing an updated version of his Cocoa book. He declined, and he suggested I write it. I was nervous. I remembered him saying to the Cleveland Java Users Group that he had thought he was an OO "badass" when he was working at Sun on Java but that working with Objective-C and Cocoa made him realize he wasn't at the time. That thought was what stood at the core of this book for me. I didn't want to walk through Cocoa APIs and just teach you tools. I wanted to look at the techniques that would make you an OO badass.

Thank you, James.

Appendix A

Bibliography

[App06]   Apple, Inc. *Coding Guidelines for Cocoa.* http://devel-
             oper.apple.com/mac/library/documentation/Cocoa/Conceptu-
             al/CodingGuidelines/Articles/NamingMethods.html, 2006.

[App08a]   Apple, Inc. *Cocoa Bindings Programming Topics.* http://
             developer.apple.com/documentation/Cocoa/Conceptual/Co-
             coaBindings, 2008.

[App08b]   Apple, Inc. *Cocoa Bindings Reference.* http://developer.apple.
             com/documentation/Cocoa/Reference/CocoaBindingsRef,
             2008.

[App08c]   Apple, Inc.   *Cocoa Fundamentals: Communicating
             with Objects.*   http://developer.apple.com/mac/library/
             documentation/cocoa/Conceptual/CocoaFundamentals/
             CommunicatingWithObjects/CommunicateWithObjects.html,
             2008.

[App08d]   Apple, Inc.   *Garbage Collection Programming Guide.*
             http://developer.apple.com/mac/library/documentation/cocoa/
             Conceptual/GarbageCollection/Introduction.html, 2008.

[App08e]   Apple, Inc. *Interface Builder User Guide.* http://developer.
             apple.com/mac/library/DOCUMENTATION/DeveloperTools/
             Conceptual/IB_UserGuide/Introduction/Introduction.html, 2008.

[App08f]   Apple, Inc. *Key-Value Coding Observing Guide.* http:
             //developer.apple.com/documentation/Cocoa/Conceptual/
             KeyValueObserving, 2008.

[App08g]   Apple, Inc. *Key-Value Coding Programming Guide.* http: //developer.apple.com/documentation/Cocoa/Conceptual/ KeyValueCoding, 2008.

[App08h]   Apple,   Inc.   *Notification   Programming   Topics   for Cocoa.*   http://developer.apple.com/DOCUMENTATION/Cocoa/ Conceptual/Notifications, 2008.

[App09a]   Apple, Inc. *Automated Unit Testing with Xcode 3 and Objective-C.*   http://developer.apple.com/mac/articles/tools/ unittestingwithxcode3.html, 2009.

[App09b]   Apple,   Inc.   *Blocks   Programming   Topics.*   http: //developer.apple.com/mac/library/documentation/Cocoa/ Conceptual/Blocks/Articles/bxUsing.html, 2009.

[App09c]   Apple, Inc.   *Concurrency Programming Guide.*   http: //developer.apple.com/mac/library/DOCUMENTATION/General/ Conceptual/ConcurrencyProgrammingGuide/Introduction/ Introduction.html, 2009.

[App09d]   Apple, Inc.   *Introduction to Core Data Programming Guide.*   http://developer.apple.com/documentation/Cocoa/ Conceptual/CoreData/cdProgrammingGuide.html, 2009.

[App09e]   Apple, Inc. *Memory Management Programming Guide for Cocoa.* http://developer.apple.com/mac/library/documentation/ cocoa/Conceptual/MemoryMgmt/MemoryMgmt.html, 2009.

[App09f]   Apple,   Inc.   *The   Objective   C   Programming   Language.*   http://developer.apple.com/documentation/Cocoa/ Conceptual/ObjectiveC, 2009.

[DA02]   James Duncan Davidson and Apple Computer. *Learning Cocoa with Objective-C.* O'Reilly Media, Inc., Sebastopol, CA, 2002.

[DA09]   Bill Dudney and Chris Adamson. *iPhone SDK Development.* The Pragmatic Programmers, LLC, Raleigh, NC, and Dallas, TX, 2009.

[GL06]   David Gelphman and Bunny Laden.   *Programming with Quartz, 2D and PDF Graphics in Mac OS X.* Morgan Kaufman, San Francisco, 2006.

[Tho06]   R. Scott Thompson. *Quartz 2D graphics for Mac OS X developers.* Pearson Education, Inc., Boston, MA, 2006.

[Zar09]   Marcus Zarra. *Core Data: Apple's API for Persisting Data under Mac OS X*. The Pragmatic Programmers, LLC, Raleigh, NC, and Dallas, TX, 2009.

Index

D

E

More Core

Core Animation for OS X/iPhone

Have you seen Apple's Front Row application and Cover Flow effects? Then you've seen Core Animation at work. It's about making applications that give strong visual feedback through movement and morphing, rather than repainting panels. This comprehensive guide will get you up to speed quickly and take you into the depths of this new technology.

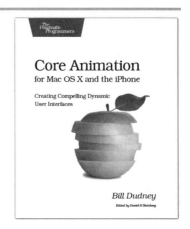

Core Animation for Mac OS X and the iPhone: Creating Compelling Dynamic User Interfaces
Bill Dudney
(220 pages) ISBN: 978-1-9343561-0-4. $34.95
http://pragprog.com/titles/bdcora

Core Data

Learn the Apple Core Data APIs from the ground up. You can concentrate on designing the model for your application, and use the power of Core Data to do the rest. This book will take you from beginning with Core Data through to expert level configurations that you will not find anywhere else. Learn why you should be using Core Data for your next Cocoa project, and how to use it most effectively.

Core Data: Apple's API for Persisting Data under Mac OS X
Marcus S. Zarra
(256 pages) ISBN: 978-1-93435-632-6. $32.95
http://pragprog.com/titles/mzcd

More iPhone and iPad

iPhone SDK Development

Jump into application development for today's most remarkable mobile communications platform, the Pragmatic way. This Pragmatic guide takes you through the tools and APIs, the same ones Apple uses for its applications, that you can use to create your own software for the iPhone and iPod touch. Packed with useful examples, this book will give you both the big-picture concepts and the everyday "gotcha" details that developers need to make the most of the beauty and power of the iPhone OS platform.

iPhone SDK Development

Bill Dudney, Chris Adamson, Marcel Molina
(545 pages) ISBN: 978-1-9343562-5-8. $38.95
http://pragprog.com/titles/amiphd

iPad Programming

It's not an iPhone and it's not a laptop: the iPad is a groundbreaking new device. You need to create true iPad apps to take advantage of all that is possible with the iPad. If you're an experienced iPhone developer, *iPad Programming* will show you how to write these outstanding new apps while completely fitting your users' expectation for this device.

iPad Programming: A Quick-Start Guide for iPhone Developers

Daniel H Steinberg and Eric T Freeman
(250 pages) ISBN: 978-19343565-7-9. $34.95
http://pragprog.com/titles/sfipad

More Productive

TextMate

If you're coding Ruby or Rails on a Mac, then you owe it to yourself to get the TextMate editor. And, once you're using TextMate, you owe it to yourself to pick up this book. It's packed with information that will help you automate all your editing tasks, saving you time to concentrate on the important stuff. Use snippets to insert boilerplate code and refactorings to move stuff around. Learn how to write your own extensions to customize it to the way you work.

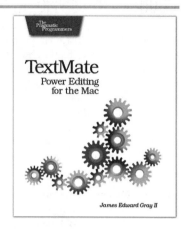

TextMate: Power Editing for the Mac
James Edward Gray II
(200 pages) ISBN: 0-9787392-3-X. $29.95
http://pragprog.com/titles/textmate

Pomodoro Technique Illustrated

Do you ever look at the clock and wonder where the day went? You spent all this time at work and didn't come close to getting everything done. Tomorrow, try something new. In *Pomodoro Technique Illustrated*, Staffan Nöteberg shows you how to organize your work to accomplish more in less time. There's no need for expensive software or fancy planners. You can get started with nothing more than a piece of paper, a pencil, and a kitchen timer.

Pomodoro Technique Illustrated: The Easy Way to Do More in Less Time
Staffan Nöteberg
(144 pages) ISBN: 9781934356500. $24.95
http://pragprog.com/titles/snfocus

More Techniques

Debug It!

Debug It! will equip you with the tools, techniques, and approaches to help you tackle any bug with confidence. These secrets of professional debugging illuminate every stage of the bug life cycle, from constructing software that makes debugging easy; through bug detection, reproduction, and diagnosis; to rolling out your eventual fix. Learn better debugging whether you're writing Java or assembly language, targeting servers or embedded micro-controllers, or using agile or traditional approaches.

Debug It! Find, Repair, and Prevent Bugs in Your Code
Paul Butcher
(232 pages) ISBN: 978-1-9343562-8-9. $34.95
http://pragprog.com/titles/pbdp

SQL Antipatterns

If you're programming applications that store data, then chances are you're using SQL, either directly or through a mapping layer. But most of the SQL that gets used is inefficient, hard to maintain, and sometimes just plain wrong. This book shows you all the common mistakes, and then leads you through the best fixes. What's more, it shows you what's *behind* these fixes, so you'll learn a lot about relational databases along the way.

SQL Antipatterns: Avoiding the Pitfalls of Database Programming
Bill Karwin
(300 pages) ISBN: 978-19343565-5-5. $34.95
http://pragprog.com/titles/bksqla

The Pragmatic Bookshelf

The Pragmatic Bookshelf features books written by developers for developers. The titles continue the well-known Pragmatic Programmer style and continue to garner awards and rave reviews. As development gets more and more difficult, the Pragmatic Programmers will be there with more titles and products to help you stay on top of your game.

Visit Us Online

Cocoa Programming
http://pragprog.com/titles/dscpq
Source code from this book, errata, and other resources. Come give us feedback, too!

Register for Updates
http://pragprog.com/updates
Be notified when updates and new books become available.

Join the Community
http://pragprog.com/community
Read our weblogs, join our online discussions, participate in our mailing list, interact with our wiki, and benefit from the experience of other Pragmatic Programmers.

New and Noteworthy
http://pragprog.com/news
Check out the latest pragmatic developments, new titles and other offerings.

Save on the eBook

Save on the eBook versions of this title. Owning the paper version of this book entitles you to purchase the electronic versions at a terrific discount.

PDFs are great for carrying around on your laptop—they are hyperlinked, have color, and are fully searchable. Most titles are also available for the iPhone and iPod touch, Amazon Kindle, and other popular e-book readers.

Buy now at pragprog.com/coupon.

Contact Us

Online Orders:	www.pragprog.com/catalog
Customer Service:	support@pragprog.com
Non-English Versions:	translations@pragprog.com
Pragmatic Teaching:	academic@pragprog.com
Author Proposals:	proposals@pragprog.com
Contact us:	1-800-699-PROG (+1 919 847 3884)